I0824153

praise for **We Are the Stars**

"Want to know what it's like to spend time with someone so funny and wise and so brutally honest that your jaw is permanently on the floor and your heart is singing? Gina's memoir quite simply broke me open. Her powerful poetic mixture of truth, humor, hard-fought wisdom, and unblinking authenticity radiates from every page. From the first paragraph it dawned on me that this is unlike anything I have ever read before. I can't wait to give this book to everyone I love. Read it."

HUGH JACKMAN

"'I am a storm wrapped in skin,' writes Gina Chick in this book full of bliss, sorrow, earth, and stars. I love Gina's courage, her strength, and her joy. Above all I admire the life force that guides her through the worst of times—facing death and grief without evasion, without hiding—to emerge on the other side of that dark river with a truly rare perspicacity. A wild, creaturely memoir that shows us how to really live."

CHARLOTTE WOOD, author of *Stone Yard Devotional*, shortlisted for the Booker Prize 2024

"As debuts go, they don't come more heartfelt or electrifyingly honest than *We Are the Stars*. Gina Chick is a force of nature, and so is her story. It's a book to ignite your soul."

MARKUS ZUSAK, author of *The Book Thief*

"A book like a huge wave of saltwater; raw and real and true. Chick has gathered a whole life's worth of lessons, recorded them here with honesty, and the result is a completely unique philosophy of life. It wrecked me and woke me the fuck up."

BRI LEE, author of *Eggshell Skull*

"YES is the clarion call, the anthem, the bass drumbeat that infuses Gina Chick's insistently joyous memoir. *We Are the Stars* roars with life. Chick not only sits with grief or pain or sensuality or love—she meets them head-on. This book is a defiant embrace of both living and dying, calling readers to see the wonder that is being mortal. Yes is the only answer to Chick. Yes. Over and over."

AILSA PIPER, author of *For Life*

"One of those rare books that goes to the quick of existence on almost every page. It is raw, lyrical, passionate, and wise, and I cannot recommend it highly enough."

Sydney Morning Herald

"There's nobody like Gina Chick and this book pulses with her intelligence, authenticity, and vulnerability, but most of all, with her passionate love of life."

LEIGH SALES

"Gina's eyes are wolf, her limbs the trees, her heart a moon, her mind the sea. *We Are the Stars* is an exhilarating story of a life uncontained and it will travel with me forever . . . an excellent manual for making a friend of life's intrepid roads and the wisdom that ensues. Let her words churn you up and inspire you to admire your deepest sorrows, laugh when you shouldn't, and above all, make a god of curiosity."

POH LING YEOW

"Gina Chick showed Australian audiences she can survive alone in the wilderness longer than anyone else. Turns out she can also write better than most too. *We Are the Stars* is a glorious, lyrical, heart-thumping account of a remarkable life by a remarkable woman. Gina Chick has gifted us a book for our times. May it land in the hearts of many."

DAVID LESER, author of *Women, Men and the Whole Damn Thing*

We Are the Stars

Gina Chick

a memoir

This book is dedicated to
my beautiful ghosts.

Frankie*, who started it all.*

Dan Arthur*, without whom
I would be a husk.*

Blaise*, who taught me that love is
always worth it, even when it hurts.
And love will always hurt.*

Charmian*, my wild, sad, brilliant
grandmother, who was born too
big for the life she was given.*

And Star*, loping endlessly across
the night sky, light raining from
her dingo paws like diamonds.*

contents

prologue

My daughter taught me many things, mostly after she was gone. But this one she tattooed into my heart with her tiny butterfly kisses: without death, life cannot be. We can't fully love one without embracing the other.

I would hate her for the lesson, but how can I hate her, she who made me in her undoing? All I can do is learn it, over and over; I who lusts for life with a burning fire that sears me whole. She's right. If I am to love life, I must revere its ending, which is a beginning, which is an ending. You see how it goes.

This is not her story, although in a way it is, as every step led either to, or away from, her. Like death, she is the tapestry into which this life is woven. The invisible locus around which worlds swirl. But the tale is mine. Her sister, friend, enemy. Her mother, the body who birthed her, whose tongue sang her secret name until she sang back and we danced this life together for less years than a handful of fingers. I have to utter it again now, under my breath, before I let her fall back into the ocean, to swim the darkling deeps until she's needed again. She is first and last.

Goodbye, love. Go back to sleep. I love you.

part one
Storm Girl

the year of 6

Frankie arrives today. The three of us jump around, pestering Mum and Dad: "How long till he gets here?" Frankie is a strange wonder. He's different from most people, which means he has to live on his own out past Wagga Wagga and has a lot of dogs and not many friends. When he comes to visit, he brings presents to "feed our minds." We play Mastermind and he says I am a genius. He doesn't know I cheat by peeking when he isn't looking.

His car pulls up. Monty Python blares from the cassette player: "This is an Ex. Parrot."

He's still laughing as we barrel into him. He picks us up easily, one by one. Danni and Kris run inside to tell Mum and Dad.

"Frankie's heeerrrrrrrre!"

I fold my legs like a spider and wait while he pulls his bags out. His back muscles and shiny brown calves are big silvery chunks of Plasticine. Everything about Frankie is wide, including his laugh. Mum says he'll never have kids because he's a homosexual. Frankie says he doesn't want any because he could never have kids as great as us, so why bother.

He bends to sit on the grass with me and says, solemn as a tree, "I have something for you."

A book peeks through his huge hands, like it's shy. It smells ancient, with a faded red cloth cover and embossed writing. I go to take it, but he holds it so I have to look into his eyes. Frankie doesn't use many words, so I listen with my skin as well as my ears when he does.

"You're a funny one. Not many people understand you, do they, Gina?"

I shake my head.

"Sometimes books understand us better than people. I think this book will understand you very well."

The silence between us pushes at my breath as he releases his hold on the book. Circles of sweat darken his shirt. Ants scratch hieroglyphics into the dirt. I feel a tremble, the moment just before a wave breaks, when a hopeful blade of water tries to cut the sky, before clouds push it over.

The book lands in my hand under the wide brown stare of this huge, mysterious grown-up god. And then I forget him as I examine it.

Chipped gold writing on the spine. *The Jungle Book* by Rudyard Kipling. I like it already, if it's a book about jungles. It smells like old people. I get that familiar feeling: the world is full of hidden doors and I'm fumbling smooth handles too big for my little hands.

"Thanks, Frankie," I offer, not sure what else to say.

"You'll see," he says, unfolding upward. His knees pop like fireworks.

In my room, I write my name on the first page in large, looping letters. Gina Chick. 6Y. I'm nearly seven but it's too hard to write six and three-quarters.

That night, in an earthy den in a place called India, I meet a skinny village boy named Mowgli who wanders into the night, away from the safety of the fires, and is chased by a tiger into a wolf den. I shudder as Raksha the mother-wolf snarls at the enormous head of Shere Khan, who can't fit in the den, although he tries.

Even the giant tiger backs away from a mother protecting her cubs. I meet a panther named Bagheera and fat, sad Baloo the bear. I meet glorious wolves, who live in packs with laws that make sense, and talk to each other and protect their kin, even when one is a strange man-cub who has no fur and runs on two legs. Bagheera buys Mowgli's place in the pack with a fresh-killed bull. No wolf may now harm Raksha's new cub because the law is the law.

The walls of my room dissolve into purple shadows, alive with capering creatures and an endless shout of wet heat. Words paint cascading pictures inside my blood. I don't know some of these words, but the story is alive inside me and the blanks fill in by themselves. I'm not reading, I am *remembering* something my heart always knew. My room grows more humid. Strange sounds gradually overtake the mournful call of the boobook until the owl is gone completely and a different symphony arrives, crashing in a fervent dream of screams and gibbers. Layers of sound rise and splash around the island of my bed. I am lost, found, lost, found, in the heaving howls of monkeys and elephants and the eerie heartsong of wolves. Winding through it all is the call of the jungle.

We Be Of One Blood, Ye And I.

Mowgli drums his heels into the ribs of Bagheera, who could kill him with a single paw swipe but does not. The boy is covered in scratches from playing with his wolf brothers and sisters. Kaa the snake tries to hypnotize him and cannot.

He belongs. He *belongs.*

I am home in a way I have never felt at home. Far from my family and our familiar beach and the merciless kids at school. Vines thread through my skin, pierce my eyes, wind up my legs. Their flowers smell of wonder and wounds. Jungle mosquitoes attack my face. The waterhole of my belly is a calm pool where all animals may drink in peace. My hair is a nest for birds and wild bees, groomed by law-breaking monkeys. My feet are hard leather, my ears know all the songs of the jungle.

Frankie was right. This book understands me. I am all the way awake. The world has torn apart and will never be the same again. My mind splits open. For the first time in my life, I have friends. Mowgli and Bagheera and Baloo and Akela. Rikki-Tikki-Tavi the mongoose, who fights a cobra and is bitten so many times he dies, then comes back to life again.

We be of one blood, ye and I.

Curled under the sheet with a flashlight, I quiver as Mowgli's story writes itself onto my skin. Very, very carefully, I tear the corner of a yellowed page, avoiding ripping into a single precious word, until a triangle of paper sits on my finger. I fold up the speck of old paper and put it in my mouth, chewing it to brown pulp. It tastes like freedom. I tear another corner, and another. Little wads of paper melt to nothing. I swallow. If I could eat the whole book, I would, but then I wouldn't be able to read it again. I want to read this book every day of my life. I hunger for it so much I keep tearing, keep swallowing, to take it inside myself, and then maybe when I wake up, I'll be in the jungle with my wolf pack and I'll be a boy and I'll be free.

In the morning, the house looks and sounds the same, but I'm different. Nothing will ever be the same again. My sisters' laughter fades, and the sun shines through their bodies. Behind them is jungle.

I take the book everywhere. To the beach, where Frankie teaches us to make dribble castles with wet sand. To the old ruined lighthouse we scramble over like Mowgli's friends, the outlaw monkeys. Whales pour foamy dreams high into the air; we count the spouts from the top of the tumble of sandstone. The book isn't heavy but its weight is a stone I feel against my ribs. Frankie stays up all night talking with Dad. The murmur of their deep voices becomes the growl of Shere Khan, stalking Mowgli. Dad's drifting pipe smoke is the tang of jungle rot. All the paper I've swallowed sits in my belly, holding Mowgli in place. I've eaten the story. He can never leave me now.

Frankie's weight is heavy on the couch, where I'm stretched out, reading. The big words make me frown.

"Do you like it?" he says. "Does this book understand you?"

I cannot answer. "Like" isn't even a word for what this feeling is. I just nod, sour paper caught on my tongue, and his eyes search mine. Then he nods, smiles, and pats my hair, which I hate if anyone else does it. His huge hand covers my whole head. I hear words underneath his hand, where it touches my hair.

We be of one blood, ye and I.

the year of 10

Saturday morning is for the birds. Literally. Mum is taking me birdwatching and I'm so excited I can hardly breathe. I've been poring over the big *Reader's Digest Complete Book of Australian Birds* for so long now I feel like each bird is a friend I've yet to meet.

I want to look through the eye of a bird. Would its world be the same colors as my world? Would everything bend and ripple like a crazy mirror at the fair? Most birds have eyes that face sideways, so they can see predators coming. I must look like a predator to them, with my forward-facing eyes, like a big, featherless owl. I flap my arms, imagining how big my wings would have to be to lift me off the ground. It seems impossible, which it is, because my bones are dense and heavy while birds' bones are intricate, hollow chambers filled with air. Eagles can telescope their vision in to catch prey, which makes them superheroes, better even than Wonder Woman, my favorite. I want an invisible airplane and silver bracelets that can deflect bullets. I want a whip that makes people tell the truth. I'd take it to school and lasso all the girls who bully me and ask them why. Maybe I could lasso the whole universe and make it tell me everything.

The heath is a stretch of unforgiving scrub, bristling with nasty hakea bush. The leaves are spikes as long as my finger and prick like a bastard, Dad says, while Mum shushes him for swearing. Birds love hakea because they can hide in there from things that want to eat them, which is pretty much everything. Poor birds. They're afraid of me and my owl eyes, so I talk to them in a low voice, telling them I won't hurt them and how beautiful they are.

My binoculars only work if I squint one eye. If I use both, I get a headache. Mum carries a pair of brand-new field guides with different pictures from the ones I'm used to, so these are perfect treasures. They spill over with reams of silhouettes and flight patterns and nesting habits. I could burst with happiness at the riches in the pages.

"Chip-chip-zazou."

"Look, Mum, a gray fantail." We look it up together while the small bird waggles its tail and hops close enough that I can see its pale, whiskery eyebrows and bright eye, which looks right into me.

"Do you want to read about yourself?" I ask the bird. It shimmies, chirps, then darts into the air to snag an insect.

"Mum, it fans its tail to change direction in mid-air! Like a fighter jet. Woah."

The heath suddenly cascades into a symphony of urgent cries, then falls utterly silent. A shadow flickers over us. We stare up at the dappled underbelly of a cruising eagle. There isn't a sound from the bush, only the sleepy hum of bees. I imagine all the birds with a feather to their beaks, whispering, *"Shush, shush."*

"It's an osprey," I say, hopeful. I love ospreys and want one as a pet. Mum is ambivalent. I don't know why. I could keep it in the chook pen and catch fish for it. Mum says I'd have to catch fish every single day but I reckon I could feed it cans of tuna on the days I have to go to school. I don't see what the problem is. She says its shit would be profoundly awful and stink up the backyard. Never mind there would be a bloody great big osprey eating the chooks.

The silent shape circles.

"Is it an osprey?"

"Not big enough," says Mum, flicking pages. "And it's the wrong color. It's a little eagle."

"Doesn't look very little to me."

The jam in my sandwich has oozed perfectly into the bread and across the slice of warm, sweating cheese. It's delicious, especially washed down with steaming tea from the thermos and followed by a couple of arrowroot biscuits held together with a thick slab of margarine. Daddy's Biscuits, or DBs, they're called, and they're a treat for birthdays and birdwatching. I feel like the luckiest kid on earth and lick all the grease and crumbs off my fingers.

As we wend our way back to the car, a flurry of feathers and sharp, piping calls stops me. Two white-cheeked honeyeaters berate us. They grow more agitated and fierce as we walk by. Something makes me look deeper into the banksia they flew out of.

The nest is perfect, cunning, a woven wave of twigs enclosing a cup of pure feathered softness. Four small, speckled eggs nestle within. My heart tries to jump out of my mouth.

"Mum, Mum, it's a nest, it's a nest, look, there are eggs and they're so small, Mum can I take an egg and hatch it, please can I can I?"

The parents dart and make repetitive calls as we peer into the nest.

"If you handle the eggs the parents might abandon them," says Mum.

"No, they won't. I'll just take one. Hey, mummy bird, can I have one of your eggs and hatch it so it will be my friend? I'll look after it, promise."

The birds keep sounding their alarms. I know I shouldn't take the egg but something has hooked in my guts and even if there was an earthquake or a tsunami right now, I couldn't stop myself. I quickly scoop out one tiny perfect ovoid and nestle it in my hand, backing away. I will protect this egg with my life. If the eagle comes back, I will fight it.

The birds dart into the banksia.

"Look, the mummy is sitting back on her nest. It's fine, she won't abandon the others."

Back home I make a pretend nest from a coffee tin with sand in the bottom, as if the egg is a dragon egg like in the Pern books. I aim my reading light into the tin to keep the egg warm, and spend hours watching it, in case it starts to hatch. My eyelids droop but I hang on, not wanting to leave my baby alone. Dad comes downstairs eventually and tells me I have to go to sleep or he'll take it away.

I take a long time to fall asleep, and when I do, I dream of flying.

Morning arrives with the scent of heat and the rich sound of classical music from the speakers Dad built from scratch and jerry-rigged together in a tangle of wiring so convoluted, the last time we were broken into, the speakers were left sitting in the middle of the living room and the would-be burglars had fled, empty handed, unable to figure out how to disconnect them. Mum said they must have been good kids really because they washed up the glasses they used for a drink of water. Dad said not so good because they were breaking into houses and stealing people's stuff.

Danni and Kristie argue in the next room, which is painted like a jungle. Mum used to paint huge stage sets for her church theater group when she was young. When we moved into this house, she took to our rooms in a riot of color and varnish. We all helped paint some of the animals. My room is better; it's the ocean. My bunk is high, with wardrobes underneath and a ladder to climb up. When I lift my bum off the bed, I can touch the sky with my feet. There are dirty footprints all over the ceiling. The main cloud looks like Kimba the White Lion.

I lie awake for a moment, listening to classical radio from upstairs; Mum and Dad are up and about already. Nan and Grandpa are here from Sydney, which means we'll be having boiled eggs and toast, Grandpa's favorite. Or maybe he thinks it's our favorite, which is why he always serves it when we stay in the house in Cremorne that smells like lavender and sherry. Mrs. Cat is a warm knot on my legs. She purrs when I squish her ears.

And then I remember the egg.

I leap up, sending Mrs. Cat flying. I pull the light out of the way and grab the Milo tin, then scream and drop it, sucking my fingers. The metal is scalding hot. Too hot. Way, way too hot. I'd positioned the light in the mouth of the tin because I hadn't wanted the egg to cool down, and had inadvertently created an oven.

"No no no, please be all right, please please please."

I reach my hand in, hissing when my skin touches metal. Even the sand is too warm to touch. The egg is hot.

I've cooked it.

I am inconsolable.

Mum and Dad are used to my tragedies. They don't say "I told you so," they just cuddle me while I wail with snot and tears smeared across my face.

"Are you sure it's dead?" I plead, anguish twisting my belly.

"Sorry, lovey. It definitely wouldn't have survived in there."

"I was just trying to keep it warm. I didn't know the tin would get so hot. Mum, I killed the baby, I took it away from its mummy and then I killed it."

This is the worst feeling I have ever had, worse than being picked on at school, worse than having no friends, worse than seeing the boys throw rocks at the magpies, until I run and scream at them and they back away from the crazy kid.

I killed the egg.

I sit in the backyard, nursing it, rocking, and crying "I'm sorry I'm sorry I'm sorry," over and over. It's so perfectly shaped. I wonder how the baby can even fit in there. I decide I want to see what it looks like.

I crack the egg, and the tiny baby bird flops into my hand, looking peaceful. Its bulbous eyes are huge in its head and there are little wet tufts of feathers all over its body. My tears stop. I have a real baby bird in my hand. I hold it up to stretch out its featherless wings. I play with its feet, counting the teensy claws. They curl up when I let them go. Whichever way I turn it, it's fascinating.

I want to show it how much I love it.

I spend an hour drawing the scrap of feathers and skin, paying attention to every part of it. When I'm done, Mum exclaims over how lifelike the drawing is. I decide to bury the bird, give it a proper funeral, and make a little hole in the dirt and lay the body in gently. When I cover it up, I feel funny in my belly. I go to play with my sisters but can't stop thinking about the bird, so I dig it up and carry it around with me, talking to it. Then I bury it again. Then dig it up.

Nan doesn't understand.

"Suzie, you have to tell her to leave it alone. It might have *diseases*."

Mum knows better. She leaves me to my devices. Later in the day I notice a strange, cloying smell. I wander around the house, sniffing in corners, but it seems to be everywhere. It's sticky and sweet. I keep playing with the bird. The smell grows stronger. It's a smell of wrongness and it keeps getting in the way of my games. Then I smell my fingers and recoil.

"What's that smell?" I say.

"That's the baby bird," says Mum.

"Why does it smell?"

"Because it's dead."

"Oh."

All of a sudden I'm revolted. I don't want to play with it any more. It's rotting. It's going to fall apart and be covered in maggots and that is what dead means. I never really knew what dead meant inside myself, but now I do. Dead smells broken in ways that make my skin tingle. I quickly bury the bird again and tamp the dirt down so it can't wake back up and crawl out, even though I know it won't. Dead is the place where life isn't, and it smells really bad. I'm sorry I killed the baby bird, but I don't like it any more. It's not my friend.

Nan shakes her head and tuts. It takes three goes with the nailbrush to get the smell out of my fingers and even then, I catch sickly wafts every now and then.

Danni and Kristie beckon from downstairs. They're up to something. Danni shows me a few silver coins in her hand. Kristie has a couple too. I don't need any encouragement. I tiptoe to the coin jar and sneak my hand in like it's a snake stealing eggs from a nest, feeling for the straight edges of a prized fifty-cent piece, wincing when I clink a couple of coins together.

"Shhhh," says Danni.

The grown-ups are outside on the front deck but Mum's got voodoo telepathy skills and calls out, "It's awfully quiet in there. What are you lot up to?"

"Nothing, Mum," we chorus, snorting and giggling.

I poke my head around the door. "We're just going for a walk to the shops."

Mum flaps a hand, which is yes in Mum language.

The road is a black Mordor furnace, and gobs of melted tar stick to our bare feet when we cross. Knickers the dopey cocker spaniel sniffs all the places where dogs have peed like she's reading the dog newspaper, her eyes droopier than her long ears. We leg it through the section where the magpie bombs us, waving towels above our heads. The maggie clacks its beak when it swoops, scattering sharp cries that would stab us if they could. I get nailed by a bastard patch of stabby little bindi-eyes and hop the last few meters out of maggie territory, then sit in the gutter, pulling prickles out of my feet.

A couple of super-tanned boys with bleached hair walk past.

"Are you boys?" one of them says.

"Maybe," says Danni.

"Are you twins?" says the other.

"Maybe," I say.

"Weirdos," says the first boy.

We don't care. Danni and I get asked if we are twins all the time. Kristie's the odd one out; she's so blonde and she's little compared to us. None of us wear bikini tops, so people think we're boys. We think it's funny. "Don't need one don't want one don't have one," is our standard answer when people get upset because we're girls without tops. I don't understand why I should wear something silly and pointless when my chest looks exactly the same as a boy's.

I want to be a boy more than anything. I beg for Tonka trucks for my birthday and play with them in the sandpit, which can get gross 'cause the cat poos in there. Boys are better than girls in every way. I hope I never, ever, ever get boobs. If I get boobs my life will be over. A teacher at our school is flat like an ironing board. I hope that's what my boobs will look like. Like nothing.

"Come ON," says Kristie, hopping from foot to foot as I pull out the last of the bindis.

"Let's race," I say, dusting dried grass from my shorts.

"No," she says.

"Yes," I say, because I am the biggest and I know I might win.

I take off, and Danni chases. She's perfect like a doll, and is good at everything, including making friends, and she has a neck like a swan and always does everything right. I only beat her at things because I am a year older. I don't let myself think about what life would have been like if she had been born first.

Danni beats me to the shops and we huff and puff in the shade of the big tree. The guy who owns the toyshop asks, "Where's your little sister?"

"She's coming. You know her leg doesn't work right."

Danni looks stricken, obviously thinking about little Kris running by herself in the sun because we left her behind. Mum says Danni is the "sensitive one" and "the peacemaker." I don't know what that means, other than she knows how to suck up to grown-ups.

"She'll be fine," I say.

When Kristie arrives it's at a thumping run, or her best version of it. Her face is crimson thunder, her lame leg rigid at the ankle as she galumphs along. She never asks us to slow down or wait for her. She simply refuses to be left behind.

When Kristie was born, one of her feet faced completely the wrong way. Club foot, it's called, and to fix it she had three operations in her first six weeks of life. We were living in Tenterfield, which was pretty different from where we live now, in Jervis Bay. Lismore Hospital was a couple of hours away, so Mum had to leave newborn Kristie there to be doted on by nurses. Every other day she'd load up the tiny red Mini and even squish in old Sam the cranky kelpie to visit our baby sister. Bridgette the goat never came with us. There wasn't room, although when she did ride in the Mini, she stuck her head straight up and out of the small sunroof and the wind wobbled her lips and made her mouth look like she was smiling.

When Kris finally came home, she had plaster casts and Frankenstein-monster scars up the inside of her ankle and calf. When she was two, she had another operation. Afterward, at night she had to wear red boots that were fixed at the heels and toes with silver bars, to hold her feet into the right position and teach them how to be feet.

"No, Daddy, no, Daddy," she screamed and sobbed every night as Dad strapped them on. "Please, no, nooooooo, I don't want them, please, it hurts, don't." She cried herself to sleep most nights. Dad always went straight for a big glass of whiskey as soon as she was quiet. I could tell his hands were shaking by the way the ice clinked in the glass. Her foot mostly points the right way now, but she doesn't really have a calf muscle and her ankle doesn't move, so when she runs, she looks like a pirate.

Kristie is taking too long to finish the last fifty meters I head for the shops. Danni looks back at our red-faced, puffing sister, obviously torn.

"We should wait for her."

Kris and I fight a lot. We hate each other. I don't want to wait for her. She always slows us down and she sulks all the time.

"Hurry up," I yell, and Kris shoots me one of her dagger glares, finally limping up to the candy store like a dingo about to bite.

We pool the loot from our heist. Altogether we've snagged ninety cents from the coin jar, so we're millionaires. Most of the candies are one or two cents, but some are half a cent each, including milk bottles, which are my favorite. We'll get a decent bag each. We point and choose, arguing about whether red frogs are better than licorice and which flavor Chupa Chups is the best. It's obviously pine lime.

Soon we're sitting outside, swinging our legs, sucking artificial colors and flavors into our mouths to prepare us for the hot walk back up the hill. Danni farts into her hand and holds it in my face. Her tongue is bright green. I lick my finger and stick it in her ear. "Wet Willy!" Kristie pushes me off the bench, so I tickle her until she runs away.

"Hoppo boppo," she shouts, and we drop our candy bags, fold one leg behind us and hop-smash into each other, laughing so hard I almost pee my pants.

The cool boys from before side-eye us from the shady tree. I can see one of them wants to join in but his mate is doing that boring chin-up eye-roll thing with his arms folded.

"Whatcha doin'?" says the nice one.

"Playing hoppo boppo."

"What's that?"

"You have to make the other person overbalance so their other leg touches the ground."

"This is dumb," says his mate, pulling him away.

"Hup-e's dupumb," says Danni.

"Dupumbuper thupan dupogshupit," says Kris.

"Dupumbuper thupan upa bupag upof upelupaphupant pupoo," I say, and we lose it at how good elephant sounds in Upenglupish, the secret language Dad taught us by putting an "up" before every phonetic vowel.

"Upelupaphupant!" Danni shrieks, high on candy, not that she ever needs an excuse. She starts jumping around like a maniac, making elephant noises and waving her arm like a trunk. "Upelupaphupant! Upelupaphupant!"

It's not wise to play hoppo boppo on a hard surface but we do it anyway, fueled by sugar and summer and most of all sisterhood, which means we will always have each other, even when we fight, and none of us cares about the bruises.

We're in Queensland on a wide beach, eating a picnic of hot french fries that the seagulls steal raucously, demanding more, more, until I throw the whole bag at them in fright.

I'm freshly wise with the secrets of the surf, which Dad revealed over lunch as he unwrapped the chips and the seagulls jousted over scattered morsels.

"You dive under the waves, grab hold of the bottom tightly, with your hands, like this, like you're hanging on to a blanket. That way you always know where up is, you see?"

I don't but figure I'll work it out on the way.

"Then, when the wave goes quiet above you, kick to the surface and wait for the next one."

I nod seriously; it feels like a rite of passage, my father instructing me in the greater mysteries. He takes a stick. "It's you, this stick, see, it's even got stumpy little arms."

I laugh when he makes the stick swim in the air and dive under an imaginary wave.

"You make your body stiff to catch the wave. But if you get dumped, and you will, just grab the biggest breath you can and roll up in a tiny ball. You'll get bounced around like socks in the washing machine, but if you're all curled up the wave can't hurt you. You got that? It'll scare you, but as long as you stay curled up, you'll be right. If you're all stretched out, what do you think will happen when the big wave lands on you?"

"I dunno, Dad, what?"

He holds the stick in his hand and drives his other hand down, a stiff blade. The stick snaps in half, one of the arms breaks off.

I stare at the splinters. He smiles to make it all right.

"Curl up in a ball when you get dumped, don't fight it. The sea is bigger than you and I put together, and you can't fight it when it's made up its mind." He grins into my face, which is scared now, the stick in three pieces. The sea isn't friendly, it's mean.

"I'll come out with you, show you how. Come on."

Sure enough, it's fun, awesome fun. I dive under the waves like an otter. Dad shows me which ones to catch, you swim like crazy till the wave picks you up, launches you down the glassy face, you're going to die for sure, keep your body stiff and your arms out and the wave pushes you along, it's the best ride, more, Dad, more.

That one's a dumper, see how it's curling over at the top? Don't try to catch those, they hurt.

I grow too confident, go for one too big and am thoroughly dumped. I curl up like he said and the world is in a million places, but it ends, finally. I have sand in every crevice of my body, and he's hugging me. You did it, see? It's not so bad.

He leaves me to my play while he teaches my sisters the same lessons. Soon all three of us are bobbing in the water, joyous water babies.

I drift down to the place where the waves don't break, the water ironed and foamy and calm, the shore a long way away, getting further, caught in a rip. It's the place where all that piled-up water escapes out to sea, a turbulent channel of fast ripples, an elevator the gleeful surfers ride. I hurl my arms desperately at the receding shore, but the sea's arms are stronger, pulling me out, and out, and down, until Dad's suddenly out here too. I hang on to his back and he swims sideways until the sea lets go.

"You didn't tell me about rips, Dad," I cry, hysterical, betrayed. "You didn't tell me."

Dad's in trouble again. This time it's a doozy. He's always a little bit in trouble from Mum, but it's that in-trouble that grown-ups have with each other when they're still smiling underneath the words and don't really mean it. He told me once that whenever Mum asks him to weed the garden he pulls out all the herbs, pretending he doesn't know what weeds are. And when she asks him to get herbs for the salad, he brings back weeds. She gets so nearly-mad she never lets him do either. Dad is the smartest person in the world, until he isn't.

He's usually in trouble for one of three things.

The first is that when he does home improvements for Mum, he makes contraptions that are efficient instead of beautiful. Mum is an artist. Everything she sees is a living painting and absolutely must be beautiful or she gets a migraine. She arranges the house so the scarlet vase leads your eye toward the cerise painting, which sets you on a visual adventure through light and space. It hurts her eyes if something is bog-ugly. Literally everything Dad creates is bog-ugly, including his outfits. He combines stripy chintz pants with a cheap nylon paisley shirt he bought when Mum wasn't looking, or completely shaves off his moustache and most of his chin, leaving his bushy beard intact from the jaw down, without telling her first. She makes him sleep on the day bed until it all grows back and he looks like himself again.

His solutions to problems are always innovative and unorthodox, if somewhat lethal, like the powered hedge-trimming contraption he cobbled into a full-body harness, and then climbed the rickety ladder with it whizzing and whirring, leaning out in a precarious trapeze act over the naked chainsaw blade. He got in a lot of trouble for that one, but the hedge got trimmed, mostly, and he was undeterred.

The second thing he gets in trouble for is that he doesn't feel pain like normal people, which means he always trips over his gigantic feet, or runs into sharp edges, or cuts himself with a saw or an axe, or somehow clocks himself with a lump of wood. He drips blood everywhere, which makes Mum totally lose her mind. I'm reading one day when he staggers into the house, mopping his head with one of the nicest bath towels, covered in streams of blood. He'd been riding his bicycle home from playing squash, head down like a bat out of hell, and looked up just in time to see a parked trailer. He crashed into it, hurtling through the back window and landing inside with his arms and legs in a painful tangle. He shook himself off, cleaned up most of the shattered glass, and wrote a note for the owners. Then he carefully let himself out the side door, picked up his mangled bike and walked home the rest of the way, pulling bits of glass out of his head and face. He was lucky he didn't blind himself, but Dad is always lucky. The bike and caravan, not so much.

The third thing is that he does exciting, amazing, dangerous stuff with us *all the time*, which we adore but Mum hates. She hides upstairs while we're jumping off the high top deck into his arms, or he teaches us how to chop wood barefoot with an axe he's sharpened to a samurai razor, or we're climbing the biggest tree in the backyard.

Danni and I learn the hard way that sometimes Mum's caution is called for.

The family car is a fifteen-seat minivan. Right now, all the seats are removed so Dad can transport paintings for an exhibition Mum's art class is putting on. It's a Thursday, which means sports day, so we're wearing our school sports uniform: yellow T-shirt, tiny blue wraparound skirt, and blue nylon knickers called PE pants. While we wait for Dad to do boring grown-up art things, we kick off our sneakers and balance on the fences outside the exhibition hall. There are crocodiles in the quicksand, and if we fall off, they'll eat us or we'll just drown. Dad takes ages. I get eaten by two crocodiles and Kristie nearly drowns in the quicksand, until Danni and I make a human chain to pull her out.

The sun has vanished into an inky veil studded with stars by the time he finishes, and we pile into the van to go home for dinner. It's a forty-five-minute drive from the back country road out near Shoalhaven Heads, where the paper mill spews a yeasty stench into the air and black dairy cows graze across a lush floodplain.

Danni and I wobble-stand at the back of the hurtling van and sing a school rhyme we made up, hitting our hips together on the beat. It's a bumpy old potholed road. We jostle and giggle as Dad hits the bumps, on purpose, because, Dad.

Sha-la-a-BOOMsi-ay
There is no SCHOOL today
The teacher PASSED away
with COLgate
We threw her IN the bay
She frightened the FISH away
We pulled her OUT
She smelled like SOUR trout.

Dad sings tiddley pom out of key and makes the car dance around, which throws us into each other more. Kris is asleep on the floor; she's only seven and it's been a long day. Danni and I sing louder and louder, and Dad dances the car more erratically, with the headlights spearing into the dark and moths kamikazeing into the windscreen with tiny splats.

And then.

All sound vanishes into a vast velvet cave, I am flying and the sky is huge and inky and all the stars spread out like glowing grains of sand on an endless indigo beach. There is no moon in the whole sky. I have all the time in the world to locate the Southern Cross; those extra-bright stars are the two pointers, which means that's south over there in the far darkness. I float on a cushion of wonder. This is the best feeling. The night takes cold nips between my spread fingers. This must be what birds feel like. I wriggle my fingers like feathers. I'm flying, for real. It lasts forever. Time has stopped and gravity cannot touch me.

Until it does.

I churn in a washing machine for a long time. When the world finally stops its crazy rotation, I'm somehow standing in a dark field. A distant sound like a whistling kettle gets louder, and now it's screaming. It's Danni. I hear another sound and it's me, screaming with her. We've fallen out of the car in the middle of nowhere; I wasn't flying, I was falling. Two red tail-lights disappear around a bend. Forever was actually only a few seconds. Dad mustn't have noticed we've fallen out.

"Danni, get up." I pull her upright. "Dad's gone home without us. We're going to have to walk."

"Dad's gone?"

"Come on, we have to walk home." We're forty kilometers away, but that's not important. I'm determined to get my sister home.

When Dad tells the story later, he says it was all laughter and fun in the van until there was suddenly just silence and a swinging door. He turned the car around, unsure which side of the road to drive on. He didn't know whether we'd even be alive or if another car would hit us before he could get to us. Then he saw two figures in the headlights, covered in blood, running alongside the road.

I see white lights and the familiar shape of the van. There he is, leaping out, all angles and arms and legs like he's made of pipe cleaners. He hasn't left us behind, after all. He noticed we were gone. I don't have to be the big one any more.

Dad is some ashen color I've never seen before. His voice doesn't sound like him.

"Do you want to go to the hospital or do you want to go to Mum?" he says, lifting Danni into the car as I hobble after her.

"MUM!" we both scream; of course we do, and it's all he wants too: safe harbor.

"Faster, Dad," we say. Then, when the bumps jolt us around and it hurts, "Owwww. Slower."

The thing about falling backward onto a road at a hundred kilometers per hour wearing a T-shirt and a pair of undies is that anything that sticks out has no skin left. Knees, bum, ankles, toes. There's a chunk missing from Danni's shoulder where the road chewed a piece out of her, like a tiger bite. I see white things in it, parts of her insides that skin usually hides. Her knees are okay, though, which means she can lie on her belly in the back of the car. I wasn't so lucky; no part of me can touch the floor, so I crouch and hang on to the bar behind the driver's seat while Danni cries herself to sleep in the back, screaming, "My bum, my bum." Kristie sleeps through the whole thing.

I can't sleep. All I know is that I have to keep talking to Dad, whose voice is still all wrong. He feels broken somehow, on the inside where I can't reach. I talk to him to let him know I'm okay, that everything will be all right. I chatter about silly things and his hands unclench a bit from the steering wheel.

About halfway home I say, "Hey, Dad . . ."

"Yes, lovey?"

"Can I swear?"

The laugh sounds like it's been wrung out of him, like he's a dishcloth being squeezed. It's awful.

"Of course, lovey."

"Well shitting bloody hell." It's the worst swear I know. His laugh sounds more normal this time and his hands relax a bit.

"Can I tell a dirty joke?"

"Yes please, kiddo."

"What's the definition of a thumbtack?"

"I don't know."

"A Smartie with a hard-on."

This time I laugh with him, both at the joke and that I'm telling dirty jokes to my dad while clutching the back of his seat after falling out of the car on the road and shredding my school uniform and a fair expanse of skin. Laughing hurts, so I stop.

I cling to that metal bar and talk to Dad while the headlights reveal the next stretch of road, until finally we pull into the driveway. He carries Danni, and I limp next to him. The sliding door flings open, and Mum thunders onto the deck, shouting, "What have you done to them this time, Doug?"

It's like a spear flies through the night to puncture whatever was keeping him upright. I feel him pop like a balloon. After the last forty minutes of pouring myself into keeping him afloat, I'm angry at Mum for stabbing him in the heart when he is already splintered inside, and I'm scared he will never be fixed.

Kris yawns, bleary and sleepy, watching while Mum checks Danni and me. There's no doctor in our sleepy seaside village, but the local pharmacist is a friend, so the call goes out. He opens up the pharmacy and checks us out, turning our bodies to examine the huge, weeping patches where skin used to be, black gravel scattered through the shiny red ooze. He shines lights in our eyes, pokes and manipulates our joints and makes us stand on one leg to see if we can balance. He dresses Danni's tiger bite.

"These are very lucky girls," he says to Dad. "Looks like no broken bones. They need some disinfectant, and you should really clean all that gravel out of the wounds. Don't put any dressings on them, just let them air out. Hospital will just traumatize the girls at this point. Keep an eye on them tonight and take them in if they don't seem right. But the best place for them is with you."

Dad says it's fantastic old-school frontier doctoring and tries to give him some money, but he won't take it.

When we're back home, Mum and Dad pour Mercurochrome all over us, which is like taking coals from the fire and pressing them into every bit of torn flesh. It burns twenty times worse than lemon juice in a thousand paper cuts. I've read about Tarzan being swarmed by fire ants. I reckon this is what it must feel like, but if Tarzan can do it, I can too.

Dad says Mercurochrome is mostly mercury, which is on the periodic table, I can't remember where. Near the end. All I know is I'd rather fall out of the car ten times than be painted with this red stuff ever again.

After we stop hollering, we arrange beanbags under our shins and bellies. This means we can lie down, which is a revelation. After the pain from the Mercurochrome fades, I feel euphoric. Danni babbles happy nonsense, which is really just Danni on any Tuesday. Mum mutters something about endorphins and turns on the tiny black-and-white TV we're only allowed to watch *The Goodies* on, and *Doctor Who*, and sometimes *Tarzan* and *Catweazle*. There's a movie playing, *The Bridge on the River Kwai*. It's a war film, but it's a grown-up film so we feel really special. We get cups of tea with as many Daddy's Biscuits as we want, and Kristie gets some too, even though she didn't fall out of the car.

I feel warm, and safe, and loved. Mum and Dad sit on the floor next to us, with Kris cuddled up in Mum's lap. And then we write limericks.

Two girls by the name of Chick
Performed an amazing trick
In the dead of the night
At speeds faster than light
They fell out on the road on their dicks.

After we all finish wiping tears of laughter from our eyes, Mum reckons we might just live, though she'll never forgive Dad. Which isn't true; she already has, mostly. She'll never let him live it down, though.

I've never thought about skin before. It's just the stuff that gets sunburned and scratched and salty and super freckly in summer. But now I realize it's there to keep the outside out and your insides in. When large patches of it seep, cracking and bleeding as they heal, skin becomes a lot more important.

Mum or Dad have a few goes trying to pick the gravel out of my wounds, but I pretend it hurts and stop them. That's just because I want to do it myself, which is gross and thrilling, all at once. It's the same when I have a wobbly tooth. I wobble it nonstop for a day until I can give a mighty twist and pull it out with bits of shredded gum still attached. I'll dig at a splinter with a needle until it's out, even if it takes hours.

Extracting gravel from my scabs is better than watching TV. Hairs keep getting caught in the sticky surface, which dries to a crust. Pulling them out is the best. Mum gives up scolding me. She calls me a monkey. Dad says you're one to talk, squeezing my blackheads all the time. Mum says thanks for reminding me and makes Dad sit still while she squeezes the big one on his back that never goes away. Dad doesn't feel pain ever until Mum squeezes a blackhead, and then he yelps like a seal, while Mum slaps him to make him sit still.

"Serves you right for dropping them out of the car," she says.

After a few days, beanbags are too uncomfortable to sleep in, and we start sleeping back in our beds, which brings its own challenge.

Every morning the alarm goes off, and I gather all the sheets around me, head upstairs and run a bath. I slide in with the sheets and slowly soak them off from the places where they've stuck to my wounds in the night. Danni jumps in to do the same. The sheets go in the wash with some bleach and now we can get ready for school.

Wounds, scabs, broken bones, and scars are all currency at school. My injuries bring unexpected popularity and income. Boys pay five cents to pick gravel out of the scabs, and also want to talk to me for the first time ever, especially when they hear I fell out of the car on the highway at full speed and didn't die, like a stuntman. I play it up, exaggerating the story until the car was doing two hundred and I was hanging on to the door with my feet scrabbling along the road until my fingers gave way and I fell.

The glory.

For a couple of weeks I feel what it must be like to have friends. Then someone tells on me to the teachers, who are horrified and disgusted by my scab-monetization business and popularity plan. They shut down my enterprise, and with it any chance of people to sit with at recess. I go back to climbing the tree to talk to the magpie. It's a bit harder with all the scabs getting in the way, but I find a new way of flipping backward up onto the branch like a gymnast, so all in all, the whole falling out of the car thing was worth it.

I'm no longer Gina the stuntman. I'm back to being Gina the weirdo. Luckily, I've found *Jonathan Livingston Seagull* in the library, so nothing else exists. I don't usually read skinny books but this one has me rapt. Jonathan is an outcast seagull and he doesn't join the flock; he just keeps going further and further away from it until he discovers the secrets of everything and can see through the fingers of the world.

This book requires deliberate attention. I tear the small corners of these pages precisely, folding each triangle first instead of my usual careless rips. I chew each piece fifty times. It's hard to count and read at the same time. The pulp tastes different from *The Jungle Book*, *White Fang*, *The Hobbit*, and *The Lord of the Rings* and *Watership Down*. All the little pieces will join up inside me and teach me how to fly.

There's a hole in the sky where the moon comes in. It hangs near the horizon like a spider's orange egg sac, swollen and strange. Sand squeaks under our feet. It's no color at all. Un-color. I tremble with a dark and secret wish to understand what people are saying when their lips move and sounds come out. The words those lips form aren't true; I've learned that the hard way. They're just feathers and muscle. It's the bones I'm after, and nobody can point me to them, no matter how much I peel apart the skin of things.

Dad tries, though, in his way. Tall as mountains, familiar as my scattered freckles, as the gap between my teeth that's a gift from my mother, along with my wide mouth and love of music. His hand sweeps across a skein of stars. Whenever we walk at night, he shares new revelations about atoms and elements and the hidden workings of the universe, stitching for me a cloak of mysteries that makes me feel like the most special person in the world.

Dad takes me on walks when it's been a bad day at school. I don't know how he knows, but he does. Today was a bad day.

He says: some of the light splashing my eyes is from suns that died when the universe was born billions of years ago, and it's been flying through space aiming right for me, for all that time. If we hadn't come out for this walk, if I'd gone to bed with my sisters after dinner, I would have missed this piece of light forever. It would have crashed into the beach like a shooting star, and most of it would have been absorbed and lost. But because I was walking on this beach and looked up, I caught that tiny piece of light in my eyes and my brain stole it and turned it into a picture and now I get to keep it forever. Starlight is inside me now.

"So is my brain like a photo album, Dad?"

"Kinda, kiddo."

I imagine all the light from all the stars radiating out in a zillion spheres, like ripples on the water when it rains but as luminous balls hanging in the sky, growing bigger and bigger through endless waterfalls of space.

"Woah."

My toes scuff sand so fine I'll be sleeping with it tonight, no matter how well I wipe my feet when we get home.

Where beach meets bush, Mrs. Cat leaps from tussock to tussock, avoiding getting her paws sandy. She's a silent wraith, but sometimes I catch her out of the corner of my eye. Mum says she's never heard of a cat going for walks like this. I like that she's different. Like me.

"What else is true, Dad? Tell me something else."

"Maybe you can tell me. Is glass solid or liquid?"

"It's solid, of course."

"Is it?"

He bends to scoop a handful of sand, which he deposits into my hand.

This must be a trick.

"Okay, it's liquid."

"No," he says, and I feel his grin, even though I can't really see his face.

"It's not solid, and it's not liquid?"

"Correct."

"Then what is it?"

"It's called an amorphous solid. That means it's caught halfway in-between."

I know glass is made of melted sand, which is silica on the periodic table. This sand in my hand could make a glass to drink from.

"Doesn't it get confused being half one thing and half another?"

"I don't know. Do you get confused being half one thing and half another?"

"What half things am I?"

"Well, you're half a kid and half a teenager. Does that get confusing?"

"Every day."

"You're half made of Mum's genes and half of mine."

"Definitely confusing."

"Have we talked about entropy?"

"That's the thing where everything in the universe is falling apart."

"Yup. But very, very slowly." He pauses. "What if we call things names so we can think they won't change, but really everything is on its way to being something else? What do you think, kiddo?"

Dad's secrets are always a bit too big for my brain, but I like the way they make me feel. If I know enough of them, maybe everything will come into focus.

I know about focus. Mum and I develop photos in the darkroom Dad built in the bathroom for her. I help whenever I can, feeling like a wizard, making spells with chemicals and light. I love rocking the tray, eyes watering from acrid fumes, watching shapes bloom under the red light, trying to guess what the picture is. And then the invisible turns itself inside out, from nothing to everything. It was there all along, waiting to be asked.

I'm supposed to use tongs to get the photo out but I use my fingertips, very carefully at the edge of the paper, letting the developer run off before sliding the sheet into the fixer.

"Quick," Mum always says. "Don't let it overcook."

There's magic everywhere in the world, hiding behind familiar shapes and the words that describe them. In the cracks between objects lurks another world, I'm sure of it. It keeps leaking out. Maybe there's a world behind that one. Maybe one day I'll burrow into one of those cracks and end up floating in space surrounded by spheres of expanding light, and then I'll understand everything.

Dad waits patiently for me to return from my moondream.

"Do you want to know what the biggest lesson of all is, Gigi-love?"

I nod. I sure do. His face is dark against the moon. He looks like he's been cut out of the sky.

"Levers."

I puzzle this one over, turning the bones of the idea around in my hand along with the cool clump of sand. It seems like an anticlimax.

"What does that mean?"

"You know what a lever is?"

"Ye-es."

I do, on the surface, but not in whatever portentous way he means. He lets me stew for a bit.

"Um. I guess. A seesaw is a lever."

"How?"

"I—"

I can't explain. Shapes collide in my mind.

"When you understand levers, you understand everything," he says.

"But why, Dad?"

I want to understand the universe, which is unfathomably complicated. Then maybe I'll understand people, who make no sense at all.

"Have a think about it. Let me know when you figure it out. What's infinity times naught?"

Infinity is forever and naught is nothing. I see them as pictures and put them in a paper bag and shake it up. When I look inside I see stars.

"Infini-naught," I say, and he laughs all the way off the beach and up the road and back into the rambling house on the hill that smells of jasmine and books and dogs and cats and sisters.

Mum's still grading exams, which are spread out over the floor. She swears when Knickers runs to greet us, scattering papers. Dad makes her a cuppa and rubs the back of her neck. Mrs. Cat yowls at the door to be let in, furious we've left her behind, and her with sandy paws and all. She's so good at being invisible it's easy to forget she's there at all. Knickers wags up to her as she leaps through the door as though it will bite her. The cat hisses from habit, not malice.

It's one of those days when heat is a fist, clubbing the girls until their meanness bubbles over. Sweat trickles down my back, a shivery cool finger tickle-tracing my spine. Paper-dry grass gives way to pebbles and bindis prick through my uniform.

These girls have claimed the only shade in the playground, directly under my usual roost, the twisty tree where the magpie scans baked earth for wriggling things. Because they're there I can't climb the tree.

A tiny sliver of shade ripples against the fence. I press myself into it like a small leaf. I'm nearly at the end of *Jonathan Livingston Seagull.* My heart feels wide. It's too big for my chest. I stare into nothing, into everything. Sunlight stripes my legs. Fat blue sky might hold a seagull. Ants clamber in dead grass.

A radiant circle of girls, all wearing trendy desert boots. No matter how I plead at home, I have to wear black shiny school shoes, because they're the uniform. Mum doesn't understand how black shiny shoes make me a target. Not that shoes would make any difference, not really.

It's not what I wear, it's who I am. Weirdo.

Melinda braids Alice's hair. Her fingers are deft, twisting strands into small, honey-hued ropes. They hang like magic spells alongside Alice's tanned neck. Hands flutter next to mouths and giggles echo like birdsong, except if the girls were birds I'd know what they were saying, and these pretty creatures are a cruel mystery, one I can never solve. Melinda glances up, catches me staring. I look away as cupped hands catch whispers and laughter explodes. They sound like lorikeets. Mum calls the lorikeets bullies when we lay seed out on the deck for all the parrots. They're small, but fierce as dragons, and screech at the big, gentle king parrots until they fly away.

"Just goes to show, beautiful doesn't mean kind," Mum says, shooing the gaudy birds away when they harass the crimson rosellas.

A green ant bites my leg, startling me out of the daydream. No seagulls are visible from my hiding place under the fence.

I'm striped with shadows like a tiger. Like Shere Khan. I wonder what it would be like to eat a person. I reckon they'd be crunchy. Everyone's scared of tigers, and they aren't scared of anything, except maybe a mama wolf.

I go back to watching the girls.

Joanna has curly red hair that catches the sun and looks like Dad's copper wire. Her plaits are twice as thick as everyone else's. I wonder what it must feel like, to have someone playing with your hair, little bony fingers tugging and twisting, giggles and gossip and the fruit of secrets.

"Did your mum use the mixing bowl?" the girls taunt when they walk behind me on the way to class. My fringe is crooked where Mum never gets the scissors level. "Bowl cut bowl cut cake head fake bread."

Mum says with my short hair, at least I'll never get nits. Sometimes I wouldn't mind nits to know what it feels like to be in the middle of the knot of twittering bodies.

Melinda's staring. I've been noticed. My tiger stripes have failed. I retreat further into the fence shade, but it's too late. The girls are bored and hot and they help each other up, shaking grass from their tunics. They stand over me in a half circle, a sea of legs like prison bars. I stab a stick into the ground, but it's too dry and hard, and the stick breaks.

"Wiener Dick," says Helena. "You're a disgusting weirdo. I heard you were getting the boys to play with your scabs and you nearly got expelled. I betcha did more than that. I betcha showed them your scabby fanny. It's the only way anyone will ever like ya."

"Bianca saw you eating your scabs," says Andrea.

"Gross," says Melinda with her pretty mouth screwed up so it looks like a cat's bum. "Scabs are so inhygienic."

"It's *un*hygienic," I say without thinking. "And scabs are the body's healing mechanism. They're perfectly natural. They're really clever, actually. They seal off the wound from the air so it can heal."

"You're such a freak. Didja eat a dictionary?" Melinda kicks my leg. It would hurt more if she was wearing a shiny school shoe. If I kick her back it will make a huge bruise. Shere Khan would eat her in one bite.

She kicks me again. "You think you're so smart using big words."

Heat makes me defiant.

"Unhygienic isn't a big word, it's a dirty word. Colossal is a big word. Or gargantuan. Or behemoth."

I should know better. It's not worth talking back or showing them how stupid they are, it just makes the whole thing last longer.

Melinda and Helena cross their arms, sharpen their tongues into dagger points, and start cutting. Their faces look so ugly, screwed up like this. They may not know big words, but they sure know mean ones. I've heard them all before.

I fade the meaning out, making the sounds random bird noises, lorikeet screeches. After a while I don't even hear them, which isn't true. My skin has holes in it now from where the road bit me. Vicious words don't slide off any more. They get stuck inside me like hakea spikes. Maybe I can pick them out with the rocks and bits of gravel later. I'd better, otherwise, when the skin heals, they'll get sealed in.

I feel nasty spider words crawling around inside my skin and shudder, wanting to brush them off. I keep my head down until the girls get bored and fly away to harass some other wounded animal.

I'm glad they don't know how boundless the world is when you know the best and biggest words. I can hide in whole countries, continents, planets, and solar systems, and they'll never find me, because their words are so small and can only paint tiny pictures. It's like being color blind, but worse.

After they finally leave, I lie back on baked earth, turning my head a little so a sizzle of sunlight falls through a crack in the fence into one of my eyes. I'm lying on a whole planet. It stretches as far as I can feel in all directions. Gravity keeps me stuck onto it. It holds my body with invisible arms. If gravity stopped, I would just float away. Everyone would, millions and billions of people and animals and trees all floating with nothing to stop them. Even the oceans would float away.

Small scritching sounds from a burrowing beetle scribble lines of sound into my ears. I turn to hear better, pressing my ear on the ground. Beneath all the ordinary noises something else rolls, something immense and indescribable. Does a planet have a heart? It is so very old and big, its heartbeat must be slow, like mountains creaking. Bah. Boom. Bah. Boom. Silence waits under everything I know, under even the heartbeat of a planet. It grows loud enough to pound inside my eyes. I tremble on the edge of an idea so fat it clicks my teeth, smooth and hard and shocking. The idea wants to tear the sky to ribbons. I'm afraid of what might be on the other side but the whistle blows and it's time to go to class.

In PE the teacher takes us to the quadrangle and asks us to walk around in a circle. I step outside the circle and walk the other way, chin up, ignoring the stares, taking the wrong way on purpose, shoulders back, eyes straight to show I don't want to be like the others, not even if it means I have a friend. It doesn't even occur to me to walk in the circle in the same direction as everyone else.

There's a place in my room where I talk to things that aren't there. They're alive in my mind, though, so bright and loud I can see them. I wish with all my heart that Doctor Who will arrive in his Tardis in my room and poke his head around the door with his long, multicolored scarf flapping and a big goofy smile, with his goggly eyes staring right at me.

"Come on," he'll say, beckoning. "What are you waiting for?"

Just like that I'll be the next *Doctor Who* girl. I'll be a huntress, like Leela, and we'll have adventures all over the universe, and I won't be scared of the big green slime maggots or the giant leech or the Daleks.

He never comes, not once.

More often, I just pray to the aliens. I send a letter to outer space, folded into a paper airplane so it can break through the hook of gravity and the earth's skin of atmosphere, which is thick and slows down spaceships. In my mind I write in big, neat writing, like Danni's, which is perfect. It's always the same message.

When you figure out what I am, can you tell me where the others are?

I like the red lipstick best, although I always seem to go outside the lines of my lips, no matter how carefully I put it on. It smells a bit stinky, like flowers that have been too long in the vase. Kristie and Danni paste blue eye shadow all the way to their eyebrows, which looks really grown up. I pass Danni the lipstick and hold out my hand for the eye shadow, slurping my Milo. I made it with more Milo than milk. The unmelted bits crunch under my tongue. I'm wearing the long pink and black dress from the dress-up box. Mum used to wear it out to posh parties before she had us. Having babies turned her sensible, Dad reckons, in a voice that sounds like he misses who she was before she was sensible, when she wore the see-through babydoll mini to a costume party with a white bra and knickers and he was in his undies with a rabbit tail on the bum and rabbit ears on his head. That photo is on the mirror. Mum's legs are so curvy they look like she's an ice skater in the Olympics. Dad doesn't have a beard, which just looks weird.

Danni's wearing the cream dress with the frilly cuffs that looks like the lady on the Cherry Ripe ad. Kristie's in the babydoll nightie. It goes almost to the floor on her. She spills her Milo and sucks it up with her mouth from the bench before she can get in trouble.

"Oh god, you rascals are going to get my lipstick everywhere. Be careful. It'll never get out of the carpet or the curtains," says Mum, poking her head into the room. Kristie looks guilty but Mum misses the Milo splashes in the general mayhem.

"Do I look like you, Mum?" says Kristie, pouting in the mirror. To me, she looks like a short, chubby clown, but I know Mum will get angry if I say it.

The corners of Mum's lips twitch.

"You look beautiful, darling."

Mum's adopted. Her dad died in the war and her mum died in childbirth, so we'll never get to meet them. Nan couldn't have babies of her own, and Grandpa's sister was the matron in the maternity ward. She said this baby was special, which is how we know Mum's real mum was famous.

We make up the best imaginary mothers for our own mother, who is so beautiful it's hard to think of her as ever being a kid like us.

"I think your mum was a Russian princess, and you have her mouth," says Danni. "Russians have big mouths, you know."

"No, she was a famous ballet dancer and you have her legs," says Kristie. We all look at Mum's muscly calves and nod. This is definitely a possibility.

"She was a famous opera singer and you have her voice," I say, and again we all nod. There is no arguing with Mum's voice, which even has the proper wobble like opera singers on the radio and is so loud it can cut through walls and even skin when we're in trouble. I think opera sounds screechy and awful. It must be one of those things that you need to be a grown-up to like, like olives or anchovies.

"She was a famous painter and one day you're going to see Chick written on a painting in a huge museum or on a school trip or something and it will be your mum, and we can buy it and put it on our wall next to your paintings and you'll be famous too," says Kristie.

"Don't be silly, that can never happen because Mum's real mum's name isn't Chick. That's Dad's name. We don't even know what her real mum's name is. Can we find out, Mum?"

"Nan and Grandpa are my real mum and dad now," says Mum in her That's Final voice.

"What's it like to be adopted?" Danni says while she smears lipstick across her mouth. "Do you miss your real mummy?"

"Well," says Mum, "I don't remember because I was just a tiny baby. I grew up thinking Nan and Grandpa were my birth parents until they told me I was adopted, and I just felt really lucky to have such wonderful parents. There was something I only realized when I had you girls, though. Adopted people don't grow up seeing faces that look like them. As soon as Gina was born it was the first time I saw my face in someone else, and then you, Danni, and you, Kristie."

"Even though I have blonde hair?"

"Even though you have blonde hair. You still look a bit like me. My history doesn't go backward like everyone else, only forward, with you three. It means I love you more than anything in the whole world."

Everyone says Mum's face is a postcard from my future. I don't know what that means but I get a funny feeling in my tummy when she pulls out the old black-and-white photos of herself as a schoolkid, and they look like me, but with different haircuts and old-fashioned clothes.

Sometimes Mum looks sad and I know she's thinking about her mum who died.

Most of the time, though, she spends her time playing the guitar so we can all sing together, or lays out all the colors on the front deck so we can paint, or teaches us rounds we sing for hours on our family adventures, or shows us how to take proper photos on the big camera, or takes us on bushwalks when we're camping so we can see the pademelons and pythons and huge mountains that touch the clouds, or buys us huge towers of books every Christmas that take the whole holidays to read. She presses native flowers under her art textbooks until they are flat as paper and warbles when she's adding to the paintings in our rooms so they're a jungle and an ocean. Best of all is when she unzips her dressing gown so we can all climb in like baby possums. She's the best mum in the whole universe.

"Douggie, can you take a photo of our gorgeous daughters, please?" Mum calls down the stairs. Dad appears with his camera. Mum stands in the middle while we do modeling poses with our posh made-up faces, wearing her old dresses. I can tell she's trying not to laugh.

Six puppies and six kittens roam over the day bed, where Knickers and Mrs. Cat take turns to look after them. When Mrs. Cat had her kittens first, Knickers stole them one at a time in her soft spaniel mouth, and Mrs. Cat stole them back, holding her head high so the mewling, dangling bundles wouldn't drag on the ground.

When Knickers birthed her puppies, the mothers decided to share the responsibilities. Puppies and kittens push to suckle at whichever mother is closest. When one of them goes off for a wee, the other rounds up the whole dozen. We help, of course.

Being a mother looks like hard work. Knickers and Mrs. Cat chase each other around the house, blowing off steam. Knickers isn't allowed upstairs, so Mrs. Cat perches up there, a haughty queen, licking her tail like she hasn't seen the dog and isn't teasing her on purpose. Then she launches onto the pine dining table, scoring deep scratches into the wood, while Knickers takes off after her. The cat leaps onto the other day bed and Knickers plows onto the rug, which skids and bunches across the floor. Mrs. Cat leaps over her head and streaks back up the stairs.

"Oh, for god's sake," says Mum, tripping over the dog on her way to the waste basket. Then, "Gina! Will you get that bloody blue-tongued lizard out of the bin?"

"Mu-uuum. I've got nowhere else to put it."

"Can't you let it go?"

"I've got to check its foot. I think a rat bit it."

"Well bloody well hurry up so I can throw the paper away. And can you get that pupa off the light cord? I nearly squashed it when I turned on the light."

"No, Mum. It's nearly hatched. I can't move it in case I hurt it."

Sunshine pools around Danni, finishing off the crocheted leash for her duck, Plop, which lives up to its name by squirting a giant green shit all over the floorboards.

"Ducks OUTSIDE! OUTSIDE! And clean that up!" Mum shouts, skidding in it.

Kristie's duck, Boffy, nibbles geraniums on the front deck while Danni mops up duck poo. My duck, Gobbleguts, squirms under one of my arms. I juggle masks and snorkels for all of us with the other, stuffing them into the beach bag.

"Sunscreen! Hats! Do you have water?"

"Yes, Mum," we say. Dad slings the snorkeling bag over his shoulder, freeing me to wrestle my duck. Knickers raises floppy ears at the word "beach." Beach means rabbit burrows, which means disappearing for hours and emerging with no rabbits. Instead, she lugs her body weight home in extra sand, which we have to sluice out of her fur with a high-powered hose.

A puppy nudges at her. Her ears drop. She sighs and returns to the more important business of licking her babies. No rabbit chases for new mothers.

"I'll be down soon," says Mum, settling into a chair with a cup of tea and a book.

We don't really need leads for the ducks, which we imprinted when they were hatchlings. David Attenborough says that baby birds and mammals attach to the first moving object they see, so we had to make sure that was us, so they would think we were their mothers forever. Dad brought them home as balls of yellow fluff from the agricultural department at the high school. Year seven kids get to imprint three-day-old ducklings and look after them, and Dad snaffled three extras for us. He said they'll be useful, because they lay eggs twice the size of chook eggs and can live in the chook pen. We're running out of room what with the guinea pigs and the mice and the chooks and the ant farm and all my rescued animals and the red-bellied black snake Dad caught in the woodpile that's now coiled into an oily knot in the spare mouse cage. He hasn't told Mum about it yet. She'll make him take it up to the golf course later to let it go. I want to come with him and watch.

The ducks have grown into giant white terrors the size of geese whose entire purpose in life is to shit. They must be males because the only eggs in the pen are from the chooks, who are not impressed at having to share their run with the water-hogging marauders.

Finally, we get out of the house. The ducks follow us like slow dogs, stopping every few steps to waggle their tails. It's good to have the lead on a duck leg when we cross the road, in case they get spooked and fly into a car. Cars slow down and rubberneck. Whatever.

The nor'-easter hasn't hit yet, so the water's flat as paper and throws light around. At low tide, the Rock is partly exposed. It looks like a crocodile and is alternately a fort, a palace, a launchpad, a pirate ship, a castle, a dragon, a home for fish, a rocket, and a million other things, depending what game we're playing.

Today it's a place to escape from ducks trying to scramble onto our backs when we're swimming. Their claws tear long rips in water-softened skin. I'm on a mission to catch fish for the aquarium. Freshwater fish were a bloody disaster. They kept getting pop eye, which is when one of their eyes bulged out until they died, or they caught a gross skin disease called Ick that looked like something from *Doctor Who*. I think Ick is the best name for a disease I've ever heard. Because, Ick, right? We flush the fish down the toilet when they die.

Dad came up with the idea for a saltwater aquarium and it's brilliant. The eroded sandstone rocks we've foraged from the beach have caves and hollows for fish to hide in. If (when) fish die, we just catch new ones. Danni caught an angelfish the other day, which Mum said was appropriate 'cause she's an angel. Kris and I pretended to vomit where Mum couldn't see but Danni could, and the hurt in her eyes was obvious. She's such a goody-goody I don't care. Mum sometimes says, why can't you be more like your sister, and I want to say, I don't know how. But really, I wouldn't even if I could.

I'm on the hunt for a moray eel, which Mum says are only on the Barrier Reef, but you never know, one might be lost.

"You have to keep the ducks so they don't try to climb on me when I catch an eel," I tell my sisters.

"Bossy boots," says Kris. "Why do you get to go for a swim? It's not fair."

"You do it now, and then I'll mind them so you can both have a swim after. I'll be quick."

"You always take ages, Gi."

"I'll be quick this time. I promise."

I jump in before she can argue anymore, which doesn't stop her. I dive down to block out the sound, into the cool world hiding beneath the skin of the sea. It's anything but silent, alive with strange clicks and pops and the soft background shush of sand under wave. If I close my eyes, I'm in an alien world, which in a way is true. I wonder if the clicks are fish talking to each other. Maybe I can learn to speak ocean. I sing into the snorkel so it sounds like a dolphin and look around to see if any dolphins want to come to play.

I can hold my breath for a long time. I practice whenever I swim. Dad used to be able to hold his breath for the length of the whole swimming pool. I dive to the bottom and count one, two, three . . . When I see stars at fifteen and my belly heaves, I scrabble for the surface, popping water out of the snorkel, heaving in air. Dolphins can hold their breath for ten minutes or more. I want to be a dolphin. I hold my ankles together and kick as if I have a tail. Then I see a school of little neon fish hiding under an overhang in the Rock and go after them. I manage to get two and hold my hand over the net while I wade to shore, where the bucket is. I dive back in before Danni and Kristie notice.

Back at the rock, I start to hunt properly. Most of the fish are too big. There's a sea slug, which shoots out purple ink if you squeeze it. I put it on the rock to throw at my sisters later. We call them green goo, and when we have a proper green goo fight, we end up covered in purple ink, which stains our swimsuits. I yank off my flippers and crouch on the edge of the rock, peering into the pools and seaweed.

A piece of rock moves. My mask is fogged. I push it onto my forehead and look again. I can't see anything until the rock moves again, and there is a flash of bright blue in small circles, which fade, then return. And then I know what it is, and my heart tries to jump out of my eyeballs with excitement.

It's an octopus. A blue-ringed octopus, which can kill you in a few minutes. When we went on a holiday to Heron Island, the lady ranger told us about a man who was collecting shells illegally and he put them down his swim trunks. One of the shells had a blue-ringed octopus in it and it bit him on the willy. He nearly died and his willy never got better. The only reason he lived was because the octopus must have bitten a lot of the shells before it got to his willy, so it ran out of venom.

The sides of the ranger's mouth kept twitching when she was telling the story. Dad shuffled around and looked uncomfortable, but Mum just laughed and said, "Don't steal any shells, Doug," and he said, "No fear, it's not worth it."

While we were there, I found a white heron that was covered in oil and caught it. It tried to stab me with its long, sharp beak, but I told it we were going to get it cleaned up so it could fly again and it stopped trying to stab my eyes. We washed the oil off and dried it with a towel and took it to the ranger lady, who said I was a budding conservationist. Mum bought me a T-shirt in the Heron Island shop. It said Oil And Water Don't Mix, Save The Reef. I wore it every day for the rest of the trip.

The blue-ringed octopus is getting away. It takes a couple of tries to get it in the net, but finally I do. I jump around and dance because I am so happy. This will be the best thing in the aquarium, better than a moray eel. I hold the net up close, to look at it, all mottled and perfect, covered in bright blue pulsing circles. It's so beautiful I want to cry.

I crouch on the rock, looking closer. It uses tentacles to pull itself along and crawls up the handle of the net. Then one of the tentacles wraps around my finger, and it pulls itself onto my hand and I suddenly realize this is not ideal and I might die, like right now.

I shake my hand but the octopus is stuck, so I grab it and pull and shake and it comes free, arcing through the air to land on the beach. I wade and run to get it and scoop it up again, then put it in the bucket. It pulses impossible, electric blue, swirling around the bottom of the red bucket making octopus calligraphy. It's the most wonderful thing I've ever seen.

Danni and Kristie have made a fort for the ducks to play in and are making dribbly castles with wet sand along the top. I run up with the bucket.

"Guess what I caught for the aquarium? It's the best thing ever. Look."

"What is it? Is it a seahorse?"

"It's better."

"Nothing's better than a seahorse," says Danni.

"This is!" I am triumphant. "It's a BLUE-RINGED OCTOPUS!"

"Woaaaaaah."

We all peer in, letting this awesome thing be true.

"It'll eat the other fish. We can't keep it," says Kris.

"We can catch other fish. It's a BLUE-RINGED OCTOPUS, and it got on my hand but it didn't bite me because it likes me!"

"Betcha Mum makes you throw it back."

"Stop it, Plop, get out. It'll bite you and you'll die."

We crouch over the bucket and shove at the ducks to keep them from trying to stick their heads in. Dad wades over to see what the commotion is. He's never seen a blue-ringed octopus before, either.

This is the best day of my life.

When we slide it into the aquarium, it hides under the rocks, then sits on the sand and gradually turns more and more pale, until the only way I can see it is by holding the shape of it fixed in my mind. Then it explores all the glass walls. Its underside looks a bit like a starfish, but squishier. I wave at it and introduce myself.

"Hi, I'm Gina, and this is your new home. Do you like it? Mum, it waved a tentacle at me. It heard me. I have a pet octopus."

I stay by the aquarium for hours, just watching. I wonder if it's hungry. It hasn't tried to eat any of the other fish yet. I'll catch some crabs for its dinner.

I run back down to the beach and spend an hour catching small crabs in rock pools by pressing on their backs, then picking them up by the sides of their shells so their pincers can't reach my fingers. When I've got a few in the bucket, I run back up the hill to give them to the octopus, which must be really hungry by now, because I am.

Nobody's around. Mum's asleep with a book over her face on the couch. Dad's building something noisy in the garage, and Danni and Kris are playing Uno downstairs. I consider telling them I'm going to feed the octopus but decide not to. It's my pet and I want to feed it so it gets tame just for me. Most pirates have a parrot on their shoulder. I want to be a pirate with a deadly octopus on mine.

I pull a crab out of the bucket and look for where the octopus is hiding. I can't see it so I go to the other side of the aquarium. I can't see it there either.

Five minutes later I yell, "Mum, Dad, the octopus is gone."

"Whaddya mean gone?" Mum's voice is thick and groggy.

"It's not in the tank."

"It's just hiding under a rock."

"No, it's not. It's NOT HERE AT ALL."

Mum walks down the stairs like a zombie and rubs her face.

"Right. Let's find your octopus."

Five minutes later she opens the front door and yells down to the garage.

"Doug! DOUG! You'd better get up here."

Danni and Kristie follow the commotion, and we have a family meeting.

The octopus. Is gone.

A quick flick through *Encyclopaedia Britannica* confirms that octopuses have only one hard object in their bodies: their beaks. They can squeeze through any space their beak can fit through. We all stare at the openings where the air and heating lines go into the tank and come to the same conclusion.

Crap.

A small, lethal blue-ringed octopus that can camouflage itself to its environment is loose somewhere in the house.

"You wanted a house full of animals," Dad says to Mum.

"Not helping, Doug," says Mum.

We spread out. Where would an octopus hide?

"Anywhere it wants," says Dad, and Mum gives him one of her Looks.

I find my errant pet at the stop of the stairs, making a bid for freedom. It flashes blue warnings at me, like traffic lights. When I deposit it back in the tank, it scoots under the rock and changes color from carpet to stone. It is immaculate. A marvel.

"You can't keep it, Gina. It'll keep escaping," Mum says. "And, Doug, that red-bellied black snake has to go. No venomous animals in the house."

"Mu-uuuum. We can plug up the holes in the tank so it can't escape again. I can tame the octopus, I promise. And the snake isn't in the house, it's in the shed, and it's in the old mouse cage so it can't run away."

"The octopus is too dangerous. What if it escapes in the night and crawls into someone's bed?"

"It won't if I train it."

"No," she says, in her this-is-final voice. "And the snake has to go, Doug. Now."

"That's all right, Dad," I whisper. "We can let it go in the roof and it can eat the mice."

Mum flips.

"NO YOU CAN'T LET THE RED-BELLIED BLACK SNAKE GO IN THE ROOF! AND GET THIS BLOODY BLUE TONGUE OUT OF THE WASTE BASKET. AND GET RID OF THIS FUCKING OCTOPUS."

For some reason Mum puts her head in her hands. The moment smells like razor blades and vinegar. It's the smell that often billows around her in the kitchen, when we all hide downstairs as the catastrophic clanging and crashing of pans is only overshadowed by the volume of her swearing. Mum loathes cooking as much as she hates eating peas or fish.

"I know—I can put the octopus in our museum," I say. "I'll study it like a marine biologist."

The museum started out as a playhouse for us and our awesome cousins, who are the same age as us and with whom we have the best adventures every school break at their farm out past Bathurst, or at our house on the beach.

Last break, the playhouse turned into a science project. It's filled with skeletons of birds, a turtle shell, nests that blew down in the rain, Mum's pressed flowers, a nautilus, a mummified weedy sea dragon, fossils we found by smashing rocks, an assortment of feathers, and my prized discovery, a white-bellied sea eagle's wing. Everything has a scientific name if we can find it and a list of facts in my messy writing, or Danni's neat cursive. Now it will house a blue-ringed octopus, *Hapalochlaena maculosa*.

I find a jar and half fill it with alcohol. When I tip the octopus in, it hisses and dies immediately, stretched rigid, glorious colors sundered and the exquisite blue circles reduced to dead gray lines. It's the wrongest thing I've ever done, except for accidentally cooking the bird egg. I cry myself to sleep all week, so sad for the octopus I stole from the sea so I could study it. It will never swim again. All its beauty is gone. My heart is a stone made of ache. I vow never to preserve another living animal again. I will only collect ones that are already dead.

Our tin roof thunders with rain. Giants galumph with heavy boots, kicking up huge sprays of water. My hair is electric. I can't sleep, it's all too wonderful.

When Mum and Dad finally creak up the top stairs to bed, I wait for ages just to be sure, then slip out the front door in a T-shirt and undies. The rain is so cold it shocks me into running. I hug the shadows, in case Mum and Dad are awake after all, looking out the window. Streetlights throw curtains of jewels as I flit like Mrs. Cat, not that she'd be out on a night like this. I'm drenched and freezing, but I don't care. This is apocalyptic and I feel all the way alive.

My feet know their way to the beach. The sand is colder than the rain. I run, shouting and crying at the same time, around the rocky point, into the full force of Storm.

Luckily it's low tide, so the promontory of flat rocks is exposed. It's studded with sharp periwinkles and limpets, but my feet are hard as couch leather and anyway, I can't feel anything over the howl of wind and spray. I see only darkness, so I must hear and feel my way. I know these rocks like I know my sisters' faces. They won't shrug me off. We're family.

Water everywhere, in my eyes and ears and teeth. Waves snarl and gnash, reaching for me. I hear words in their black faces. *Mine. Mine.* They're monsters that want to devour me, but I'm safe here, at the edge of the rocks, although the spray is ferocious. Lightning spears high above, count one, two, three, and the answering crack shocks me so hard I nearly slip over, even though I'm braced for it.

This is pure maelstrom chaos. This is the storm that happens in every cell in my body as it burns energy to fuel me. The storm in my nerves as they pass information along synapses. In my heart muscle as it beats. The storm of my emotions, my abyssal loneliness, my love for life. Somehow, I'm not afraid. In the middle of this whirlpool of insane fury, I feel quiet and calm, buffeted by wind, sheets of water, and throbbing darkness. I spread my arms as if they're wings, catching whipping eddies in my fists. This is how big I feel inside. This feels true to the bone. This is what I am. I make sense.

I'm not a human; I am a storm wrapped in skin.

I'm blue lipped and shivering when I let myself back into the house, dripping water on the carpet. My fingers feel like swarms of bees are trapped inside them, they're buzzing so hard. In the morning I wonder if it even happened, but for the faint outline of sandy wet feet stitching an unsteady line from the front door to my room.

Mum's worried about me again. I smell this as fresh-cut orange and mothballs. She's reading one of her revolving-door books about raising kids. The three of us hide when she comes home with a new one and wait to see what fresh hell will ensue. It's my job to sneak upstairs while Mum is in the garden and read as much as I can to find out what we're in for.

This one has a chapter called "the influence of friends," and my belly churns. I don't know what a friend is. Apparently you have to "make" a friend. I don't understand how to make one. Is it like baking a cake? Maybe there's a recipe in the book and I just have to find it. I scan but find no instructions for friendship. I tear off the corners of a couple of pages and eat them, just in case.

"Did you play with any friends today?" Mum asks, every afternoon, with that cut-orange and mothball smell. I lie and say yes, loads, we skipped rope and played tag.

Mowgli has friends, so I know it's possible. I study groups of kids to figure out what they're doing that I'm not.

Dad says I need to find common ground, things the other person is interested in. That sounds easy, so I approach a girl in my class after a test and say, "I got 98 percent. What did you get?" Her face goes red and her hands shake. She doesn't even reply. I ask a boy the same question. He shuffles his feet. I approach a group of boys and tell them about the feeding habits of New Holland honeyeaters. After a while they get up, one by one, and walk away, until only Donny Rigdon with the thick glasses is left, staring at the ground.

I steal coins from the coin jar and find the cool kids, the ones who always seem to be playing rowdy games. They obviously know how to make friends. I offer them money, twenty cents and ten cents and even fifty cents. They take it with wary eyes, like it's a trick. Later I feel hungry and ask for the money back so I can buy lunch. They call me an "Indian Giver" and throw the money at me and then toss dirt in my eyes.

I don't understand what makes someone a friend.

Mum asks again, "What did you do today? Did you play with some friends?" I tell her about my friend Jonathan Livingston Seagull, and that the library is my favorite place in school. The cut-orange and mothballs smell grows strong.

Mowgli and Bagheera chase each other through my room at night. Buck from *White Fang* pulls a sled through the icy wastelands that close around my heart after a really bad day at school, while wolves howl in the forest and the curling silence of snow throws spells of wonder over the acid pain of rejection. Bilbo, Frodo, and Sam sweep me into forests that speak and introduce me to elves and dwarves and spiders the size of houses. Tarka the otter dives and twists in figure eights through the water of my blood. Fiver and Blackberry and all the rabbits from *Watership Down* gambol with the moles of *Duncton Wood.* I have young Gerry Durrell and his animals, related or otherwise. I have Grandpa Chook—"first with the head, then with the heart." Storm Boy is my brother, Mr. Percival another. Over and over, I push through the wardrobe into Narnia to melt the icy winter of my heart. Aslan pads through my room.

Worlds within worlds within worlds.

My belly clenches around all the paper I've swallowed. When I'm not reading, I tap at mountains to free the songs trapped in their old cold bones, which swell inside me to burst out as music. I crawled onto the piano and taught myself to play when I was little. Mum says I have a good ear. My hands ripple across the old ivory keys of our heavy purple piano as music chooses me from some place I don't ever see, but it reaches out to touch me, to tell me I'm loved, and pours itself through my fingers in skeins of melody and harmony.

Life is a series of stories. I have the best friends in the whole world.

And then I meet Modesty Blaise.

She's the most exotic thing I've ever seen. Smoky dark eyes smolder from the silver cover. She's wrapped in a tight, shiny black jumpsuit that's zipped down to her belly button and high-heeled boots. The book smells musty and exciting. I'm sure it's too grown up for me, so I don't tell Mum and Dad I'm reading it. As soon as the words unfurl into pictures behind my eyes, I know this is who I want to be when I grow up. Many page corners do not survive the first reading. So much paper fills my belly it hurts a little.

I devour the Modesty Blaise books, then immediately read them all again. She is a retired criminal who used to run an organization called the Network and still has contacts through the underworld. Her lieutenant is a blond giant named Willie Garvin, who is a savant with knives but can't use a gun. He adores her but will never sleep with her. It's an honor thing.

She's a master of combat and carries a carved wooden piece called a kongo in her hair, which she uses to strike pressure points in a fight. She's lethal but also kind. She and Willie train in any style they can find. Judo, karate, quarterstaffs, and archery. They have adventures called "capers," which always involve their lovers getting in trouble and needing to be rescued in some way. Willie and Modesty fight the baddies and win. After the caper, she always cries, but only on Willie, then gets angry with herself for doing so.

I resolve not to cry in the middle of things, like when the girls at school pick on me. Only afterward, where nobody can see.

My body hurts, all the time. Since falling out of the car, I can't sit in one place for longer than half an hour without pain thumping around under my skin, all fat and hot like some creature from *Doctor Who*. I shuffle and toss around the bed to ease the throbs and aches chewing at me from the inside, mapping my whole skeleton in gnawed bones. Dark bruises bloom under my eyes.

Mum and Dad find a chiropractor in Nowra who specializes in putting bones back into their right places. He says when we fell out of the car, the bones in our spines got shoved out of position, and our muscles are really tight because they're trying to push the bones back in place.

He has a chair that reclines, with the word "RELAX" on a small square sign on the ceiling. The nurse holds me down when

I struggle, so he can try to rip my head from my shoulders with a horrendous cracking sound. If he doesn't get the result he wants the first time, he enlists Dad to press his whole weight onto my shoulders so he can try again and again, ignoring me when I plead for him to stop. I can't move my neck for days afterward.

Eventually Mum finds an osteopath, who massages before he manipulates and teaches Dad the basics. When Dad massages, it's like being poked by an Ent with crowbars for fingers. Danni's fingers are strong and kind.

Danni and I knead each other around the winter fire in our red dressing gowns while our sandwiches toast in the coals. Egg and cheese, banana and honey, bubbling hot margarine to make the bread and escaped cheese super crunchy. I sit behind Danni while she keeps one eye on the pie iron, my elbows in the tops of her shoulders. We know where the sore spots in each other are, but the pain never actually goes away. I sleep in short jabs, but the pain even follows me there.

What would Modesty Blaise do? She's been shot and stabbed and broken most of her bones. She walked through the Middle East barefoot. She's even been tortured. She wraps pain in velvet and puts it somewhere where her mind can't find it.

I've read a book of Dad's on hypnotism. When I can't sleep because of the pain monster crunching my bones in its awful, tender teeth, I imagine a candle in my mind. I focus on the blue part at the bottom of the flame, falling into it until it's louder than all the hurt.

The pain never leaves, but sometimes I fall back to sleep. Most of the time, though, I just turn on the light and read more *Modesty Blaise*, or James Bond, or cuddle a pet lion in *Born Free*, or look at the pictures by Ainslie Roberts in my favorite book of Aboriginal stories, *The Dreamtime*. Those pictures are better than a doorway to Narnia. They suck my whole room away until I'm floating in the sky with an emu made of ten billion stars. My room echoes with the click of clapsticks and the yowling drone of didgeridoos. Dirt flips around my bed from stamping feet, and firelight reflects from teeth and eyes in the darkness of the time before time, when animals spoke in human voices and humans wore animal faces and even the trees and rocks could talk. They still can; it's just that grown-ups can't hear them.

If the story is good enough, it swallows the pain for a while.

A triangle of paper dissolves on my tongue, drowning out the schoolyard squeals and shouts. Modesty fights for her life in a cave of icy water. The baddie, Sexton, is undefeated in unarmed combat and thinks he'll kill her easily. She's covered herself in grease so his hands slide off. I want to be Modesty Blaise so badly I bite hard into the wad of paper, catching my tongue by accident, and the yearning tastes like iron.

A shiny, impossibly yellow-and-red plastic packet lands in my lap with a rustling thump, startling me out of the book. For a moment I have no idea what it is, or even where or who I am. I stare at it, trying to figure out what just happened, coming back to schoolyard anarchy from the dark cave of black water where Modesty has gone under, with no ripples to show whether she's dead or alive. I'm terrified she may be dead, and now there's a packet of cheese Twisties on the page.

My favorite.

Where did they come from?

I look behind me, see a figure running away. Long gray socks. Shorts. Sandy hair, ears that stick out a little. It's Jesse Walker. He's in my class and he talks to me sometimes when nobody else will, which is mostly.

I look at my book. The packet of Twisties is still there.

I like Jesse. He has a kind face and he knows some birds. He can do a magpie call that sounds really awesome. It seems he knows I like Twisties. I shrug and open them, eating the whole pack. When they're gone, I scrape the salty cheese paste off my fingers with my teeth and lick them clean.

After that, every day there's another offering and a pair of tanned boy-legs running away. Chips. Cheezels. A Mars bar. After a couple of weeks, another boy brings a note. It says:

Will you go with me? Jesse.

I look at the boy. I think his name is Ben. He sits with Jesse most days and does the best yo-yo tricks, Walk the Dog and Around the World. Yo-yos are banned, not that it stops anyone.

"Tell him I said yes."

"You have to write it," he says. "Otherwise it doesn't count."

I write *YES* in big letters, going harder over the bit where the pen didn't work.

The next day Jesse delivers Twisties in person and sits with me at recess, and we talk about lyrebirds and stink bugs and dolphins and barn owls, and I don't care that I'm not allowed to watch *Grease*, or my hair is crooked, or I have a gap between my teeth. He's getting a bug catcher for his birthday. I tell him to bring it to school and I'll bring mine and maybe we can look at what we catch under the microscope I got for Christmas.

His eyes are wide and light colored, and his hair has sun streaks like the girls get from putting lemon juice in theirs. His smile jumps into my bones and squirms around like puppies. I want to protect him the way Modesty Blaise protects Willie Garvin. I need to learn to fight like Modesty. If aliens try to take him away, I'll be able to kick them and break their alien fingers so they can't have him and then we'll escape. I'll be able to fly. I'll fly us up and away like Jonathan Livingston Seagull and show him how to fly past the edge of the sky.

The next note asks if we can hold hands.

YES, I write, heart pounding. But disaster comes in the form of Narelle, my nemesis. She likes Jesse as well. I see her whispering in his ear at lunchtime and looking at me. He turns to stare, with a terrible expression on his face. I don't know what she said to him. When I go to ask, he walks away, and the next day Ben tells me I'm dropped and won't say why.

Storm Boy by Colin Thiele is a wind-driven shriek in my blood. When Mr. Percival dies, I am cloven. Why do animals always die in all the books? The boy is just like me on the inside, but in boy skin. I'm pretty sure I'm a boy on the inside and there's been a mistake. Can I send my body back and get a different one?

The Boy hears the song the earth sings, and the sea, and especially the wind. He knows what the waves say and all the ways currents show what's really going on. If he was at my school, he would be my best friend, but the whole point is he isn't at school; he's where he's supposed to be, wandering the estuaries and lakes, blown by the best breezes, free to roam.

If he's Storm Boy, I suppose I must be Storm Girl. All I need is a pelican, but really, I want an eagle. I want an eagle so badly at night I dream I am one, twitching to change direction, higher than all the other birds except the hunting swifts that loop like fighter jets, up where the air is rare.

Dad thunders up the stairs and into the house on giant size twelve feet with thick nails that invariably slice through the ends of his shoes. Mum and I are at the table, each with a fat book open in front of us, squinting over the tiny writing.

"Ooh, Mum, this one. 'Coruscating.'"

"How do you spell it?"

I spell out the word, then say, "It's a word for the play of light on water. What a banger. Light coruscates, Mum."

We both stare out the sliding glass door to the sparkling bay, alive with glowing silver discs.

"It certainly does."

I tuck the word into my ribs for later.

She glances at me across the table. She has such a kind face, with heaps of laugh lines and a big smiley mouth, and she loves me so much it sometimes feels like seeing all the colors in the paintbox at once and they hurt my eyes.

"Gina, you know that school is only a tiny part of your life. It's not forever. You'll grow up and follow your enormous talents into worlds you can't even imagine now. One day, you'll find your people, the ones who love the same things you do, and love you as well."

"I'm okay, really."

"Or they'll find you. I promise."

Mum's finger tracks down her page like a hunting crane, spears a wriggling word, and delivers it onto the table. "Nadir. It's the opposite of apex."

"So school is my nadir, Mum?"

She smiles like I'm already a grown-up and we share a secret.

"Something like that."

Dad shakes his head. "You two playing Dictionary again? You do know there are about two thousand actual books in this house?"

"Make us a cuppa, love?" Mum says, leaning back. He rubs her shoulders and kisses her forehead.

"Of course. You, too, Gigi?"

"Yes, please."

Piping soprano voices from ABC Classic radio cascade around us in streams that braid and billow. I catch the notes on my tongue like snowflakes in Narnia. When they swell into rivers, the water flows right back out of my eyes. Mum's just as bad. Her voice quavers on a hovering arc of dissonance and we both gush tears when the final chord resolves and releases us from the tension.

Music paints the spaces in the house. Joan Baez and Joni Mitchell and Neil Diamond. *Hot August Night.* Billy Joel, Elton John, us kids know all the words and take turns choosing which record will deliver booming magic through the latest massive speakers Dad built in the garage, about five times more powerful than the room needs. Records are spells that change the world. I handle the black discs with my fingertips so as not to scratch them.

Classical music tells the best stories, ones you see in your mind, like books. *Swan Lake* and Beethoven and Bach and Handel's *Water Music.* When we were little, we followed along to *Peter and the Wolf,* dancing to all the parts while Mum explained how the music told the story. That string melody, that's Peter, wandering through the forest. Those French horns are the wolf sneaking up on him. Every time "In the Hall of the Mountain King" played, we'd push the carpet back and stomp and whirl like the wild rumpus in *Where the Wild Things Are* until we fell in panting heaps, Dad included.

Mum has a huge contralto voice that sounds like a dark angel is kicking down the door to my heart. Danni and I have high voices that Mum says are like boy sopranos. We harmonize to Mum's melodies and sing with Mum in the Lydian Singers, a madrigal group that does concerts where we wear our white dresses and everyone tells us we're angels.

Kristie doesn't have a musical ear, but we aren't allowed to tell her that, or tease her when the notes are wrong. It's really hard for me as anything that's even a tiny bit out of tune sounds like the ending of worlds. I see all the chords in my head and don't understand how everyone can't pluck harmonies out of the air. It's just a matter of picking out the ribbon of music that's hanging in space, waiting to be captured, and following where it leads. When nobody's looking, I reach out my fingers to play with the notes like they're harp strings hanging in space.

Mum shudders and shouts *Ohhhhhhh* as Fauré's "Requiem" fills the room. *With drooping wings, ye cupids come.* Dictionaries forgotten, Mum and I sing in tight harmonic thirds. Her voice sounds like a cello. The song is so sad I feel like my chest is made of shattered glass.

Danni and Kristie barrel into the kitchen, breaking the spell with their ruckus. We all sing the different parts of our favorite rounds at the tops of our lungs as we make sandwiches for this weekend's adventure. Maybe we'll go visit the baby penguins in our little boat with the thirty-five-horsepower motor that's just powerful enough to pull us up on the waterskis Dad made. Dad's banned from singing because of his tin ear, so he tiddley poms for comic effect.

The front door tut-tuts, maybe it doesn't like the tiddley poms.

"Hello 'ello 'ello," booms Dad in his huge grown-up papa-bear voice, wandering down to see who it is. Sounds of mumbling and murmuring float up the stairs, then I'm summoned. I don't know what I've done wrong.

The neighbor from the squat house with the red roof down the road smiles at me. He offers a scraggly bundle wrapped in a tea towel. A baby crimson rosella twists and struggles in the folds. It's all mottled green, with red patches and a pink beak and scruffy pin feathers.

"You're the bird girl, right? This one was in the backyard; our cat had it. I think it's a king parrot."

"It's a juvenile crimson rosella," I say. "You can tell it's a juvie 'cause of the pink beak, and its colors haven't come in yet, which is why it's all red and green. It's a male, so will be all red when it matures, with that blue patch just here next to its beak. The females stay green. Also, see these feathers that have funny white stuff on the bottom? They're the sheaths of grown-up feathers. They just flake off if you roll them between your fingers."

The neighbor looks at me strangely, then shrugs and hands the bird over.

I take the squiggly bundle, wrapping two fingers to firmly grasp the back of its head so it can't bite me with that strong parrot beak. Even juveniles leave a nasty bruise and can break the skin. I've learned this the hard way.

"Keep the tea towel," says the neighbor. "You can bring it back later, Bird Girl."

I take the rosella to my room and shut the door so it can't escape. It perches on my finger, wobbles a bit, shakes itself, and shits on the seagrass mat that annoyingly presses ridges into my bum, but also hides the inevitable flakes of fallen crayon, biscuit crumbs, acres of sand, and globs of crap from various animals until Mum cracks the shits and makes me vacuum.

I scratch around its beak, rolling the pin coverings between my fingernails to scrape off the sheaths and release the feathers rolled up inside. The bird drops its head to let me scratch it, eyes closed in bliss. It makes low begging sounds. I feel its crop, which is empty, and the begging intensifies.

"Hungry, huh? Let me look at you first."

I spread the bird's wings. They seem fine. It probably blew down in last night's storm and was too wet and silly to fly. I chew up seed, grimacing a bit at the taste, and push my lips around the pink beak. The baby makes wheezing noises and lets the paste go in with a bobbing motion. I'll be picking millet husks from between my teeth all night.

Once its crop is nice and full, I find a sock and hold it open so I can get the bird in, tail first. Only its head is visible. It closes its eyes, warm, fed, and contained. When I open my wardrobe, a row of similar socks stir, and tiny heads poke out. Yellow maws gape and little lungs wheeze as my other rescues beg for their next meal.

The babies are Bourke's parrots from the aviary, which I'm taming to sell as pets, next to a honeyeater with a bruised wing and a finch hopping around with a broken leg, which Mum and I splinted with a split matchstick and some cotton. It looks like the leg is dying, though; we may have to amputate it with Mum's sewing scissors.

I add the rosella to the shelf and traipse upstairs to mix up the next batch of egg and breadcrumb mix, which is a baby bird formula. You're supposed to use a syringe to get it into the baby birds' gullets, but it's easier just to spit it in.

Birds shock and die easily, especially when they live with two cats and a dog, but a few of mine make it, and I let them go once they can fly properly. They often hang around for months because they've imprinted on me as their new mother. When I go outside, random birds try to land in my hair or on the handlebars of my bike when I'm riding down to the shops.

Poor Mrs. Cat is traumatized because every time a bird flutters, someone throws a shoe at her, just in case. Now, whenever she hears bird wings, she bolts under the couch. Knickers wants to retrieve the scrabbling scraps of feathers when she finds them, but she's so daft she doesn't notice them half the time. Mum says she's probably dreaming of rabbits. Dad says she's just a gorgeous dope.

*

Mum's floating around the house, humming her Christmas hums, like Pooh Bear. Christmas Day is when she was born to her mysterious and undoubtably famous dead mother, then abandoned, before being adopted by Nan and Grandpa.

"It's terrible being born on Christmas Day," she says, often. "Nobody comes to your birthday party."

We've spent our whole lives making up for her lack of birthday parties. Christmas must always be a huge fuss. Every year, we head into the local pine forest to choose a suitable Christmas tree, which is inevitably too tall for the four-meter ceiling in the living room. This year, Dad's rigged a new system for holding it in place, a series of bungee cords roped around the base, which last precisely four seconds after Mum catches sight of the tangle of bright orange and blue cables at floor level, with another three up the tree, holding it to rusty nails in the wall.

She bursts into tears.

"DOUG! What have you DONE? It's HORRIBLE. You've RUINED Christmas."

"It's beautiful, lovey," he says. "Look, the tree stays in place, it's easy to decorate, you can duck under these ones. It's perfect."

"It's ugly as sin and you have to take it away RIGHT NOW."

Christmas is fraught. Any tragedy on the news or courtesy of Dad breaking Christmas brings home to Mum that she's adopted, and she trails through the house, singing carols and weeping in equal measure.

We go back to using stacked garden rocks in the pot, as usual, and the tree lurches to one side when Knickers chases the cats and they run up the middle of it, scattering tinsel.

Mum decorates the tree as if it's the ceiling of the Sistine Chapel. I'm banned from helping because I throw tinsel anywhere. Danni's perfectionism means she's enlisted. We have to hang the precious glass balls up high, out of reach of Mrs. Cat, who bats at her reflection and smashes untold treasures. The huge, ancient star that's been handed down from Nan and Grandpa goes to Dad, because he's the only one with long enough arms to balance it on the waving tip of the tree.

Mum warbles as she works, telling Christmas stories we've heard a gazillion times.

"When I was a girl, our church choir would go through the neighborhood, carrying candles and singing carols for all the houses."

"Why don't *we* do that, Mum?" I say, suddenly fired up by the romance of it.

"What, here?"

Vincentia is hardly sophisticated. Mum misses the shows, exhibitions, concerts, and plays of her young years. She makes up for it by putting on musicals and art exhibitions. Living here is part of the sacrifice she made to have a family. It's worth it for the beaches, our sprawling house, weekends bushwalking and camping and adventuring up cliffs and in caves. The one thing we don't have nearby is "culture."

"Yes, here. Mum, it'll be awesome. We know all the carols, we can practice and get really good. We can bring a hat and people can give us money."

"It's not Halloween, Gina. We're singing to spread Christmas spirit, not ask for coins."

"Come on, Mum. It'll be fun."

We kids wear our angel dresses as our little orchestral choir floats through the neighborhood, knocking on doors. They open to reveal delighted faces as we launch into a slightly wobbly, but passable concert. Knickers wags her bum and goes up onto porches for pats, and Mrs. Cat flits through the shadows like we're all idiots, but she doesn't want to miss out.

We have a book of Australian Christmas carols and we sing them, along with the old favorites.

The north wind is tossing the leaves
The red dust is over the town
The swallows are under the eaves
And the grass in the paddock is brown
As we lift up our voices and sing
To the Christ child, the heavenly king.

We giggle and mumble the Christ child bit, but the rest is lovely. Mum leads, of course, with her guitar and her big voice. Dad plays the clarinet because he's not allowed to sing, and I sing harmonies and join in for the non-singing bits with my recorder. Danni and Kristie sing and bang triangles and tambourines and maracas, sometimes even in time. Mum's ecstatic and cries all the way back up the hill. I clutch the loot of Christmas chocolate various neighbors handed over as payment and stay up with Danni and Kristie super late eating it so we can finally see Santa. Danni makes me leave some out for the reindeer, but I wait until she's asleep and eat it anyway. Everyone knows chocolate is poisonous for reindeer, same as for dogs.

The next day Mum is so happy she can't stop crying. She says it's the best Christmas ever.

Above Mum and Dad's bed, the whole wall is a bookshelf. There's another wall in the little study of floor-to-ceiling riches. I've read really grown-up books like *One Flew Over the Cuckoo's Nest*, which made me cry for hours, and *Sophie's Choice*, which is the most awful book I've ever read, and *Catch-22* and *Zen and the Art of Motorcycle Maintenance*, which I loved. *The Clan of the Cave Bear* crawls into my brain and won't leave. I want to be Ayla and invent fire and hunt animals with a sling. Mum's Agatha Christies are interesting, but not compelling. I don't seem to care whodunnit, unless it's on Mars, and then I'm captivated.

Along with his Wilbur Smith and le Carré sections, which I've devoured, I've found Dad's towering expanse of science fiction and power my way through the titles. *Hothouse*, *Have Space Suit—Will Travel*, *Fahrenheit 451,* and the Andromeda series. Niven and Pournelle fill my brain with ramjets and hydrogen scoops and Moties. Asimov shows me Mars and robots. Piers Anthony offers strange space sex and tarot. And Frank Herbert?

He gives me *Dune* and changes my life.

From the moment I begin reading *Dune*, the book wakes me up like nothing has since *The Jungle Book* and *The Lord of the Rings.* Every word writes itself under my skin. Scenes unfold with such clarity I have to shake sand off my hand to turn the pages. Every word of the book is perfect. It is entirely itself, a pure story so true it must be true, somewhere. Mum comes down to kiss us kids good night and tells me to turn out the light.

"Just one more chapter," I beg.

"One more. School tomorrow, you need to sleep."

Two hours later, Dad pokes his head around the door and growls. "Lights out."

I flick out the light and toss and turn beneath images of Paul Atreides with his blistering, charred hand in a box, Gom Jabbar held to his neck by the ancient Bene Gesserit priestess Reverend Mother, promising instant death should he not override his animal fear of pain. My room tastes of spice and treachery. The mournful rhythm of a boobook owl is a thumper on broad desert dunes, calling sandworms to be ridden by hooded Fremen. The whites of my eyes gleam blue in the dark. I slip out of bed, turn on the outside light, and jump back into bed to hold the book up to the light.

It's the first time I read through the whole night.

I finish the book as kookaburras take over from the boobook owl. My eyes feel strange, gritty with sand, or maybe my eyelashes are turned inside out. I have more eyes than the ones in my face. I have eyes inside my body, and they have all opened at once. I see things, lines of power and meaning, rivers of consequence. I died in the night, under the spell of the book, and a new Gina wakes in my skin. I am an astronaut after all. I have visited far worlds and brought them back inside me as seeds, which I will nurture where nobody can stomp on them. At school, the girls tease me as usual but I don't even notice, or care. I recite the fear mantra, over and over.

Fear is the mind killer. It is the little death.

I know what it is to ride a sandworm, and my veins are full of spice, and each drop of water in my body is a miracle beyond price. The world will never be the same again. I know what I want to do.

I want to be a writer.

the year of 12

Mum's latest child-rearing book is *How to Parent* by Dr. Fitzhugh Dodson, and we love it because he says negotiation is better than discipline. As far as I can tell, negotiation is just knowing what Mum wants to hear and saying it so she'll give us what we want.

Dr. Dodson says children should be allowed to learn through exploration and can be trusted to make their own decisions about the world. We tell Mum we're prepared to be responsible and do our chores if she increases our privileges, like an extra hour of TV. I'm working on getting to see *Grease* at the movies; Mum says it's too adult. Everyone at school sings the songs at recess and lunch, and they don't sound grown-up, just fun. Girls wear their hair back in ponytails like Olivia Newton-John. My short boy-hair and horrible bowl-cut count me out of the *Grease* games, not that I'd be invited to play, anyway.

I buy my way into the boys' soccer game with a soccer ball I begged for and received for my birthday. I'm a terrible player, but they need the ball, so they let me play. I tell them my name's George, that I'm really a boy, and invite them to punch my stomach as hard as they can to prove it. Even the biggest boys' punches bounce off. It's a trick, but I don't tell them that. I tense the muscles in my stomach as hard as I can, and nobody can hurt me. If someone punches me by surprise, I'll go down like a sack of spuds, so I keep my belly tensed all day, just in case.

Danni has committed the ultimate crime. She's wearing my His Pants For Her knickers again.

"Give them back, ya stinky stealer!" I am outraged. She's such a goody-two-shoes and always gets away with everything.

She shakes her head, pushing me away. "These're mine—I cut the tag off, see?"

"No, I cut the tag off and mine have pink and purple spots."

"Yours have green spots."

"No they don't."

"Yes they do, vagina face."

"Shut up, penis breath."

"VAGINA FACE VAGINA FACE VAGINA FACE."

We've been through our first official sex talks from Mum and Dad, courtesy of a book called *Where Did I Come From?*, which uses all the proper words for things like breast and anus and scrotum and vulva. My sisters love that the word *vagina* has Gina in it. So do the kids at school, of course. Sometimes I'm angry that Mum and Dad didn't think my name through. Why did they call me a name that's in *vagina*? What were they thinking?

Danni zigzags past me and runs up the stairs. She's faster than me, but I'm bigger. I tackle her to wrestle my undies off her. Knickers thinks it's a game and barks and jumps around.

"Mum, Gina's picking on Danni again."

"Shut up, Kristie, ya little snitch."

"VAGINA FACE VAGINA FACE," Danni shouts and giggles as I tickle her in a vain attempt to release her hold on the elastic, which stretches and pops as we tug back and forth.

"For god's sake, you two, sort it out," Mum says. "And get out of the way—I can't get down the bloody stairs."

"Muuuum, she stole my undies."

"Did not."

"Did too."

"Did not VAGINA FACE. Owww!! That hurts! Mum, she's HURRRTING me."

Mum trips over the dog and swears. "DOUG, will you DO something? I have to finish grading." Mum's stressed in the mornings, especially when her students have exams. She's always grading endless papers, rolling a hot cup of tea across her forehead. Exam time smells like migraines.

Dad looms over us. He prods the nearest rib with a giant leathery foot. It looks like it belongs to a dinosaur. His toenails are as thick as my fingers and bayonet sharp, especially when he cuts them with tin snips and gets in trouble for leaving the sharp clippings lying around.

Luckily Dad hasn't clipped his toenails for a while or Danni and I would have sharp gouges in our skin as he pokes us.

He solves the undie conundrum by pouring a big glass of water over us.

"Daaaaad, now they're wet," Danni says, spluttering.

"Good. I'm sure you can find another pair. Why don't you all just write your names in them? I don't understand what's so special about your his or hers special undies. They're just undies."

"Ginaaaaa." Kristie's voice is muffled. "Eric's escaped again."

I run upstairs to Mum and Dad's room, which is at the top of the house, next to the piano. The top deck looks out across the bay. Sometimes we see the waterspouts of humpback whales. Jervis Bay is along their migration path, and they come in to rest in the protected waters. A mother whale weighs six elephants. The babies jump out of the water like the grown-ups. When there's a whale, I run down to the beach to get as close as I can and put my face under the water and sing whale sounds, because sound travels for miles underwater and I want them to know I'm their friend. Maybe one day I'll tame a whale and it will let me ride on its back. I scan the water but can't see any white spray.

"Ginaaaaaaa."

Kristie's manky foot points inward, her pajama-clad bum wiggling almost as much as Knickers's furry one as they both investigate the space under Mum and Dad's bed.

"Got it!" Kris says, and the dog's tail stump goes into a frenzy. My sister hands the blue-tongued lizard back to me. Eric instantly settles into the warmth of my hand. I don't understand why reptiles are called cold-blooded. Their blood is warm. Their skin can be pretty cold, though.

"Hang on, what's—" Kris's voice stops, then there's a dragging sound and she emerges with a magazine.

I know what it is immediately. I found Dad's stash of *Penthouse* magazines a couple of years ago and have explored their illicit worlds at length, especially when I play hooky and stay home from school, reading four *Modesty Blaise* books in a day, playing piano, and eating cheese and Jatz.

"Mum, this book has NAKED LADIES!" Kris shouts, clomping down the stairs. "Why does this book have naked ladies?"

I'm hot on her heels, in an ecstasy of horror. What will Mum do?

Danni pops up from downstairs in a different pair of undies.

"Naked ladies? What naked ladies?"

"Look! I found this book under their bed, and it has all these pictures of NAKED LADIES."

When I grow up, I want to master the secret language of Looks. Grown-ups have whole conversations without saying a single word.

Dad looks a little embarrassed.

Mum clears her throat. "It's only natural, kids. It's a magazine about sex. There's nothing to be ashamed about."

"Is this what Gina's boobies are going to look like when she's in high school?" Kristie points to the picture.

"Maybe. Eventually. But not for a few years yet. Maybe not at all."

I hope not. I don't ever want proper boobs at all.

"Gina's got great big FLABBY, puftaloon TITS," my sisters chorus in unison.

I have a raised, painful lump in each nipple and a small tuft of dark hair promising changes in my near future. My sisters are merciless about all of it.

I kick Kristie's bad leg. "You're going to have them one day, too, Kristie, so shut up. I hope yours are huge and ugly, like you."

Danni takes the magazine from Kristie and giggles as the centerfold unfolds. "Wowww. So, we can look at it?"

Mum sighs, giving Dad another Look.

"Yes. For a little while. Five minutes. Then you have to get ready for school."

What? I did not see this coming.

I dump Eric and scramble under the bed to retrieve a fistful of magazines. We dive in, shrieking and pointing when we get to each photo. Mum pretends to mark her year twelve exam papers, but her foot twitches and she gives Dad a whole new flavor of Look I've never seen before. Dad seems unfussed, but who knows with grown-ups. They say one thing, but there's another layer under that thing, and currents beneath that, and underwater tidal waves and earthquakes and sea dragons. They never tell kids any of it.

I can't believe we're allowed to look at the sex magazines.

I go straight for the section called Penthouse Forum, which is where people write in their sex stories. I've learned more about sex from these over the past year or so than the sex ed classes at school, which are super lame and embarrassing, especially when Miss Tindall tried to put a condom on a banana and couldn't get the packet open and then the banana squished and everyone laughed. I reckon when it comes time to have sex I'm going to be really good at it because I've memorized all the things in Forum. I know that if my washing machine breaks, if I call for the repair man to come and fix it, he'll want to have sex with me. So I had better learn how to fix washing machines for myself.

Kristie and Danni twitter over a magazine, laughing more with every page. Mum's twitching grows more pronounced until Kristie screams, "Gina! Quick, come look. He's DRINKING her WEE!"

"Right," says Mum, slamming the table with her hand. She jumps to her feet, spilling tea and a snowstorm of papers. "That's enough. Get ready for school."

She retrieves the magazines and disappears them back upstairs. And that's the end of Dr. Fitzhugh Dodson and his book of liberal attitudes. It's also the end of the *Penthouse* magazines, which vanish from their hiding place under Dad's side of the bed. I ferret them out from a high shelf in the garage next time I play hooky.

Today's the last day of year six. I'm so excited to go to high school. Mum and Dad are teachers at my new school, and they say it's one of the biggest year sevens ever. So many new kids who'll have no idea I'm toxic.

Every person is just a story that everyone around them writes on them. When we meet new people, the story changes. This school break, I'll lie out in the sun and bleach off all the stale old words, especially the nasty ones, until I'm blank as the chalk of sky on a cloudless day.

Our excursion for the last day of school is to Kangaroo Valley, where we'll have a picnic. I've brought a pot of snails I've been feeding lettuce to for a week. I'm going to make a fire and cook them for lunch.

Jesse and I have been spending a lot of time together, after school and every weekend, now that he lives two blocks from me. We're explorers, mapping new lands where dinosaurs roam in the sprawling network of stormwater drains that run under the land like a secret world, carrying our supplies and flashlights and hard-boiled eggs for lunch. We watch dusk gather all the best colors and drag them into the ocean, throwing back ink and silver like a consolation prize. He doesn't talk much, but I don't mind. Sometimes I talk enough for both of us. Sometimes we don't say anything at all.

Under the faintest shower of light, he tells me what different stars are, and we follow the steady trails of satellites, like shooting stars that never fall. I want him to kiss me but I'm scared he will. We went to the Nowra Show together this year, and he gave me an opal necklace in a little box when he came to pick me up, his dad patient in the car, waiting while Jesse delivered the gift at the front door. My heart fluttered like a bird under the small, cool circle of silver somehow trapping a chip of fire and ice on my skin. His hands shook when he did up the clasp. We held hands and he put his arm around me on the rides. I felt like I had swallowed a secret. It was warm and tasted of honey.

Jesse's coming to Bomaderry High next year. We're going to be boyfriend and girlfriend forever. I'm wearing the necklace today because it's the last day of primary school and we can wear whatever we want. Also, I want to show him I love him.

When the school buses arrive, ravens pick up their black skirts and scatter, dropping curses. Cicadas screech. Kids swarm across the grass, scattering bags and drink bottles in their hurry to get to the water.

Kangaroo River is wide and filled with smooth stones that tumble over and over. The freezing water sings an old song, one I almost know the words to, or I will in a minute when I stick my head underwater and listen properly. I strip down to my swimsuit and start gathering perfectly shaped stones to make a dam. Jesse is still under the big camphor laurel tree, so I wave him over; hurry up, it will be the best dam ever. He's taking a long time to come over. I have a huge pile of rocks and he still isn't here. I flick back my wet hair and run over, panting.

"Whatcha doing, slowpoke?" I flick water at him and he flinches. "I've got heaps of rocks. You coming to make a dam? It's so fun."

He evades my eyes and mumbles that he doesn't feel like it. The more I ask what's wrong, the more he retreats. Something's happened. The beautiful colors between us have gone suddenly gray.

I already know the world can change in a heartbeat. Birds die, all at once, even when they look healthy. I've watched an eclipse through my fingers, seen the sun eaten by a huge black werewolf, until only a circle of light remains, like Sauron's eye of doom. Kids can be nice and then mean in no time at all. But not Jesse. He's like me. Isn't he?

He won't look at me. Life drains from my day. I taste sour metal, old blood. I don't understand. The opal necklace burns on my throat as the magic leaves it.

I make the dam on my own, but the stones keep getting washed downstream, no matter how well I stack them. The current is too strong to do it on my own.

Later Ben finds me crying under a tree, cooking my snails on a little fire. They're super rubbery once they're boiled. He shifts from foot to foot, chewing his fingernails, and looks at his feet when he tells me Jesse says I'm dropped.

"But why?" I wail.

"He's embarrassed 'cause yer bloody twelve, not three, and yer still not wearing a bikini top and ya need to wear it 'cause ya have, like, boobs now and everyone's talkin about it, even the teachers. Kids are gonna complain to their parents and ya mum and dad are gonna get in, like, heaps of trouble."

He turns to leave, then comes back, scratching his hair.

"Fuck, think I got nits. Can I've a snail? Are they totally gross?"

I nod, chewing and crying at the same time, and hold out the pot. "You have to pull them out of the shell. They're really chewy. French people eat them all the time in restaurants, but they must do something else to them to make them taste good. Maybe I cooked them too long."

Ben pulls on the little brown twist of flesh.

"Looks like a turd."

He curls his lip a bit, sniffs it, then shrugs and throws it in his mouth.

"Doesn't taste like anything. Maybe ya need salt. Anyway, like, sorry. Ya should maybe put a top on."

He spits out the half-chewed snail, then walks back to the noisy group of kids scattered under trees and in the water. If I squint, they could be a flock of parrots, feeding in the grass. It occurs to me they've been whispering and pointing all day; I'm just so used to it I hadn't noticed. I regard my naked chest with its offending tiny bumps and sharpen the hate that I'm not a boy. Everything would be easy if I was a boy.

Jesse isn't looking in my direction at all. He's talking to Narelle, who stares at me, just once, with her chin up.

My T-shirt is all the way over by the bus. I'll have to walk past everyone to get it.

In the heartbreak of Christmas holidays without Jesse I discover Tom Robbins. *Even Cowgirls Get the Blues* is a shining wonder, as is Sissy Hankshaw, she of the enormous thumbs. Sissy falls into bed, and my fantasies, with the irrepressible Bonanza Jellybean, who puts Sissy's one remaining large thumb to good use. Bonanza Jellybean is even sexier than Modesty Blaise, or at least, that scene is. I tear so many edges off those pages I can find the passage by braille, simply by feeling the outline of the book. I still don't want to be a girl, but if I have to be one, I want to be one like Bonanza Jellybean. For the first time I realize it's possible to have a girlfriend instead of a boyfriend. Maybe I'm a boy and a lesbian, at the same time.

But every time I catch a beetle, I miss Jesse like there's a chasm in my chest and have to play piano for hours to make the ache go away.

the year of 13

Bomaderry High School is a sprawling expanse of two-story concrete buildings and portable classrooms, as gray as a prison, surrounded by sports fields and dry gum trees hanging their heads in the heat. Trails go off into the bush, where kids nick off for a cheeky ciggie or to smoke bongs, or ditch school for the day. There's a long driveway down to the teachers' parking lot and a scrappy patch of scrub I've played in with my sisters a hundred times over the years, when we walked up from primary school and waited forever for Mum and Dad to come out to the car so we could go home.

I know how high school smells when nobody's in it, like stale farts and BO and weary despair. I know the fastest way to get from A Block to C Block, how to take the stairs three at a time, and which toilets run out of toilet paper first. I know the best place to sing is halfway up the stairs in B Block, where you sound like a rock star with all the echoes. I know all the teachers' cars, and that Mr. Hackleton keeps a bottle of whiskey under the front seat; if you look through the side window, you can see the top poking out where his feet will go.

And now I'm in year seven and this is my school. It's where I'll make my stand, carve out a place for myself away from the bewildering torture of primary school. There are 365 kids just in my year. Three hundred of them have never heard of me. It's statistically impossible that I won't find one person to be my friend.

Now I'm here, high school is a roaring ocean with its own wild weather, tossed by rips and big waves, eddies, and cross chop. Dangerous currents wait to suck an unwary kid under. Whirlpools around the bubblers, packs of menace ready to pounce. Huge surges of bodies pound through corridors, up and down stairs, into and out of classrooms. Cigarette smoke pours from the toilets in rancid clouds, along with packs of girls with bright blue eyeliner and uniforms so short you can see their bum creases when they lift their arms up. Older students strut around like they've stepped off the cover of magazines, especially the seniors, who look like grown-ups and stare down their noses at anyone in a junior's uniform.

In the first week, groups quickly form: sporty kids, cool kids, tough kids, delinquent kids, nerdy kids, grommets, Aboriginal kids, and the flavorless groups floating somewhere in the middle, unremarkable and therefore camouflaged. I linger around the edges of a couple of these. Playing handball. Poking fun at Mr. Bell's stutter. Talking about the scandalous *Thorn Birds* TV series like I've watched it, which is a lie because Mum will never let us watch anything on the commercial channel, especially not a miniseries that has sex in it. But I've read the book and think Dane is the best name for a boy. I make up a boyfriend named Dane, who goes to Nowra High and is an exchange student from Europe.

For the first couple of weeks, I'm almost normal. Then, like a tap turning off, the other kids stop talking to me. All of them. When I walk through corridors, they pull away, so there's always a space around me, like reversed magnets. Joseph had a technicolor dreamcoat. I have a coat of no-man's land.

I'm kryptonite again and have no idea why.

Jesse finds me in the heaving sea of bags and uniforms piling through a choke point between A and B Block. He holds out a piece of paper but doesn't meet my eyes.

"I thought you should see this," he says. "Narelle started it. I'm sorry."

He's tall now, and even more good looking, though his arms and legs all move in different directions like a praying mantis. His voice sounds disconnected from his body, like it can't make up its mind where it wants to sit in his throat. We haven't talked about The Topless Incident At The Year Six Excursion, but it revolves in the air between us, ready to coalesce if he stays too long. When we run into each other, he's always polite, and almost apologetic, and a thousand miles away. Whatever was between us, it's broken forever.

After he bolts, I unfold the paper.

Petition: Gina Chick Should Wear A Bra. More than 150 signatures spool down the page.

In one move, Narelle's doomed me.

I sit alone on the hard plastic suitcase that brands me a nerd, and that Mum won't let me switch for a soft bag like everyone else has, reading *The Lord of the Rings* for the fifth time. I want to be Galadriel or Aragorn. Nobody sits with me, not even the other nerds. The magpies talk to me, though. So do the beetles, and the little purple butterflies that rest in the clover. I make daisy chains and learn the language of ants, who teach me about rain and perseverance, and that size isn't everything. Trees catch stories from far places in their high branches and the wind gives their leaves language: rustle and sigh. Gum trees are generous with light; they throw it around so plenty lands on the ground for small orchids to drink. Clouds taunt from the high vault of blue, pulling themselves apart with endless pale fingers. All the water that ever was is still on the planet. My blood is as salty as the sea, which I hear surging through my heart when I stick my fingers in my ears. The tears in my eyes used to be a cloud, worshipping the sun. Nothing ever dies, not really. It just changes form.

Grass scratches at the back of my neck and legs, and the hot, dry scent of dirt fills me as I fall upward, counting time. I can outlast high school, no problem. It's just six years. I can read ten thousand books in that time. And then I'll be a grown-up and I can do whatever I want.

Katie, the toughest girl in my year, rubs rotten oranges into my hair during gym. I don't stop her, just wait for it to be over. I lie to Mum about why my uniform is sticky and gross, some accident with a spilled drink. I stamp on the uniform in the shower, washing out the memory of her freckles and crooked tooth.

"I don't like you, Gina," Katie says, really rubbing the orange in, while her cronies throw extra pieces at me until I'm dripping.

In my mind I have all the witty comebacks, like "Thanks, Captain Obvious," and "That's a relief! I thought you were going to ask me out." But I never say anything. I never say a single word.

Rain beats at the roof like it's trying to convince me of something important. I push up onto my shoulders and make more grubby footprints on the painted cloud that looks like Kimba the White Lion.

Feet are really weird when you look at them properly. My toes are long. I practice picking things up with them and even clutching a pen and scrawling ragged loops of letters on butcher's paper, just in case I lose my arms in an accident. There was a boy on *60 Minutes* who had no arms, and he played the guitar and the piano with his feet. Try as I might, I can't make my toes stretch far enough apart to play "Für Elise."

More smudges on Kimba. The cloud blurs into a sea of stars. I pick them up with my toes, juggle them around. They turn into atoms; colliding, joining, coalescing into molecules, each one the size of a planet, trillions and trillions of them in my body.

A universe revolves inside me. Inside each atom is the energy of a sun.

Sunshine tastes like love. So does a storm.

These are things I know about love.

Dad's made-up bedtime stories about Grumpus the dwarf. All three of us practicing our musical instruments at once; the cacophony is nightmarish. The scrabble of dog claws adding more scratches to wooden floorboards. Harmonies. Caroling magpies. Rumbling conversation from Mum and Dad's room. Mum grabbing Dad's arm in the car, screaming DOUG so it scares the shit out of all of us; maybe she saw a murder, but it was only the color of a cloud so beautiful it broke her heart and burst out of her like rage. Summer breaks. Sandwiches toasted in the big fireplace Dad built from copper and rivets that set the house on fire twice. Lemon delicious pudding and barbecue lamb chops with crunchy burned fat bits.

Sand in the sheets and scratchy sunburn and stabbing a fork into the last piece of avocado in the salad bowl before my sisters get to it. Dad's rough beard, Mum's soft face. Snoozing bodies scattered through the house, covered with animals. The rasp of turning pages, the taste of torn paper. A huge tattered monolith of cloud, painted gold at its apex and indigo at its base. The underside of the sea eagle's pure white belly, a fish the size of my head writhing in its talons. The yellow gape of a begging bird. The last gray gasp of wave before it tumbles to its death. Muddy toes. The heart-colored center of an orchid. Raindrops hanging from a leaf.

My feet stir the night sky into whirlpools. Filaments extend from my toes, my skin, twining through scrub and forest, into insects and moss and creeks and the birds waiting in old socks for their next meal. Tendrils wind through to my sleeping sisters, to my parents, to Knickers's furry paws, to my cousins, to the horizon beckoning from a beach as familiar as my freckles. They quest toward the kids at school, and here they stop—repelled, repellent.

Love. Love. Love.

Only with family, Gina. Not with others. Not for you.

At singing practice on a Wednesday night, I hang out with a girl my age whose grandmother is in the choir. She has a face shaped like a heart and her eyelashes are almost white, even though her eyes are dark and wide, like a horse's. In the break when all the grown-ups talk about boring things, we walk outside the hall and throw stones at a streetlight. Her eyes look even bigger in the dark. The night doesn't seem real, which is probably why I ask her, this stranger I'll probably never see again. Somebody else has my voice.

"Have you ever kissed a girl?"

She looks shocked, and I want to bite my tongue; I've done it again, said the thing you shouldn't say. But then she comes up and suddenly her lips are on mine and my eyes are open and so are hers, but they're so close I can't focus and the light is stark above us and I can see through her pale eyelashes. Her lips are smaller than mine. She tastes like cherry lip gloss. Afterward, while my heart thunders and my knees wobble a bit, she says "slut" and walks back into the hall without looking back, then ignores me completely until her grandmother takes her home.

The thing about being on the outside is that you get to notice everything. It's hard to notice things when you're inside them. I squint so the kids in the playground blur into creatures. Antelopes and lions, wrens and hawks, otters and orcas. Humans are just animals and animals behave in certain ways to survive. With a tree at my back, watching packs break and re-form, it seems to me that humans have one motto: if it's different, kill it.

I obviously smell wrong, like some baby animals whose mothers reject them. If I don't figure out how to make friends, I'll die, because humans are pack animals and aren't designed to live on their own. Lone wolves don't survive in the wild.

So, I watch. And watch. And watch.

Near the end of the year, I ask a group of girls if I can sit with them in their "area." They put it to the vote and say no because they only have one seat, which means most of them sit on the concrete and there's daily tension over who gets a bum off the ground each break.

Seats are the most precious commodity in the playground. Our year color is yellow. These lemon-hued seats are more precious than gold. Any group lucky enough to have one has it chained and padlocked to stop pilfering, and even then, there are swooping raids with bolt cutters.

"Gigi-love," says Dad on one of our night walks. I've just told him about the girls saying no to me joining them, and he replied with a description of the atomic dance of protons and electrons, and how their electric charge creates the bonds around which all matter revolves.

It's obvious: if I'm an atom, I am not carbon, beloved by other atoms, destined to connect in endless combinations with hydrogen and oxygen and nitrogen to create life. I'm an outlier, chemically inert: krypton or xenon or radon. Even elements have hierarchies.

"Gigi."

"Hmmmm?"

The picture spun by his words has me rapt, caught in the nucleus of a Neptune-sized atom, while moon-shaped electrons whiz in orbit like giant dragons.

"Why don't we build a seat? I reckon those girls will be happy to have you then. Find the thing they need. Levers, remember?"

Shock ricochets me into space.

Could it work?

Dad and I toil in the garage after school, sawing, nailing, gluing, sanding, and then painting, a perfect bench seat. The making is a magic spell, a weaving, a prayer. In fairy tales, an object can become alive. A doll becomes a real boy. Red shoes dance all by themselves. I whisper into the seat all my dreams and accidentally seal the magic with blood from a banged thumb.

"Ow!"

Dad barely looks up from his sanding.

"Any bones sticking out, kiddo?"

"Nah," I say, squinting. I suck the shocking pain into my mouth.

"You'll live," he says, examining and dismissing the tear.

Blood always tastes like adventures with Dad. Mum says this isn't a good thing; he's teaching me his risky ways. Dad says I'm not afraid of life, which is the best thing of all.

We give the seat three coats of paint.

"Do it properly," says Dad. "It's got to last you a few years."

Our white van fills with a sharp chemical smell all the way to school. Kristie makes a big deal out of holding her nose and complaining about the stink. I squish my fingers into a couple of bubbles where the paint is still wet under its hard skin and try not to think about what's coming.

Dad wants to help me carry the seat, but I stop him.

"No, Dad. It's bad enough that you and Mum teach at my school. I have to do this myself."

My heart thumps fit to burst as I drag the long seat out of the van, bumping it along the concrete. It's cumbersome and heavy, and trumpets the promise of glossy, mindless happiness in bright paint, that eternally optimistic shade little kids use to color in the sun. Half the playground stops to watch what the weird Chick kid is up to this time. The seat bashes my shins as I lug it past the stares and glares, to the spot in front of A Block where a clutch of girls tan their skinny legs.

There's no fence around their territory, but I feel an electric buzz when I cross the invisible threshold.

"Can I sit with you now?" I say, dropping the seat in front of them with a final grunt. The seat glows, proud, pearlescent, promising years of prestige and comfort. It's spectacular, the essence of seat. It's what the tired, beaten seats of the playground yearn to be when they grow up. Its yellow is the yellowest yellow imaginable. It's the yellow of envy that every other kid will burn with once the seat finds its rightful home. This seat has been kissed by the sun itself. To reject such an offering would be like saying no to a trove of dwarf gold or a ring of power.

Magpies salute the day and stab iron earth with stiletto beaks. My feet sweat in my hideous black school shoes. Thwacks of handballs hitting concrete, shouts of protest, random cheers from kids playing basketball. I shuffle from foot to foot and chew a thumbnail. Eyes from everywhere crawl over me like spiders.

From the girls, a final set of frantic whispers, then a sea of nods.

"Sure," says a tanned girl with streaked blonde hair, nonchalant as summer, as if I've asked for nothing more serious than to borrow a pen. Her smile is a waterfall, cool and inviting.

I drag the seat the final couple of meters to meet the one they already have, a ragged, splintery thing with half its bolts missing. Bums shuffle along.

"Yay, another seat." A girl sits next to me. "I'm Rhiannon."

Then another. "This is such a cool seat. What a great idea; did you make it yourself?"

"With my dad."

"Mr. Chick, hey. He's funny. He's my math teacher. He wears that safari suit and always says *diddle iddle iddle* when he's drawing on the board."

"Yeah, he does that at home as well."

"He got us to stand on our heads to teach us about gravity," says a tall girl with wild hair and a big smile.

"But he did it too," says Leanna. "His legs were waving around in the air, and then Mr. Rankin came in 'cause he thought there wasn't a teacher in the class, and Mr. Chick just waved at him, and Mr. Rankin told him to come and see him after class. I think he got in trouble."

"How can teachers get in trouble from other teachers?" says a pretty girl drawing a heart on her leg in marker.

"If they're my dad, pretty easily," I say. "Mr. Rankin is his boss."

I don't tell them Norm Rankin, the deputy principal, is a rascal, and he laughed about it later with Dad at a barbecue at our place. It feels strange to be talking about my dad with these girls.

"Mum made that safari suit for him and crocheted the belt. He's too tall for the pattern, which is why his legs stick out at the bottom."

"I'm Shari. We're in Art together. I love your mum."

Someone holds out a bag of chips. I take one, crunching it slowly, scared to breathe too loud in case this miracle evaporates. My heart is painted the same color as the seat, the color of hope.

Mowgli's place in the pack was bought with a bull killed by Bagheera. Mine is bought with a bright yellow seat and the love of my father.

"How'd it go, lovey?" Dad says in the car on the way home.

"Yeah, did you bribe some kids to be your friends 'cause it's the only way anyone will talk to you?"

"Shut up, Kristie." I burst into tears and lean against the window, sobbing like the world is ending.

"Kristie!" Mum twists around in her seat, giving my sister a don't-even Look. Kris rolls her eyes. Danni leans forward.

"Did they like your seat, Gi?"

I can't talk for crying. Sounds come out of me I've never heard before.

"Shit," Mum swears under her breath. "It didn't work. What are we going to do with her, Douggie?"

"They're poo-heads," says Danni. "It's a great seat. They don't deserve you."

"Yeah. Stuff 'em," says Kris. "Silly bitches."

"Bitchy witches. Witchy bitches," Danni says, bouncing in the seat, winding up for one of her episodes.

"Don't worry, Gigi, they'll come around," says Mum.

"Snitchy bitchy witchy witches."

"Shut up all of you! And d-d-don't call them bitches!" I shout. "They're my F-F-FRIENDS."

Mum and Dad stare at each other.

"Gina, you are a funny one," Dad says.

"I knowww," I say, and cry whole rivers into my hands.

That night I can't sleep.

I know how this goes. The seat is only the doorway.

I don't know the rules about how to be a person, and what I don't know will kill me. Mum says I'm too dramatic, but she doesn't understand. This is life-or-death stuff. I have something to lose. I have friends now.

I have to be an octopus. I don't need to change my insides, just the patterns on my hide. It's okay to be different where people can't see. When Tarzan came out of the jungle and went to England, he put on a suit to hide his wildness, but inside he was himself because the jungle was who he really was.

I've made a seat, now I need to sew myself a human skin, and I have to do it fast, before my new friends decide I'm too different and eat me.

I use my pocket money to buy fluorescent off-the-shoulder shirts and leg warmers, hoop earrings, and high-waisted jeans and sport a series of perms that make my head look like an orange cabbage until they grow out, when they look like a flat-top pyramid. I watch *Flashdance* and *Ferris Bueller* and *Footloose* and *Dirty Dancing* and *Sixteen Candles*. I discuss the respective merits of the Brat Pack and which one is my favorite in *The Breakfast Club* (Judd Nelson, of course). Record endless mix tapes that are swapped and listened to on a huge ghetto-blaster that eats batteries like Cookie Monster and devours all my Christmas money. I ask Dave at the newsstand to give me advance copies of *Dolly* magazine, so I'm right there on the yellow seat with the page opened to our sex education guru, Dolly Doctor, when the other girls arrive. I talk about boys and carry pictures of Simon Le Bon from Duran Duran and squeal when "Careless Whisper" comes on the radio.

I'm humaning, and mostly it's almost okay. Until I bring one of my baby birds to school and kids catch me chewing up seed and spitting it into its mouth. Or I say something that feels normal but it's like the record stops on the world, and everyone stares, or rolls their eyes, or sniggers, or doesn't talk to me and I don't know where I went wrong but it's obvious I've fallen into another trapdoor, we're all playing snakes and ladders and I've slid right back to the start again.

Every night I play out the day until something goes ka-chunk inside me, and I see the thing I said or did that isn't normal, that marks me so horribly *other.* For everything I catch, there are five hundred things I don't see.

Why can't I understand what I'm doing wrong?

At a beach party, Cheryl takes pity on me and explains.

"Gina, like, you're just too big."

"Whaddya mean?" I look at my body.

"No, not literally. You just . . . sometimes you're, like, too much."

"Too much? Too much what?"

"Too much EVERYTHING," says brash Kaleisha, waltzing past, chugging Diet Coke straight from the bottle. "Fuck me, chicken Twisties. Even ya cheekbones are too fuckin high. And ya mouth is fuckin enormous, ya could fly a fuckin plane into it. And ya sing all the time, like, really loud. Like ya think yer Madonna. And yer always doin weird shit like pukin in birds' mouths. Yer not . . . normal. No offense, but ya know what I mean?"

I didn't.

"Ignore her, she's a grumpy bitch, and she's jealous 'cause she wishes she had cheekbones like yours," says Cheryl as Kaleisha giggles past. "Just stop, I dunno, trying so hard."

I touch my face, prodding under the skin and muscle. What's a cheekbone and where's it supposed to be? It just feels like general face to me.

Shari always finds me when I've fucked up somehow with my new friends.

She tells stories about her goofy family, or falling off her horses, or how she makes up names for paintings in her art exams to make the teachers laugh, like "Sloppy Clocks by Salvador Dalí." Occasionally she brings random competitions for us to enter. Sometimes we even win them. She's funny and kind. I'd share my lunch with her, but she's a vegetarian.

"Relax," she says about whatever bewildering social storm blew me into the only safe harbor I know: the library. "The others will get bored and forget about it. It'll blow over."

Relax? How can I relax when every day is a fight for survival?

the year of 16

His white shirt is untucked and contrasts his tanned skin. A breathy murmur stirs through the science class when he prowls in, shoulders back. He runs his hand through his hair. Actual muscles shift under his shirt. Girls nudge each other and giggle as he talks to the chemistry teacher, Mr. Patrick.

"Oi, you lot, this is Felix. Behave, you horrible animals."

Felix is gorgeous. Proper, drop-dead gorgeous, with strong legs and dark flicked hair, a clear jaw, and a smile that twinkles the corners of his eyes, which have lashes so long and dark they stir the air when he blinks.

There's only one spare seat in the whole class. It's next to me because nobody will sit with me. He's walking toward me and smiling. I think I may die. I hear the girls in the class gnashing their collective teeth as they realize he'll be sitting there. My isolation has suddenly become my salvation. He pulls up the stool next to mine.

"Hey," he says, nonchalant, slinging his bag under the big science bench and sliding onto the stool. Our legs touch and I startle, like I've put my finger on the heater element in the bathroom. I haven't shaved my legs for a couple of days. Oh god, he will have felt the stubble. I'll shave them every single morning, just in case our legs touch again. I tuck my shiny black school shoes under the stool. He has desert boots, of course. He's already the coolest kid in class, and he's only been here five minutes.

"Um, I'm Gina."

"Great name. I've never met a Gina before. You like science?"

"Um, yeah. I do."

"Me too. I'm going to be an engineer."

"Oh. That's cool. Like, building bridges and stuff?"

Gina, you're an idiot.

"Yeah. And stuff."

He smiles again, and I'm riven.

"Hey, I don't have a textbook yet. Can I share yours?"

"Uh, yes. Of course. I'll, um, just, hang on."

I fumble in my bag, which regurgitates onto the floor with an exploding clatter. He jumps off the stool to retrieve rolling pens and tubs of lip gloss. I leap to snag the tampons before he can get to them, my face on fire. I don't even care that the whole class is laughing at me. He isn't.

Felix doesn't know I'm toxic. He smells like warm, toasty sausage rolls and cinnamon. He smells like detergent. He smells like a blanket I want wrapped around my shoulders. I want to touch his skin, which is golden. If I do, I think my finger might go through it into his muscles and veins. He asks me questions about my life, and tells me about his, over months of kids setting things on fire, blowing wet paper spitballs at the teacher through empty pen tubes, tying hairs around blowflies to make pets, making weird giant blue copper sulphate crystals in beakers. I don't notice anything but the deep, dark wells of his eyes.

I doodle his initials in my diaries and dream fervent dreams of togetherness. But he's already hooked up with Samantha Lane. I hate her so much if I was a dragon I would burn her to ash with a single breath.

Dad plays clarinet in the local Gilbert and Sullivan *South Pacific* production, which rehearses in town every Thursday night. I'm singing in the chorus. Dad always gets a block of Old Jamaica chocolate for the drive home, which he shares with me. I hold each piece in my mouth until the chocolate melts away and all that's left are raisins and a faint flavor of rum.

I know most of the singers from the madrigal group I've been in for years now with Mum and Danni. They dunk their biscuits into tea and ask how Mum is, and how's school, and what do I want to do after year twelve. Everyone in the production is well over forty-five, except for me and a lanky guy in the orchestra.

Mark's twenty-seven and flies helicopters on weekends. He also plays the trumpet. He's tall and a bit goofy with a wide, white smile. He kisses me under one of the gum trees, and suddenly, to the scandalous delight of the girls in my area, I have a boyfriend, eleven years older than me. It's all ladders. For once, I'm ahead.

He takes me on a real date, to a restaurant. I have nothing to wear.

"I need sophisticated clothes, Mum. It's a posh seafood restaurant."

She comes to the rescue, even though she really isn't keen on me dating a guy that old. She knows she's got bugger-all chance of stopping me. She drives me to town, and we pick our way through Kmart racks until I have a spotty shirt with big shoulder pads and a thin *Footloose* tie, a dark pencil skirt, and a wide red belt. Red hoop earrings and I'll wear red lipstick. Patent fake-leather heels from Target. My perm is so fresh I can still smell the chemicals. I don't recognize myself in the mirror.

"You look gorgeous, love," say Mum, and even pays for the clothes.

Mark picks me up, and as I slide into the plush car seat, he says, "Is this your sophisticated outfit?"

Something about his face.

"Uh, no, I decided to leave it."

"I didn't think so," he says, and my cheeks burn. "Still, you look nice."

At the restaurant he holds a chair out, but I don't know what he's doing so I go to the other one and sit in it, then realize my mistake when he turns red and looks around to see who noticed, before sitting quickly in the chair he'd offered to me. I'm getting this wrong already. I always get it wrong. I watch what he does with the napkin and copy him, draping it across my new skirt. Mum always talks about lobster mornay, so that's what I want. Mark orders a seafood platter. It's got everything, prawns and oysters and crab and lobster mornay and mussels. He orders champagne as well. We clink our glasses.

Champagne tastes weird and sour, and the bubbles go up my nose when I drink from the tall glass. I snort and sneeze, and the woman at the table next to me giggles with me when I catch her eye.

The seafood platter is like a thousand Christmases at once, all stacked high with fancy garnishes. The closest I've ever come to fancy is a prawn cocktail with Thousand Island dressing out of the bottle at one of the parties the local squash club threw, everyone in silly hats. Us three girls in charge of taking around the finger food and being pretty.

"Horse's doovers," Dad called the morsels, but he was more interested in the keg of beer and grabbing Mum's bum when she had her back turned.

"Look at your beautiful girls, Suzie," said Margie when I leaned down to offer her some Jatz and cheese with little green things on top that tasted like the inside of a McDonald's cheeseburger. Margie scooped three of the bikkies into her hand and spoke through a mouth full of crumbs and wine breath. "Like Degas girls. They're all lookers, aren't they? And that broad back of Gina's. Thanks, pet, if I have any more, I'll need a bloody wheelbarrow and one of these fine men to manage me home in it. And I don't think they'll be managing anything other than a Bex and a lie-down after this lot."

Mum took us home early, leaving Dad to rampage with the blokes.

It's strange having oysters so big, and without bits of shell and grit in them from smashing them on the rocks when the tide is out. The prawns are as big as my hand. Juice runs down my arms into the cuffs of my new shirt when I pull the heads off. I crack crab claws in my teeth, sucking out the sweet flesh. Mark says, "Use this," and hands me a nutcracker.

"Oh."

The woman at the next table leans across to catch a piece of crab shell when I get the angles wrong and send chunks flying.

"Here you go," she says. "You'll cut a powerline with one of those bits if you're not careful, love. Like bloody ninja stars, aren't they?"

"Sorry, it's my first date ever."

"Oh, how exciting! You look familiar? Local? Wait. You're one of the Chick girls? Your mum taught my boys art? You home from uni, love?"

She's so funny, every sentence is a question. Her smile is kind.

"I wish. I'm sixteen, in year eleven at Bomo High. I'm gonna be a vet. Or a writer. Or a ranger. Or a marine biologist. I can't decide."

"Sixteen. Right."

Not a question anymore. Her lips purse and she stabs Mark with lethal mother side-eye, like knitting needles with barbs. It makes the crab shell ninja stars look like soft toys.

Mark shifts in his chair.

"Gina," he says under his breath, his lips barely moving. "You can't say that."

"Why not? It's true."

I use my finger to mop up the mornay sauce, which is delicious, but stop myself from licking the plate when I see the look on Mark's face. The woman next to me winks and licks hers. If Danni and Kristie were here, we'd all be licking the plates, probably singing some silly song about the waiter with the snooty face and playing tag in the parking lot afterward to burn off steam. I carefully file away all the details about the restaurant, to make my sisters laugh when I get home.

Mark pays with a real credit card like in the movies and I feel like a grown-up, out to dinner with my boyfriend. I feel like Baby in *Dirty Dancing.* Nobody puts Baby in the corner. Mark is my Patrick Swayze.

Back at his house I wander around, looking at his books, and he hands me another glass of champagne. It tastes worse than the one at the restaurant. Surf pounds the beach, rattling windows. He unbuttons my shirt.

"You're going to have to do it sometime, might as well do it now, don't you think?"

My head surges with the sound of waves. I didn't know IT would be this soon. Barely three weeks since he kissed me. His face is rough where a beard would be if he didn't shave. I thought I was grown-up, but I'm scared now and just want to go home.

"Uh, I guess."

I don't know how to say no, so I say yes.

My imaginings about sex come crashing to earth. It's the most awful thing that has ever happened to me and hurts worse than falling out of the car as he forces his way into a body that has all the doors and windows closed. I float above my body while he does things to it, wondering why anyone chooses this on purpose.

Someone is inside my skin, all the way in my center, and I don't want them there but there's nothing I can do to stop this, it's already happening. I untether from the feeling and turn away as the world grows faint, although the pain and speed of it all is astonishingly bright and keeps me from disappearing altogether. How can the Penthouse Forum stories all be so wrong? This is catastrophically horrible. All the lights are on so I can't even hide in a cocoon of darkness.

Finally he is in, and something happens to him. He goes crazy, grabbing my shoulders and jiggling me so fast I bounce around like at Nowra Summer Fair, on one of the rides. Then he's done, heavy on my body, panting. That's it. I'm not a virgin anymore. I should feel something. I press at the place where feelings live and find only bruises.

When I sit up, to my complete horror, a huge fanny fart splits the air. A trail of blood streaks the bed.

"You're bleeding," he says, tying the condom off. "Got your period?"

"No! God, no." I'm still mortified about the fanny fart and the lights on and his eyes between my legs, watching my face.

"What, then? Not . . . damage?"

I really stare at him now.

"Are you joking? It's called a hymen. I was a virgin, remember."

"Oh. Right, of course. I'm having a shower. Want to come with? You can wash the blood off."

I'm dazed.

"Nah, thanks, I'll wait."

My body hurts where it's never hurt before. I search for some glow of satisfaction, now I'm through this rite of passage. I'm a woman now. I have joined the ranks. This is adulthood.

There's no glow. Adulthood is a long gray tunnel to nowhere, and I've been tricked by all the books and stories into thinking everything will be okay. Nothing will ever be okay again. I thought Mark was Bagheera, but really he's Shere Khan. I thought I was Mowgli, but I'm nothing but a stupid, stupid girl.

When he drops me home the next day, I go straight to my room and close the door until dinner. Mum looks worried as she dishes out mashed potatoes and sausages, so I keep conversation light and brash, making the flying-crab-in-the-restaurant story extra funny for my sisters.

I can't even cry myself to sleep. The tears are wrapped up in some thick veil and I can't feel where they're hiding.

I don't have a friend I can tell. The girls at school want gossip. I don't trust them with what's real.

Frankie. I could tell Frankie, but Frankie's long dead. I suddenly miss his wide brown eyes and deep voice. I miss the way he used to look right into me so I felt like I wasn't alone. I pick out his small red book with the gold embossed title from the bookshelf. His gift warms my hands, like his ghost is giving me a hug. I open the front cover and sniff the pages, letting comfort steal in with the humid jungle melange of musk and madness and the acrid den-stink of wolves.

There's my name. Gina Chick 6Y.

Ten years ago, Frankie gave me this book, when I was just a little kid. Now I'm a woman and I'm more scared and confused than I ever was back then. I thought I would have figured out the world by the time I was this big.

I tear off a corner of paper and chew it to smithereens, turning pages as the familiar story sweeps me away from the sharp edges of my body. As long as I don't move my legs to wake up the pain between them, I forget everything except the reassuring safety of Mowgli's adventures.

"I did it," I say to the girls at school, and it's like throwing seed to a flock of lorikeets.

"What?" "When?" "How?" "How was it?" "You didn't!" "Tell us everything." "Was it fun?"

"He left the lights on and didn't know what a hymen was."

"Noooooo." "No waaaay." "Whaaaat?" "For real?"

"It hurt a lot. And then he went kinda mental like a crazy jack-rabbit, thought my eyeballs were going to pop out of my head and roll around on the floor. It was pretty weird, to be honest."

Rhiannon looks worried. "Really? Does it always hurt?"

"I hope not. I think it's just 'cause I was a virgin."

"It didn't hurt me at all," says Kaleisha. "Except when my head kept hitting the panel van door. Mind you, I was pretty out of it on bourbon and Coke."

"I guess some hymens are thicker than others. Unlucky, Gina," says Cheryl, our resident sexpert.

"Yeah, unlucky," I say. "Probly be fine next time."

Rhiannon's face is a bit white. I feel bad for scaring her.

"Don't worry, it's kinda like riding a roller coaster and getting your ears pierced at the same time," I lie. "Oh, and wait for this bit. It was sooooo embarrassing. When I sat up after, I was all full of air and—"

"Fanny fart!" squeals Shari. "Oh my god, no. Whaddid he do?"

"I wanted to literally die. He thought it was a real fart, and then it was open season on farting. And he asked if the hymen blood was because I had my period."

"Euuuuuw. He thought you were on the rag? Is he brain damaged?"

"As if anyone would have sex on their period."

"I can't believe he didn't know virgins have hymens. Like, isn't he supposed to be experienced?"

"How big was his thing?"

I spread my fingers and their eyes widen.

"Yeah," I say, feeling my insides clench. "Ouch."

"Are you gonna keep seeing him?"

"I guess," I say, closing down on the panic. "He's my boyfriend."

"It'll get better," says Cheryl, with authority. "Practice. It just takes practice. It's only your first time. I didn't love it the first time either."

I don't want to practice ever again, but I don't know how to break up with Mark either.

Raksha the mother wolf said no to Shere Khan when he stuck his head into the cave. She was ready to defend the wandering baby man-cub Mowgli with her life. She scared the tiger so much he left.

I practice the word "no" in the mirror for hours, but next time I'm with Mark my words dry up as soon as he starts kissing me and I vacate my body, leaving it to his attentions. It hurts again, just as much. More, even, on the raw bits that broke last time. I watch the rag doll of my body from somewhere else. When it's all over I return to my body for the cuddles, which are nice, but deep down I'm angry with my body for all this pain and for tricking me into thinking sex will be wonderful when in reality it's utter shit and the biggest disappointment of my life.

I fake orgasms to make Mark stop what he's doing and am haunted by his eyes, always watching. I see those eyes everywhere, in the painted walls of school corridors, in the clay I knead in art classes, in clouds tossing themselves into jet streams far above the school, where I can't follow.

I fade into a restless ghost, floating through the walls of my life, broken inside. In queasy dreams I hear the constant tinkle of a spring rattling around in a toy that won't work. Sometimes, on waking, I wobble my head to try to shake it out but it's stuck, and so am I. I stop washing my hair, throw books away half-read, shout at my baby birds. Over and over I shatter like a dropped cup, and inside I am nothing but emptiness. At school I giggle about my boyfriend with a sick smile plastered on, then on the weekends he picks me up for another two days of hell and I die a little more inside, until I'm hollow as a balloon and there's nothing left of me but a thin film of misery. I punch myself in the eye one day, over and over, just to feel something. The eye puffs and swells until I can't see out of it. I tell everyone I hit it with the back of the hatchet when I was chopping wood.

Modesty Blaise saves me. One weekend I tell Mark I have too much homework and go to bed and stay there, reading all the Modesty books, one after the other, devouring and digesting her ferocious badassery. She would never put herself through this. With a belly full of matted paper, I pull her on like a sealskin and zip myself inside. She's the ultimate protector. I just need her to protect me.

The next time he arrives to collect me, Modesty Blaise sits in the car next to him.

"Can you just drive down the road a bit? I need to tell you something."

He's got Chopin playing on the radio. He pulls away from the house.

"Yeah, all right. What's this about?"

"Just park down the beach, okay?"

"Is everything all right?"

I wait until he parks and take a huge breath, and Modesty Blaise speaks the words that choke my throat.

"Mark, I can't do this anymore. I just can't."

He's freshly shaved, with a nick where the razor bit. Hair short at the sides. His Adam's apple bobs. The car seat hugs my back. I pick at my fingernails.

"Do what?" he says, picking up one of my hands. I pull it back.

"This. Us."

"Whaddya mean? Wait. Are you breaking up with me?"

"Yes. I am. I can't. Do. This."

He doesn't understand why and I can't tell him I'm dying every time he has sex with me. It's hard enough just to do this.

"But it's so good," he says. "The sex is so good. It's the best sex of my life."

"Not for me, it isn't."

"What? Why didn't you tell me?"

"I'm sixteen, for fuck's sake. Why didn't you ask?"

I walk up the hill to the house as he drives away, and for the first time in two months, I hear the birds again.

It's too late, though. The damage is done. I ooze with a sticky, stinking secret, hidden where nobody can find it, not even me, although it surfaces to bite whenever my back is turned.

Because of it, I know the whereabouts of every public toilet. I know the ones less traveled. I can describe their filthy floors, their acrid stench, the taste of the soap I use to wash out my mouth from plastic dispensers—bubblegum pink or Smurf blue. I know my swollen face in their scratched mirrors, eyes red with the occasional burst blood vessel, slime and ooze dripping from my hand and sometimes even out of my nose. I know the faint, bilious smell in a fresh cubicle that tells me some nameless other shares my monster.

My body, which has always been so strong and true, is a greasy house of hate. All the words I've ever heard about myself aren't just written on my skin. They've sunk deeper. They peck out my eyes every time I eat until my belly will burst, and twist into me as I crouch over a toilet, hands dripping, stinking of vomit, emptying so I can eat again. I eat to fill the gaping chasm of this hate, but it's impossible.

Every morning, I vow I'll eat healthy food, I won't buckle, I will resist the monster now living in my guts, the one that would eat the whole world and still be ravenous, never satisfied.

It's futile. That monster is me.

Shari pulls me aside at recess, jumping up and down.

"Have you heard?"

"Heard what?"

"Felix broke up with Samantha."

"No way."

"Way. And he told Matt he likes you."

"He did not."

"He totally did. Gina, you have to make a move."

"What am I supposed to do? Cook up a love spell in a beaker in chemistry?"

"Hey! That's actually a great idea. I could—"

"No, Shar, we are not putting his name in the freezer or whatever that witchy shit is."

"All right, all right, just offering to help."

"Thanks, but I'll take it from here."

"Ooh, I'm so excited. You two will be an adorable couple."

"Quit it, Shar. We're not there yet."

Shari manages to keep her Cupid arrows sharpened and bides her time. On my seventeenth birthday, on the beach where Jesse used to point out stars and give me notes asking to hold my hand, a bonfire hurls crazy shadows along the sand, under a clear night free of any moon. Stars gleam like the eyes of forest creatures, stalking through the dark. A group of us hands around a bottle of tequila, playing truth or dare.

Shari dares Felix to kiss me, of course. He takes my hand and we walk away from the fire and lie down on a sleeping bag. Mist from breaking waves blows salt across my face. This feels so inevitable.

We click together like magnets.

Homecoming. There is no urgency. My skin is on fire, every hair on end. I didn't know a kiss could be like this.

"Wow," he says, and kisses me again, and again, and again.

Raucous laughter deflects from the fire as somebody is dared something ridiculous. Whoops and a splash, then hysterical squeals. Moonlight drifts into the breaking waves. I can just see leaping silhouettes in the foam.

"I like your friends," he murmurs, as I nuzzle into his armpit. He smells so good.

"Huh," I say. "They are, aren't they?"

"What, utter lunatics?"

"Friends. They're my friends."

"That's what I said. I like them."

"Yeah, me too." I smile to myself where he can't see. I'm suddenly really, really tired. A yawn splits my face.

"Oh, I'm sorry. Am I keeping you up?"

"No. I mean yes. I mean, shit, sorry."

"Don't be sorry. I'm not. You're a comfy place to sleep. Especially this bit." His hand cups my boob.

I fit into the curved island of his body. My eyes droop and I drift into some indigo ocean of return. The frantic vibration trapped in my cells slowly loses its buzz.

Safe. He's safe. Years of loneliness melt under his heavy arm, thrown across my ribs.

He burrows into my neck, murmurs something I barely catch. A minute later I decipher it, just as a huge warm wave of sleep pushes me all the way to the bottom, where ancient tides wait to carry me away.

"Yes," I whisper before my edges fold all the way in. "I love you too."

part two
First Flight

the year of 21

Fledglings think they're adults, but really, they're just snacks waiting to happen, unless they wise up fast. Life has teeth. I've shepherded many young birds into the wild, felt the delicate tattoo of hearts stuttering through fragile breastbones as they work up the courage. Now I understand their hesitance, wobbling on the branch, instincts leaning in to whisper, "Fly; this is what you were made for, the world awaits," but how do you truly know you can until you do? The first leap is of faith alone.

I've launched now, sure enough, flung myself skyward on wings I've spent twenty years feathering, but nothing about adult life is as I imagined it. Living in the city, away from the perfect blue arc of Jervis Bay, away from my gloriously tumultuous family, away from the deep, persistent bell of the boobook and the ceaseless sigh of waves, is hard and lonely.

My hard-won lessons about the rules of humaning crumble in the bewildering new shape of university life. It's fast and vast and unforgiving. For all my encyclopedic reading, I'm naive as a kindergarten kid about the greater world and keep running into my own ignorance and privilege at great speed. Among some of my classmates, eyes roll and sniggers erupt and I am as confused as ever about social cues.

I've found a clan, though, a bunch of fellow strangelings who feel like friends. I laugh too loudly, say the wrong things often, but my friends don't seem to care and together we muddle through sociology, post-modernist theory, Marxism, and gender studies. I secretly wonder how I'll ever work as a journalist, or in PR or advertising, as I'm supposedly being trained to do. It all feels surreal.

I've snagged a part-time job on the reception desk at a Mosman gym and found Hugh, my uni bestie, a job there as well. Danni works out at the gym, which is nice; we live together in a little flat close by. She's studying commerce law on a scholarship at Sydney Uni. She always was the brilliant one.

Felix is studying engineering out in the west. We limped along for the first year of uni, adjusting to a relationship away from the goldfish bowl of school. Now, at the end of second year, he's quit school and found a job in the city, and we're drifting apart. He talks a lot about his boss, a ball-breaker in power suits who wears too much makeup. I love him but am restless and prickly whenever he visits. He feels rough on my skin, like a sweater that's shrunk in the wash.

Nothing fits. I miss my piano. I miss my birds. Spilled city lights murder the stars and I mourn their pale brilliance. I can't hear the drum of the earth under the shriek of trains and the taste of hot metal. Sometimes a storm bursts overhead before I even know it's there. Maybe it's my skin that's shrunk. It feels too small for me.

I feel lost all the time, and my books are no help, which is the biggest betrayal of all. The city is too noisy for me to hear the words. None of my true friends, the ones who live between the pages, can find me through the stink of traffic and the relentless hum of millions of humans, thinking so loudly I want to put my hands over my ears and scream.

It's still dark, but that doesn't deter the early birds, bundled up and stamping their feet, waiting for me to fumble with the keys. They're here for their fix of endorphins, never mind it's eight degrees outside and they've been waiting for fifteen minutes for me to arrive with the keys.

I flick the lights, punch in the combination for the burglar alarm, sling my motorbike helmet and thick leather jacket behind the reception desk. Riding in Sydney traffic is often downright terrifying, but when I'm on the bike, at least I feel free and all the way alive.

The in-house personal trainer is first in the door after me. He swaggers to the desk, all pecs and bravado.

"Gina Big Tits. Another fine morning." His voice sits high in his head, like a girl's. He pushes back his thinning hair and unholsters the grin that melts his female clients. Rumor has it he's available for private sessions. Really private.

Behind him, regulars stream into the gym, saying g'day and reaching over the counter to slide keys into pigeonholes and help themselves to the stack of towels I've placed within reach.

"Morning, Muscles. I see the steroids haven't reached your calves."

"It's called a bar body for a reason," he says, flexing. "I only need to look good from the waist up. Chicks don't realize I'm hung like a hamster until it's too late, and by then they're too polite to throw me back."

I flick the switch that pipes music through the gym.

"You're just a walking advertisement for the male species, aren't you?"

"I aim to disappoint."

"And I'm sure you do, Muscles. I'm sure you do."

A young woman clears her throat, waiting to hand her bag over. She's a model, my age, with huge, slanted eyes the color of sapphires and dark hair pulled back in a ponytail. Muscles whistles as she walks away.

Hugh starts work at 8 a.m. I'm bursting for him to get here because I have news. I finally spent the night with my neighbor, Dean, who I've been perving at through the peephole in my front door since Felix and I broke up a couple of months ago. Felix got together with his boss, the one with all the makeup. I wonder if it tastes like chemicals when he kisses her. When he told me it was over, I spent a whole night walking around in the rain, wondering why I was in the city at all.

"Hey, Gi," Hugh says, gangly and tall, appearing in the door juggling takeaway cups. "I brought you coffee."

"Quick," I say. "I've been waiting forever for you to get here."

"Righto," he says, handing over the cup. "She has news."

We settle onto our stools while I tell him how smitten I am with Dean, who's part Samoan and a graphic designer and has a bad-tempered cat called Mooch.

Behind us, through the glass, fifty G-stringed bottoms bend and flex as the gym owner dishes out his latest old-school high-intensity moves. He plays Jurassic rock and beams a huge double-teeth grin like Max Headroom. Muscles drifts in and out to collect the next client chasing the dream of the perfect body or, failing that, his perfect body. The twentysomethings cycle in and out of the tanning beds, trailing that peculiar baked-on smell of cooked skin. Hugh wanders off to chat with whoever's throwing dumbbells around in the weight room.

And then the phone rings.

"Physical Factory, Gina speaking, may I help you?"

"Gina, it's Mum." Her voice sounds strange. My belly drops. She never calls the gym.

"Mum. Hi. Are you okay? What's wrong?"

"Nothing's wrong, love. It's just. You know how I wanted to find out the name on my birth certificate, now that Nan and Grandpa are both gone? Well, I wrote to find out my mother's name. I just wanted her name. That's all."

"Wow, good for you, Ma. Did you find out?"

"That's the thing, Gigi-love. I did. And. I know the name. I think."

"What do you mean, you know the name?"

"Her name's Charmian Clift. I don't know if it's the same woman, but it's not a common name so it has to be. She's a writer, a good one. She might even still be alive. It was a common story, with adoptions, to say the mother had died in childbirth."

"Holy cow, Mum. Does that mean your mum *is* famous, like we always said?"

"I think so. It's all a bit of a shock. I just wanted to let you know. I'm going to call the others now."

"Danni's here in the gym. I'll tell her. There's a bookshop across the road. I'll grab her and go see if there are any books by your mum. C.H.A.R.M.I.A.N Clift. Is that right?"

"Oh. That's a good idea."

"I'll call you right back. And, Mum, what's your real name?"

Her voice sounds hollow. "Jennifer."

"Woah. Jennifer Clift. That's you. Does it feel weird?"

"Everything feels weird right now, Gigi."

Mosman Bookshop has a center stand, and there, at eye height, are four books by Charmian Clift. Danni pulls out *Peel Me a Lotus* and I flick through *Mermaid Singing*. Danni turns over her paperback and gasps. There, on the back cover, is a photo of . . . Mum.

Danni's eyes are the size of basketballs. Mine feel like they'll fall out on the floor. It's inarguable, inescapable, impossible.

This is our grandmother.

I quickly flick to the inside jacket and read that she was a groundbreaking, renowned author, who married another writer named George Johnston, who wrote *My Brother Jack*. From the date of Mum's birth, he's not our grandfather. The woman behind the desk has more information. They lived in the Greek islands and had three kids who must be Mum's half brothers and sisters. Charmian was Australia's first female weekly newspaper columnist. She died in 1969. The year I was born. While Mum was pregnant with me, her extraordinary, trailblazing mother, who refused to compress into the box society built for her, took her own life.

"Fuck," I say. "Danni, she's dead."

She's dead. Our famous grandmother. She's already gone.

"Oh no," says Danni. "We'll never get to meet her. Poor Mum."

I run my fingers along the spines of the books my grandmother wrote, feeling the skeins of stories rippling inside, bursting to escape. I spread pages, inhale. I can't rip a corner but breathe her in through the sharp, clean smell of paper and ink and the hidden jostling of words. Something shifts inside me. A tiny, tiny voice so quiet it's a sigh swallows the knowing of this huge, wild figure whose blood flows in my veins, whose womb cradled my nascent mother, while she in turn grew the egg that made me, and breathes out a single, shaky breath.

"Well, that's all right then," the voice says. *"This explains everything."*

the year of 23

Midnight peals with turgid bells, not that any stars hope to gleam through the muddy light bleeding upward from the city, stained with lurid horns and an occasional drunken shout from the local pub. Cars litter the verge. From here there's no sense of music, just a distant tap of bass. It's enough to kick my excitement up a notch. Waiting for my friends to get their shit together, I stretch my legs. By the end of the night my hamstrings will scream and my blistered feet will throb and burn.

But not yet. Now is for the hot, quiet breath of beginnings. This night is a perfect mystery, leading me into a hidden pearl in myself.

Where once my knobbly legs wore pajamas and I stared up at the god of my father as he revealed the intricacies of atoms and molecules against a backdrop of shooting stars, now I'm wrapped in small, sewn strips of black leather, my height raised by platform boots that see me tower above mortals, and the only stars I'll see tonight will strobe and flash, shedding discs of dazzling rain from my plated silver bra.

I'm a long way from Dad's wandering lessons. My pocket bristles with small plastic bags of chemicals to help steer my way along my own peculiar trail of party science. These days I pursue chemistry of my own, experiments that take place in my bloodstream, but the building blocks are the same. Carbon, hydrogen, oxygen, nitrogen. I've hacked and mapped my own bio-code.

I recognize half the people leaving cars and emerging from cabs—tight bodies in *Barbarella* outfits spilling laughter and feathers, slabs of impossible muscle shrink-wrapped in tights and cutoff shorts scattering sequins and benedictions. Through it all, there's a sense that something's happening, some essential human earthquake. We're poised on the head of a pin, and what we do here matters. Or maybe it's just the drugs. Ecstasy is a wave that lifts me up from the inside. I've timed it so it doesn't peak before I find my way into the middle of the dance floor, but only if my friends hurry the fuck up.

"Come onnnnn."

"Keep your knickers on," says Rebecca.

"You know she isn't wearing any," says Jodie.

Bec straightens, locks the car, smiles that devastating smile. Why do I fall in love with my straight friends? Jodie pushes her.

"Get a move on, you nitwit."

We wrap arms around each other and follow the streaming lines of dark-delving denizens sniffing at the scent of bass like it's a creature to be stalked and captured in our steaming hips and pounding hearts. Wait in line under the bored gaze of giant security guards, checking bags and taking payments in drugs for the odd illegal entry. Wrist stamp, check our coats, more waiting. Energy builds under our heels and we jiggle in place on fractured beats finding their way from the pumping core of it all.

Now, finally, in we go, rocked on our heels by the brutal thumping throb that comes weaving through the crowd at the doors, into the wide, wet wall of solid skin-slap humidity and the tooth-rattling bass that reaches up through our bones to shudder our sternums, doosh doosh doosh, growing louder and louder until we're close enough that those pulsing waves resolve into some kind of treble.

Excitement fizzes like the speed in my bloodstream, like the glitter left on my skin from a drag queen's hello-darling kiss, not quite the air kiss she meant to make, she overbalanced on her seven-inch platforms and smeared a spray of fractured oil-slick flakes across my cheekbones, dagger-divine eyelashes scraping my face like they're made of death metal and she's going in for the kill. One inch to the right and she would have taken out one of my eyes. Glitter all over, but I don't mind. It's pointless trying to rub it off, gets everywhere.

"Well that's me back in the fuckin toilets for another half an hour, smeared my makeup to fuck, haven't I, sweetie?" she snarls, and I reassure her she's still utterly fabulous. That makeup wouldn't move in a hurricane.

Rebecca is so gorgeous she makes my heart flutter. We dance closer and closer, hips in time, until we're one body made of music and her arms are around me and our lips find each other. It's the kiss of all kisses; it always is with Bec. We fit like we're made for each other and stay here, standing and dancing, while Jodie pokes us every now and then with her water bottle.

"Oi, you two," she says finally. "Fuck off and get a room or pay attention. Show's about to start."

"I'm straight," says Bec, as she always does, unpeeling from my embrace. "It's just Gina."

Music grows into crisp, sonic flowers. Harmonic fragrances weave and bloom. It's an anthem I know and my heart grows wings. The rush that sends gooseflesh pinging all over my skin is part endorphins, part ecstasy, part communion, and the sense that here we go, we're on this ride again. My body moves in time with ten thousand other bodies. We're one organism with a million hearts. We don't mind rubbing against other people's skin and sweat; we're all the same in here, we're family and this is home.

A gorgeous shirtless guy with a square jaw and a perfect body grooves up, huge smile on his face. "I've never said this to a woman before," he shouts. "But will you have sex with me?"

This isn't the first time a gay man has propositioned me. I think it's the shoulders.

"Awww, thanks darling. But I don't think it would work once you got to the pink bits. Pink bits pink bits pink bits."

He grimaces, and I laugh. "See? Aren't you glad we got that sorted with our clothes on? I'm Gina. These giggling wombats are Bec and Jodie."

"I'm Stevie. You're fabulous, darling. Shall we be friends?"

"Absolutely. Wanna bump instead of bad sex and embarrassment?"

We dance like we've known each other for years.

A show erupts just as my drugs kick in. I'm flying on wings the size of sails. Dean and Hugh find us, with half a dozen friends in tow, all in flamboyant outfits. My engagement ring gleams in the lasers.

The roar that echoes from every throat lifts me higher as I fall off the edge of a roller coaster into unity. Dean and I wrap sweaty arms around each other's waists, riding the radiant crescendo of euphoria. I understand why people sing gospel in church. It's that same feeling, of tribe and togetherness and oneness and the feeling that everything's going to be all right.

Nobody outside the scene understands this experience when I try to explain, so I've given up. The people who judge usually do so while half-drunk. Droning lectures tinged with ashtray and booze-breath that Drugs. Are. Bad.

I don't try to explain anymore and have taken to lying about where I was on the weekend, although it's obvious enough when you know what to look for.

My tacit passport into queer nineties subculture is my haircut. I shaved my head on a dare while tripping at a barbecue and have left it close-cropped around my face.

It's in my hips, grooving in the thrift store to background music cloned straight from dance floors, somehow homeopathically effective even beneath the flickering hum of fluorescent lights.

It's in my athletic body, sculpted from dancing eight hours solid, three nights a week, on the spurs of amphetamines and eternally aching feet. Dancing as if my life depends on it, which it does, until the evil fuckers turn on the ugly lights and it's time to spill into the gutter, honked at by crisp, clean people in crisp, clean cars on their way to crisp, clean jobs, and here we are, sprawled and blinking like sticky human flotsam on a filthy shore. Our outfits, so fabulous in the dark and glittering maw of night, now hang sad and limp from white skin that rarely sees the sun. Eyes huge in dehydrated faces. Pupils black holes to forever. Time to face the day, although I generally don't. Instead, I hole up at someone's place with the curtains drawn. Chill-out music with a lyrical kick props up the fading fizz of dying chemicals and the resurgent lift of top-ups. Puddles of melted bodies, with eyes like dinner plates; inner cheeks chewed to the shithouse and still gurning; carelessly draped limbs; massaging each other's feet; smoking weed and picking at food that won't go down because amphetamines suppress your appetite.

I telegraph my subculture in the way I weave through passers-by on the sidewalk with determination and purpose, effortless after so many hours of practice threading through thousands of heaving bodies. The way I exchange easy smiles with a passing queen or butch in absolute and instant recognition, like some people in certain cars give each other a fleeting highway wave. Nothing needs saying because we're singing the same song together across space, and we both know the words because they're true.

From the outside, any explanation I give sounds like a clumsy rationalization for being a junkie, and let's face it, I am.

We're all junkies in a way, chasing the hit, the high, but it isn't just the chemicals. If it was, we'd happily stay home and ping our heads off with headphones on. We're addicted to the feeling of unity, and for me, it's personal. After so long staring into living rooms firelit by friendship, circling the edges of warmth but never shaking the outsider's chill from my bones, I've finally found my pack, and I'm drunk on communion with friends who are blood brothers and sisters. I understand at last what it is to be completely accepted in all my freakish edges and loved not despite but because of them. There's a name for my kind after all.

Queer.

We be of one blood, ye and I.

The queer scene is every book I've ever read, every magic carpet I've ever wished for, every genie lamp I've ever dreamed of finding. It's the Narnia wardrobe for real, it's riding every dragon in Pern, it's the wild rumpus, every night of the week.

Sometimes it's as much heartbreak as euphoria.

Stevie, completely recovered from wanting to make his only foray into heterosexuality and who is now one of my best friends, calls me, voice shaking. "Have you heard? Mustache Sally's died. We're scattering her ashes at Sleaze Ball."

I startle and accidentally stick myself with the needle I'm using to sew neon stars onto my Sleaze outfit. "Fuck. Ow. Noooooo. We just saw her a few weeks ago. I didn't know she was sick." Mustache Sally's a baby drag queen; we recently crammed into the Albury hotel with three hundred gay men and a few women to see her parade on the bar covered in feathers, miming to Celine Dion. Dean meets my gaze, tears in his eyes. It seems like every week we hear of another funeral.

At Sleaze, we gather in the Royal Hall of Industries while Sally's weeping lover pours ashes for us to dance through, toast the fallen with pills and K-bumps and amyl and ethyl and shots of vodka, first libation for the dance floor, *salut* and fuck life and fuck death and it's all a cosmic fucking joke anyway so we might as well dance.

I've peeled back the membrane of the world to find another one hiding in plain sight, with colors more rich and vivid and tastes so potent my tongue sizzles and my eyes water. The mind-blowing creativity of shows and outfits. The sharp whiff of danger and hellish crashes. Bringing flowers to friends recovering from being battered by homophobes or police, or in Ward 17 South dying of AIDS. The constant expansion of my belief structures and the challenge to my edges, seeing things I can't reconcile and having to adjust my mind accordingly.

I don't party in the straight scene and only encounter those straights who turn up at gay venues or the big parties or at DCM, the Studio 54–esque nightclub that's my second home and whose labyrinthine line I bypass three times a week with a nod to the bouncer, taking the stairs two at a time.

I head straight for the left-hand platform and clamber up to dance full-throttle until the lights go on at 7 a.m. Occasionally, I'll feel a touch on my leg and look down to find some steroid-inflated straight drug dealer with the body of a Greek god pressing a small pill into my hand, obviously enjoying the show.

I ricochet through gay picnics and queer pool parties and adventures to the mountains on LSD and mescaline with our tribes within tribes, a group of us scrambling down a cliff face to play like seals around a pristine waterhole, every surface lined with golden threads.

Fair Day, Andrew Boy Charlton, Harbor Party, Sleaze Ball, Inquisition, Mardi Gras, various camping trips and houseboat adventures with Stevie and a twitter of beloved queens in ornate outfits. I'm the one who erects the tents, pulls up the anchor, parks the houseboat, makes the fire, and scares away spiders.

No matter how much space I take up, the queens love me for it, and so, without any judgment to keep me small, I expand into the space provided, fluff out my feathers, stretch and spread my wings, stitching my flight into an endless sky of aching color. Some future version of myself hovers at the edge of my vision, a speck on the horizon beckoning as I peel apart the known and fall into worlds beyond my ken. More, says that silhouette. More.

I dance in shows at big parties and small, sniff into the shadowy corners of after-parties, sex parties, subculture parties, kink parties, fetish parties, queer parties, all-girl play parties. I lift every rock in my own sexuality, then come home to tell Dean about my all-girl adventures. He doesn't bat an eyelid. "Explore," he says. "Whatever you need. I love you."

Through it all, for the first time in my life, I feel accepted.

Mum's words resonate in my ears from so many years ago. "One day, Gina, you'll find your people."

I've found my people, and they live large and bright.

Through it all flows the music written just for me, delivered into my veins by godlike DJs who somehow know my hopes and fears and drop *that* track like they're reading my mind, bringing me to euphoric tears, the music that threads itself into the spaces between my cells and lifts me on a wave of sound I can see and taste.

I dance with absolute abandon, the way humans have been dancing since someone banged a couple of rocks together to make a drumbeat, around campfires with the moon unfurling overhead like liquid fire, dancing to unmake all the baggage and trauma and the mundane grittiness of being in a body when you're made of star metal.

When I dance like this, I remember who I really am. I soar through time, Jonathan Livingston Seagull in flight, past the terrible jagged tooth of the world, into pure potential. Everything disappears into this perfect point, this solitary presence, but I'm not alone, I am home. I scribble my dervish love song into space with swirling hips and feathered fingers, and every joyous second I dance is the best moment of my whole fucking life.

How can I explain this to people who've never dived into life this way? Either you know it from the inside or you never will.

"I can't believe you're getting married," says Hugh. I'm sitting at the piano at his dad's place, in cutoff jean shorts and bare feet as usual. Hugh's a tall drink of water, as a friend says. He's lying, limbs akimbo, on the carpet. More than a brother, less than a lover, he's just Hughby and I love him with my whole heart.

He's made some god-awful pasta mess that smells like cat food.

"Believe it," I say. "You're the MC. You'd better show up for this one, Hughby, or I'll bloody kill you."

"Of course I'll be there."

"Yeah, right. Maybe I should organize someone to be my plan B for when you get a better offer."

He unfolds a telescoping gangly leg and nudges my bum with his foot.

"As if I'd miss your wedding, you wombat."

"We'll see. You got your ticket to the Deception?"

He smiles, dazzling the irritation out of me.

"Can't wait. Wedding, reception, Deception, check. How many of us are kicking on?"

"About forty, I think. After we've packed up the hall, we can bugger off and get changed, hit the warehouse about 1 a.m., and have the real party. I've got a few spare tickets if we have any latecomers. Wait till you see what I'm wearing. It's filth."

I close the lid of the piano. Outside, a lawnmower whines and someone shouts at a dog to shut the hell up, ya stinky mongrel. I lie on the carpet, my head on Hugh's hip, and pull at his leg hairs.

"Thanks for doing this, Hughby. I couldn't have you as a bridesmaid, obviously."

"Well, you could. But your mum would lose it. Ow. Y'right, there?"

"Sorry." I twirl the fringe on the rug instead. "God. She freaks out enough about my life. A boy bridesmaid would tip her over the edge. I reckon you'd look great in a black dress, though."

"Thanks, think I'll stick to MC. Dean's changing his last name to yours, hey. I've never heard of anyone doing that."

"Yeah, nah. Dean was the one who suggested it. My family's pretty much adopted him. So he's gonna be Dean Chick. He has to change it officially. His work mates are giving him so much shit. They can't cope."

"That's awesome."

"I'm going to be Mrs. Chick. That's just weird. Mrs. Mrs. Mrs."

"You're such a great couple. I'm really happy for you, Gi."

"I can't imagine life without him."

"I never thought I'd hear you wanting safety and security. Does he remind you of your dad?"

"Eeuw. Why would you say that?"

"Y'know what I mean."

Hugh's dad putters around the other room, singing to himself. Hughby's mum left when he was little, so his dad has to love him extra hard.

"I guess. He's kind like Dad. He's just steady and there without making it obvious, y'know? He doesn't make me feel like I'm too big."

I slide off his hip and lie next to him, staring at the ceiling.

Silence is easy with Hugh. Sometimes we talk for hours, sometimes we don't say anything at all.

He pulls me upright. "C'mon, let's eat. I'm bloody starving."

"Not that disgusting cat food. I'd rather stick pins in my eyes."

I spot a corner of sheet music on the piano.

"You've got *West Side Story* coming up next week, hey, Hughby? Lead role?"

"Yeah. You're coming along?"

"Are you kidding? Of course, I'll be there with my pom-poms and popcorn, front row. Gotta catch you before you fuck off to Hollywood and get all famous and forget about us mortals."

Hugh and I met on the first day of uni. The friendship was instant. We talked nonstop in the low-ceilinged room in the basement of the UTS tower building, which permanently smells of the five-spice in the two-dollar fried rice we all still live on and stale beer spilled on the hideous carpets in the uni bar. We missed the first day of classes, sitting in those fluorescent orange plastic chairs, yakking away like we'd known each other forever. It freaks me out a bit when I think about it. I don't believe in any of that past life nonsense, but hanging out with Hughby makes me feel like the universe has holes in it and something is poking its fingers through and he's on the other side, making faces at me.

the year of 25

Carols wind through the rambling blue house on the hill, around the red profusion of Christmas bush Mum harvests every year and places in huge vases where it will catch the morning sun. Music fills the backlit cerulean glass bottles glowing on the high window, circles the row of nautilus shells, birds' nests, feathers of every hue, and family photos in a riot of frames, then settles finally on lumps of bodies belching, farting, and snoozing after Christmas lunch.

Kris potters in the kitchen, emptying prawn shells into freezer bags and trying to stuff the gigantic ham we always get but nobody eats until it gets thrown out, green and slimy, in a month's time. But Mum needs it, it's part of the Christmas tradition, and this Christmas is extra meaningful because in the time since she found out her famous, brilliant mother's name, she's written a book, called *Searching for Charmian*, which burst into the Aussie bestseller lists, and now Mum is a bit famous too.

Her book was released right after the adoption laws changed, enabling people to write to receive their birth certificate. Australia is buzzing with the aftereffects. Thousands of people open envelopes to discover wanted and unwanted news. Mum's the poster child for the adoption movement. On the book tour, she beats her breast and tells the story of finding and losing her famous mother on the same day. There isn't a dry eye in the house.

Where before, she spent every Christmas wondering about the story of her mother, this Christmas she has all the evidence, and it's scattered across the table. Photos and letters, a treasure trove of stories about Charmian and George.

I've heard it all so many times now it's become family history, with the quality of memory.

In 1954, Charmian and George Johnston moved to the Greek island of Hydra/Idra to live a life that from the outside looked idyllic but from the inside was much less so (as is so often the case).

Charm was Australia's first female columnist, a beautiful essayist and novelist, and her weekly column was groundbreaking and beloved.

She wrote about multiculturalism and racism when the prevailing patriarchal winds blew women's sails toward baking or looking immaculate to please their hard-working men, and the country was in the grip of the White Australia policy. She shook up the status quo and made a stand for something deeper and richer, using her profound voice to change the world she lived in.

Leonard Cohen is part of her story. When he first came to Hydra in 1960, he met the couple, who took him under their collective wing, and put him up in the spare room of their house until he bought his own. They spent years together, tavernas and songs and alcohol-fueled nights with a growing expat community of bohemian artists and creative dreamers.

On the table, among sketches from Cedric Flower and black-and-white photos of a Greek harbor with sponge divers and fishing boats, peeks a famous photo from *Life* magazine. Charmian leans against Leonard Cohen's shoulder as he serenades revelers at the taverna around the corner from their house. She's rapt, lost in the music. I see Mum's face in hers and wonder what life would have been like if we'd known my grandmother.

It all ended in tragedy. Charm took her own life. George died of tuberculosis. Two of her three other children took their lives. Charm was stalked by shadows with dark wings.

Mum was removed from what would become the unhappy tempest of her mother's life, riddled with arguments, alcohol, and affairs, and delivered into a family of kindness and safety, rules and obedience. Yet Mum always felt the call to rattle her own cage, bring something life-changing into the greater world. Anchored by three children, she's been frustrated, but now her voice roars into the wind and she's gathering momentum.

Alongside the trove of Charmian relics sprawl maps and printouts and passport application forms.

Mum and Dad are about to travel overseas for the very first time, in their fifties, using the advance from the book. They've planned to be away for a year. First stop is Greece to retrace Charmian's footsteps, then they'll buy a camper van and wind their way through Europe. Mum's got all the art history books out; she finally gets to visit the paintings and sculptures she's spent her adult life teaching to bored kids. I see her in the Bomo High hick-filled art classes, passionately expounding while teenagers flick clay at each other and mix all the paints together to make sludge.

"Look at the translucence of the marble in Michelangelo's *David*. The delicate flow of light and shade, bringing the eye to his focused gaze on the giant. The tension in the hand with the sling, veins pulsing, poised to unleash."

"Why's his willy so small, Miss? Was there something wrong with it? Did he ever get laid?"

Copies of Mum's book line the bookshelves, the floor, the table. In breaks between planning the Europe itinerary she signs title pages, packages them up, and sends them off. Newspaper clippings of all her interviews complete the stacks of paper everywhere.

She's finally made her scratch on the world.

Dean and I lie on the lounge with our legs intertwined. He's reading, while I'm studying for a naturopathy exam. I'm in my third year of learning about bodies and how to keep them healthy. I practice on Dean with foul-tasting potions and supplements, and we both reek of the garlic and ginger combo I make us take every morning. He never complains, just chugs the horrible mess down.

Danni's come home with us for the weekend. She pulls Dean up from the couch to help make a salad for dinner. I tune out their chatter to focus on my exam and feel a guilty pang. Dean fits perfectly into the pandemonium of my family. Everything's easy with him. We're the "perfect couple." For six years he's loved me so deeply I've remembered how to love myself. It's years since I crouched over a toilet with my hands dripping vomit. The monster in my guts retreated to its cave, where it grumbles occasionally, but most days it lets me be. The huge well of loneliness that was drowning me alive has been filled with love, but now I don't know what to do with all this kindness.

I feel like we've skipped straight to being married for fifty years, not two. The only thing missing is heat. We're like two magnets of the same polarity, without the friction required for passion. He doesn't know how to fix me, and the frozen wasteland of my sexual psyche isn't thawing. I can't imagine life without him, but with him I feel scratchy and hemmed in.

Dean needs, and deserves, a safe life, which for me is a cage.

I wonder, if Charmian had kept Mum, would my mother have become part of her story of tragedy? Does all wildness end in death? I feel my grandmother's genes pushing at my insides. Fly, they say. Touch the sun.

I need to follow the strands of my sexuality away from the safety of Dean's gaze, even if my wings melt. What's dead in me won't heal until I do.

We've lived together for six years, been married for two of them, and deep down in my belly, where musk-pelted creatures pad all light-pawed, I know I'm about to leave, and when I do, it will break his heart.

Six weeks later, puffy-eyed, I move out to a small flat behind Taylor Square, single again, podium-dancing my guilt away four nights a week. I feel the loss of Dean most just before I sleep, when the ghosts of our blissful years gather in the corners of the room. His familiar, gentle eyes, no longer loving but darkened with hurt, follow me through fitful dreams.

There's nothing to hold me back now. Oxford Street swallows me whole.

Dance, Gina.

Dance.

part three No Perfume Like Innocence

the year of 27

I travel the river Styx naked, shorn of strength. Die on its shore as the unsullied must, crawl among scattered bones to learn who I really am, and discover I am not made of the feathers and promise I see in the mirror, but stupidity worthy of the ancient stories. Old, cold iron. Despair.

There's no perfume like innocence.

In the beginning, of course, it's magical. That's how this whole thing works. "Take your heart's desire," sing the gods, delivering my deepest yearning on a plate with an apple in its mouth and hooks in its flesh.

"Now eat."

*

Grayson approaches me in a cocktail bar while I'm back in Sydney on a whirlwind weekend from Perth, where I've been living for two years.

I'm here for Mardi Gras. Rebecca and Jodie kidnapped me straight off the plane for a cocktail party at Taylor Square with all our gay and lesbian friends.

In the squealing welcome of homecoming, I realize how isolated I've felt in Perth. After Dean and I split, I'd followed a bodybuilder to the other side of the country, thinking the relationship would last a couple of months and then I'd head off overseas.

Somehow, I'm still living there, managing a chain of bodybuilding gyms. Even though I've made a life, I don't realize how tense and miserable it is until I'm back in Sydney and see how small I've become.

The DJ's a dream on the decks in her trademark cowboy hat and drops the black mix of "White Horse" just for me. Already I feel like I've come home. I glance back down the stairs to see a honey-blond god staring up at me, slight bones under all the steroids. Insolently good looking, with broad shoulders and a wide, easy grin, he holds my gaze as he climbs the stairs.

"Who are you and why haven't I met you before?"

"Gina. I've been away."

"I'm Grayson. You caught me staring with your double look back. Cheeky."

"You're worth a double look."

"So are you." He takes my elbow and leads me to the bar, and we don't leave each other's side for the next three days, while my heart tremors in strange shivers and every hair on my body stands on end whenever we touch.

The connection is voltaic. I've never believed in love at first sight, yet here I am. Smitten, blazing toward the sun, waxed wings melting in great gobbets as I burn myself up in the radiance of his regard.

Electricity forks around this barb-tongued creature. He crackles with ominous secrets, shadows of past hurts, sharkish stories of business deals to catapult him into the stratosphere; he'll never need to work again and will bring me with him on his journey of success, spoil me with ambrosia and kindness until my hurts fade to mist.

He's Willie Garvin to my Modesty Blaise, in the flesh.

I refuse to sleep with him until I've tied up the loose ends of my life, so our encounter is chaste, mostly. In our three days together, his tales seem plucked straight from my cells.

"Have you noticed most people are walkin around half-asleep?" he says, rubbing sunscreen on my back at Bondi Beach on the day after Mardi Gras. Fading waves of drugs fizz in my bloodstream, painting my world with glowing euphoria.

He gestures to the throngs of people on the sand. "Look at them. Muggles, like in Harry Potter. Settling for a life that's small, can't handle anyone with fuckin imagination. People underestimate me all the time. I bet they underestimate you too."

"I've always felt too big," I say, as his fingers knead my shoulders.

"Yeah, but that never came from you, did it? It came from everyone else. Hey, what's something you've never told anyone?" he says, turning my face to meet his.

My stomach tremors. His eyes are two chips of sky. Do I dare tell the truth? I've never been asked anything like this.

"You can trust me, Gina. I've got you."

My heart hammers. "Um. Okay. Sometimes . . . I think I'm a wolf. Instead of a person."

I drop my eyes so I won't see the ridicule that will be shining in his face. He turns my face back to his and his voice is gentle.

"I used to have a wolf, y'know. He was actually a Malamute, but they're wolves. He weighed seventy kilos and was totally wild. Nobody could touch him but me. He was my spirit animal."

I'm lost in those eyes. I couldn't speak even if I had words to say.

"See? You're not so strange," he says. "Just misunderstood, hey."

My eyes blur. He strokes my jaw with his thumb.

"You've had a rough ride, haven't you? I'm here now to take care of you. I'm not afraid of you, Gina Chick."

"I'm not afraid of you either." My voice feels hollow.

"That's good." He sounds satisfied. "You and me, we're the same. Us wolves gotta stick together."

Some invisible bell rings in my bones, like we've made some kind of pact with the gods. I want to say *I love you* but don't have the courage.

We all have our Smaug point, the missing scale on our belly. That one place where a perfectly aimed arrow can slice through our wisdom, our sensibility, our hard-built defenses.

Loneliness is mine. My kryptonite. I'm too big, too much, too loud for anyone to truly love me, or so the voices whisper. I believe Grayson when he gazes into my eyes and says, *It's you, I've been looking for you my whole life, and now I've found you.* I believe him because in my secret heart of hearts, I yearn for this exact love story.

He's the answer to every question I've ever had, presses himself into my pain points and shape-shifts to fill them. I surrender in a single breath, gather all my power into a solitary pearl, and drop it into his palm for safekeeping, trusting him, simply because he says he'll never let me down.

I sell my ancient, furred pelt to craft a pretty collar to keep me chained. Turn my back on the wild voice that's been my constant companion since I first crawled in dirt and danced with storms as if I was made of lightning. Stop my ears to the siren song of the moon. Capture my struggling heart and place it in a cage, then hang the key around his neck. All these things, and worse.

He prepares the noose, but I go willingly to it. Such is the shattering of innocence. The fairy tales warn us, but only the stain of blood teaches the true cost of Bluebeard's secrets. We learn these lessons through the bloody belly of experience.

At the end of our brief flush of days, Grayson begs me not to return to Perth. If I stay and we move in together right away, everything will work out. We're soulmates, after all. We're the same.

"Don't go," he says. "Don't go. It will be different, if you go."

"If it's real, it'll still be real in a couple of weeks. I have to tie up my loose ends; I can't just walk out on everything. If I'm going to do this, it has to be clean."

In Perth, I end my relationship and pack my entire life into a tiny blue car to move back to Sydney. It takes weeks to get everything organized.

In that time, I moon and daydream, write atrocious love letters and terrible poetry. Grayson and I talk for hours every day. I learn about his life, his friends, his tormented past, which of course I yearn to heal.

"I'll never hurt you, Gi," he promises when I express fear about how fast this is all happening. "Wait till we go to Paris, you'll see. We could even live there for six months, get a nice apartment, learn to speak Froggy. You and me, we'd tear the place up. Wolf style."

I fall more in love every day. My breath hitches in my lungs. I'm giddy. I can't work, eat, or sleep. I drive everyone I know completely insane with my endless gushing about Grayson The Amazing And Perfect WonderMan.

Finally, the day comes for me to fly to my new life, my dearest love, my happily ever after. He's picking me up from the airport and will take me to our apartment so we can fall into each other's arms and finally make love for days.

I land in Sydney after five hours on the plane in a state of jittery, over-caffeinated excitement, leave him a message from my Nokia brick-phone that I've arrived, then collect my bags at the carousel and head to the meeting place we've agreed on. He isn't there yet, so I grab a coffee and sit down to wait.

And wait.

And wait.

And wait.

Airport scenes unfold in waves of pathos, human origami tessellating into patterns of reunion and separation. Lovers succumb to the gravity of the heart, pulled together or sundered across time and space. Parents farewell children launching skyward on youthful adventures, their brave faces falling once the kids are out of sight. Tears sketch tracks of loss across grieving cheeks.

None of these people is my person. None of these stories is my story.

Still Grayson does not come, and the stone in my throat drops into my belly. An awful truth writes itself across its rough face, one I won't read, but it murmurs anyway from the growling wolf pacing through my guts.

He's not coming.

The air that steals in from the parking lot, whenever the doors open, chills and cools to winter. Darkness crawls from the shadows outside, into the sky and across my eyes. I call Shari for the fifth time in as many hours. Since leaving school we've been on wild adventures together in her life as the girlfriend of a billionaire, and I'll always love her for talking to me as a teenager when nobody else would. Over the last few weeks she's been my one-woman cheer squad, workshopping the minutiae of every phone call with Grayson.

I finally break as she picks up.

"He's not here," I cry, surrounded by scattered bags and carefully wrapped presents adorned with handwritten cards. "He's not answering his phone. It just rings out."

"Maybe he's been held up," she says.

"Something's wrong." I smear mascara deeper into my puffy eyes. "He wouldn't just not turn up. He must have been in an accident. I need to call some hospitals."

"Get a taxi to my place," she says. "I've got a spare room. Come and stay. We'll figure it out. You can call the hospitals from here."

Shari's apartment is in a lovely building overlooking Hyde Park. I collapse on the floor while she makes tea and pats my arm.

"It'll all work out," she says. "You'll see. He'll call soon."

He doesn't call that day, or the next, or the next. His phone rings out when I call. I don't have the numbers of any of his friends, the ones I've heard so much about. I don't know his address or where he works. I don't know anything, it seems.

Gradually, the stone in my belly thickens. He's not coming. He hasn't been in an accident. He's just not coming.

It's worse than being at school, thinking I'm humaning just fine, and then out of the blue, something I've said or done brings banishment. Here, in the scabbed detritus of my broken heart, all my buried demons come out to play.

I'm a freak. I'm a freaking freak and it wasn't true. None of it was true. I've just blown up my life for a mirage. I'm a fool.

He lied to my face and I believed him.

Shari flutters around, making soup and tea. She tells me she's pregnant by Richard, her billionaire boyfriend. I can stay until the baby's born. It will give me a few months to get myself sorted and figure out what to do. I crawl into the spare room and hide under the covers in disbelief. This can't be happening.

My life feels like a twisted dream. There has to be an explanation. There's no way it's all a lie. I can't be this wrong about someone.

I need answers.

City Gym is the one detail of Grayson's life that I know; he trains there daily. It's just around the corner. I haven't eaten in days and my cheekbones are so sharp they'll give him paper cuts. The dress I've chosen shows off my shoulders, which I know he likes. I rehearse what I'm going to say, although I'll probably just ramble like an idiot. If he's even there.

Seeing him is like walking into an icy waterfall.

He's over by the mirror, throwing dumbbells around with another 'roid boy. When he sees me, he reddens, then throws his chin up, shoulders back, a swagger in his hips as he walks toward me. Not a care in the world.

"Here she is," he says, smiling. "The wolf herself."

I stare at him, shaking inside.

"Where were you?"

He babbles glib excuses about phone batteries.

"No," I say. "Not here. Come to the apartment for a proper conversation. You owe me that at least."

To my surprise, he nods. "You're right; I do."

Shari leaves for the afternoon to give us privacy. When he turns up, we sit in my room, surrounded by my books and textbooks and unpacked gear. My chest is full of thorns. He flicks his hair back, takes a deep breath. I don't know where to look.

"Nice place," he says.

My hands are shaking, so I shove them under my thighs. I don't know if I'm afraid or angry. "What happened?" I say. "You left me at the airport for hours. Then nothing. No word."

Even when he's abashed, he looks like he just stepped off the cover of a magazine with that wide smile and perfect skin. Like an action hero, too good to be true. I just want to fall into his arms and have him tell me everything's okay.

"Sorry, hey, Gi. I had a medical emergency, it totally freaked me out and I just, I dunno, panicked or something. I didn't know what to do or how to tell you I couldn't make it."

"Medical emergency? What kind? What's wrong?"

He stares at his deeply bitten fingernails, chews his thumb.

"I don't want to talk about it till the tests come back."

My anger evaporates. He's sick. Oh no.

"Fuck. Is it bad?"

He looks scared.

"Could be. I'll know in a coupla weeks."

He wraps his arm around me. "I know I should have been there. And then my phone battery died and I couldn't call to let you know. That musta been really shit, waiting for me."

"I knew something had happened; you wouldn't just not show."

"Of course not. I'd never do that to you. I just lost the plot for a minute, hey. If it's what they think it is, it's bad."

"Fuck, Grayson. Is it cancer?"

His eyes mist and he looks away. "I can't talk about it yet."

"Jesus. Where is it? What kind? What can I do?"

"I'll tell you about it when I know more. But I can't be with anyone right now, not until I get through this, make sense?"

"Of course, love. Just let me know what you need."

"Just a bit of space. Course I still love you, and I wanna be with you when I'm through this; it's just all overwhelming right now. Be patient, yeah? You'll be okay staying here with your friend?"

"Don't worry about me; I'll be fine."

He still loves me. There's an explanation after all.

That night I read *The Clan of the Cave Bear* for the tenth time, losing myself in Ayla's journeys as a prehistoric human, hunting with her sling, making fire by rubbing sticks together, surviving with her lover.

Grayson and I will beat this, whatever it is, together. We'll gallop across the plains on horses we've tamed, finding ways to survive in a changing world. We're destined to be together. I hang on to this with the grip of a drowning woman. Grayson is my soulmate. If I just give him space, and we hang out as friends, we'll end up falling back into life together, because it's impossible we could be apart.

In my bones, a wolf howls. I twist down until the sound falls away. Tarzan left the jungle to follow Jane. He sacrificed his wildness for his one true love. I can do the same. I will never give up on Grayson. He needs me.

Grayson's room is bare apart from the bed he rarely sleeps in. He keeps his hair products and perfumes on the floor instead of in the shared bathroom. Sometimes I go in and sniff them, to remember what he smells like, then feel grubby and ashamed. There are a couple of T-shirts and some cargo shorts folded on the bed. Without them you'd never know he lives here.

My room's a mess as usual, a mattress on the floor and clothes piled in the corner in a tangle of platform boots, sequinned bras, and leather harnesses. Naturopathy textbooks and piles of novels make towering sculptures along one wall, sporadically hung with chunky silver necklaces. Photos of my party friends smile from above the bed, next to a couple of blu-tack stains where the odd photo has fallen off. Carlos Castaneda lies open and dog-eared next to my pillow.

The apartment is expensive, on the twelfth floor, with a balcony that looks toward the city and smells of Grayson's cigarette butts. The leased fridge just arrived, so we can finally store the organic food, vitamin supplements, and smoothie ingredients he needs to deal with his medical procedures.

I measure out two small bottles of herbal tinctures to support his digestive system for when he starts having chemo next week. If the chemo doesn't work, he'll have a few months to live, and I can barely wrap my mind around it. Knowing he's dying makes my hands shake. Not knowing where he is most nights makes it worse.

"Why don't you just move your stuff in?" I ask him, often.

He always smiles and snaps his fingers. "I'm a nomad. You know I can't be in one place, Gi. I need to travel light, be ready to move out in an hour, y'know, like Robert De Niro in *Heat*. It's what they taught us in the Commandos." He talks about being in the special forces a lot, which I think is sexy. But then, everything about him is sexy, except that he won't touch me, which drives me insane.

I throw on my favorite aqua dress, scrape my fingers through my hair, and move through the apartment, snagging my bag and car keys. Today isn't a hospital day; instead I'm picking him up from the gym and driving him around on his errands. I'm his volunteer personal assistant while he's still healthy enough to work, helping him sell "bespoke" chamois towels, although to me they just look like the ones people use to clean their cars, except with logos.

Dance music blares in the little blue bubble car as Grayson jumps in, still sweaty from the gym, slinging that careless smile along with his satchel, one landing in the footwell, the other in my heart. I can tell he's in a great mood because he's wearing his lucky *Friends* T-shirt.

"Hey," he says, kissing my cheek, turning down the radio and lighting a cigarette. "You look nice. Been on a date?" He winds down the window to blow the smoke outside, but most of it stays in the car. My hair will stink for days.

"No!" I say. "As if."

"You should. You need to get out, find someone for yourself."

He's more tanned than usual. He must have been to the beach in the last few days, although he said we couldn't hang out because he was working, so maybe it was a sunbed between clients. The tan makes his eyes even bluer. I love walking around with him, catching all the envious glances from pretty girls. Having him push me toward dating makes me feel trembly and scared.

"Where we going?" I say through a foil-bright smile, turn signal ticking.

"Nowhere yet." He grins extra hard. "That letter you wrote for Rip Curl came good. They're making an order."

I twist in my seat. "What? No way. How many?"

"Fifteen thousand units. We'll get a 10K commission. High five, kiddo. We did it. You're a bloody genius and we're an awesome team, hey."

We slap palms, and I tingle at the unexpected touch.

"Thank fuck. I can start to pay back the bloody bank loan."

"Toldya it would all work out. Half for me, half for you. Head down to George Street, willya?"

I start to move into the weaving lines of Sydney traffic, then brake.

"Wait, I thought we agreed I'll get the commission for any sales I land."

He ashes out the window as a taxi hoots and swerves. I pull out behind it, feeling nauseous.

"Well, yeah, of course you do, but Gina, it's through my work and I still have to do all the follow-up to make it happen. Fifty-fifty's fair, dontcha think? Anyway, I thought we could go out to a movie to celebrate. My treat. Whatcha wanna see? *Big Lebowski*? *There's Something About Mary*?"

"Uh. *Big Lebowski* sounds good. But . . . the commission. It's just not what we—"

He sighs, faces me with that I'm Being Patient face, and speaks slowly.

"Gina, it's not just the sale; it's everything else. I have to make sure the designs on the towel are right and, y'know, keep the client happy, hey. It's ongoing."

His cigarette stinks, but it smells like him so I don't mind, not really.

"I'm still a bit confu—"

He taps my arm with his fingers. It's hard to focus on anything when he touches me.

"Think about it, Gi. This is just the beginning. Once we've got these bad boys in a hundred and fifty stores, other clients'll be lining up. Rip Curl's a big deal. We're gonna be in Paris in no time, living the life. Left up here, I've got an appointment with another brain doctor. Then we'll go out, I'll spoilya a bit. You worked really hard on this. You know you're my best friend, right? We're the same, you and me."

He turns up the car stereo, sings our current favorite party anthem. "Everybody's freeeeee . . ."

I don't want to be his best friend. I want to be his girlfriend, but he won't let me in.

"What doctor is this one?" I shout.

"Just a second opinion." His fingers drum on the open car door frame, head bobbing to the beat. Grayson refuses to let me come in for his medical appointments, or even talk about them in anything other than vague terms, no matter how much I press. He won't even let me wait while he has radiotherapy. He says it's because he needs to do this part alone.

He turns up the music some more, looks at me, smiles, and pokes my leg a bit.

"Come on, y'love this song, chicken-lips. Lighten up."

I'm worried about money. Another overdue bill in my name sits crisp and clean in my bag and they're adding up, along with Grayson's endless promises. I follow a stream of cars into the city, working up the courage.

"When I got the loan, you said it was temporary. How am I supposed to pay it back without income?" I have to bellow over the music.

"I toldya, just keep using the loan money to make the repayments until these sales start racking up. It's short term, kiddo. Now drop it why dontcha; you're freakin me out."

"But I'm paying our rent, and all the leased appliances, and I'm getting a bit scared that everything's in my name and—"

Grayson massages the bridge of his nose. The corners of his mouth harden and his voice is a blade.

"Jeez, Gina, sometimes you'd suck the fun out of a clown's dick. I can't cope with your bloody neediness. Y'know I can't be stressed right now. I've got a lump the size of a tomato in me fuckin melon and they're upping the radiation this week. We've had a big fucking win, can't y'just go with it?"

My eyes well and his voice softens. He turns down the music. "Trust me, Gina. I'll look after you, I promise. We'll get that loan paid back in no time. Now pull up here, willya. I won't be long." I crane my neck to see the medical center. All I see is a couple of pawn shops.

He's out and away, moving pretty fast for a sick guy. The car smells like an ashtray.

the year of 28

"Gina, I don't think he has a brain tumor," Shari says, as we apply our makeup in the marble bathroom, ready for a night out with friends of hers. It's her first since giving birth to Paula, who's six months old. I'm smitten with the kid and keep peeling off to sing her silly songs and play peekaboo. The nanny shoos me away. "Stop razzing her up, go get ready." Shari's swathed in lime-green silk, by some designer whose name I always pronounce wrong. Gold heels encircle her dainty feet. My only shoes are platform boots.

"Here," she says, handing me a gauzy dress. "Why don't you wear something pretty? Cheer yourself up."

★

"He doesn't have a brain tumor," says Stevie, as we dance across a heaving midnight ocean of bare male chests, each more magazine-worthy than the last. Stevie's an eye surgeon, so he knows medical things, but I know in my heart he's wrong about this. I take a hit from my bump bottle. Expanding detonations of ketamine smooth the pain from my aching feet. The bass is a beast. We ride it like gunslingers.

★

"He doesn't have a brain tumor," says Jodie. Rebecca and I roll around on the couch, drinking Long Island iced tea at Gilligan's, clad in outrageous outfits that don't raise an eyebrow here. "Of course he doesn't," says Bec. "It's been a year and he isn't dead yet. He doesn't deserve you." She kisses me hard and long to take away the sting.

"Run away with me," I say.

"I'm straight," she says as always, and kisses me again.

"Gina, Grayson doesn't have a brain tumor," Dutch says, half-laughing, handing over an intoxicating pile of books. When he smiles, the scars on his face don't move, which only highlights their jagged brilliance. He spent all his money on plastic surgery a few years back, after cancer ate his face. This is the result. It must have been awful before the surgery.

I don't notice the twists in his skin any more. They're all part of Dutch, whose face I love, even the parts that don't move. A photo from before the plague shows his long, salt-bleached hair, wide, easy smile, golden skin. Men went crazy for him. I can't imagine him unscathed. All I know is this version: pale skin against thick, jet-black hair, chewed ragged by viruses and cancers, condemned to an early death, which he defies daily. HIV doesn't seem to touch him, except to throw up more cancers. Most of the time, he talks to them and they go away. He's the longest-surviving HIV patient in the Southern Hemisphere, has beaten cancer five times now. I reckon it's all the speed and gin. He's pre-embalmed.

"Cancer isn't an enemy," he says. "They're *my* cells. I'm not going to hate my cells. I just tell cancer, or Hep, or HIV, that there's room in this body for everyone to share space. But if they get carried away and start taking over the joint, I'll have to call in the guys in the white coats, and none of us want that. Last time they *burned* my *face*. That's what I tell cancer. Behave, or we all get nuked."

Somehow, it works.

Ironically, I met Dutch through Grayson, who introduced us over a drug deal, then watched aghast as we fell into immediate mutual adoration and hasn't stopped bitching that I stole his friend.

Dutch is on a roll.

"Grayson is unfairly pretty, preternaturally cunning, but ultimately an idiot who'll self-destruct and take everyone around him down as he goes," he says. "He's done it before. If you don't snap out of it, there won't be any pieces for me to even pick up."

Without Dutch's ceaseless mentoring, I think I'd be in an asylum. My friend is Bagheera in man form, a panther with a mighty paw to cuff an errant fool, which he seems to think I am.

He shakes his head as he taps a little mound of yellowish crystals onto the glass table, then uses a credit card to squash them into powder, hands deft and sure, without a trace of quiver. He bends, inhales in a swift arc and shakes his head again, either from the acrid sting of speed or from my stupidity. He can't believe I still trust Grayson's stories.

"He doesn't have cancer, Gina," he says again, pointing to his scars. "I know what cancer looks like. And Grayson doesn't have it."

I shake my head, stubborn as a tree. At the center of a labyrinth of bones and tears lies my need to believe Grayson's story is true. I've staked my life on its veracity, planted a spear in the clearing, and hung myself on it like a dog soldier. All my choices in the past year flow from that one decision. They surround me now with thickets of devastating consequence.

If this isn't true, then none of it is and I'm so far down this path there's no retracing my steps. It has to be true, never mind the increasingly loud yammering in my guts from the prick-eared, flick-tailed creature who doesn't think in words.

"He has *symptoms.* Things he can't know."

"Because that's so hard to fake. Are you still leaving your naturopathy textbooks lying around? Chapter seven, brain cancer."

I don't answer.

Dutch racks another line, hands me the rolled note. It's 4 a.m. and we'll be talking all night again. We nearly got hit by lightning walking down his street last week. Afterward, the smell of ozone hung like cordite. He didn't stop talking the whole time.

The speed burns, then sharpens my focus. He presses crumbs with his finger and smears them on his gums, beneath a painting of him reading on a throne, looking noble. Another painting of a blue torso, naked, with a huge cock, hangs above the glass table. There are books everywhere; we swap every time we meet. He's returning *Chaos* by Gleick and I'm taking William Gibson's *Burning Chrome* and *Snow Crash* by Neal Stephenson, along with Mary Oliver poetry and a book on women murderers. I reckon he hopes the last one will give me ideas.

If it was anyone but Dutch, I'd be home right now with these new riches, diving into the matrix and the metaverse. I don't tear the pages of his books; well, mostly. Every now and then my fingers sneak in a sly rip when I'm not paying attention. Cyberpunk tastes sweeter, seasoned with a small stab of guilt. I hope he doesn't notice, but of course he does. He notices everything.

His eyes are always kind, even when his words aren't.

"Grayson seems to find these symptoms every time you're about to leave his toned, tanned arse. Funny, that, don't you think?" His drawl lengthens when he drinks red wine, which stains his lips almost black. In anyone else I'd find this repulsive, but it's Dutch.

"Sometimes I don't love you anymore."

"And yet you keep coming back."

"Only for the drugs."

"Liar."

Hip-hop bass gathers in the corners of the room where the light doesn't reach, among mounds of dust bunnies. The community housing walls must be thick; that or his neighbors are deaf. Speed fizzes under my skin. I wriggle in my chair to the beat.

He splashes more wine into his glass. He knows better than to offer it to me; alcohol isn't my drug of choice. It rarely seems to affect him, no matter how much he drinks.

"He doesn't have cancer."

I grit my teeth, obstinate now. "But how could he lie about something like that? I don't understand. I take him to the hospital for chemo and radiotherapy."

He sighs.

"Gina-girl, you're one of the smartest people I know, but when it comes to men, you're dumb as a bag of hammers. Haven't you learned this about Grayson yet?"

He lights a cigarette, blows a perfect smoke ring. Ash falls onto the table, grubby with smeared fingerprints and stray crystals of speed.

"If his lips are moving, he's lying. Use your considerable brain. Just because he has the tattoo, it doesn't mean he was *in* the Special Forces. He's not an international man of mystery, just a petty hustler, and not even a good one, which is why he's always broke."

I shake my head, trying to reconcile Dutch's words with the fantastic stories Grayson regales me with.

My friend is relentless.

"Don't you think it's amazing how he still has his hair with all that brain chemo and radiation? No burns on his skin either. Amazing. I bet he's never let you go to the hospital with him, has he?"

He sees I'm close to tears.

"Let's not fight about it, Gina-girl. You're still in love with him, and he doesn't deserve you. Love is the most foolish force in the universe. Go on, play me that new song you were telling me about. As long as it's not a love song because you're absolutely crap at those."

Dutch used to work in the music industry, signing fresh talent. Last week, I played him a new song, and after the last note faded he said, "Gina, that's astonishingly . . . awful. Don't ever play me that hippie shit again."

He doesn't just slaughter my darlings; he eviscerates them.

My fingers hit more wrong notes than right ones as I tune the guitar and begin to sing. I only know three chords and stumble over them.

Did you ever lose your way, just one day, turn around and wonder
how the hell you got here?
Did you ever lose your light, in the night
Wake up in a cold sweat with a void where your faith used to be?
I've been there
You've got concrete in your boots.

Dutch closes his eyes, tapping his fingers and bobbing his head like he does with hip-hop, which is a good sign. He doesn't lie. Ever. Which makes his feedback terrifying.

I hold my breath. "That one's a hit," he says. "Well done." I exhale.

I go through my very short repertoire of Dutch-approved songs.

"Time for you to play at a singer-songwriter night," he says. "You need practice with an audience. And a microphone. And something to get you outta this god-awful obsession with Grayson. Live a little. Get yourself laid by someone who can actually get it up."

"I love him. I've tried not to. But I do."

"Of course you do. He's a gorgeous, gold-plated narcissist, who's told you everything you wanted to hear, and you believed it. The only thing he's dying from is a lack of conscience, too many steroids, and not enough Viagra."

I don't answer. Even though we've been having these discussions for over a year, I'm not ready to admit he's right. All my friends are. I'm the only one who's not ready to see the truth. I think I'm so smart, and I've broken my life by falling for the oldest line in the book. You're beautiful and I love you.

Another Sunday recovering from the night before. I lie in bed, looking up at the glossy patchwork of photos from the early nineties, sun-bleached Polaroids, edges curling, a pastiche of fading memories I long to flee back to. If I tap my heels, maybe I can fall into one of them. We were all so young and beautiful and innocent.

Those first years in the queer scene, I thought anything was possible and nothing could ever harm us.

Eight years on, the rose-colored glasses have well and truly cracked.

Many of those glowing young faces on my fridge are dead, from street and police violence or HIV/AIDS. One friend will never be the same after he was beaten in a back street by a gang of men, one of whom had a crowbar. Two of my friends are in jail for dealing drugs, a couple more in psychiatric hospitals. A few have simply disappeared.

Kings Cross, home of the straight scene with its bikers and gangster turf wars, has spilled its corruption onto Oxford Street. The nights of gazing across a hall of fifteen thousand people with their arms in the air and huge ecstasy grins are just stories us old-timers tell.

My beloved scene has changed. Ice and the designer drug GHB replaced the pills. The love-fest of the early nineties morphed into something far more edgy and sinister. It's the difference between hanging out with your hippie aunt, who wafts around the house in a sea of incense and mildly irritating aphorisms, and an unwelcome visit from your nasty next-door neighbor who shouts at his kids and belts the missus and poisons your dog.

I stagger through a haze of back rooms and the relentless endorphin crashes of Eccy Tuesday, which turns into Eccy Wednesday and Thursday. Dancing all night, once a haven of joy, is now a desperate chase for escape. I throw my body skyward in a sordid parody of bliss, which never comes. I stink of cigarette smoke and bad comedowns and crawl around the carpet, looking for crumbs of weed or speed to pull a veil of oblivion over the jagged holes in my mind.

When I come home in the wee hours, Grayson is usually out. We're barely roommates anymore, and I still pay all the bills.

I have grown-up debt, a huge bank loan and two maxed-out credit cards. I borrow money from people to pay people I've borrowed money from, and every day the hole gets a little deeper. Grayson's world-breaking deals are always about to materialize, the money just about to come in. It never does.

My part-time massage shifts in five-star hotels barely cover my rent, unless I receive a decent tip. All day I walk around with a voice in my head repeating over and over, in time to my steps: "Oh fuck, I'm fucked."

No matter where I look, my life is in tatters. Bills keep coming in with red OVERDUE stamps. I don't have the money to pay them. All I have is ashes.

I'm a wolf in a trap, considering how best to chew off my leg to escape. Nights crawl for too many hours as I'm chased by creatures with black teeth. It's no better when I wake and realize there's no trapdoor to save me, no way to wake from the real nightmare, which is my life. So I rack another line, drop another pill, and dance, and for a few hours pretend everything will be okay.

"O fuck, I'm fucked."

A sultry woman slides up to writhe with me in some dark den. She's my kind of wonderful. A connected friend tugs me into a corner.

"Chick. Stay away from her. That's The Big Fella's girlfriend."

"Who?"

"You know. *Him*."

My blood turns to ice. For all my fascination with sharks in these waters, The Big Fella is the greatest of great whites.

"Fuck."

I look up to see The Big Fella walking, dead-faced, through the crowd toward me. He's a fridge with eyes. Bodies part around him so he never touches flesh.

"Get outta here," says my mate.

I bolt.

Hell hath no fury, it turns out. The Big Fella's girlfriend bears a colossal grudge about my sudden departure and is connected in her own right. Paying back my debts becomes less of a worry than surviving the year intact. I don't know what she's actually capable of, but the word on the street isn't pretty.

I take to walking between streetlights with my keys protruding from my knuckles, hairs standing up on the back of my neck like a thousand antennae. I flit from light to light, avoid alleys, leave from the parking lot rather than the main entrance to the apartment building. Every footstep behind me sees me flinch. I never walk the same way twice, avoid routine, learn to spot her silhouette, and live with the feeling of being hunted.

I snap one night when I come home to see her familiar car outside my apartment again, three or four large shapes inside.

Something breaks in me. I howl like a valkyrie and run at the car, berserker-style, ready to kick in every panel, fight every one of them, *just stop fucking following me you fucking fuckers.* I almost hope they'll pour out of the car like ants, beat me or kill me, and put me out of my misery. At least it will be something.

The car guns it and screeches off in a cloud of blue smoke as I get close, leaving me panting and strangely disappointed under a lone streetlight. I lose my shit, thrashing and screaming in the street, kicking garbage bins, and setting off a car alarm when I fall onto the hood of a badly parked Mazda. Two rubber balloons filled with water explode next to me with sounds like gunshots, making me jump like a scalded cat. A nasal voice from on high shouts *shut the fuck up, willya, some of us need sleep. Fuckin hobo.*

I collapse into a gutter and weep. The fading scent of burned rubber smells like despair.

I just want it over. I want all of it over.

On impulse, I try calling Hugh, but he's Wolverine now, in Hollywood being a famous movie star, and the phone rings out.

Turf wars rage up and down Oxford Street; there are more shootings and violence. I'm stoned from first light till bed. The lease ends on the apartment, and Grayson moves away somewhere, barely a goodbye, just gone one day, leaving me with all the bills, three months to go on the lease, a fan of scattered promises, and one last indignity. One of his friends spills the beans. Turns out he's had a girlfriend the whole time. I wonder if he's been spending my money on her. I decide not to even go down that path. Better not to think about it. Better not to think about it at all.

A tinny melody from my bag, then old mate Bricka's in my ear, so excited I barely understand him.

"Slow down, Bricka." He's a shady character from the Cross, face like a dropped pie, deals drugs and god knows what else. I nursed him all night once when he was ODing and he's old-school loyal to the bone.

"Fuckin got 'im, Gi. He's fillin up petrol behind me."

"What're you on about, Brick? Who?"

"That fuckwit cunt Grayson. He's shittin' himself, saw me spot 'im, knows I hate his lyin' guts. Wait. He's just goin' in to pay. Gimme the word, Gi. I'll break both his knees right now. He'll never walk again."

"Bricka, no. Absolutely not."

"Fucker can't be allowed to walk around. He'll do it to someone else, ya know he will."

"The fuck, Brick? No. I'm not having that on my karma, or yours."

"Karma? This? Get real, this is fuckin nothin'. My karma's already well munted. Might as well enjoy fuckin it up some more. I'll do it for free."

"No. Don't. I absolutely forbid you. A long life looking out of his own eyes. That's my curse on him. Living in his own skin."

"Forreal? Ya witchy shit might take awhile but. Lemme make it a painful ride in his skin, hey? Dontcha reckon? A long life crawlin' insteada walkin'."

"No. Not in my name. Not ever."

"Gina, he's a slippery fuckin weasel cunt. Might never get another chance."

"I'll never speak to you again if you do this."

"Your call, mate. But say the word, hey Gi. Any time. Be my pleasure."

"Thanks, Bricka. Do me a favor: don't do me any favors, okay?"

I crawl back to Jervis Bay and slink upstairs past worried parents to the daybed with a book I'm revisiting: *Women Who Run with the Wolves* by Clarissa Pinkola Estés. I fall into the waiting stories as if they're a map, hunting a path out of the trap I've assembled around myself with my terrible decisions. I'm captivated by the story of Bluebeard. An innocent girl marries an exotic, handsome man with a beard of blue, who offers her the run of his whole fine house as long as she stays out of one small room in the basement. Of course, she opens the door, to find the murdered bodies of his previous wives. Her innocence is shattered. He discovers her perfidy and tries to add her to the pile of corpses, but she is saved by her brothers, her protectors, riding over the horizon. Where are mine, on all their fine horses, hooves striking sparks as they thunder to my rescue?

I've always trusted my choices. Now I live in a world of my own creation. What I thought was instinct was blind hubris. If I'm wrong about Grayson, I can be wrong about everything. How can I ever trust myself again? How can I have been so blind?

Clarissa Pinkola Estés climbs into my body on rope ladders of words. She reaches her small and tender fist into my chest and squeezes until I gasp. Her barefoot kick to a rusty padlock springs the cage in the basement of my heart, where she falls to her knees, weeping at what she finds. The emaciated creature curled nose to tail in a corner barely twitches as she cradles its head and strokes its long nose, singing in a guttural language of croons and growls, until its eyes slowly lift. She takes a small silver knife from her hair, digs the blade into her liver, and pulls out a strip of raw and bloody flesh, which she chews to mince. She spits gobbets into the creature's mouth and strokes its throat until it swallows.

Downstairs, from my huddle on the daybed, I hear Dad pottering around in the kitchen, filling the house with mouthwatering smells. Mum warbles Joan Baez songs as she fills a giant vase with native flowers from the garden.

She turns the vase until golden latelight catches on the red grevilleas, just so.

"Gigi-love," Mum calls, aglow. Even in my misery, I marvel at her beauty. She's so perfectly herself. "Dinner."

Woven into the walls, the carpets, the paintings and ornaments, I almost see myriad small sequins of love, like motes of dust hanging invisible in the air until the light hits them. The salad tastes of it, the lamb chops are perfectly, lovingly crisped where the fat's caramelized, and Dad passes a chop by tossing it across the table to land on my plate.

"Doug! What are you . . . DON'T WIPE YOUR GREASY HANDS ON YOUR LEGS."

"It's better than wiping them on my shirt."

"And now you'll get into bed without having a shower and get grease all over the bloody sheets. God, you're a heathen. Gigi, can you get some paper towels?"

Dad twirls his fingers in his beard then licks them.

"No need, see? Clean."

Mum puts her head in her hands.

"How's Sydney life treating you, Gi?" Dad says.

I smile my fake smile. "Doing great, thanks, Dad. Chuck us another chop?"

"Doug, no, NO—"

I snag it out of the air before it can land in the waiting wide crocodile grin of Barney the kelpie.

"Thanks, Douggie." I feed Barney some fat, but not much; it's too delicious to share.

"Gi," says Mum, helping herself to a piece of avocado. "I watched a show on the TV about a really interesting scientist. He was brilliant and quite strange. He counted everything. Steps, ceiling tiles, even how many times his toothbrush moved when he brushed his teeth. He didn't know how to connect with people. Just talked at them about the thing he was obsessed about. He has a condition called Asperger's. It's a kind of autism, apparently."

"Sounds like Pop."

"Exactly. He reminded me of Pop so much. And you, actually."

I look to see if she's making a joke, but she's serious.

"Are you saying I'm autistic, Mum?"

"I just feel bad, love. When you were young and you went through that terrible, terrible time at school. We had three little kids and we were so busy, and once you got big enough to play together, we didn't really pay attention to things like that. We always knew you were different, but we didn't really know there was something wrong with you. It would make sense, something like this Asperger's."

I put down my chop bone.

"Something wrong with me?"

"You know. Not *wrong* wrong. But maybe if we'd gotten a diagnosis, you wouldn't have had such a rough time."

"Mum, what you call wrong is what makes me *me*."

"Doctors can do things, love. There's medication. And maybe if we'd known, we could have helped you."

"I don't want them to do anything. Jesus, Mum, are you saying you wish I'd been medicated?"

"Of course not. But it's not just for you; it's the impact it has on your sisters. Look at all the photos of Kristie in the photo albums. She's rolling her eyes at you in most of them."

I have absolutely no idea what she's talking about. I've looked at those albums hundreds of times.

I pull out an album, then another.

Mum's right.

"She was a brat to everyone, Mum. She was fourteen."

"She's not a teenager anymore, and she still does it. Maybe you could ask her some questions about herself, instead of only talking about yourself all the time. Which is apparently a symptom of—"

"Drop it, Mum."

"I didn't mean to upset you, love."

"My mum telling me something's wrong with me? Nah, not upsetting at all."

"I feel like a walk down the beach," says Dad as we finish off the washing up. "Feel like joining me?"

Mrs. Cat is long dead but Barney's keen for a nighttime sniff at the local doggy news bulletins. Mum pleads a cuppa and a good book, one of her endless crime novels. I still don't get the appeal of crime, unless it's *The Girl with the Dragon Tattoo* trilogy, which I've read three times now. I'm devastated Larsson's dead and can't write anymore.

Barney pounces on small hopping things in the tussocky grass. Dad doesn't say much, and neither do I. I barely notice the stars or the squeak of sand under my feet. For all my outrage at the table, Mum's voice barely penetrated the ice.

In my belly, though, something stirs, a shadow of growls and a wet nose whuffling at someone's footprints in the sand. My footprints. I recognize the high arches, the spread toes. Nose down, woken by the words of Pinkola Estéz, my shadow follows these small depressions into the gloom.

Pay attention. There's a way out of this.

"You know we're always here, Gigi-love," says my father, tucking me under his armpit. "I don't know what's going on, but it looks bad. You could just come home for a while. We'd look after you."

"Thanks, Dad. I know. But I have to figure this out for myself."

"Attagirl. You always were a problem solver. Find the levers."

"You and your bloody levers." I squeeze his waist.

At the littoral margin, bioluminescence flares blue sparks, then fades.

Like me, I think. Fading. I'm Frodo after the black knife pierced his shoulder. A deadly shard burrows toward my heart, and Galadriel is nowhere in sight.

Barney leads us back up the hill to the house, lost in twisted trails of scent. Dad gives me a long hug that says the words that live underneath every cup of tea, every laugh, every casual touch in this airy house of art and light. Mum squeezes my hand as I go to bed. I squeeze back.

A sleep of sorts swallows me whole, shredded paper clumped between my teeth. In my dream, rivers of blood tumble from a tiny key. They gather to form a rising lake around the island where I pace with webbed feet. On the shore, a giant with a beard of cobalt rampages. The air smells of iron. Bobbing shapes move in the blood lake, skeletal grasping hands, long, matted hair, the gibbering, yawning skulls of lost women. Baba Yaga's house of chicken feet hurtles out of the forest, leaps on the giant, and pins him to the earth with yellow, curved claws. He roars earthquakes as skeletons of women fall on him, chewing his flesh, and as they do, their bones plump up with meat, and pulsing veins snake through white webs of nerves.

A crone older than time peers over the hut's balcony, and I know I have to hide or she'll eat me next. There's no hiding. She's older than all the stories.

Baba Yaga spears me with a rheumy white eye.

"There are no brothers," she says, clear as morning. "There never were. There's only you."

Dad's voice echoes. "Find the levers."

Fucking levers. They magnify force, but to do so they pivot on a point, around which the mechanism rotates. A good con is all about levers, human ones. The con learns the mark, learns their pressure points, and when they've found the sweet spot, the pivot point is so simple. All that's necessary is to say the thing the mark most desperately wants to hear, in their secret heart of hearts. The thing they most want to believe can be true.

A tiny amount of force, merely a few whispered words, can magnify and multiply exponentially, generating enough energy to shake apart a life, destroying the structures and foundations it balances upon.

Every heart is a house of cards, easily undone by the right lever. The right words. The con whispers a spell; the mark activates it and confers the power to self-destruct, simply by believing it. That's the kicker, with a con. They set things up so we willingly take the gun they've so lovingly prepared, turn it on ourselves, and pull the trigger.

Shari's boyfriend's apartment is light and bright, but I barely notice through the ever-circling windstorm in my mind.

"Oh fuck I'm fucked oh fuck I'm fucked."

There's a gathering in full swing. Suited men reek of money and power. Designer-wrapped women sip champagne from cut crystal, shedding light in diamond curses. I'm a long way from the familiar grime of the queer scene.

Stooped into itself, a piano beckons with sweet purity. I'm grateful for the balm of music. My fingers sing, unwinding bolts from their grooves, springing hinges, releasing tides long pent up behind a tall white wall. Here it comes now, a whirlpool of heartbreak and sorrow in rippling notes that steal the breath from my lungs. Melodies soar into the space. I almost see their fluted edges. My eyes are dry. These notes are the only tears I can cry any more.

After the final melody fades to a thread, I smell Arthur's powdery aftershave as he limps the distance from the kitchen to the piano. He's a courtly English gent in his sixties, some kind of international statesman, quite a big deal, according to Richard. Quirky with old-school manners and perfect grammar, I know he'd love me to be his paramour, but I've never shown the slightest interest and he's too polite to push.

His hand's a bit shaky as it pats mine. He sits on the piano stool.

"Gina, I have to say, you're not yourself lately. Is everything all right?"

It's the first time someone apart from Dutch, Stevie, or Shari has truly asked how I am, and the kindness in his eyes undoes me. There are cracks in the wall after all; the music has burrowed into them and released the water behind.

He flutters around like a big kind moth as I sob, then passes me his handkerchief, which for some reason makes me laugh and cry at the same time.

"I think I'd better take you to lunch," he says. "Come on, dear. Come with me, and you can tell me all about it."

Over a superb meal of delicate fish I barely taste, and salad my dry throat won't swallow, I turn myself inside out like an old handbag, emptying the whole sordid story onto the table. It flops around, dying in the light.

"I fell in love with a con man," I say, and as the words hang in the air, I know they're true. "He faked a brain tumor, and I believed him. I am so fucking stupid."

It's such a relief to stop pretending everything is all right.

I tell him everything, even the darkest parts, the parts I won't even tell myself. Grayson's whispered phone calls, his midnight excursions in dark clothing. Me, complicit, funding it all with my own ignorance. Words spill and spread like ink across the white linen tablecloth.

"Oh dear," Arthur says.

The tears come again, hot and shameful.

"How bad is it?" Arthur says, fish forgotten, salad wilting.

I tell him, and he blanches. "Gina, you could buy a small apartment with that."

"I know," I wail. "I've got no way of paying it off. I'm twenty-eight and I've fucked my life."

Great walloping waves of tears pour out of me, all the water that's ever been in my body coming out at once.

Arthur is distraught.

"But that's horrible, dear. Truly horrible. What are you going to do?"

"I don't know. I'm proper fucked. I don't know how I got into this mess."

We sit in silence for a while, as my breath goes *whu whu whu* and I try to get the tears under control. His hanky's saturated. I blow my nose on it.

"Sorry," I say. "I'll wash it."

I feel better, for talking. Telling this gentle stranger what I've never fully admitted to myself.

He bobs his head to meet my eyes, which are so swollen I can barely see.

"Gina, what if a wealthy friend helped you?"

For a moment I don't understand what he's saying, then I laugh without too much bitterness. "Get real, Arthur. I'm not that stupid. Wealthy friends want payment in kind for that sort of help."

His head shakes, no.

"What if that wealthy friend just wanted to get you back to square one?"

Lightning burns behind my eyes. The cage door swings ajar. He's offering a no-strings-attached, get-out-of-jail-free card. In his compassion he would give me all the money I need, this aging suit in shining armor, and ask nothing in return.

It's the answer. It's all the answers. I'm saved. For long seconds I stare at him and see he means it. The money is mine.

A few months ago, courtesy of Dutch, I read a book called *Damage* by Josephine Hart. It made me feel queasy at the time. Suddenly, terribly, I know why. A quote rises up from a corner of paper I ate, words buzzing as they find me from wherever words hide.

"All damaged people are dangerous. Survival makes them so. Because they have no pity. They know what others can survive, as they did."

My glamor falls away and underneath is rot.

We become that which shapes us. I've been in the orbit of a shyster too long. I'm stained by his damage, and I see, all at once, that I have to hit parachute from the whole bloody mess. Stop this thing now, right now, exactly now, before I become another version of Grayson. What Arthur offers is a trap masquerading as a solution.

I have to grow the fuck up.

The shift is tectonic. Plates rumble and grind against each other in my deepspaces.

It's so obvious, now I see it.

Grayson's web is a barbed wire cage, infecting me with his decay. I've internalized his world of scarcity, savage manipulation, survival at the cost of tender-bellied prey too soft to notice the predator, and therefore deserving of death. As I was.

I've been so hell-bent on chewing my way out of the trap around my leg I've failed to notice the bars of the zoo. I've become institutionalized. There's a deeper cost to loving Grayson, far beyond the financial and emotional ones I've been paying for in blood and obsession. He's a strange attractor, pulling my trajectory into twilight.

My fascination with darkness, my need to explore those who mirror my own, has brought me to this pivot point. Whichever way I angle the lever either it will tumble me down a shadowy road from which I may never return or I can choose to turn and open my eyes in all directions, use my will and integrity to inch myself back up the sheer cliff I've pinwheeled over.

All this in a few scant seconds. My mind is a snowstorm of the possible, tracking expanding ripples of consequence, and I see it all.

Arthur stares at me, uncomprehending, as I unravel.

This moment is the hinge on which my life turns. The shadows of my power cavort like beasts on the wall. For the first time in my life, I really know myself, belly to bone, and I Do. Not. Like. What. I. See.

A con creates a con. I've angled Arthur toward this moment. Manipulated his kindness. Worked his levers. This kind, good man in front of me is my mark, and I've been unconsciously playing him.

For a last silken second, I hang on to the solution Arthur offers, Grayson's voice howling that I'm mad, this is the golden ticket. Then the shift inside grows a voice, a wise old voice I'd thought gone for good, but here it is, against a backdrop of moss and ferns, redolent with jungle rot and good earth and the blistering soul-quake of endings.

We be of one blood, ye and I.

I sigh, and release my hold on the kite string of possibility Arthur offers. The single red sail of it streams straight up, to be drunk by the perfect cup of blue, until it was never there at all.

I smile. My first good smile in what feels like years.

"Arthur, thank you, from my deepest heart, but I can't accept."

"What?" he says, puzzled, fork hovering over the remains of fish and the black shards of damage tinkling from my heart onto the plate.

I squeeze his hand, suddenly overcome with gratitude for his kindness, and for what he really offers, which is an opportunity to choose well.

I speak slowly, figuring it out as I go.

"Grayson didn't hold a gun to my head. I got myself into this mess, and unless I learn the lesson, I'm going to do it again, but next time I could lose my parents' house, or my marriage, if I have one. I can't learn about money if you fix this for me."

He looks confused.

"I don't understand. It's a gift. You can use it to get back on your feet."

"I have to save myself to learn that I can. Otherwise, I'll always be looking for someone like you."

"You're saying no?"

I laugh and stamp my feet under the table, scattering seagulls. They wheel back instantly, in hope of scraps.

"I am," I say, feeling the insane wonder, the dizzying freedom of it. I'm not hiding anymore. From anything.

Relief.

I finally know what to do. I'm clear for the first time in eighteen months. On the harbor esplanade, children giggle and the distant thunder of a plane trails a net of expanding snow across the sky. How can every color glow so brightly?

I hug Arthur, and kiss his cheek, which casts the scent of aftershave across my skin.

"You dear, dear man. Thank you for lunch, and thank you for your kindness."

Arthur pays for our meal and leaves, an old man in an expensive suit, limping along the foreshore. Pigeon wings offer whirring music, caught by the hands of a clapping child, as he drifts away.

A waiter clears the debris and I stop him.

"Mate, could I could borrow a pen and paper, please?"

"Certainly, ma'am."

I stare into nothing and calculate, scribbling numbers onto the scrap of paper, adding it all up for the first time: rent, electricity, phone, credit cards, loan repayment, food, ganja, then divide to find my weekly expenses. For a moment I quail. It's a lot.

I need a job, a real one, that pays real money.

My university time taught me I'm not suited for the things I'm qualified for: PR, advertising, journalism. Naturopathy simply won't pay enough.

Could I do crime, for real? Lurk in shadows, make pacts with demons, always looking over my shoulder, dealing slow death in little plastic packets?

I stare at my hands, these overlarge hands that grasp life with such fervor. Hands that paint and draw. Hands that caress music into being. Hands that sing life into dying birds. Hands strong and webbed with veins from massage, bringing warmth to whomever they touch. When clients ask how I know where their places of pain are, I always answer, "My hands are smarter than I am."

These hands will save me.

I start my full-time bodywork business with forty-five cents in the bank and a heart full of optimism. I visit the manager of the local print shop, tell him I need business cards and have limited funds, but can give a massage as payment. When I press my thumbs into his trapezius, he says *Yes, and let's make your cards four color, in gloss.*

With business cards still smelling of new ink, I find every opportunity to knead the shoulders of a fellow passenger on the bus, that woman in the supermarket, those peaking revelers riding waves of bliss in a club. Within a week I have clients trickling through. Within a month it's a steady flow. I sign a lease on an apartment that's expensive but overlooks the harbor, and where I massage all day, every day.

My shifts in the five-star hotels feed my business. Their gyms are patronized by hungry young lions from the stock market and finance sector. I cruise around in tight black pants and a fitted black top, all muscles and attitude, inviting the highfalutin finance boys to try a bodywork session. When they love my iron elbows, I invite them to walk through the park to my studio for their next treatment. My thumbs seal the deal.

I'm a strung bow, held at tension for too long, finally released, and the arrow flies true.

I work, and in the work find redemption and a doorway to freedom. Under my questing fingers, bodies seem to be made of music. It's a revelation and homecoming. I massage from dawn till nearly midnight, six days a week, feeling every nuance of the body I'm working on until I see its miraculous nature with my elbows and palms, and all that exists is the beautiful dance of muscle and sinew. As soon as I lay my hands on a client, my turmoil vanishes. I'm good at this thing, know exactly what to do, can help someone feel safe with the subtle pressure of my fingers, the warm, heavy weight of my forearm. There's intimacy here, a wordless dance far beyond the strivings of personality, whole conversations without words.

Hour after hour, day after day, month after month, bodies teach themselves to me, offering up their secrets, which I hold as tenderly as any of the newly hatched chicks I cradled as a child. When I massage, I feel only love for the person unraveling under my hands and gratitude for their trust. I forget I'm broken, fly on wings of connection and hope, float on an expanding sense of possibility and renewal. Smoking weed increases my focus and helps me forget everything but the dance of fingers on skin, breaking me into the perfect purity of the moment I'm in. It's only once the last client leaves that the rapture breaks and I remember how bone-exhausted I am, how heavily stoned I am, and how many years it's going to take at this pace to pay off my horrendous debt.

Shari is once again my savior. She buys tickets to the A-list balls she attends with her friends from the horse racing scene and brings me along. I borrow dresses from her incredible closet. Men swarm around us. I take lovers from the high-society scene, men dripping with money and privilege, men who've never had to work, men who never stop working. Women in between. I learn their world.

One of these men is a banker. Not a greet-you-at-the-counter teller, but an immaculately dressed finance whale not much older than me, who swims in the digital oceans of commerce, where money isn't real, is simply a concept passed around in phone calls and on balance sheets. In his towering aerie overlooking the whole city, he sums me up in a glance.

"I have a book for you," he says, walking naked from the window, then handing me a thin yellow paperback from the floor. "It's a treasure map, and it will save your life."

I never see him again, but I read the book over and over until I hear whole sentences in my dreams. It's called *The Richest Man in Babylon*, and it does indeed save my life. I tear and eat the corner of just about every page, digesting the paragraphs that tame impossible torrents of numbers into an orderly dance.

The Richest Man in Babylon is a parable. It sums up the catastrophe of my life in the simplest language imaginable and offers a way out. Every word is meant for me. I digest the story, and from the seeds it plants, I grow a forest.

I put aside cash from my bodywork sessions. Write down every cent I spend and hoard my saved money, counting it obsessively.

I've never noticed that money smells like cocaine, when you get up close. Mine quickly grows to be a pile. The next time a bill comes in, I pay it right away. The thrill of this, actually having the money to pay the phone bill, gives me the first good night's sleep I've had in months.

I follow the map, call all the companies who've sent OVERDUE letters, and renegotiate. Design payment plans with friends who've lent me money. Every month, when the bank loan repayment rolls around, I walk into the branch with a deposit slip and a handful of cash. The teller counts it all out, mostly in tens and fives.

Every month I vow I will never be in this situation again, never in my whole life.

Dutch is in a foul mood, a hepatitis flare-up that stains his eyes yellow and twists him into a pain-stunted dwarf. He doesn't pull any punches when I tell him silly stories about bodywork clients pushing my boundaries. The stories aren't really that funny, but it's the way I get through when things are rough.

He arcs up, stabbing his cigarette out in precise flicks.

"I know you had a shitty time at school, Gina, but if you don't get over it and start sticking up for yourself, Grayson's going to be the least of your worries. Where's your self-respect?"

"I have self-respect."

He snorts. "Really? When was the last time you said no to something you hate? Like that disgusting little troll who keeps flashing you. It's not okay. It's abuse, and you're saying yes to it by not saying no."

"But if I call him out, he won't come back, and I need the money. He comes in once a week. That's food, Dutch. I don't have a choice."

"Of course you have a choice. How much is the money costing you?"

"I don't know why you're angry with me."

"You know I have no tolerance for willful stupidity. Easy money is never easy money. There's always a cost, in the way you contort. After a while you forget any shape but the box you've put yourself into."

"It's just until I get out of debt."

"Oh, great. That's going to work out just great. Five years . . . ten . . . letting douchebags walk all over you. You'll end up in debt again to some other fuckwit who needs a doormat. How'd you get yourself into this situation in the first place? If you don't learn that, you'll be in the hole again before you know it."

"Fuck off, you cheerless bastard."

"If I die next week, nobody's gonna have the balls to tell you this. You're too smart to be this stupid, Gina. It's okay to get angry when people are cunts to you and to tell them to fuck off. After a while there are no cunts left in your life, and believe me, it's a much better view."

One of my clients is a serial sex pest. He stands naked in my room, watching to see if my eyes will flicker to his crotch, which he sporadically rubs, and which I ignore, keeping studious eye contact no matter how hard he jiggles his balls.

He wriggles on the table when he's face down, and I know he's using the movement to stimulate himself, which makes me feel queasy. Halfway through the session I hold the towel so he can turn underneath it and immediately retrieve another towel to place over the first one. In the time it takes me to turn, I hear the familiar shhhht-wssshht, and when I turn back, the first towel is off his body, and his small, stumpy erection stares at me. I immediately cover it with two towels. Whenever I turn to get more oil, or another towel, or change the CD, suddenly there's Stumpy.

Every week it's the same. After the massage he walks around my apartment naked, then asks if he can use the shower before he goes to work. I don't want to think about what he's doing in there. I tell myself that all my other clients are respectful and that I can grit my teeth through the weekly dance. But I feel nauseous when he turns up, and want to scrub my skin, and the money he hands over when he leaves.

Today I've had enough. I don't even realize it until he pulls his signature move. Stumpy waves around in a bed of ginger pubes almost longer than it is.

Something parts in me with a small sigh. Maybe it's Modesty Blaise, stretching into my body. Maybe it's Dutch's voice, fresh in my ears from my recent excoriation.

The Pest watches through slit eyelids, which flicker.

I take the towel I've just picked up and, instead of covering Stumpy as usual, I stare at his penis as if it's a beetle in a bug catcher. And then I slowly, deliberately start rolling the towel, the way I used to with my sisters when we'd chase each other through the house, flicking stinging fire-ant bites into fleeing skin and squealing every time one landed with a perfect whip-snap.

Roll. Roll. Roll.

A tremor runs through The Pest's corpulent belly, and Stumpy starts to shrivel like it's trying to run away, which, of course, it can't, being attached and all. I hold the towel for a second as if I'm going to flick, and The Pest's eyelids flutter extra hard. Then I take the end of the rolled towel and reverently curl it around Stumpy's retreat, around and around until the towel sits like a blue soft serve ice cream on a pale expanse of doughy flesh. Stumpy is completely contained by the mound of towel. I leave the rest of The Pest's pasty body completely exposed.

I hum during the massage, taking my time. He twitches often, opening his mouth to speak, and I place my finger on my lips. Hussshhhh.

Afterward, he throws on his suit in a world speed record, flings cash on the table, and flees. The last impression I have of The Pest and Stumpy is a clean bathroom, unsteamed, unsullied, and smelling of lemongrass rather than cloying aftershave. My shower is mine again.

Gorgeous George is a barrister, a great one, according to George, who will be a QC one day, and then a judge. He specializes in making appointments, and then, with ten minutes to go, calling to cancel because something came up.

The day after my duel with Stumpy, and only three days after his last cancelation, Gorgeous George rings.

"Okay, Gina, I'm rescheduling today's massage. I'd like to come in on Monday."

"Hang on, I'll just check." I turn pages. "No, nothing on Monday."

"Really? Wednesday night then."

"Nothing available there either."

"Hmmm. Okay, I'll squeeze it in Friday afternoon."

"I don't have any availabilities on Friday."

"Gina, when can I make a booking?"

"You can't, George," I say. "You're fired."

Silence settles through the phone in a chilly drift.

"You can't fire me—I'm the client," he says eventually.

"I just did," I reply, and hang up.

A week later, he calls back.

"What do I have to do to get un-fired?" he says.

"Pay the fifteen cancelation fees you owe me," I reply.

"FIFTEEN?!"

I go through my diary, reciting dates.

Two days later a check arrives in the mail. Modesty Blaise purrs as I use it to buy two months of freedom from the bank loan. Only five years and eternity to go.

From the outside, I look like I have my shit together. My bodywork business is thriving and nobody knows of my struggles.

I'm a bodyguard, one of the most recognizable faces of glamorous all-female Charlie's Angels Security Service. Modesty Blaise at my shoulder, I prowl in a sleek black suit, platform boots, and a Madonna mic, welcoming immaculate guests to the floating marquee at James Packer's wedding, then guard the stage as Elton John plays on a grand piano lifted four stories by a crane. I escort four million dollars of diamonds being transported to a gala on a swanlike neck of epic loveliness, some It Girl who'll be lambasted by the media in a week or a month for some transgression or other. I shepherd visiting movie and rock stars past adoring fans to some event or launch.

I look like I have my shit together in the social pages with Shari at horse races, the polo, charity balls, A-list openings, and various parties where cocaine is the drug du jour. Its manic glitter is not my drug of choice, nor, thankfully, Shari's. She's an old-fashioned champagne gal.

I look like I have my shit together turning loop-the-loops and aileron rolls in a Russian decommissioned fighter jet, a MIG trainer brought to Australia by a client who lets me not only ride in it with his ex-RAAF pilot, but, once we've taken off and are in clear air, fly it.

Ironically, I look more physically beautiful than I ever have. I take lovers, more men than women. I tell them there's zero chance of me falling in love, and it's true. My heart is a wasteland.

"Ask me no questions and I'll tell you no lies," I say.

I don't have my shit together. I've lost connection with the girl who danced with storms and talked to birds. Forgotten what it is to follow a flickering shadow, tracking the scalloped breast of a hunting eagle, primary feathers splayed, micro adjustments to keep its body suspended on a cushion of air. I can't remember the last time I walked barefoot in the bush, lit a fire and slept beside it, caught stars on my tongue, let the boobook's haunting refrain circle my dreams.

My heart is a ragged pile of mincemeat, falling through the gaps in my fingers. I try to stuff it back into my chest, but the pieces keep falling out, to be pecked at by birds. Whatever I touch leaves a bloody stain, reminding me that everything I thought was true is a lie. Love is the biggest lie of all.

Tartarus chews my bones. Even Asclepius could never stitch me back to life.

the year of 30

The millennium clicks over, the Y2K bug does not, in fact, crash civilization, and I still have four more years to pay off the loans. No matter how much the bodywork sessions bring me joy, the schedule is punishing. Working fifteen hours a day, six days a week, is an impossible pace to maintain. My adrenals are down to fumes. Sometimes I even fall asleep mid-massage, jerking awake as I'm about to fall onto the back of a client.

I'm not in pain, I'm just too tired to trudge anymore.

I'm done.

—*if one more thing goes wrong I am out of here*—

Oh fuck I'm fucked oh fuck I'm fucked oh fuck I'm fucked.

—*One more thing. And I'm gone*—

It's a calm and peaceful thought.

A thought I dangle from when my hands are too tired to massage anymore. I turn it over and over like a smoky gem in my pocket, rubbing the facets till they're as familiar as my smile once was, when the world had color.

For seven months I polish my secret stone and wait for that one more thing to go wrong. I tell no one. I dream nightly about a silver door. My fingers rest on the handle, waiting to turn it.

Music drifts from the other side, where there is peace.

The very next thing to go wrong will be the last thing. And then I will be gone.

I wait for that thing to happen, yearn for it, hunt for it.

It doesn't.

For seven months, in a final cruel move from jackal trickster gods, now that I'm ready to leave, nothing goes wrong. Not one single thing.

I'm at a training session for Charlie's Angels, to get my firearms licence. I spend the day shooting Glocks, feeling the sting of power in these compressed metal vipers. At lunchtime I head to a corner shop with the rest of the trainees. On the way back I trot across the road, then scold myself.

Gina, you didn't look for traffic. You could have been killed.

And then I realize. I care.

I care.

I care more about living than dying. It's like finding a seedling growing in the rubble of an earthquake. Life plants itself in a scrap of green where the wind can't reach, roots tiny filaments, and starts to grow.

"Wanna come watch the Olympics here?" says Kristie. She's sunbathing on Mum and Dad's back deck. I skulk in the shade, squinting at all the light.

"Figured I'd be here for it. I've rented out my apartment, so I'll need to move out."

"For the Olympics?"

"Yeah, a gay couple from San Francisco. They've paid fifty percent deposit, and I get the other three grand when they get here."

"Six grand all up? You serious?"

"I know, right?"

Kris and I have dropped into a much deeper friendship since I took Mum's advice and started asking her questions about her life. It's like she was waiting for nearly thirty years for me to notice her properly. I can't believe I didn't know. Maybe I do have that autism thing.

"Hey, Kris. Sorry if I was an arrogant shit who stole all the oxygen when we were kids. And adults."

"Nah, fuck off, Gi, I was a total teenage brat, sulking all the time. I woulda been horrible to be around."

"I was worse."

"Were not."

"Was too."

She adjusts her hat, squints at me, then sits up. "Hey, Gi."

"Yeah?"

"I'm selling my car. It's a shitbox, but it's been serviced and it's a Toyota so it'll go forever. I was gonna ask four grand for it, but you could have it for three. Wanna buy it? I know you've been working your arse off with this whole Grayson thing. Why don't you drive yourself somewhere nice and have a proper holiday over the Olympics? You won't be able to massage anyone if you're moving out."

I sit up as well. "Your gray Corolla?"

"Yeah. It doesn't look like much, but it's reliable. The heater won't turn off so you have to drive with the windows open."

Fireworks go off in my mind.

I kiss my sister on the cheek, hard. "Fuckin love you, sis."

"Love you more. Camel scrotum."

"Fanny fart."

Time speeds up. Life claims me. The Olympics comes to town and the fever is like the old days, when Oxford Street was a riot of color and life. It's the party of the century, and I'll be missing it. I'm not sorry. The highway has hooks in me, and I barely sleep the last couple of nights before I leave.

House contents packed into storage, keys handed over, I take off out of Sydney like a slingshot released.

Kris was right. The car's heater won't turn off so all the windows stay open as I drive north for five days, alternating which foot roasts on the floor.

My passion surges back; vivid, fragrant, flooding me with sensation. I'm hungry now, starving after so long without appetite. I sniff the future, the edges of myself, sighing fields and forests, the long humming rhythms of traveling.

I smell roadkill before I see it. Sweet, cloying carcasses, smashed eagles killed where they'd been picking at dead ravens, themselves hit where they'd been picking at flattened rabbits. The canny ones, still alive, lazy over their lunch, barely flinching as I swoop close enough to ruffle their feathers. Skeins of sky flash bobbing white tails as they bolt, folding into horizons I'll never catch. The joy of the hunt. Color bruises my eyes. I lick the air with my tongue. It tastes like a promise. One tanned arm, always out the window, sometimes flying on its own, holding up the wind. Singing for hours, the radio pumping through crackling speakers. Sometimes I thrash like a lunatic so my hair falls in my eyes.

The road, the road. It smells like a pack-a-day lover's tarry kiss, and I inhale every carcinogenic molecule deep into my belly. Having been trapped in glacial time, caught and glued and stuck for eons, here at last is movement, here is the road, and I'm free for a fortnight, free of it all, clickety-clack. I flee captivity, a songbird aloft. Driving ever away, not thinking about what it's going to be like to come back to my cage of debt.

Five days traveling north, sometimes more than twelve hours at a time, and I'm running out of Australia. I'm glued to the car seat with sweat, muscles cramped into all sorts of wrongness. Every time I stop for fuel, people are clumped around small TVs, cheering the green and gold. I pass cars whose windows shout cheerful slogans: Aussie Aussie Aussie Oi Oi Oi, Go for Gold, Cathy 4EVA. Houses hung with green and yellow tinsel, Olympics T-shirts and caps, every radio tuned to Triple J. Laughing so hard at Roy and HG's tongue-in-cheek wrestling commentary I nearly crash the car.

A tiny village called Mission Beach calls me coastward. I settle on a bed and breakfast run by a flamboyant queen who greets me in a peach chiffon kaftan, promises the best bacon and eggs I've ever tasted, and invites me in to watch the four-hundred-meter Olympics final. Our girl, Cathy Freeman, is running. Home crowd. It's the race to stop the country.

Every hair on my body crackles electric as the starting gun snaps and she floats, right from the beginning. Everyone else seems to scrabble in the dirt, but she has wings on her heels, and the crowd is an animal roaring into my heart as she accelerates, it isn't possible but the gods lift her into some rarified place where there is only grace. Gooseflesh studs my arms; my hair stands up. I wipe my face to discover tears I didn't know were there as she soars. Still, she accelerates, on the howl of the crowd, on twenty million people all around the country cheering at their TVs, on the joy of her mob and her ancestors lifting her up and up and up. She takes me with her. She takes us all and wins, still accelerating.

Afterward, she laps the Sydney stadium with an Aboriginal flag and the Aussie one. Her focus is transcendental. She is the perfect slice of moment, the dervish's closed eye; the place where she ran is utter stillness while the universe whirled around her.

She is. Entire.

Something of that finds its way in. It gifts water to the ruptured seedling reaching for the sun.

The next day, desperate for some exercise after five days in the car, I book a sea-kayaking experience. I talk the guide into letting me have a single kayak, despite never having paddled before.

Homecoming.

If the rolling road has been freedom underfoot, this is the flight of my dreams. I soar like a seabird taking flight for the first time. I know this thing in my bones, love it like oxygen. The ocean reeks of life, slaps me sane. The tour group lunches on Dunk Island, and I spend the whole time itching to get back on the water, to the briny beat of paddle and muscle and the rocking slip-slap of chop against the boat. I could paddle forever.

My drive back down the coast is slow and serene. No hurry to get home. I crane to snatch glimpses of coastline, frustrated I can't see the shore, although the salt breeze brings postcards from the blue. If only I was in a sea kayak. I'd see it all.

I return to Sydney suntanned and headstrong, burning with an insane idea. To paddle the east coast of Australia. No woman has done it.

I have exactly three hours of paddling experience.

I buy an enormous map and plaster it on my wall. Pore over the Yellow Pages until I land on a paddling teacher down near Bega. His name is Charlie.

"Hi," I say over the phone. "I'm thinking of paddling the east coast of Australia in a sea kayak, and I need to talk to someone about it."

"Right. You don't say," he says. "Ballsy. I like that. Aimin high, pet. How long you been paddlin?"

"Err . . . well . . . that's why I need to talk to someone. I've paddled once. But I was good at it."

"Were you now?" His laugh is friendly, not mocking.

"Yes. I . . . err . . . yes."

He doesn't laugh again.

"When can you come out on the water? Best place to have a yarn about this kinda thing."

I like him already.

"This weekend?"

"Come down Saturday. Let's have a look atcha."

It's one of those perfect days when the ocean promises only kindness and the sky is a begging bowl for gulls and terns. It's hard to believe my land life is a torment, out here where horizons tug my bindings loose. I find myself in the swish of paddles, the unrushed conversation and easy silence of my teacher.

Charlie watches me with a shrewd eye. We round a point and paddle into a headwind, spray stinging my eyes while I laugh with delirious joy. The boat he's given me glides like it's on ice. At the end of the day, we tug our kayaks on to the shore and sit without speaking for a long time while the last light ebbs from the sky. Gulls trace incomprehensible patterns overhead. I scribble idle circles in the sand with my toes.

"I'm kinda jealous that this is your life," I say. "Always been a paddler?"

"When I was a kid, yeah, up north. But here, pretty recent. Before I started this business, I worked on oil rigs."

"Wow."

"It was hard on me wife, though. I was away a lot, missed the kids' birthdays. That shit's just not cool. We moved here, it's a fuckin good life. I'm around for me boys now. And look where we are. Fuck me. I get to do this all day. Straya is fuckin paradise."

Cormorants arrow in to land in a huge tree, then spread dark wings to dry in the fading sun.

Charlie squints at me. "And now you've turned up with your mad bloody plan to paddle six thousand kilometers with no fuckin experience and no fuckin idea. You're a bit of a unit, arentcha? Got guts but."

"You don't think I can do it."

"Do *you* think y'can do it?" he says. "That's the important thing."

I really think. I've now paddled a grand total of twice. It's not much to go on.

"Yeah, I do. It sounds nuts, but I do. Is it insane?" My eyes are bright.

"Insane? Probably." He smiles. "But fuck, who wants to be boring? You're a natural, pet. An instinctive paddler. I can teach you the expedition and safety stuff. As long as you've got that covered, it's temperament and fitness that'll make you succeed or fail. Temperament isn't something I can teach you. I reckon you might have it, but. In spades."

"So you do think I can do it?" I ask, a little anxious.

Again the long stare. Then the slow smile.

"Gina Chick, you're dead set mad as a bag a'snakes, but I reckon you can. Let's give it a go, hey? This'll be fun. Gimme a bit of excitement in me old age."

The seedling grows more leaves. I begin to live.

I still work fifteen-hour days paying off my debt but take weekends off to train. I spend spluttering hours eskimo-rolling in surf, practicing deep-water rescues. Charlie teaches me the liquid language of the paddler. How to glide across a river mouth, around a bay, read the wind from the texture of the water, how to land a sea kayak in surf. He's methodical and uncompromising. We pore over maps, gathering weather information, tracking seasonal winds. We plan concentric rings of redundancy to keep me safe. Strategies for capsizing, for whales, sharks, rogue waves, reefs, crocodiles, gales. He pushes me hard, training me through dehydration and hunger.

I shift my bodywork schedule to give me mornings off. Every morning at dawn I push a kayak out from Rose Bay, winging across to Manly, dodging container ships and ferries, speedboats and yachts. After a stretch and a sandwich, I turn back for the fifteen-kilometer paddle home. Sometimes I'm met by castles of purple cloud with brilliant white crenellations rearing impossibly high, rain or hail hazing their undersides. I paddle flat out through the freezing wind of the southerly buster to make it home before I get blown out to sea or lightning finds my carbon paddle, shaking my head at the sheer madness of it all.

I paddle at least 150 kilometers a week and am fitter than I've ever been in my life. I've stopped smoking weed, I'm eating well. I should feel fantastic.

I feel terrible.

Something's wrong with my body. I wake up heavy. Purple bruises flower under my eyes. I guzzle vitamins. Paddling gets harder, not easier. I push through. And push. And push.

And then the pain hits. Pain I've never felt in my life. Acid sears my insides. I hole up at Stevie's house, gasping, wrapped so deep in myself I can barely speak.

In the morning, he takes me to hospital.

The doctors in emergency tell me there's nothing wrong and send me home time and again for three days. Finally, on the third day, with Shari creating a ruckus about my lack of treatment, the surgeon tells me he'll do a laparoscopy to "have a look," and if there's something wrong, which he doubts, he'll deal with it. I'm hallucinating by the time I go in for the op, at midnight.

I wake to the anesthetist's voice, saying, "It was your appendix, one of the nastiest we've seen."

"Gangrene?" I ask a nurse later, after reading my own chart. "Really? How long have I had that?"

"Looks like a few weeks. And then three days with it ruptured. You're a very lucky girl."

When the registrar visits, he apologizes.

"But I told you," I say. "I kept telling you there was something seriously wrong with me."

"I know," he says. He has the grace to look abashed. "I just didn't believe you." His pager beeps. "There's a high chance of infection," he says as he leaves.

I don't know what that means, but I find out soon enough.

I go home and a week later am carried back in with a complete bowel obstruction and a pelvic abscess the size of an orange. For some reason it takes another two days before the senior surgeon operates. Stevie says I'm too lucid when I'm in pain. I have Douggie's high pain threshold. I should be screaming and incoherent to be taken seriously.

I wake. It's a long swim through molasses, this wakening. Tangled in the spine of some machine, I hear its blood hissing, its heart beeping, its soldered breath echoing inside me. Everything's bleary.

"Gina, you're on a morphine drip, honey, this is the button, look, I'm putting it into your hand, you have five minutes after you press the button before it'll work again, see, you press, that's it."

The red button is right there, in my hand. I press.

I dream of Shere Khan, wake in the claws, the jaws. Fumble in slow motion. Stab the red button repeatedly in the trembling eternity before whiteout.

Wake again, fumble, press, red button, how quickly I learn. Pavlov would be proud. Pain slices me awake. Before the morphine caves in on me, I wonder if I'll be triggered by red traffic lights when I escape this prison of machines.

A leech digs, burrowing, wrapped into me. No, it's a face rustling through the quiet dark, just the electric underhum, not all the big noises. Something slides under my tongue.

How's the pain?

Horrible, I say. My body's swollen to bursting. Without the staples holding me together I would pour liquid, a river. I'm a jellyfish drowning in my own fluid. A cloud, shiny with rain.

Press.

The leech is thirsty, it drinks and drinks. I watch fluid pour from my insides into a clear bulb attached to its feeder, which disappears in my belly. What does it look like in there, what horrors and marvels does the blind leech see?

Press.

How did I get here?

Press.

And press.

I wake, properly now, hazy and heavy but awake. The ceiling is pocked, looks like dirty polystyrene. Same as high school ceilings. Long, lazy summer days, rocking back in the chair, staring at the ceiling, daydreaming of Felix. The chainsaw burr of a trapped blowfly, chasing freedom against the glass. Orange time. Time chopped into five-minute segments, bite-sized portions.

Here there are segments within segments. Nights are the longest. Nothing to distract me while I wait for the nurses' visits. And through it all, the relentless five-minute dance, blowfly against the red glass, knocking itself endlessly, questing the sky.

Press.

Thirty-six staples snake down the front of my swollen belly, six stitches from the first appendix op, a morphine drip in one arm, saline drip in the other, catheter, tube down my nose into my stomach that makes me gag, and an abdominal drain. A plastic balloon rests on the end of a tube that goes inside my body, draining gushing fluid from the infection, which is probably antibiotic resistant and rips through my body like a bushfire.

One minute I'm the fittest woman in the universe. The next, this.

Charlie visits. I don't recognize him in his town clothes. He surveys the mess of tubes and paraphernalia.

"Don't think I'm going anywhere for a while," I say.

His face is helpless.

"I'm not usedta seein ya like this."

"Me neither." I try to push myself upright. "At least it didn't happen on the water. I'd be dead for sure."

A treacle-slow nightmare follows; three weeks on the morphine drip waiting for my insides to remember how to function.

Noah, my favorite nurse, listens to different parts of my belly for the twentieth time. In the first few morphine-hazed days, I recognized him as a familiar muscle queen from the Midnight Shift.

"You look different with your shirt on," I said.

"I'd recognize those lips anywhere. Sorry to see you in here, gorgeous," he replied. "I'll bring in some glitter; we'll have a party for two. Looks like they've got you on the good stuff."

"I fucking hate it. Prefer eccies any day."

"Don't we all," he sighed. "But you'd be pretty sorry without this little drip." He patted my hand. "Don't worry, we'll have you out in no time."

"You know what peristalsis is?" he says now, pressing the stethoscope to my ribs.

"Sure. Smooth muscle contractions that push food through my guts."

"That's the puppy," he says. "Trouble is, when your intestines are in shock, which yours understandably are after your appendix exploded gangrene everywhere, that wave stops, and without it, nothing moves inside. You can't digest food and, eventually, you'll die. We're waiting for you to fart, which tells us everything's working again. Until then, it's nil by mouth, I'm afraid."

"My survival hangs on a fart?"

"Fraid so. So you may want to cook up a beauty for us. Everyone'll cheer."

"Do my best. Can I listen?"

He gives me the ear pieces. Cold metal nuzzles against my belly. No gurgles and hisses. It's silent as the grave.

Blur.

My parents and sisters drift in and out, spilling worried stares and outrageous stories to make me laugh, which hurts astoundingly, but it's worth it. Mum takes photos of me with all my bags and tubes and tries not to look scared at how skinny I'm getting. Kristie tells jokes for hours until the whole ward is in love with her. Danni turns into a pony and gallops around neighing. Douggie pats my hand and looks a bit helpless.

It's hard to find me in the wall of flowers around my bed. I task nurses with distributing the huge bunches, first through the whole room, then the ward, making gradual headway against the ubiquitous antiseptic reek of misery.

Stevie visits nearly every day. He gets special privileges because he's a surgeon, reads my chart and murmurs to the nurses, keeping his face schooled. He watches me struggle to sit up, shuffle to the toilet, refusing his help.

"I need to do this," I say, waving away his hands. "Otherwise, I'll never heal."

Underneath his concern lies something darker. I see it in his face.

I'm dying.

From some bubble of lucidity in the numbness, I think: anything that stagnates in nature dies. I need to move.

I scoop up the bagged bulb catching the fluid from my insides and thread my feet through the clear tubes going into my veins from the drip bags on a pole next to my bed. The pole has small wheels. One of them points in the wrong direction and whickers mindlessly, like an errant shopping cart. I shuffle the length of the corridor, doing laps, white pressure socks to my knees, hunched into queer positions around the knives in my guts. Up, down. Up, down. Back to bed to rest, then gather my motley and shuffle up and down the corridor again. Up, down.

The wise old voice in me is insistent.

If you don't move, you will die.

I dwindle to an angular arrangement of bones trying to burst through skin. In the mirror, my eyes are too large for my face. Infection rages and chews through me, dissolving flesh to fluid which gushes into the clear bulb, day and night. IV antibiotics and morphine blow out the veins in both my arms, so the nurses go to my feet to find a vein while I sob and beg them to stop.

I loathe the morphine. After nearly a decade of recreational drug use, my opiate receptors are affected and my tolerance is high. The drug barely blankets the pain. I feel heavy, stupid, hot, and sticky, a fly in amber. Pain is a cruel marauder, stomping all over the morphine.

The anesthetist visits, blue gown and shower cap, kind eyes.

"Were you ever an IV drug user?" she says.

I'm shocked. "Never," I say.

"You're medicating yourself with levels we see in heroin addicts."

"Morphine doesn't work. I hate it. Can you give me something else? Not an opioid?"

"There isn't anything," she says. "It's all versions of morphine."

"There has to be something."

She shakes her head.

I press the red button every five minutes, to hold back the knives. Shuffle. Up. Down. Day and night.

I'm dying.

I see it in the faces of the nurses, the doctors, and my friends, especially Stevie and Dutch, who can't hide themselves from me. My legs are matchsticks, but still I walk, nodding to the patients I know, nodding to the new ones, nodding to the nurses and doctors. I imagine a faceless, dark cowled shape reflected in the window. Or maybe it's not my imagination after all.

Up. Down. Red button.

It's groundhog day. Three weeks tick over in eternal five-minute slices. I know every chip of paint on the ceiling. Patients come and go. They wave goodbye and wish me well. Out on parole.

"Get square," I say as my latest roommate leaves. "Don't wanna see you back in here." I'm a lifer.

The room is quiet after she goes. I'm on my own with my tubes and drips and the empty silence inside my belly.

I think about the hidden mystery of intestines, slippery and cunning, nestled together in their watery home, never seeing light. And then flesh opens, light spears into layers of muscle sliced and spread by scalpels and clamps. A doctor's plastic-coated hands reach in and pull blue ropes and ribbons and organs out, into the air, away from each other. What do guts think, when sunshine pierces their essential darkness? They're never meant to see light. Now in an icy metal dish, cold air, scorching lights; roughly handled and scrubbed and splashed.

No wonder my insides are on strike. They're in shock.

I put my hands on my belly, avoiding the long central zipper of staples.

And then.

A brilliant white light switches on at the base of my spine, a glowing ball of strangeness. Then another a little up from it. Then another, then one in the center of my chest, then my throat, forehead, top of my head. Those are chakras, aren't they? I thought they're supposed to have colors. All I see is dazzling white.

The palms of my hands blaze.

This has to be morphine. I have never, in all my years of recreational drugs, hallucinated to the point I believed it. Maybe I'm dying, right now. My mind's throwing up visions.

Light pours like honey out of my hands and through my perforated insides, cooling and mending, how could this be but oh, and oh, and oh. If this is a hallucination, it feels incredible.

I feel held. I feel safe. I feel a rush of joy and peace.

A nurse bustles in the quiet. Thermometer in and a pat on the arm.

"Ah, well done. Your temperature's down, love," says Noah. "You're on the mend, gorgeous. You'll be back on that podium for Mardi Gras."

It's another week before there's a gurgle in my belly, and the day nurse's face lights up. She gives me the earpieces.

"Listen," she says. "That's the sound of survival. You're gonna make it. But your first bowel movement's gonna be a horror, after all that morphine. I don't envy you. I'd start on laxatives as soon as you can."

The gurgles grow stronger, and as promised, the ward cheers when I let rip with a big fart. My insides have decided to live. I'm allowed to drink some water, slurp some soup. It's a few more days before I'm strong enough to leave.

The anesthetist visits. She's blunt.

"You're going to have withdrawal issues," she says, handing over a script for oxycodone. "Stay in touch."

"I don't want it," I say. "I'll never take that shit again. Give me something else."

She looks skeptical but writes a script for Indocid, an anti-inflammatory for rheumatoid arthritis and terminal cancer patients, and adds it to the Endone.

I emerge, newborn and shaking under a collapsing sky. Stevie helps me to his car. I take an Indocid as soon as I'm settled. As it disperses into my blood, the pain in my guts loosens its talons and

I feel relief for the first time since this whole thing began. I tear up the Endone script.

Stevie tries not to look worried. I weigh forty-five kilos, down from seventy-five; muscles wasted and morphine-sodden mind confused, so thin a gust of wind could blow me away.

He hatches a plan for my recovery.

"Here, look at this place," he says, showing me photos of a Robinson Crusoe treehouse on a small tropical island.

"Looks spectacular, Stevie."

"Pack your bags. We're going."

Haggerstone Island is a remote coral resort in Far North Queensland. Stevie rents it for a week and brings four of our nearest and dearest along.

We frolic on the wild frontier, six hundred klicks north of Cairns, weave outfits from palm fronds and wear them to dinner. Snorkel over beautiful unspoiled reefs, pulling slick-scaled fish from the deeps and shivering when we see saltwater crocodiles. Haggerstone Island only sleeps six guests, so we have it to ourselves. Every day the owner, Roy, takes us out in the boat to catch our food for the day, which he cooks on deck, before bringing us to all his favorite secret wilderness spots. The Milky Way streams like a giant galloping dragon from one horizon to the next. I make sand angels. Shooting stars fall around like snow.

My ravaged body fills out, and I start to feel peace. This place is good for me.

At the end of the week, I ask Roy and Anna if I can come back to the island to work.

Anna's voice is soft, impeccably English. "Gina, I know you've had a lovely time, but it's a very different experience as a guest. Staff work hard, from dawn till late, seven days a week. You might not enjoy it."

"I'll love it. I work hard," I say.

"We don't pay much."

"I don't care about the money." Without rent, and with nothing to spend a meager salary on, the pay will be just enough to keep my loan repayments kicking along.

"Keep in touch," she says.

Six months later I pack a huge suitcase with enough clothes to last a year and set off to Haggerstone Island.

In the constant labor of sweeping paths, tilling orchards, preparing food, washing boats, lugging supplies, making beds, chopping wood, and looking after guests, I grow strong again, fit and brown.

Underwater, I'm as sinuous as an eel, stalking avenues of coral with a spear and reliably bringing back lunch of crayfish and coral trout. That atavistic joy is a drug more potent than any I've ingested on a dance floor. I'm a hunter, it seems, and live for the chase.

Everywhere my eyes fall, beauty strikes me mute. Time ties itself in gentle knots, delivering me into myself anew.

And still I work, hands callused, back ridged with ropes of muscle, every day, all day, losing my pain, finding the pure diamond bones of will that hold up my cage of flesh. The wild devours me whole, spits me out, devours me again, until I no longer remember the Gina of nightclubs and concrete and heartbreak, and instead, Storm Girl walks the beach and dives the sea. Creatures pad, trackless, at my heels. Endless, agonized conversations with Grayson's ghost drop away, lulled by the returning chimes of tide and wind, the manic cackle of chickens, the squeal and chitter of flying foxes, the slap of dying fish in the boat before my blade splits their gills and there's no life left to lose.

Every day my world is a little bigger, brighter, slower. Wrapped in blankets of silence as I work, I begin to understand the Zen masters. Chop wood, carry water—such beautiful, simple tasks in a location so exquisite my heart swoons every time I raise my eyes. Hospital memories fade like coral tree leaves under the relentless scouring tongue of the dry season, to blow away in the sea breeze.

As my year on Haggerstone draws to a close, I find to my surprise I want to be alive. Properly alive. When I chose to love Grayson, I bankrupted myself mentally, physically, emotionally, financially, and spiritually. Paying back the money is only part of the bargain of homecoming. The island is healing my body, burning out the infection and morphine. After a year roaming free in the jade wilds, Mowgli's fiery hunger for life crackles under my skin. The soles of my feet are leather-tough, and new lines radiate at the corners of my eyes. My hands bristle with calluses.

Now for the hard part: dealing with the scars I can't see. I'm ready to face the world again and, more importantly, myself.

The island falls away to a small dot under the wing of the tiny aircraft, until it finally vanishes, and I can only look forward. I'm excited to see what life has in store. I'm still in debt but feel ready to face the next stepping stones to freedom.

Mowgli drums a salute as the propellers drone on, holding up our tiny toy of folded metal against the voiceless hum of gravity.

part four Big Sky

the year of 32

Her name is Violet, but I call her Kiri, after a valkyrie. She's Peter Pan in wraparound black shades. Untameable. She asks if she can kiss me the first day we meet, then tumbles us both down the grassy knoll, shrieking.

If there's an adventure, she's up for it, full throttle, with no thought of consequence. After my interminable years of fiscal responsibility, she's a carnival, a cyclone, an ice bath, an odyssey. She has no boundaries, but like an enormous puppy, it's impossible to stay mad when she jumps on the bed with her huge muddy paws and shakes water and sand through the sheets.

When we're together, I don't feel alone.

We roll along a concrete footpath on a dare, carve our initials in wet cement, play silly pranks on each other. I drive with the top down in Pandora, my beloved Jeep, blasting the *Lara Croft: Tomb Raider* soundtrack at full volume. Kiri stands on the seat with her whole body poking through the top of the car, despite me pulling at her knees to come down. I can't get enough of her armpits and sniff them when we're walking down the street, in the cinema, everywhere. I ride a huge black behemoth of a motorbike in the Dykes on Bikes float at Mardi Gras, wearing a studded harness and leather shorts. She wraps long legs around me, waving at everyone. Half a million people line the road, throwing glitter and streamers, and the roar that goes up when the bikes rip the air with thunder like jets landing is enough to shake buildings to rubble. We drink coffee on the bench seat of a Bondi café, wearing matching black bug-eyed sunglasses, watching the beautiful people slink past. Crash our bicycles, kissing while riding on the bike path. I'll keep the scar forever.

Kiri's snoring softly next to me in my studio apartment when a huge storm rolls in across Bondi. I shake her, take her hand, and pull her down the stairs, yawning and bleary, to the beach, where waves pound and boom and the rain stings our eyes. We strip naked and push into the breakers.

"What are we doing?" she screams. I can barely hear her.

I howl, "This!" and punch and thrash at the wave bearing down on us, grabbing a watery breath to scream into the wind, which tears my voice away. The wave knocks me backward, sand in my mouth. When I surface, I do it again, shouting and punching and kicking, tumbled and tossed by marching embankments of water. Kiri's already got it, is her own whirlpool, encased in darkness and foam.

Maelstrom.

My skin softens, turning me inside out, pouring black poison into the sea. No matter how hard I punch, the ocean pushes back. No matter how big my rage, the sea is bigger. I can't stop, my arms flail. I'm crying but can't feel the tears. I plant my feet, thighs like tree trunks, and roar at the waves, "Come on! Fucking well come on!"

Somewhere in the churn, Kiri assaults the living arms of the kraken trying to dislodge us. I only know she's still there when I hear her whoops, catch the glimmer of a long arm, tousled streamers of dark hair like seaweed across her face.

Inside, I fall into a point so still a single atom could crawl into my hand and I'd feel it. An ancient, creeping horror vomits from my cells, to be swallowed by the searing maw of storm and ocean, leaving me stranded on the shore, exhausted, ecstatic, sand in every pore, tumbled by the dying edges of waves as they scratch for land.

Death. I'm squeezing it out.

Kiri washes into me, a detonation of limbs, and then we lie above the last soft fingers of water, chests heaving, legs flung over each other. Rain still pelts, shockingly fresh after all the salt.

She staggers to her feet, pulls me up. We walk back up the beach and across the road to my apartment, still naked, shedding sand and euphoric giggles, tingling and electric, not caring about streetlights and the delighted honks of passing cars. In the heat of the bath, I almost fall asleep, until she tries to stick her toes up my nose. By the time we've finished wrestling, there's water everywhere. I'll lose my bond, for sure.

For the first time in memory, I sleep the whole night through and wake in the same position my body had fallen into, rendered into warm, spreading peace. There's a fresh coffee next to the bed and a note from Kiri.

I love you. Can we run away together forever and drink chai and make babies?

I wish I could love her the way she loves me, that is to say, entirely. There's still a broken piece inside me, and no matter how hard I shake, I can't rattle it loose.

The clues are piling up, though.

Wrung clear in the aftermath of the storm, I feel, rather than see, a path. These answers aren't to be figured out, they're to be felt in the thousand miles between my head and my feet.

My body knows what to do.

When I was a child, I danced the storm inside and the storm outside as naturally as breathing. I didn't ask why, just ran into the heart of the tempest to find balance in a world that made no sense.

When did I abandon that fey creature who saw worlds of wonder hiding beyond the membrane of the real and brimmed with love for every living thing? Was it when I lost my virginity? When I started to believe the names that branded me other? When Grayson's precise strike sheared rows of carbon atoms and split a diamond to its core? Or when the rot inside carried me to the edge of my ending?

Part of me wants to stay forever in Kiri's timeless Neverland, but I know it's time to leave. Thanks to her unbridled love, I feel lightness and hope, have remembered how to play and meet the world with curiosity and joy. It's not enough. I can't find the part of me that knows how to love and be loved, and I won't be whole until I do. Somewhere, buried inside, the wildling still remembers, if only I can find her. I spent so long as a child wondering how to leave my strangeness behind, and it turns out it's the wisest part of me.

the year of 34

The fingers digging under my ribs feel like scalpels. I've partnered with the biggest guy in the room, on purpose.

"More," I grunt. He ratchets up the pressure until it feels like he's scraping my sternum out from the inside.

"More."

"Fuck, Gi, any more and I'll be in your lungs."

"Exactly. Errghhhhhhh."

Chris O'Brien paces through the rows of towel-draped bodies, turning up the volume on the well-worn *Gladiator* CD we all know by heart after a year of these workshops. The plastic skeleton he uses to demonstrate techniques hangs habitually from his hand, like a faithful dog. He forgets it's there. My eyes are closed, but I know he's grinning under deep-set eyes that can make him seem grumpy, which couldn't be further from the truth. He's awkward in conversation until you veer into the language of the body, and then you realize he's giddy as a kid.

The man's a paradox. Spends his days teaching students the quantifiable mechanics of anatomy and physiology, in particular the hidden language of fascia: silvery sheaths of connective tissue interpenetrating the whole body, compressing vertebrae and nerves, squeezing organs and pushing bones into painful shapes. Then he'll suddenly veer into the mystical. The experiences that may arise once these tissues release their vice grip can look a lot like magic.

Chris and I are recently back from a two-week training in holotropic breathwork, using our own bodies to test the work of Stanislav Grof, a seventies psychiatrist who used thousands of hours of LSD sessions to heal catastrophic trauma in his patients and then, when acid became illegal, realized those same states could be initiated with certain patterns of conscious breathing. Over two weeks, chests heaving, breathing fast and hard for hours, we've experienced things that can't be explained.

It's all science until it isn't.

As *Gladiator* builds to a riotous swelling frenzy, someone in the room starts to moan. And then I can't think about anything other than what's going on at the place where my pectoral muscle attaches to my clavicle. Big Fred's meaty fingers are spot on. Scar tissue parts with almost audible judders. The pain is exquisite. My eyes roll into my skull and I deepen my breath, barely hanging on.

"You okay?" he whispers as I writhe.

"Fucking fantastic," I grunt. "Errrghh."

"You're a bloody tank, Gina."

And then I'm in and away, following the pain, my breath, the snaking undulations of spine and neck as an old blister bursts somewhere back in my childhood, lifting me up and over one of the waves I used to catch with Dad. I go limp, tumbled, tearing inside out. Pain is a doorway to another country, my body the map. I sniff into a forgotten jungle, drink at a waterhole where my lost ones wait. Here's one now, peering from behind her fingers, birds fluttering to land in her hair. She's six or seven, amber-eyed, barefoot and patterned with lichen, and oh so alone. She's a part of me I left behind a long time ago.

I don't want to spook her.

The pain is background noise now but still loud enough to keep me here, locking me into this breath, this moment, this dance between my biggest self and my smallest.

She can't be rushed, this little Gi.

I offer her treasures from behind my back: sunflower seeds, a bee's wing, a shell that looks like a fish, lyrebird songs captured in cupped palms. She takes them one by one, solemn. She's so small and strange.

I remember her now: wide-eyed, freckled, nut brown, strong as roots and reeds.

I tell her I love her and will never leave her, hoping it's true. I abandoned her somewhere along the way. How do I know I won't do it again?

Her emotion is mine, rising through the galloping rocking horse of my body, which we ride together, faces whipped by streamers of mane, legs gripping the huge barrel of chest, held on by faith and fear. What if we fall? She leaps up, balances with her arms flung wide, whooping. Her trust that I'll catch her brings a flush of shame for all the times I didn't.

Pain is a rope we climb together. I pull us up these braided threads until I'm aware of the room again, music soft now, the pressure along my ribs gentle.

"Hi," I say to my untameable, skinny echo, my cloven other, now returned. She stitches herself into my marrow. There's nothing to say who she is or who I am; we're the same.

Who knew life could be so rich? Every step takes me deeper into a life that works. By diving into the wisdom of my body, I've learned how to heal my psyche, and the journey is marvelous and horrible in equal measure. In the thick of it, I wonder why on earth I'd put myself through this crazy dance. On the other side, I can't imagine any other life.

I don't need drugs, rule books, chants, ideology, dogma, incense, drums, or intricate rituals. I'm down to the simplest movement of all. The willingness to feel everything this body is designed to feel, which is all of it. As long as I allow my body to move in the same way a child instinctively processes a tantrum, or an antelope bucks and kicks after escaping a lion, there's an intelligence to the process that brings me safely through. After the tempest has cleared, I feel peaceful and whole.

The shadow on the wall is far scarier than the creature casting it. Humaning is simpler and more difficult than I ever thought. It isn't choosing one voice. Humaning is welcoming them all.

In the magnificent wilderness of my own body I've become a gardener, hands buried to the elbow in earth and mud and the good rot of compost, churning and turning the soil, uncovering small, sad seeds of belief that I'm not enough. It takes tenderness to plant them, right side up, water them with benedictions and a whispered spell of forgiveness. With *enoughness.*

In discovering myself in this way, I've become a practitioner of modalities that allow others to do the same. The more time I spend with my hands on bodies, the more I marvel at their mysterious perfection. I'm no longer a journeywoman. Fifteen thousand hours of touch flare in the fingers that lit my way back from the darkness, weaving webs of homecoming. I see with my fingers, palms, fists, and elbows as clearly as if my skin is studded with ten thousand eyes.

My hands dance across a woman's shame about her old, cold resentment; motherhood eroded the freedom of her life and she wrestles with the urge to just walk out. They rest on a man's grief as the knot in his shoulders resolves and he sobs into the table, never good enough for the hard-as-nails father who's now dying and still can't tell him he's loved. They soothe a sibling, dealing with the push-me-pull-you tug-of-war with a narcissist sister who demands the whole galaxy revolve around her.

A reclusive mercenary, fresh back from Afghanistan, twenty-two bullet scars his only portal to feeling. When I touch them, his eyes grow flat with murder and, for a moment, I'm afraid. We have an agreement that he won't harm me. I tell Stevie his name, just in case, although it's fake, for sure. The killer tells me he can't count the bodies. Specters sigh around the room. Afterward I open the window and shoo them out.

Questing fingers reveal the dreams of a politician's wife; her whole life revolves around him, but her fantasies are of Vienna and painting and music and a slow song of lovers under snowy bridges. *You're safe now,* my fingers whisper. *Whatever happened in the past, whatever will happen in the future, here, in this moment, you're safe.*

Awareness opens the darkest door.

We're mammals, and mammals need touch. At the end of each session, I leave my hand resting on skin. I'm here, you're not alone.

We be of one blood, ye and I.

the year of 35

The small folded lump of notes is heavy in my pocket, though it shouldn't be. I should have wings under my heels. This is the last payment of my bank loan. After today, I'm finally free.

I hand the wad of cash to a bored teller, who collects, counts, and stamps, then dismisses me with a breezy thank you. People speak in hushed voices, like it's a library and any loud noise will spook the money.

Invisible chains drop from my shoulders onto the marble floor. Cracks snake across pale stone, a stutter of rubble drifts from the high Art Deco ceiling. Nobody notices. I step over discarded piles of coiled links, barefoot, dizzy for a moment. Their dying imprint feels tattooed on my skin.

"You okay, love?" says the woman behind me. "Bit of a turn? Need to sit down?"

"Yeah, nah, fine, thanks. Just remembered something important."

It's pissing rain. Puddles ask to be jumped in. I oblige. The six-year-old kid from across the street joins me. Together we make muddy mayhem. I'm drenched by the time I reach the gate of the little house Stevie bought in Bondi a year ago and that I share with him. The homely fence, neatly trimmed hedge, curlicued porch light all look the same as when I left this morning, but the enormity of my new freedom brings this scene to life like a postcard and gilds every one of the raindrops I shake from my hair.

Seven years later it's really done. I've paid off my debt.

Grayson is a distant memory. I wouldn't recognize him on the street. He's a symbol, a code for some ancient, soul-led travesty. The girl who made the choice to love him is long dead, turned inside out, scoured and scarred into a lean and rippling creature, cloven in many ways, stronger in others. In her place walks a wiser, harder woman. That woman would say: we don't fall in love with the person, we fall in love with the lesson they're here to teach us. But she'd say it quietly, under her breath, in case the gods came looking.

The rain abruptly ceases as I take the stairs and make it under cover. I drip on the porch, shake myself like a cat, shrug out of my wet clothes, and quickly slip through the door, then pull on something dry. The front room is set up for a full day of clients, the first one arrives in an hour. There's a stack of folded towels fresh from the line; Stevie brought them in before the rain hit, bless him.

In my head, I count the cash that will come in. All the money I earn from this day is mine. I'm debt-free. Unshackled. My trajectory is my own.

I should feel more, but this day is just another day. I've learned my lessons minute by minute for seven years.

I've never been able to hate Grayson. He behaved in his nature and I in mine. I wonder if my curse follows him, the consequences of his actions a slow, creeping raft of misery and loneliness. A long life looking out of his own eyes, hearing only the hollow rattle of his stories in the echo chamber of his castle of lies.

Now that it's done, I find I don't even care.

As the rain fades to a symphony of drips and the birds carol the return of the sun, Rex the Burmese cat purrs at my ankles and his sister Lulu bats at a leaf.

I'm free.

But then again, I always was.

The kitchen smells like Arrakis; I left the chai simmering when I went to the bank. Cardamom and cinnamon, cloves and ginger and nutmeg coil into a mélange so ubiquitous it's permeated the walls.

There's time for a quick last-minute squeeze of paint onto the ornate mask I'm making for the workshop I'm heading to tomorrow. Feathers line the plaster, falling in soft waves in place of hair. Hollow night down one side, a painted edge running eggshell-sharp down the middle.

Stevie wafts in, wearing one of his many extraordinary, architectural hats, which highlights thick makeup and false eyelashes so long I'm surprised he can blink. Small jewels twinkle at the corners of his eyes. He trails a curtain of orange silk. The gossamer-fine fabric hovers in the air, stirring spice scent into fragrant eddies.

"Morning, darling," he says. "That mask looks amazing."

"I think it's finished." I hold it to my face, bob my head, birdlike. "Death mask."

He shudders. "Spooky."

I put it down. "I have muumuu envy. New outfit?"

He twirls. "Angel's in the house, darling."

"She sure is." I hug him good morning, offering a fragrant brew. "I paid off the last of the loan today. It's finally over."

He hugs me back, extra hard, while I juggle chai to avoid ruining his kaftan.

"Congratulations, darling, I'm so proud of you. What a ride that was. Chai to celebrate sounds perfect."

We're surprisingly good roommates considering he's a creature of order and I, chaos. I'm not as allergic to the cats anymore. The first six months were hell, but now, as long as I don't rub my eyes, I'm okay.

"Don't rub your eyes," he says as I hand him the cup.

"Shit."

"When do you fly out?" he says, sitting at the baby grand piano that takes up a whole room. I sneeze and wipe my itchy eyeball.

"Two in the afternoon tomorrow. I'm hiring a car at Melbourne airport. It's only an hour's drive, so I'll have time to settle in before the fun begins."

"Are you excited?"

"Kinda."

"Are you really sure you want to go back? It seemed a bit cultish last time."

"I'm not done there. Don't worry, I haven't drunk the Kool-Aid completely. Promise me if I ever come back not myself, you'll deprogram me with a broomstick."

He gives me a look that sees right to my bones.

"Count on it, darling."

The rental car smells of chemicals. Mask laid carefully in the back seat, I turn up the music, singing all the words. I can't shake Grayson from my mind as I escape the furnace of Melbourne, through dry farmland into cooler forest. His shade batters the windows of the rental car like a dusty gray moth.

"Fuck off. I'm done with you."

The workshop is at a center run by ex-Sannyasins, who spent time with the spiritual teacher Osho in the seventies. My favorite bunk in the big converted farm shed beckons. I toss my bags onto it, greeting a group of familiar faces and a few new ones. Some of the strangest experiences of my life have happened on this property. It's Narnia, for real.

We gather in one of the bush temples looking out into pristine forest. Dusk birds cavort, and the enormous magnolia is in full flower, throwing citrus streamers of perfume around like it's a funeral, which, in a way, this is.

Daricha, the facilitator, ponders us from his throne-like seat. I'd love a chair, but it's not how things are done here. I definitely haven't drunk the Kool-Aid because I'm filled with uncharitable thoughts about guru-trips.

"There's been a terrible accident," Daricha says after all the introductions. "The cook poisoned the soup. The phone lines are down, the road is cut off, and we'll all be dead in a week. There's no way to get word to anybody. All we can do is prepare for our deaths and leave letters for those who'll find our bodies."

Even though I know it's part of the retreat, which is called Dying To Live, a momentary rush of panic flushes my cheeks. What if he really did it and this isn't a game?

Under the magnolia, flinching against the earsplitting wail of cicadas freshly hatched into a shout of life, I shake out the writer's cramp from all the letters I've penned. One by one I make peace with my skeletons, the hearts I've left scattered like crushed roses, all the ways I've lied and cheated or simply haven't shown up, the conversations I've been too afraid to have. All now embalmed in ink in a huge book I may burn or bury. Maybe one day I'll atone in person, but for now, writing it all down is enough

Death presses its face to the glass, and I press mine back.

A lone cicada, alien feet hooked into magnolia bark, pushes against the crack in its shell. Down in the earth for seven long insect years, proboscis buried in a tree root, blind as a maggot, it had been unaware of anything but a world of darkness. And then in a single night it crawled up this tree, and now, with sunshine pouring into its eyes, it struggles free of its larval cage. Birth is such a brutal rending.

I didn't want to bring Grayson with me; I'm sick of him clogging up my clockwork. Yet here he is again, muttering from clouds, twisted into treetops, tapping on this cicada striving for life, following some ancient call to the light.

Like this tiny monster, I've spent seven years in the underworld. Grayson was a terminal event. He killed me as surely as this cicada now dies to itself.

Who am I, now that every step isn't in direct reaction to my choice to love him? How much have I shaped my life around that choice? If I take away the pain of my lessons, maybe what's left is love. I wouldn't be here under this magnolia, staring at a tiny dinosaur, if I hadn't believed the lie he offered. If I'd done one thing differently, I wouldn't be here. So how can any of it be a mistake?

What if love is when we say, *I will let you shape my life and I will shape yours?*

What if every choice we make to allow someone to sculpt us through our dance of connection, whether a dearest friend or most hated enemy, is an act of love? What a privilege, to be a force in anyone's life, no matter how small. Of all the people we could let in, we choose fifty or so to impact and mold us. In an ocean of eight billion souls, wherever we shine the light of our attention, we bring one out of darkness into the force of our regard. In changing, we are changed. Every person in our lives has their bloody fist buried to the hilt in our heart, and ours in theirs, monkey grip.

Choose wisely, says the cicada. *There are no accidents. Only lessons.*

Learn, die, learn, die.

A few weeks ago, I pulled up at a traffic light. In the passenger seat of the neighboring car rested the oldest person I had ever seen. Her skin looked like scrunched paper, an impenetrable map I did not have the years to decipher. For a moment I felt like I was flying over a continent, studded with mountains, riven by rivers. Her eyes were buried so deeply in folds of skin I could barely make them out. The young woman driving seemed like a dragonfly, darting hither-thither. The old woman was the river stone the girl rested on for a second, before disappearing in a whir of wings. Her great-great-granddaughter, perhaps?

The old woman's eyes had seen electricity pour through a lightbulb when it was a miracle of science, she'd seen the first motorcars, danced to the first recorded music, grieved through two world wars that stole her beloveds. The twisted hands folded like shells in her lap had held babies and buried them. Her world had spun faster and faster until it was now a dizzying carousel, on which her slow old breath now hung suspended, like ancient mist.

I saw in that moment that she'd watched everyone who knew and understood her die. She was the final tree in a clear-felled forest, towering high above the canopy as the next saplings strived toward the light their ancestors had freed with their passing. She could see forever. I saw in every wrinkle the loneliness that comes when you're the last of your kind.

The cicada spends an extra hour breathing life into oil-slick shimmers of wing, which unfurl to translucent beauty, then plump up to quiver and vibrate. A blast of sound adds to the shrill cascade of outrage from its fellows. LIGHT! its whole body screams, much as my intestines did when the doctors pulled them out to scrub death from their soupy skins. BURNING LIGHT!

Every birth is a death. Every death a birth.

I dance a labyrinth in my death mask, past the strange gyrations of other masked bodies. A blue-ringed octopus waves tentacles at my passing. Baby birds, the ones I couldn't save, wheeze. A ten-year-old girl with a ragged home-cut fringe watches through a snow globe as schoolgirls plait each other's hair. Halfway through the labyrinth's endless twists and turns, I'm back in hospital, wandering endless neon-lit halls, chased by a hooded shape of childhood nightmares. Briar tangles of tubes and bags rattle, my rickety-wheeled pole of drips can't keep up.

A hand of cold iron on my shoulder. Only emptiness under the cowl, but the thumb that comes toward me is bone-white and steaming. It presses into my forehead with a painless sizzle.

I'll have you. A voiceless voice inside my jawbone.

I fall to my knees.

Get up, says the wolf at my side.

Get up, says the snake.

Behind the cowled figure, an archway covered in millions of blossoms. Where the figure's feet fall, flowers bloom.

When the labyrinth spits me out, I throw the death mask onto a waiting bonfire.

Plaster scorches and curls, flames turn my carefully painted comets black. Burning feathers reek. Finally, there is only ash. I scrub at my forehead like something's stuck to it, but when I look in the mirror, nothing's there.

It's the end of the week and nearly my turn to "die." I'm not afraid of death, but the messy part, the dying, scares me shitless. In the bush temple I sit, cross-legged, as each of my brethren lies down. A roll of the dice has me as the last of my kind. One by one they fall, until it's just me and Daricha, sitting in his throne, master of ceremonies, relishing the theater of it all. And then I, too, fall back to breathe my last, shuck the shell of my body, marveling at the work it's done, the scars tattooing my choices.

I see the earth spin huge and blue in an abyss of time and wonder at the life cycles of stars and how meaningless our lives are when measured against them. Time is a force, like gravity. Each species on the planet pushes against it, trying to outrun the huge hand dissolving every single living thing to dust.

We're fireflies, believing ourselves gods.

the year of 38

Haggerstone Island beckons with cerulean fingers. I'm here for a two-month stint before heading to a primitive survival school in New Jersey in the USA. When I first read about Tom Brown Jr.'s Tracker School, my body rang with the persistent note that always precedes a choice that feels like fate. The wolf in my belly, I've learned, is never wrong. Listening to it is the tricky part.

In this instance, though, it was easy.

The website showed a bewitching array of workshops teaching all aspects of hunter-gatherer wilderness survival. Making fire by rubbing sticks together. Building shelters from sticks and leaves; learning how to track and stalk game, weave string, rope, and baskets from plants; how to carve traps and fish spears. Village building in the manner of our tribal ancestors. A whole syllabus of earth-based philosophy, ceremony, rites of passage. Treasure troves of primitive wisdom handed down from a Native American referred to as Grandfather to Tom Brown Jr., who'd spent ten years as a kid in the Pine Barrens of New Jersey, hanging out with the old Lipan Apache, learning everything he had to teach.

Scanning the website, I could barely stop myself from packing up my life and running away to live there. The wolf in my belly howled the house down. From Paleolithic depths, Ayla sang back.

"Have you heard of Tracker School?" I'd asked Stevie, eyes whirling.

"Uh-oh," he'd said. "I know that look. Why do you want to go?"

"I *have* to." My finger hovered over the booking link for the umpteenth time. "This isn't a choice."

"Ah. One of those."

He'd peered over my shoulder at intriguing images of people blowing into clumps of smoking leaves, or chipping stone into arrow points, or with faces and bodies striped with mud and clay. A calendar showed weeks of classes.

"Right up your alley, Gi. Which class are you going to do?"

I'd pointed to the section between March and July.

"It feels right somewhere in . . . *these* . . . dates. I don't know which class. So, I'm gonna do them all."

But first I need to make enough money to pay for it all.

Every time I land on Haggerstone's pristine sands, I work harder than I ever have in my life, hurt more, and fall more deeply in love with the wild. It scratches me with its single dirty claw and the itch never goes until I'm back here, shedding a little more of my civilized skin each day.

There are more stars than night. The beach whispers, and my heart breaks open. Every muscle in my body feels like it's been kicked by a very large horse.

This is my fourth stint on the island in as many years, and I can't wait to go hunting.

While happy guests eat lunch on the boat, I slide in to the Coral Sea without a ripple, parting the waters, slipping into an indigo glove custom-made to wrap around my body.

The sea opens her cool arms, smiles her cool smile. I free-dive fifteen meters into a bell of glass, piercingly clear, stray bubbles waltzing upward to disappear into the light. Currents breathe in time to my heart, which opens and closes, opens and closes. It doesn't beat; instead, waves break through me, salt water cascading in place of blood. The sea is my apex. I readily offer her my shining veins.

Fifteen meters down, the sea is eerie and absolute. It sups on radiant fields of sensation, draining me of all that makes me human. Deeper, deeper. My skin disappears until I am a grain of silence, suspended. All heat is leached, all the mortal passions, the reds and oranges, fires and flames. Dive deep enough and all that remains is the blue. I am a serrated edge of shark tooth, slicing myself lucid. There is no truth but this.

The hunt awaits.

There, a coral comet falling upward, telltale bridges and citadels where crayfish could be hiding. The ridge rises ahead of me. Any cray sneaking in the crevices had better scuttle far back into its hole.

Coming, ready or not.

Long antennae herald a beauty, marching out of its den in challenge. We eye each other off for a few seconds.

I grab some air, slow my pummeling heart, then dive back down. The shot's true and the cray scrabbles on the spear, then hooks its legs into the cave wall and pushes backward. I reach in a full arm's length and slowly wrestle it out before it can pull itself free.

A shark arrows in out of nowhere, then another, attracted to the wounded thrum of the cray. I kick hard for the surface, hold the thrashing cray out, and kill it instantly by pressing the spear into the central nerve plexus.

Now that the cray's dead, the sharks circle but won't risk injury by coming too close. They're not that interested in anything once it's limp meat. It's the electric dance of dying that's irresistible.

I don't ever want to dive the blue, the true deep. Huge saltwater crocs sail the currents, lazy between islands. Tiger sharks so big they bite a fishing boat just to see what it is, then come back for seconds, even though they've snapped teeth on the metal. Drop-offs run a kilometer straight down; there's nothing to stop the behemoths if they're curious.

Here, though, the reef is shallow. Kinder. Coral dazzles in hives of color and life. Trailing the cray as I swim back to the boat, I wave to the pair of sharks circling my heels like curious dogs. Hi, friends. No lunch for you today.

Bondi seems a long way away.

Huge container ships dance their slow glide between reefs, mirrored by drifting clouds. The trade winds kick in with steady sou'-easters that heave the sea into lumpy madness. When I'm lucky enough to score a day on the water as the deckie, I snatch blissful hours perched on the prow with a line from the handrail, balancing on the bow pulpit, mimicking the terns and frigate birds, teetering and skidding when the boat drop-slams suddenly into a trough. Sometimes I let go of the rope, spreading my arms to fly like a bird. The wind has glorious teeth, relentlessly chewing shards of civilization from my bones, spitting them back piecemeal into the sea.

My callused fingers barely bend, and I've lost pounds of city softness. My body loves this life, loves the work. Days curl dry and bright. The wild is a growl in my heart.

The northern blue tuna have been running, sleek predators all thick with muscle and appetite. You fish for them with tiny lures, and when they hook on, they fight like billy-o. I hook an absolute beauty; the reel squeals and I barely hang onto the rod as the line screams out, nearly pulling me overboard until I dig my knees into the side of the boat and haul and swear and churn as sweat slides down my face and my shoulders burn and it's touch and go who'll win. When I finally land the fish, it thrashes through the boat so fast and hard I wonder if I've captured a kraken. It explodes across the deck in a frenzied detonation that scatters rods and reels and terrified guests who leap for safety, perching out of reach until the creature can be killed. I didn't know anything could move like this. In the catastrophic violence of its ending something dark and fleshy pops out of its mouth. At first I think it's the heart, but it's actually the liver.

The tuna's liver gleams almost black. I've been without red meat for months. My body lusts after this wild, ferocious creature's flesh. I nibble a bit on the boat and it's clean and salty and rich and suddenly I'm starving. I slice it into perfect mini-sashimi wafers, chill it in the boat fridge, and eat it, morsel by morsel, in ecstasy. Each sliver makes me more ravenous. For a moment the boat fades, and Ayla sits beside me on a Paleolithic plain, gnawing on the carcass of something small and squealing, blood running down her chin.

Has it really only been two months? I've grown into this place, and it into me, but all things must end.

I stare at everything wide-eyed, every pore open. It could be years before I'm back on the island, if ever. It's so clear, now I'm here. I don't belong in the city. I don't belong in walls.

Stars skitter. I hang onto the beach in case I fall up. When I leave, I'll miss the silence. My ears ring with the lilt of palm and bird and wave. Sound becomes so familiar: the particular whine of your particular gate, the slam of your lover's car door, the groaning creaks of your childhood room settling into itself. Here I'm lulled by the faint throb of passing planes; the endless sigh of fronds and wind; the sea eagles' unlikely dawn quacking, the doves' papooah-papooah love calls; and the geckos growling and tussling all night.

I'm awake, awake, all my senses alive, my skin an electrified perimeter. I'm tracing the wild wide blue into my heart for keeps, for later, for smoky dull nights surrounded by walls and electric lights. Carving into my skin an invisible tattoo to keep my memory sharp when the huge sky has condensed to winding asphalt ribbons. I'm tying little knots inside me; this one a juicy pocket of sea breeze, that one the tang of ozone, this one the impossible red of a scarlet-headed honeyeater hovering in precious water spray.

Darkness crowds the edges of paths. Light splashes across dry eyes. The sun's sharp fingers rake the sand. Shadows float like bruises on the water.

Tomorrow, I leave. I don't want to go, but this is the nature of nature. Endings are beginnings in drag. I gather every nuance of this place into myself. The savage beauty of this country is alive in my blood, and I in its.

Island time speeds into modern time. I feel like the cray, grabbing on with my fingers and toes, resisting the relentless pull of the spear, yanking me into the world.

In this last pause between breaths I feel something simple and vulnerable and new.

Yearning.

I hunger for connection. I can't lie to myself any longer.

I ache for a mate. Ten years after shattering myself in the earthquake of Grayson, my heart is ready to let another in. I'm ready to be soft.

I've written a new song, and here on the beach on my final night, tears cooling on my cheeks, I sing it as a prayer whenever a shooting star pierces the night.

I haven't met you yet, but I feel your footsteps close by.
Wouldn't say I'm searching, you'll find me under this big sky.
You're a beautiful freak,
You're not going the wrong way, everybody else is,
Come fly with me.

part five We Be of One Blood, Ye and I

the year of 39

After Haggerstone's endless sea breeze, the air at Tracker School's Primitive Camp smells strange, of hot pine pitch and fragrant cedar. My bare feet scuff the sand as I search for somewhere to dump my things. Sugar-sand paths trail in all directions. Pots clang in a rickety camp kitchen where big gas burners heat enormous saucepans. A hundred new students mill around the camp, wide-eyed. More seasoned bodies tap and chip glass and stone into arrow points in a circle of concentration near the huge teaching shelter with no walls. There's a buzz of activity near a small tent structure that sells T-shirts, knives, books, and chocolate. A tanned, white-haired man sits with his back to everyone. As I stare, he turns as if pushed, spearing me with impossibly blue eyes. It's only later I realize this must be Tom Brown.

"Camp tour! Camp tour!"

Pack in hand, I saunter over to a tall, skinny guy with a shaved head.

"I'm Lee," he says.

"Gina."

"Welcome to Tracker."

He waits until a few more new students join us, then walks barefoot down a path, carefully, like he's placing his feet to avoid thorns. Like every step's a question and he's the only one who can hear the answer. He chats about the school, which he's been coming to for years. This time he's halfway through the caretaker scholarship program, which means he lives here for a year in a primitive shelter, practicing wilderness survival skills and helping out in camp during the weeks when there are classes. After he's shown us the waterhole, kitchen, and possible camp sites and answered questions from the other newbies, he bounces up to me with a wide grin.

"So you're an Aussie, huh?"

I've met his kind before. Cheeky. Charismatic. Trouble.

"Aussie as they come, mate," I say, and walk away.

A wave of illumination and birdsong scatters the darkness and blazes, relentless, over my little tent and away across the planet. The world turns. I imagine the leading edge of this tsunami flaming along forests, jungles, oceans. A wall of light igniting the world as birds lift their throats and sing to the sun. Somewhere, everywhen, it is dawn. Music foams in the ceaseless wave.

My feet have solid calluses, painted mud-black. I stretch. The knots and kinks from playing all day, then sleeping on the ground at night, say hello.

My crap is strewn throughout the tiny tent: a scatter of leaf-green pants, ocher shirts, camouflage-print tops, three knives, two headlamps; a buckskin fire bag I made myself after brain tanning the hide of a female deer and hand-sewing the edges together into a long tube; random sticks that will become fire-kit stalks; half-whittled trap parts I've given up carving and that stare at me remorselessly whenever I stumble on them while hunting for a cleanish pair of shorts or an overlooked packet of chocolate-coated coffee beans. There's a badly rinsed plate and cup, a homemade wooden spoon, a splay-bristled toothbrush that probably just pushes plaque from one tooth to the next, and spare batteries that always seem to migrate under my useless sleeping mat, which has a slow leak and which I have given up reinflating.

The nights are cold, close to zero. I'm building a leaf debris shelter that I'll sleep in all next week, without a sleeping bag. I have to make my shelter well enough that it will be waterproof and trap enough heat so I won't get hypothermia.

Oak trees provide bounty. I lug huge, heavy piles of leaves from the bottom of the camp to the very top, barely stopping for meals. I'm knackered, aching, and happy; the flavor of happy you get when you've done something with all your heart and it's paid off.

An empty fire pit beckons for a rest. I sink gratefully onto the sand.

"How you doing, Gina Aussie As They Come?" Lee asks, bare-chested, squatting beside me. His shaved head is wet from the creek.

"I stink," I say, and it's true. Three days of hard labour with the odd dip in the waterhole creates its own perfume.

"That's not a bad thing, is it?" he says.

"Yeah, nah, I love human smell. Fuckin hate perfume. I don't understand why people spray it on their bodies. And blokes who put it on their faces, and then when you hug, it rubs off on your own face and then you stink like their disgusting gross cologne for the rest of the day, errrgh."

"None of that here."

"Thank fuck. Give me human stink any day. At least it's honest. I reckon it's how we tell if someone's going to be a good partner, or make good babies. Pheromones."

Lee grins.

I'm feeling expansive, high on endorphins from my shelter building. "I ban my lovers from wearing deodorant. I love a good armpit."

Lee's eyes shine. I catch myself, sharing this with a stranger. It's intimate in ways I'm not ready for. What are you doing, Gi?

I stand, dusting off the sand, ready to return to my labours.

"No," he says. "You can't go yet. I have to know."

"Have to know what?"

He lifts his arm, makes almost insolent eye contact, and waits.

What am I supposed to do? A wild woodland creature offers his armpit, his essence, his pheromonal scent, my true weakness.

My kryptonite.

For a moment I freeze, tugged in two directions. The wolf wins.

I bend to sniff, long and deep. He smells like tannin from the creek. Danger. Testosterone. Clean sweat and the brazen health of youth. Pine needles and too many complications.

He smells like beginnings.

He takes my elbow, raises my arm. "My turn."

I protest that I've been sweating for three days in the same T-shirt, but it's too late.

He sticks his face into my armpit for a long time, then smiles.

I haven't slept with a man in years, but the flutter in my belly says it all.

It's only a matter of time.

Tracker is a chaotic, dawn-til-dusk jumble of information and skill and the bewitching, magnetic force of Tom Brown, who imparts his lifetime of hunter-gatherer survival expertise with the force of a lay preacher.

Under his guidance, I walk feather-soft on the skin of the earth without making a quiver. Everything is a track to be followed; each fleck and scuff of leaf and moss, every quiver of body language and birdsong.

I whittle and strive and sweat and swear on my journey to the moment when two rubbed pieces of wood gift a single ember into a bed of soft grass, which, when blown gently, flowers into flame.

My chrysalis cracks. Everything hurts. Sleep is impossible through the reams and streams of native wisdom being force-fed into my protesting cells. My eyes burn from days spent staring at the ground, trying to force the moment when a scatter of leaves resolves into deer tracks. The waterhole provides cool relief from the blinding savagery of sunlight on pure white sand. And still Tom Brown pours it in until I want to scream, "Enough already."

During all this, Lee floats around my peripheral vision, a stubborn bit of grit in my eye.

Endless night. My eyes are so scratchy it feels like my eyelashes are in wrong. I hope I can stay awake till dawn. I shuffle my weight so my legs span the ten long poles I'm guarding, pinning them to the earth. If I fall asleep, someone from another Scout team will sneak in and steal some of my team's staffs, a humiliation I won't allow. Worse still, the fabled Shadow Scouts may ghost through and steal them all, leaving red marker slashes across our throats to let us know that if this was real, we'd all be dead.

I slap my face hard, twice, and press thumb and forefinger into the pressure point at the base of my thumb. Spiderwebs of pain give me another five minutes before my head nods again.

The rest of my Scout team is asleep, tucked into coffin-sized holes we dug in the ground on the first day. Everyone's exhausted after creeping through the bush on secret missions, avoiding hidden trip wires that activate networks of man-trap fireworks and ambushes from the elusive Shadow Scouts, who hunt us every night.

We've called our team the Hoboninjas, and this is Scout Class.

Humid days stick-fighting blindfolded on a narrow, slippery log suspended over the water hole, the whole class watching. Huge cheers when someone falls in. Tracking and counter-tracking, ranging out on endless missions to capture the flag after a two-hour run along sandy trails. We share meals and coffee, sitting in the dirt, covered in chigger bites, passing around the talking stick in another tense meeting to hash out all the numerous ways we piss each other off. So sleep-deprived we sometimes have to poke a teammate with the talking stick to wake them up.

Before each mission, we coat each other with clay and mud, dust ourselves off with leaves and dirt, then run single file for ten kilometers through the night, carrying our bamboo poles, switching out the lead position because it's exhausting being the one to scan for the trip wires that will blow us all up. If any team hits a major ambush, firework explosions rain around and they have to head back to camp in disgrace. So far, we've narrowly avoided the shame.

We never use our headlamps, which would call down the Shadow Scouts. Noxious light from the nearby airbase stains the sky. We drift silent as owls through endless, Mordor gloom, melting into the bush when headlights spear the road from the odd random deer hunter or tobacco-spitting local.

Sometimes we sneak up on a real-life party of rednecks. The stakes are high. Americans have guns, and when they party in the forest, tearing up live trees to throw on bonfires, smashing glass bottles in piles, shouting at each other, chugging beer and bourbon and playing country music from their car stereos, they're also likely to shoot at things that go bump in the night. Beer cans, random noises, a sudden stick-snap that telegraphs the position of a huddled group of camouflaged bodies.

We crawl home in the wee hours, our adrenals in pieces, to draw straws for the watch shifts and collapse into coffins to catch a couple of hours of shut-eye before the day's classes begin. Sleep smells like dirt, and rest sounds like the peculiar muffled scratching of beetles.

I'm blindfolded, in a bathing suit and bare feet with the rest of the Hoboninjas, following the distant thump of a drum that beats once every five minutes. Dum, da daah dum.

The drum is two hundred meters as the crow flies on the other side of a swamp so thick it's impossible to stand up for much of it. We'll take about three hours to cover that distance and rack up a couple of kilometers of territory, crawling through to map a path, all of us completely without sight, even the leader.

Silent, single file, eyeless, one hand on the shoulder of the person in front, we move as a single organism through scrub and tangles of vicious barbed wire vines. We inch across big fallen cedar trees that have rotted and are covered in moss, into waterways choked with logs, oozing mud and slime. Slither and pull through strings of weed and strangling creepers, alligator-slide through quicksand, over snags and spikes and submerged dangers. Wade up to our chests in marshy holes and sulfurous pools.

My skin becomes moss. My body lengthens to grow twenty legs, ten hearts, blind as larvae, but the creature I've hatched into sees in all directions. It ducks automatically under low snags, reaches out twenty hands to steady itself against trees it can't see, traverses high logs over deadfalls without falling.

I peek under the blindfold when I step aside to let the person behind me take the lead position. Living bars of a greenbriar jail cell soften to let us pass.

With every graceful and graceless movement, I die into trust.

The waterhole is empty of people today, which is rare. I lie back to float in silence. Something tickles my fingers, and there's Lee. Covered in goose bumps, one hand held behind his back.

"Come," he says, sliding back into the water, then under the boardwalk, into a rivulet. I follow, and we crocodile-crawl through weeds and mud and old cedar roots to where the waterway opens out again.

"Look," he says, holding something lumpy.

It's a turtle with striking yellow and red markings.

"It's the third time I've caught him. I think he's getting used to me."

"Hi, little guy," I say, stroking its leathery shell. "Aren't you magnificent?"

Azure dragonflies whiz over the water. One alights on Lee's shoulder. He releases the turtle, which freezes for a minute, then dives for the bottom. Silt fans up.

"Great spot," I say, as water licks my waist, surveying the expanse. "All yours?"

"It's where I hide when classes are on."

Reflections fracture as a wind gust sends leaves spiraling onto the wide pool. A squirrel stutters from an old oak above us.

"Hey," Lee says, "I've been wanting to ask you something."

"Shoot."

"How old are you?"

"Getting personal, aren't you?"

"Well?"

Insects glide over the surface of the water. Birds pluck meals out of the air. Far off, I hear chorusing calls from camp, our primitive alarm bell. It's time to go back to class.

"I'll be forty next year."

He deflates.

"Oh."

"You?" I ask.

"Twenty-six."

Woah. That's young. Way, way too young.

"I couldn't tell. You could be twenty-one or thirty-five."

"Asians have neotenic skin. It means we don't age so much."

"Aussies have deep-fried skin. It means we do."

He crawls out of the pool, toward an old wooden seat. Sunlight casts a single beam across the gray wood. I follow, shivering. He gives me the seat, crouches on the moss. His skin is flawless.

"Are you going to have kids?"

"That's a big question to ask an old lady, Lee."

"It's a good question, though, don't you think? An important one."

He waits. He's so young. What am I doing?

"I don't even know if I can. I'm nearly forty, had an operation that went very wrong years ago, there's scar tissue wrapped around my ovaries. I don't think my body can have a baby."

His dark eyes shine.

"I bet you can. I'd give you one."

"Really."

"If you needed sperm. I'd give you sperm."

"You'd give me sperm."

"It would be good sperm."

"I have no doubt about that."

"Excellent sperm."

"I'm getting the picture about the sperm."

"Okay."

"Would you send it in the mail?"

"I'd think of something."

I stand, hold my hand out to pull him up. "I have to get back to class. Thanks for the offer. I'll keep it in mind."

"Don't mention it."

The turtle's head pops above the water. It spots us and dives back into the deep.

Tom gives an end-of-the-world scenario for our last night of Scout. We'll be hunted for real. The staff have spotlights and high-powered paintball rifles. Our trail out of camp is ambushed. Cars without lights lie in wait. Shots zing into the bush above our heads. The whiz of paintballs splitting leaves. My heart a hammering orchestra of fear. Pinned down, we crawl into the swamp, our only escape route.

Cars slow, stop. Searchlights pierce the dark. We're twisted logs and hummocks of mud, a one-mind, many-legged creature sliding between molecules of air, water, and moss, using the natural terrain, enfolded by earth. Every breath is a gift from trees whose roots protect us.

"You have great feet," Lee says, on another stolen lunch break down by the waterhole; it's becoming our spot. "Tracker feet."

They're black with ingrained dirt. One of the toes is fractured where I kicked a root, and the tape holding it to its sisters keeps falling off. The nails are ragged and filthy.

"I bloody love my feet. They hold onto the earth. I hate wearing shoes, it's like having blindfolds on them. I can't see properly."

He picks one up. "Good arches. I want your arches."

"Hold up your hand."

He does, and I place mine against his. Long fingers, big, wide palm.

"I like your hands," I say. I massage the one I've captured. Striped with sinew, callused from twirling firesticks and climbing trees. Hands that do rather than dream.

"You're strong," he says, as my fingers probe his palm's secrets.

"You have no idea."

Moon-mist hangs close to the ground, seeping at its edge through the pale, quiet limbs of lurching oaks and maples. It's stained dark as madness, as womb-blood, but that can't be right. Something about this place of sand and old stories has me seeing through the surface of things, like the air is water and I'm reaching through it, fingers swimming, grasping now at an elusive shadow, snaring it between thumb and forefinger. It wriggles and hisses and bites.

Bad moon rising.

I tell myself I'm not sure why I've snuck up the back trail to Lee's camp tonight, but of course that's a lie.

I've known exactly what I've been doing since we traded pheromones around the cold stink of the fire pit, in the manner of wolves. The musk reek of him in my nose for weeks. I know what I'm doing when I arrange myself where he habitually pops out from a sandy trail on his way to the kitchen. I know what I'm doing when I laugh extra loud so he'll look up from the flint-knapping pit, or flirt side-eye with one of the instructors where he'll notice and express his frustration, monkey style, with impossible acrobatics in the cracking tip of a huge pine tree.

If I'm honest, which it seems I haven't been—but the red mist burns away my lies and obfuscations, so my machinations are revealed—I've been laying myself along this path since I turned my back on him on that first day, Gina Aussie As They Come. And, well. Here I am, my protestations come to naught. Now that I balance on the blade of this moment, I'm overcome with sudden fear. If I take these last few steps, I will slice my life to ribbons.

I hesitate for a moment while the moon laughs in her high, watery grave and the mist thickens. There's still time to turn back.

Who am I kidding? The wriggling shadow is the shape of all my excuses, and I'm too far down this path. It's already done; I just have to catch up with myself. I step on the shadow, ruthless as a bear, and keep walking, toward the clearing he calls home.

Lee's face beckons from the small circular entrance in his tepee, which rises through the moonlight in a glowing swell of pale canvas, flickering like a huge lamp from the fire inside. It's open to the elements. Uneven crisscrossing poles come together high at the top, so the smoke can escape.

He's wearing what looks like a dressing gown crudely stitched from a heavy woolen blanket. The kind of blanket that smells like mothballs and childhood. His calves are skinny underneath the hem. With the pointed hood on, he looks like a strange young wizard.

I follow him in. Another Narnia moment. My life is a series of doors, each more improbable than the last.

The tepee is big inside, but with both of us in here it feels small and quiet. Dirt floor. A futon mattress nestles on the ground, covered by a giant shaggy brown blanket. Bushcraft projects line the curved walls. Treasures to make Ayla weep: two small skulls, long polished by ants and weather; immaculately handwoven cedar-bark rope; an entire translucent snakeskin draped over a stick. In the firelight it shudders and writhes, and for a moment the red mist is back, until I shake my head to clear it. Knapped stone points, a leather sling, reed baskets, a bag of firesticks, trap parts. All beautifully crafted with an artisan's eye.

A rough bookshelf made from scavenged wood holds half a dozen well-thumbed paperbacks, mostly by Tom Brown. Cormac McCarthy's *The Road* is on top of the pile, neat paper squares jutting from the pages.

I sit on the bed because there's nowhere else and rub the furry blanket. "Cozy."

Lee paces. He looks taller and skinnier in here. Even younger, if that's possible. I try to count the years since I slept with a man. Maybe I've forgotten how. Maybe I'll be crap at it.

"You wouldn't believe how cold it gets here. It snows in winter."

"Must be freezing, you've got no insulation and a bloody big hole in the roof. You've already been here six months, hey. How d'you stay warm?"

He's making me dizzy with all these laps.

"In here it's pretty easy, just keep the fire going all night. I wear the capote a lot when I'm out."

"Capote?"

He flaps the arms of his blanket robe.

"It's wool, so it's still warm if it's wet. Apache scouts survived for months in the wilderness with only a blanket. You don't need a sleeping bag. I can tie it like this. Or this."

Whichever way he ties it together, there's a lot of leg poking out the bottom.

"Their feet musta gotten cold."

"Check this out. I just stop and light a tiny fire until I warm up. Crouch over it and pull the capote over and now it's a little tent, see, warms me up, and doesn't make any smoke, so if anyone's following, they won't be able to see me."

I picture him in the middle of a snowy path, crouched with his blanket over his head, breathing in hot smoke.

"Who's following you?"

"Well, now, nobody. But . . . warlords. When Red Skies comes."

Red Skies, the prophecy of Grandfather that presages the collapse of the modern world. The end of everything we know, where the only humans to survive are the ones living the old hunter-gatherer ways, far away from towns and cities. The children of the earth.

I'm drawn to the space where the tepee opens its arms to the orange moon. If I move my head just so, it balances between the poles, cradled. I squint, imagining a blood moon throwing light across a burning world. Thousands of blanket-wearing people beelining for the forests with their Go-Bags and survival kits.

"You really believe it, then? Red Skies?"

"Don't you?"

"I don't *not* . . ."

Jigsaw pieces fall together from our conversations. I can't believe I didn't see it before. I've stumbled into the dojo of a young warrior monk, training for apocalypse. Every single thing inside this tepee is a reflection of a grueling regime and singular purpose. I knew he was a devotee of Tom Brown, but this is a more focused life choice. When the end of days comes, he'll be ready. He already is. I feel suddenly ashamed of my voyeurism. I'm inside Lee's brain, in a way, poking around in all his secrets.

I ponder the end of everything I know.

"Sure, there are too many of us, and humans only change when we see it's too late, which means we'll never turn it around in time. But what if it all takes seventy years? Or seven hundred? What if you spend your whole life training for something that doesn't happen?"

"It's already happening, Gina. It's probably already happened, and we're in the lag before the inevitable."

"The end of the world is nigh."

"Supply chain issues. Natural disasters. All we need is a pandemic or two, or a tipping point in global warming. Refugees, millions of displaced people. It's when, not if. There's no way to stop it now. We're already over the cliff."

"I don't doubt we're making our world uninhabitable for ourselves. But why the skies? Why red? Does Odin paint the sky with blood?"

He shrugs. "Something environmental, maybe. Nuclear. I don't know. Disease could be a huge problem, so wherever I end up, it has to be completely hidden for the first few years, at least, until the bullets have run out and the roaming warlords have imploded or eaten each other."

"Jesus. That's grim. I thought you said you want kids."

"Yeah. I know. I guess I'm hedging my bets a bit."

"So, who comes with you when you vanish into the wild? Is it just you?"

"A select few. We'd be on the move for years."

There's weight in his look. I can't tell if it's challenge or invitation.

The fire crackles and throws sparks.

I pick up *The Road*, flick through it. It looks brand new.

"Have you read it?" he says.

"No, should I?"

"It's good. Pretty dark, but good."

"Huh."

I scan a page, then place the book, open and face down, on the bed. Lee's face quivers.

"Can you. Not. Leave the book like that?"

"Like what?"

He reaches over, scoops it up like it's a threatened child.

"I can hear it screaming," he says. "When you do that."

"What, leaving it open like that bothers you? It's a book." I take it back and flick the pages, noticing the unmolested corners. Choose a Tom Brown book at random. Then another. "You don't dog-ear."

"Are you insane? Of course not."

"This may never work between us. I eat the corners of pages." I mock-tear and chew.

Real horror on his face. He gathers up all his books. "And I was going to lend these to you. You're a sociopath."

"I can probably behave."

"Probably isn't enough. I'll report you to the RSPCB."

"They've got a dossier on me. I'm on every wanted list. Give me that."

"No chance."

"I'll play nice. Go on, give it. If it screams, take it back."

He hands over *The Road* with a show of reluctance that isn't all an act.

I settle back on the huge brown blanket, turning pages. A man and a child scavenge through a hellish, lifeless landscape of bleak misery. The language is sparse and clean, the world gray and hopeless. If this is our future, I want to be living deep in the wilderness when it happens.

"Humans are completely insane," I say.

Lee places wood carefully. Flames leap. I'm not ready to follow him into this future, and I think he feels it. "Not all humans."

"What if," I say.

"Yes?"

"What if it's possible to be at home in the wild places because it's beautiful and magical and feels good, and if, along the way, the world ends, we'd be ready. But in the meantime, it's about connection, not having a bloody great scythe hanging over our heads. I just . . . can't . . . live with that fear day in and day out."

He pokes the fire. "How about we stop talking about the zombie apocalypse?" he says, and pulls a book from the bookshelf. "I want to read you a story. Palate cleanser."

"Hope it's a bit more cheerful than *The Road*."

He holds it up. *The Wee Free Men*, by Terry Pratchett. It looks like a kids' book.

"Ooh, I haven't read that one."

He spreads long limbs onto the blanket, flicks his headlamp on, says, "Come on, get comfy."

I lie next to him, nearly close enough to touch but not quite. Firelight tints the action as twelve-year-old Tiffany Aching, armed with a frying pan, gives something nasty a wallop to save her annoying little brother and makes friends with a bunch of psychopathic, murderous, blue-painted, kilt-wearing tiny men to save the world, or, at least, her cheese.

Lee, it turns out, is a spectacular mimic. He bends his voice into every accent, especially the Scottish of the Wee Free Men. This is better than a movie. It isn't just a book, it's a Story, magnificent as any bedtime tale could dream of being.

I snuggle closer and he raises his arm so I can lie on his chest in that maddening pheromonal armpit scent, while Tiffany's adventures play out on the tepee walls. A critter rustles, or maybe it's the tiny, ferocious Pictsies swearing blue murder and getting up to untold mischief. My limbs twitch like puppies when they sleep.

When he puts the book down, I protest, but there's something in his eyes, and I realize it's now now now now now. My heart flutters in its nest of bones.

In the end, there's nothing to be nervous about. We fit together, and it's good, wonderfully good.

Afterward he says, "You hold everyone, don't you? But who holds you?"

"Me," I say. "I hold me." But I don't meet his eye.

He tucks my head onto his chest.

"Well, if you need a rest from that, I can hold you, Gina Chickerel. I'm good at it. Why don't you put it all down, just for a while. You can pick it back up, later, but for now, I've got you."

A crack snakes right down the center of me, soul-quake. Riven, I burst. Decades of tears erupt in a mess of snot and water. He says nothing at all, just wraps his arms around me and hums until the last shudders fall away. I don't know what this feeling is. It's the absence of tension. It's bone peace.

"Been awhile since you had a good cry, hey?" he finally says, passing me a handful of tissues.

"You could say that," I croak, and blow my nose. My body's so heavy I'm made of earth itself.

He recites Mary Oliver poetry from memory as I fall asleep, enveloped by the blanket, my drying tears, and the sweet-sour scent of sex.

I wake slowly, wrapped in animal fur, to the cloying smell of smoky hides and the unwashed, acrid stink of humans and herd animals. Metallic clinks and clangs, stamping hooves, throaty laughter, a hoarse shout in some tongue I don't understand but is as familiar as a lullaby, rasping inside my skull. I open my eyes in slits. My eyelashes make rainbows out of the pearly light. A mouse scuttles along the inside of the tepee. The fire is long dead. Sunshine flings oak shadows onto the canvas. A warm arm rests on my waist. I turn to face Lee, and his eyes are slanted and dark, wrapped in a hood of animal fur. They belong to the strange language evaporating with the bustle of animals and people, like dew, until it's just us, and he smiles under the bearskin that isn't a bearskin after all, it's a blanket, there's nobody outside but a deer and some birds, and I'm all the way here.

Mine, I think, leaning against Lee, feeling myself soften. Mine.

"He followed me home, so I kept him," I tell friends, glib and triumphant.

Aussie summer sun beats through the car window, which Lee winds down to let in the hot exhalations of eucalypt forests. Eight in the morning and it's already a scorcher.

The bay sparkles its own sweet seduction as we turn up the drive to the sprawling house of my childhood, but he's unmoved. He's been in Australia for three months after a year in the Northern Hemisphere wilderness, and it's lucky we have so much passion to ride us through the turbulence.

"Growing pains," say my friends.

My *Brady Bunch* fantasies about our communal house are in ashes. Stevie and Lee, the two most important men in my life after my father, bring out the worst in each other. I watch helplessly as my dreams of family picnics and shared off-grid adventures evaporate under muted judgments about how to live in a house. Stevie retreats to his partner, Andy's, apartment more and more, and I miss him. I thought Lee would love Bondi, but along with his dismay at the conditioned cages of city life, he doesn't understand the easy congeniality of the locals. In the London schools where he grew up, direct eye contact is an invitation to fight, and he bristles at passers-by who are just giving a cheery g'day.

"It can't be real. Nobody's that nice, are they?" he says, head in his hands, while I knead his shoulders after another misunderstanding.

"Yeah, love, they're just friendly here."

"I think I'm having to remember how to be a human."

He reeks of wildness, disappears each dawn to the local park to climb trees, obsessively makes fires in the backyard, and covers every surface of Stevie's ordered house with drying hand-drill spindles, basket materials, looped strings of stinging nettle, bow staves, damp towels, wet suits, boogie board, fins, mask, surfboard, wet footprints, and his long skateboard.

And now I'm bringing him home to meet my family. This is my sanctuary, and I'm introducing a wildcat, barely tamed.

The knot in my belly tightens as we park outside the house, which is strewn with bunting and profusions of native flowers. Mum's done the Christmas thing again. Cars everywhere, relatives from all over. My sisters' laughter floats down the driveway.

"Come on, grumpypants," I say.

"It's too weird to be this hot at Christmas. Everything feels wrong. I miss snow."

It's gonna be okay, I tell myself. If I wish it enough, it will be true.

Kristie's on the deck, champagne in hand, on one of her notorious comedy jags. She spits out a full cartridge of jokes rapid fire, on a roll, she's bloody superb when she gets like this. Cousins howling with laughter, clutching each other. Danni jumps on me and sticks her spit-licked finger in my ear. Lee's whirled into a vortex of hugs and handshakes and a tour of the place. Neil Diamond belts from the speakers, courtesy of Kristie's husband, Bear.

Lee's already going under. I'm attuned to his weather now, can see the overwhelm rolling him like a dumper in a shore break. The codes and currents of my family mystify him, as does small talk and polite conversation. My family's exuberant chaos seems to highlight his homesickness for winter and an English Christmas. I watch the whole thing slew sideways. Landslide, burying me with it.

He doesn't fit in my family.

I thought I had learned all my Grayson lessons, but here is the deepest: we can't make something true, just because we wish it so.

Merry fucking Christmas.

I'm torn between the blood in my veins and the man I've chosen to spend my life with. To top things off, I'm pregnant, bone-sick with it, and deeply uneasy about motherhood. Lee's delighted, but a baby is an anchor to an existence I'm not sure I'm ready for, especially with how much we argue.

Just after Christmas, I start bleeding, bright blood, lots of it.

Lee and I flee to the bush, far from the press of walls and Christmas tinsel. We sleep straight on the sand behind a wall of white dunes on a deserted beach, sheltering from stabs of heat in a merciful tunnel of tea trees.

I'm stunned by how much miscarriage hurts. Cramps flare white and astoundingly sharp, heavy enough to flatten me. I dig a hole and bleed into it, great clots that look like chopped liver. I can't quite cry yet.

Under a pellucid night, spattered light chimes across the ceaseless thunder of waves. Lee kisses the top of my head and points to a tangle of stars.

"There," he says. "The Hunter."

We name our lost one Orion and howl like the world is ending. My womb twists and tears, squeezes and shudders. I coil around a hot squirt of shame. Maybe the baby left because of my ambivalence. Because I didn't love it enough.

The pain and bleeding last two weeks, and afterward, my periods are completely changed; blood pours fresh and bright where it has been dark and sticky for years. I wonder at the wisdom of bodies, that my womb has cleaned itself out so. It feels alive for the first time in years. Ready. I'm still not sure if I even want a child, but I can't deny my body is preparing.

Lee and I settle into a life that works. His prickles retract as he discovers the joy of surfing. Hours in cold water regulate his nervous system and give Stevie and me time for our own friendship. Sticks and twigs are now confined to our room and we have a clothesline for beach towels and wet suits. The men warm to each other.

Day by day, we find our flight paths through the house.

Lee wants to get married, partly for his residency but partly, I think, to feel safe. I'm wary of promises because the me who makes the promise isn't the me who has to keep it. How can I make a promise for future Gina? Who knows what she'll need or want? She has to live with my choices. I've learned the hard way the future is hollow.

Lee and I are two sandstorms, sometimes overlapping, sometimes whirling off on our own adventures. The space between us shifts and morphs, but we're always connected by it, by the landscape we create in dynamic tension, love seeded in every grain of sand. Something of this soothes me. I may not be able to make a promise, but I can commit to the patterns we make between us.

Stevie and a Tracker mate witness our wedding, with another friend hiding in the grass with her camera to grab candid shots. We're out on the cliffs at South Head, overlooking Sydney Harbor and the giant bare back of a rolling horizon. Lee is shirtless. I have a dress the color of emeralds, tanned skin, bare, tough feet. We stalk each other across grassy cliffs. I run until he catches me, squealing.

The sky pulsates, squandering clouds. Gulls mewl overhead. We make no promises other than to support each other's soul journeys, wherever they take us. I am a clear glass, filled with love for this wild creature who wants to share my life. The celebrant binds our hands with cordage we've spun together from stringybark.

It's done.

We all skinny-dip in a shallow rock pool revealed by the lowering tide. Light peals across wet skin. After a water fight, we make our way back to shore. A mottled octopus bulges from a crevice, just under the surface. Breathless, I extend a finger into the water. It mirrors my action, reaching out a single soft tentacle to bless my firm one.

Like we're shaking hands.

Lee and I honeymoon on Butchulla country, K'gari, Fraser Island. Hawks and eagles patrol the skies. Four-legged wraiths circle our camp, tearing apart our bags, looking for food. At night the dingoes howl fever dreams from the long ago. Pandanus branches catch their eerie night songs, rattling spiky hands in applause. Each stalk is a twisted story of the winds that shaped it. I wonder if humans are the same, if we wear the shape of our history so clearly.

Everywhere my eyes fall, they find a lesson. This country is so beautiful it cuts. I wake often to the fading sound of thudding footsteps, but when I shine my flashlight into the night, there's nothing but a careless veil of sea mist. Shadows cavort past the boundary of light. I remember the paintings of Ainslie Roberts from when I was a kid and feel like I'm peeling apart layers of time, opening into some other world, where dirt shouts through human throats and animals speak with human voices. The land sings so loud I can almost hear the words.

Lee and I make love, argue, make love again, growing increasingly tanned under the blazing sun. Our fights are turbulent, but we pull them out by the roots until they're done, and then somehow, we're friends again, but deeper, cleaner. Both of us are committed to sifting through our stories to find what's true.

We cast lines into a frothing ocean, fry flathead in salt and lemon, dive into waves to wash off the juice. Make love again in the shelter of tea trees next to a perched freshwater lake. Lee runs down the dune, all white teeth and whipping limbs as he splashes into the turquoise water.

I collect things. A wind-sculpted swirl of driftwood, bone-white. The skull of a tern. Dingo tracks. My lover's moods, fickle as weather. Silhouettes of hunting raptors. The scrape of pandanus leaves. Sand in my sleep sheet. Sunburn's wicked sting. Horizons.

I'm obsessed with fire.

With a new knife from the store at Tracker, I carve a notch into the baseboard of my firesticks, close my eyes and place both hands on the spindle. Fire spirits tickle the inside of the wood, if only I can capture their attention. I thank the sticks, thank the roots that fed them, the sun that grew them, the water that nourished them. Brahminy kites whistle in time to my hands as they fuse. The twirling stick tears old blisters, but I'm not stopping. I become the nub of the spindle, where it bites into the wood. The friction point is perfect braille. My hands slow and deepen; I don't need to look. Fire trickles from my hands into the stick, from my heart into my hands, from the earth up through the baseboard. I close my eyes, relaxing everything. My hands dance without me.

"Gi, you've got it," says Lee, snapping me out of my trance.

A tiny shaving of smoke rises from black wood dust. I sprinkle more dust on, more food for my newborn. The ember can easily be killed, extinguished by a huff of breath, scattered by a careless finger, this fragile life completely vulnerable unless I take care of it.

I tip the ember into a nest of banksia fluff and frayed grass, tender as any mother. Wrap the whole thing in paperbark and gently blow.

Fire spirits chuckle and dance, throwing out white smoke. I blow harder as sparks shoot over my hands. The coal grows and shifts, casting heat through the leaves. One more breath, this is the one. A moment of stillness hangs like a blade, then, whoomph, I am a dragon, spurting tongues of flame, juggling the white heart of a bushfire.

I quickly push the flaming ball into a structure of sticks, and blow until they crackle. Flames lick and take, snapping as they throw out heat to warm hearts, cook food, soothe a weary mind. I fall on my back in the sand, heart pounding, sweating, clutching the fire spindle to my chest. Clouds drift by. A Brahminy kite falls like a stone, disappearing over a dune, then rises again with a small, squeaking creature in its talons. Everything in the whole world is perfect.

I jump around like a crazy person, exploding with happiness.

Tracker School pulls me back, and I can't ignore the call. I'm infatuated with ancestral survival skills. Lee lives and breathes hunter-gatherer technologies, and his mastery is intoxicating. Even after three months at Tracker, I feel like I've barely scratched the surface and am starving for more. Here's a life path that makes sense. I want to be able to walk into the wilderness with just a knife and thrive, in harmony with nature, utilizing the wisdom of my tribal forebears. Rewilding is a new word for me. It sums up the skills my culture has forgotten, but I remember in my DNA and in the drumming heels of Mowgli.

I know if I don't go back to Tracker for another stint now, I'll lose the will. Lee wants kids, and maybe I do too. Once I'm pregnant, that's it for adventures.

Lee says *of course, go*. He has a surfboard. Tamarama Beach is just down the hill. Two months of surfing every day will be awesome.

Once again, I shoulder my backpack and arrive on the blinding white sand of Primitive Camp.

I'm immediately swept into Tracker life. I've enrolled in the Philosophy stream, which includes Vision Quest and Quest Protector training, plus more Scout classes. Tracking, shelter building, fish traps, hide tanning, stalking, camouflage, stick fighting, hunting. I volunteer as an assistant in the classes I've already done, gathering my strength for the new. I'm here for eight weeks straight and can't stop beaming.

Most of the day I'm so busy I think of Lee only in fleeting bursts. There's no phone reception, so I can only call him once a week when I head into town in between classes.

Six weeks in, in the moments between waking and moving, while birdsong flares and my tent is bright with sunlight, my mind turns to our last phone call. Why is it, when we care about each other so much, our calls end up awkward and tense? I'm sure he's angry with me for leaving for so long. Perhaps he won't be there when I return. I'll get home to an empty room, his stuff all gone, a Dear Jane note pinned to the wall.

It's been a decade since I've been in this position, my heart resting naked in the palm of another, at the whim of carelessly closed fingers or, worse, deliberately dropped like a bent toy or unwanted gift. Sometimes, in the wee hours, I wonder if I've made a mistake. But not today. Today, the morning stretches out like a harlequin picnic blanket. The world smells of promise.

Just before I rise, and without any conscious thought, my hand moves to my chest. I begin a familiar rolling exploration of palm on breast, as you do, probing with my fingers.

And there it is. A small, round pea.

Is it a lump? Or just gristle? My breasts are the fibrous kind, which makes it difficult to tell if uneven tissue is a cyst, or perhaps a ridge of rib. Hormones change the landscape further, and I haven't checked for six months, which might be a year, but I definitely didn't have a nodule here last time.

It's a cyst.

My fingers map. Yes, I'm pretty sure it rolls; it's a cyst. Definitely. Probably. Maybe.

I file the lump as "too hard" and put the whole thing away for reassessment once I get back to Australia. There's nothing I can do right now. While I'm busy not thinking about it so hard my brain hurts, my hand steals back upward and gently rolls the little node. My hands are smarter than I am.

The Tracker kitchen hangs together with spit and willpower and generations of creative repairs with scavenged items. Food's piled in huge coolers and cooked on massive gas burners. There are no walls.

A group of dawn Scout students staggers in, bleary around the edges, twigs and leaves still sticking to sweaters, faces gritty with dried mud from last night's camouflage. Two of them have bandages and one's limping and we're only halfway through the week.

"Good morning," I say, handing out kitchen knives and pointing to chopping boards. I'm answered with sleepy grunts and an overexcited whoop from a lad who looks fifteen but is probably twenty-five.

"You're keen," I say.

"Yessum," he drawls, downing a huge cup of coffee. "Let's DO this."

I feel old. "Dude. It's way too early for that much enthusiasm."

"Yessum."

Clack, clack, clack, knives on boards, buckets of carrots and potatoes and onions to get through. We'll be here for an hour before the call for breakfast goes out.

I sing as I chop and teach a couple of the more alert students the words. Nameless melodies lighten the work and lift weary hearts. Once they've got the tune, I soar into a harmony, and the brash lad can sing as well; he surprises me with a rich baritone and takes the third below, and now true music rattles the pots and gas burners.

I never get tired of this alchemy. Strangers' voices weave unmet lives together. Goose bumps rise on my arms.

Passersby smile at this addition to Tracker routine. I've volunteered to oversee kitchen duty every day for the past six weeks for this reason, to start the day with song. Sometimes, as I walk through the camp, I hear someone singing something I taught them three weeks ago, in some language none of us comprehend, but we understand the music, of course we do, it opens and unlocks even the hardest heart.

I'm so exhausted when I finally make it back to my tent each night that I drop into sleep without thinking about the lump, although I catch myself palpating it at odd times.

Is it a cyst? It's a cyst.

A mini tornado blasts through camp in a frenzy of whipping winds and sideways rain. The noise is catastrophic. A solid wall of water drops like a hammer. For about five minutes we hide from the downpour, then someone lobs a mud pie at someone else, and it's on.

Dozens of slippery limbed bodies slide and yell in rocky torrents of mud, swooping in on kamikaze runs to pelt and be pelted through the teeming rain.

The deluge finally relents and passes over like a tap turning off, and the pine forest sighs with streams and runnels of water and the returning calls of birds. I feel almost high, dripping, tingling, covered in mud, with an aching jaw where a stray ball of stones knocked me sideways. I've been feeling low-level fear since I found the lump, and this euphoria is its absence.

I feel my breast for the umpteenth. Roll the lump. Still there. The euphoria evaporates.

At the end of the week, I call Lee. I don't tell him about the lump.

"Hey, love."

"Hey."

"I miss you."

"I miss you too."

"You realize it's a year ago we were sneaking around camp, counter-tracking our footprints so nobody would find out we were together?"

"Meeting down by the waterhole."

"In our secret spot. With your friend the turtle. I saw it today. I wish you were here and we were back in the tepee."

He goes quiet. He's thinking about the year he lived in that tepee, wandering through the forest, dying deeper every day into earth time. I can't quite imagine him in Bondi, surrounded by noisy neighbors and coughing cars and worker-ant humans with scant awareness for the broader songs of nature. I've netted a panther and brought it to live in a house. I wonder if he can survive like this without chewing through the walls.

"How long till you come home?" he says.

"I've got Vision Quest with Malcolm next week, then I come back, love. Ten days and I'm on the plane."

"Let's not do this again. Two months is too long."

"Distraction," says Malcolm Ringwalt, a few days later, from the dais of our bush classroom without walls. I drag my gaze away from the captivating forest backdrop while the squirrel I've been watching resumes its jerky stutter-stop march up the closest pine tree.

What's Malcolm saying? Something about distraction.

"Our society, our culture, is built on distraction."

Malcolm easily commands the attention of the hundred participants in this Vision Quest.

"In Vision Quest, we quite simply remove all distractions so we can experience the moment-to-moment flow of life, inside and out, for four days and four nights."

"Sounds easy enough," whispers the chirpy lad who'd yessum'd me in the kitchen.

I'm not so sure.

I'm a rattling bag of marbles.

Caught in the last-flung net of night, we file silently into predawn gloom and peel off the main trail, one by one. I watch the scrub swallow wavering shadow shapes and wonder if I will see any of my classmates again. Perhaps, once out of my sight, they'll shrug out of their skins and evaporate in the weeping light, leaving nothing but footprints, which the wind will wash away.

All I have to keep me company for the next ninety-six hours is some water, a tarp to pull over myself if it rains, and a sleeping bag. In the mirror of nature, I'll meet myself, with nowhere to hide.

I settle down to wait. And wait. And wait. After a gelatinous hour, the sun rises, then sears. I wait some more.

Walking feels like punching through water. Humidity is a wet slap. Without enough shade in my site to take shelter, the day is scorching. How will I possibly last four days and nights here? Already I can't bear myself. This is supposed to be a spiritual experience. I've never felt less spiritual in my life.

I'm consumed with anger at Lee. We fought again on the phone before I came out for Quest. My stories line up, perch in the trees like malevolent ravens, surrounding me with vicious chirps and whistles. I rage through my Quest circle, arguing with someone who isn't even there.

But then, with the swift, sudden movement of a flickering bat, or high cloud freeing the sun, my fury is done. Something cracks and I fall onto the earth, sobbing with my face in rich soil, *I want a baby,* and the pain in my heart is so enormous I can't believe I've never known this; I want a baby, my baby, it's all I want, it's all I've ever wanted.

Inhaling dirt, I howl as this release fills me, takes me over.

I want a baby with Lee.

The desire is simple, clear as forest pools. All my ambivalence blows off the curled nub of the thing, vanishing like it was never there at all, leaving me naked in my yearning. How can I have hidden such a huge desire from myself? Fear, I suppose. Fear I'm too old, that I can't get pregnant. Fear of being a terrible, selfish mother. I haven't let myself dream it in case it never came true. Better not to want it at all.

And right then, I know her secret name. This child yet to be, still unmanifest; this far-off cloud of fireflies, this whisper of winter, this high, haunting call of a circling kite. I know her oldest name in some ancient place inside, and I say it aloud, savoring the sounds as I call her for the very first time and feel her hear me, somewhere where time is still.

I fizz, breathless with this new shape of myself, revealed. Rolling onto my back, I open sodden, muddy eyes, and the bush greets me with ordinary magic. Leaning oaks listen and rustle. The sun has passed its apex and shoots shards of light through the blueberry bushes. Glittering motes float on the afternoon haze. My eyes are wide open, I can see round corners. It's so hot my arms stick to my sides.

An enormous cloud towers on the horizon. The storm hits like a bomb. Branches whip under a heaving sky. Torn clouds flower into fractal shapes. I take off every stitch of clothing and lose myself in a frenzied dance under the purple-black canopy, cool rain blessing my skin as the sky sobs and I echo. Lightning sparks under my feet.

I call in my child.

After the storm finally passes, each drop of water hanging from a pine needle is a whole universe upside down. Perfumes intertwine; forest after fresh rain, rich loam, sour sweat. Bush music rings in the sounds of dripping water and rustling life.

A yellow and black snake hunts through low shrubs bordering my circle, while birds alarm in unfamiliar tongues and chiggers chew my belly. I find the small holes of my hate and, one by one, fill them with flowers. Lay my carapace to rest among the blueberry bushes.

Days bob and sink so slowly I feel as though I am here for months. I help a wayward ant out of a sandy depression and, to my horror, bury it through my saving. A day later it emerges, legs scrabbling. It grooms its antennae, then marches on as if it hadn't just spent a night buried alive. This is what I do. I rescue and make things worse. Woodpeckers tattoo into the night and an owl mocks *rescue, rescue, rescue.*

I daydream of a sun-freckled daughter, squealing between Lee and me as we lift her over waves and she shouts in delight.

A few days later I land at Sydney airport. Home.

The ratty backpack cuts into my shoulders. My skin feels tight and dry after too long in air-conditioning. Fluorescent lights hum and flicker in time to my buzzing skin, every hair electric. I've drunk too much coffee, am jittery to my fingertips.

He's not here. He must be parking the car. Echoes of some other Gina, that foolish naive girl-child waiting for Grayson, slide greasily around the walls.

I sink onto a bench, feet protective on the backpack. Announcements about unattended baggage. A lanky shadow slopes around the corner, a full head taller than the group of travelers thronging him. I recognize the calm walk, out of step with the milling crowd, his shoulders slightly rounded, like he's about to slip out the back door. He's wearing his Akubra and makes it look natural, not like a tourist, like he's just blown in on a westerly, crackling with wood smoke and bush dust. He looks around without appearing to but hasn't seen me yet.

I feel like a shy bride peeping around her mother's shoulder to snatch a first glimpse of the man who will soon be leaving his shoes under the bed. Fluttery and scared and wobbly. My heart, my crazy heart, it's pounding fit for dance floors, surely it's making my T-shirt jump. I wave, and he sees me, smiles, and then he's here. I forget how tall he is. He smells like a bushfire, even from a couple of feet away. His eyes crinkle.

"Hi," I say softly, in case a loud noise breaks us. We're reflected in the surface of a pool and my voice will shatter the image into a million discs of light.

"Hi," he says, just as softly, and the hubbub of the airport fades to white.

I touch him. Solid. Real. I search his face, he searches mine, and it is still all there, still all good. He's here. He's really here.

I sniff at his neck like an animal as he wraps long arms around me. "Welcome home, love."

He smells like him, spicy and musky and smoky and mine. Tiny tremors ripple through his arms as he holds me. I realize he's just as wound up as I am, just as anxious. Humans are such funny creatures.

part six The Dazzling Dark

the year of 40

Lee burns to teach kids survival skills on family camps. I'm alight with the desire to run Vision Quests. Together we'll bring our version of rewilding to Australia, or so we plan. We talk into the night, dream up programs and shelters, comparing mentoring techniques for our nascent school, where we'll teach people to be at home in the wild. He surfs, I sing, we sit together on the back deck spinning fire spindles, still driving Stevie crazy with the amount of sticks and bark we leave lying around.

Spring lays its belly down in a fragrant carpet for us to roll in. We're the first and only lovers in the whole entire world. Baby birds wheeze in the pepper tree. I pee on a white stick and the line turns blue. I stare at it, disbelieving. I've only been back a month. I must have conceived right on my fortieth birthday.

Lee's over the moon, but I can't meet him there through the creeping dread of my secret; I still haven't investigated the pebble in my breast.

In a little box room under fluoro lights, shivering from the cold goop smeared over my skin, I squint at incomprehensible squiggly gray lines scrolling on a TV screen. The technician says the ultrasound report will be ready tomorrow. She sounds bored.

That's a good sign, surely.

That night my GP calls me at home, her Eastern European accent thick on the phone. "Plis come in as soon as you can. Tomorrow, right away."

I sink into myself. Steady, steady.

"Okay," I say with someone else's voice, someone calm. "What time?"

"Come early, I fit you in first. Seven thirty."

"Okay," I say again, when it obviously isn't.

Putty-colored walls, ordinary birdsong, the smell of chai. Rex the cat batting at my toes, chasing affection. Lee heard something in my voice, he's looking at me, but he's not worried, not yet.

Someone says, "I think I have cancer. She wants me to go in tomorrow. Right away, she said."

Pressure scratches at my eyes. Lee's a statue, light hitting him at funny angles. The world, so suddenly transformed with the news of my pregnancy, flips again. I'm a conduit for life and death. Silent winds from dark, unseen lands blow into the house. My heart flutters cut paper in the gale.

This long night Lee sleeps, but I hear every tick and groan of the house turning in circles, like a settling dog.

I sleep, finally, and dream of the ocean, which rises. I am the curved wing of a seabird, I am the white bone, screaming from the crest of a wave as it rises over coral, over teeth, over end over tail over sand over water, it's a dumper this wave, it's the dreaded wave I don't catch because it catches me, where the water pulls back and there's only glistening sand or maybe rocks staring at me and it's too late, I'm past the point of no return, it has me, this is the dumper of all dumpers and if I'm lucky it won't break my neck, will only shear skin from me, sandpaper sea-scars into me, blind me with terror and adrenaline, drag me winded while the full mountainous force of wave breaks over me, pushes me flat against the bottom, pinned by the water piling heavier and heavier, a weight that will stop eventually,

I just have to hold my breath, but I have no breath, it's been driven out of me, and finally I lift and tumble and strike for the surface, except there's only foam and sand and no gravity, no clues to which way is up and surely my lungs will burst before I figure it out.

The local Bondi GP's room is coffin-dim. Lee and I sit in plastic chairs facing her, side by side.

She says, no preamble, "Iss very bad news, I'm afraid. Iss cancer. Radiologist call me at home last night, then I call you, iss very bad in younger women, this cancer, very aggressive. I'm so sorry, you must terminate pregnancy, the cancer love hormone of pregnancy, the estrogen and the growth hormone, it feed this cancer. You must not have this baby. Iss very bad news, I'm so sorry."

Terminate? Terminate?

A mystifying shimmer of meanings colliding, realities exploding. *Cancercancercancercancercancer.*

"I can have another baby, though. Right?"

"I am sorry, no. Treatment for cancer will bring the menopause."

I cry softly into Lee's shirt while the doctor organizes my next port of call, a breast surgeon at an inner-city hospital.

"He iss very good, one of best. I get you in right away. When you want book termination?" Her pen hovers like a fang. Her eyes are big in her owl glasses, watching me, waiting to pounce on the nod that will kill my baby.

Termination. The word clangs like a bell, ringing my ears. I shake my head to clear it. This is a baby inside me, and you want to terminate it, like it's a contract or a bad job or an unrewarding conversation?

Any second, I'll break like a bomb in all directions. There will be nothing left of the doctor but rubble and a pair of shattered glasses rolling end over end.

Rage, glorious rage, why do we fear it so much? We cower in the shadows of ourselves, we are good girls, we are the innocent heroines in the fairy tales, we behave as behooves us and flinch when the bitch or the witch or the whore rises up and takes what's hers. But sooner or later Baba Yaga comes cackling out of the forest and burns all our stories to ash and we find who really lives down here, and she is fine, my sweet sisters, she is a creature, a thick-muscled animal with fangs and fur and a subsonic snarl that sends the unwitting and unworthy scuttling for safety, fat chance.

Every mama who ever lived uncoils from my DNA and unites with one pure wolf voice, and in the silence I hear their chorus, clear as stars on a moonless night.

No. No. No.

Lee whittles a firestick on the back deck. His eyes are flat and glittery. I have the curious impression he's vibrating like a fluorescent light, cycling so fast you don't really notice the flicker, but it's there, and if you pay attention, it will give you a migraine.

Sinking, I think. He's sinking. And he doesn't know how to tell me.

"How you doing, love?" I ask, noticing the rigid ropes of muscle in his arms and dark smudges under his eyes. I knead the solid boards of his shoulders.

"Oh yeah," he says. "You know. Not really coping."

We trudge to the hospital, up to the consultation rooms, heavy with greenish light and the faint reek of despair, or maybe that's just me.

The surgeon palpates my breasts. There's something creepy about his hands, which feel like dry, papery insects with bones inside. His desk is bare except for a piece of paper and a mug of coffee. The mug looks like a Christmas gift from the staff, not from grandkids. It says:

TO DO:

*IMPROVE GOLF SWING

*SAVE THE WORLD

*BUY MORE JELLYBEANS

He's old enough to be my grandfather and has the bedside manner of a well-dressed stoat.

"We don't know anything yet, and it's premature to go saying it's cancer until we do a biopsy," he says as I yank on my T-shirt, feeling vaguely grubby. He pulls out needles and swabs and the walls close in.

"Um. Do you do narrow-gauge or wide-gauge biopsy?"

He doesn't look up from his orchestra of clinks and pings. "Wide."

"I read that wide gauge can spread cancer cells," I say through spreading panic. I only read it last night, at 2 a.m., four layers down like in the movie *Inception*, but it makes sense. A wider needle picks up and possibly scatters more cancer cells. Any stray cancer cells get mopped up by radiotherapy later. I don't want to set myself up for radiotherapy if I don't have to.

The doctor flushes and puts down his needle. "Wide-gauge needles are the industry standard."

"But can you tell me why? I read that—"

He says, in a clipped, why-are-you-wasting-my-time voice, "Oh, you checked out some things on Google, did you?"

I sit on my hands so I can't smash him in the face with his Christmas-present coffee cup.

TODO:BOOKZYGOMATICBONERECONSTRUCTION

I meet Lee's eyes, and he gestures to the door.

We leave the surgeon to his wide-gauge needle.

Something happens as we head back to the car. I walk through an archway nobody can see, not even me. I don't know it's there until I'm through it, but when it's done, my fear is gone. In its place is clarity.

Modesty Blaise drives me home. Paul Atreides recites the fear mantra with my voice. *Fear is the mind killer.* Bene Gesserit sing ancient songs. Ayla readies her sling.

No matter how helpless I feel, I have choice in every moment, and it isn't in my nature to give that away.

Every corner of paper I've ever swallowed comes together.

A Wolf Mother suckled the young man-cub Mowgli as her own, defending her cubs against Shere Khan when he roared and bit into the cave mouth. She named herself Raksha the demon and banished the tiger. Here in the car, her red tongue lolls, her breath steams the glass. I feel her warmth at my side, smell her rough, doggish scent of fur and fury.

Through the eyes of the Wolf Mother, my path is clear. The GP and the surgeon are not my pack. I need to find who is.

Tension drains away. My hands turn the steering wheel, my feet work the pedals, but I'm so much bigger than this small body in this small car. Paths spiral loose in my mind as I strategize, tracking possible futures, barely speaking to Lee, who's off in his own hell somewhere. When we park outside our picture-book house in its picture-book street, Lee undoes his seat belt but doesn't move, staring at nothing. I put my seat back and call a friend who's had a year-long journey with a breast lump. She gives me the number of her surgeon. I call his rooms and arrange an appointment for the next day, then turn to face Lee.

He's pale and drawn, awash with fear, overwhelm, and grief. I forget how young he is. My pool of clarity expands. I see I have the easier path because I have control. He has to watch his pregnant wife go through the unimaginable, making life-and-death decisions that affect our unborn child.

From the moment Lee and I met, we swooped and soared and dived into love, dreamed and dared and built castles in the sky.

We've planned a thousand futures and in them nobody was ever sick. We were invincible.

Now I'm mortal and it's real as a punch in the face.

Somehow, in the capital-R reality of this, I don't feel hopeless or helpless. Wolf Mother purrs. There is a way, and I'll find it. I have faith. Not in a benevolent sky god, but in my own flawed and wisening heart, leading me through the fiery center of myself.

I see Lee will be here for me in whatever way I need, but that I should treat his support as a gift, to be called on when I'm in strife, not squandered when I'm capable. We both need to conserve energy.

"Would you prefer not to come tomorrow?" I ask him. "I've got a good feeling about this doctor. I think I'll be all right."

"What do you want, Gigi?"

"I can do it on my own."

"But . . .?"

"No but. It's okay."

We cling to each other across the front seats of the car, while kids skip on the footpath and the postman wobbles down the street on his bike, delivering the mail.

I visit the new surgeon without Lee. In the waiting room, my fingers brush against the pelt of Raksha, who wrinkles her snout at all the chemical smells. Sandworms shake the ground. Anansi the trickster crawls up the window in spider form, laughing where nobody can see.

Focus, Gina. This is important.

The new surgeon is kind, listening to my questions and answering them fully. He sticks thin needles into my breast, then squirts the contents onto a slide.

"We have to wait for the biopsy report to be sure, but really, we don't need to wait. You have breast cancer, but you already knew that, didn't you?"

I nod, gulping.

He's chirpy and birdlike. Moves around the room like he's got springs in his shoes.

"There's good news and maybe not so great," he says. "We can treat you, that's the good news. But you have a full pregnancy ahead of you with those hormones feeding the cancer. Even with chemotherapy, it's far from ideal. Are you one hundred percent sure you want to go ahead with the pregnancy?"

"Yes."

He nods.

"Right, then. We can give you chemo safely in the second trimester, but that's still a couple of months away. The most urgent thing to do is to have that lump removed, under a general anesthetic."

"It that safe when I'm pregnant?"

"A general's a risk, but you should be okay. Any questions? Next week work for you?"

The medical engine revs up through its gears, sucking me into mammoth forces of metal and machinery. If I let myself be swept up, my skin will be eroded and worn by ravening cogs until I'm a jigsaw shape, tumbled, my blood replaced with mercury and my bones with wire.

Peak hour on the train home. *Rackatarackatachikchikcharackata.* People ride the carriage, ho hum, normal people with normal lives, texting on mobiles. Tinny music emanates from enormous headphones, the sound of permanent ear damage. A girl studded with piercings flicks through a trashy mag. I wonder what she looks like under the makeup. Does she scuttle into the bathroom before her boyfriend wakes, to repair the night's unraveling before he sees her face naked? Nice boots, though, buckles to forever.

It isn't enough to distract me.

I have cancer. I am pregnant. I have cancer.

I cradle my belly. My baby. This can't be happening. My little one. I'm so sorry.

Something snaps inside me.

I sob on the filthy train seat, among the graffiti and the balled-up lumps of old chewing gum and the bored commuters, suddenly not so bored. I am a wild-eyed weeping woman, a world-shaking upheaval of emotion. Out of control. I never really had it in the first place. My baby. My baby.

Commuters pretend they aren't watching. A predator prowls among us all, revealed in a ghastly glint of silver in the window's slimy reflection, sleek-shadowed in a black cowl. I recognize it from my weeks in the hospital, and from dancing the labyrinth, when it pressed its thumb into my forehead. It hisses through the carriage. What cold sigh lingers, what restless hand twitches at a throat, fingers a chilly collar? Did you feel something? Did you? Goose walked over my grave.

Always stalking, never resting. Will it be later today, when that car comes out of nowhere? Will it be when your belly overhangs your balls and your heart gasps its last?

I am the weeping woman, and the shadow has tapped me on the shoulder. Tag, you're it. A part of them knows; they're a flock and the tiger has chosen its prey. They shift away from me, give me room, in case it's catching. Wolf Mother lies heavy on my feet, head on her paws, keeping me from floating away.

Rackatarackatachikchikcharackata.

I get it all the way through, how big this is going to be. No easy answers, no simple choices.

I'd called out to the edges of creation that I wanted a child.

The gods had called back, how bad?

The medical machine changes gears, sucking me further into its grasp. I'm struck by dualities. News is good or bad, yes or no, plus or minus, give or take. Every scan and test brings results and statistics, and those numbers funnel me into a course of action. Whenever I stand up to ask, *But what if I do it this way?*, I'm met with looks that range from gentle confusion to outright alarm. I'm thankful beyond words for the medical textbooks I read while studying naturopathy in my early twenties. I'm not intimidated by medical jargon, although it's often only later in the parking lot that I fully comprehend the conversation I just had.

So. These things I know.

I have malignant breast cancer, which feeds on my hormones. The smell of fresh-cut papaya reminds me of my grandfather's hands, gnarled and brown from the sun, every line etched with good black dirt. The heart is made of muscle and nerves and somehow holds the whole universe in its red grip, which clenches and unclenches in time to the birth of stars. I'm forty years old and pregnant. Shoes feel like prisons for my feet. I am a wildish creature. After rain, a backlit tree trunk spews plumes of steam like Armageddon's flames. I have malignant breast cancer, which feeds on my hormones. There are a trillion holes in the sky but I can't quite see what's on the other side, although I've tried. I'm breathing atoms that have been around since the universe was created. I have malignant breast cancer, which feeds on my hormones. Things are about to get rougher for a while. I'm either going to die or figure this out.

So, okay.

I have a name for this thing, this disorder of my cells that hasn't suddenly happened but has been quietly pottering along with me, like a loyal hound, accompanying me to meals, movies, on planes and adventures, waiting for me to turn around and find it, oh hello, what are you doing all paw-pad at my heels? It's been here for years, they say, this multicelled catalyst for my awakening, my silent partner of the murderous kind.

Malignant aggressive grade three invasive ductal carcinoma.

Names are power. To name a thing is to begin to nail it down, to own and control it. In much mythology, to know the true name of a powerful deity is to own their essence and garners the ability to compel them. What power. Give me three wishes. Here are your tasks. Bring me that rose from the highest tower, that I may break this spell. Grant me true love. Smite mine enemy. Show me my heart's desire, no matter the consequences.

Names are also traps. They delude us into thinking we know a thing and it is therefore predictable. Nothing in the universe is fully predictable, not even gravity, which changes with mass and the distance between objects. If I jump to touch the clouds, will the earth be lighter, will its gravity change? If we all jump at once, all eight billion of us, flying upward in a radiating cloud of arms and legs and upturned faces, will the earth loosen her tender grip and grant us flight? Every time an asteroid hits the earth, the planet's mass changes, gravity shifts, just an eyelash's worth. An asteroid has hit me fair and square in the kisser, but the first shockwaves are dying away, and although I can track the taste of blood-metal in my mouth, all my teeth seem to be in place. My center of gravity wobbles, but I'm adaptable; my will to live is stronger than gravity; there's no simple scientific equation for this force of nature, but it's just as real, can lift me higher than the clouds, to where the sun breathes life and I can taste the truth of all things and know what is right.

I have a grade-three malignant ductal name for this thing. It's a beginning. I have the first strategies to tame this beast that can devour me and my child if I get it wrong. I have the stirrings of a plan and am not paralyzed with terror.

It's time to tell people.

"Dutch, me bonny wee love."

"Gigi-girl. Where have you been? I nearly *died* last week."

"For real?"

"For real. I threw up a liter of blood in the sink. It was freaky. They couldn't figure out why."

"Jeez, Dutch, you specialize in weird medical shit. I take it you're okay?"

"I'm unkillable. Like a cockroach, only way more handsome. So, what's with you?"

I still haven't got the hang of telling my friends this enormous thing. Deep breath. "Well . . . there's good news and bad news. The good news is I'm pregnant."

"Oh, that's *wonderful*, Gi. Congratulations. It will be *gorgeous.* Your cheekbones and that stunning man of yours."

I let the silence hang. He gets it.

"Okay, love, what's the bad news? Should I sit down?"

"Probably. The bad news is I have breast cancer."

"Oh *nooooo.*"

"Before you freak out, I reckon I can get through it without chemo," I say. "I've done some research about diet and alkalizing, and—"

"—mmm."

"Don't mmm me, Dutch."

"Mmm."

I see him at the glass coffee table, surrounded by piles of books, frowning into his red wine glass. I know that frown; I see it when I play a particularly loathsome song for him.

I need him to believe in me. "I can do it."

"Have chemo," he says. "I had a friend who had twins and didn't have chemo till after the pregnancy. The babies were gorgeous. She was dead in a year. Don't mess about, Gi. Cancer doesn't take prisoners. Have chemo."

"We'll see."

"Come visit me soon. We can compare surgeons. I've got frequent flyer points at all the best cancer ward in town. St. Vincent's is *fabulous.* You should see the decor these days. All new equipment and the staff are divine. Drop round for a cuppa, love. I have a new book for you, on superstring theory."

"I've got you one too. Pure mathematics, which you'll love, ya nerd. I can't understand a bloody word of it. Physics is one thing, but math is ridiculous. I need you to tell me what it's about."

"Math is the language of the universe."

"I prefer to think it's love, love."

"You and your hippie crap. Speaking of, have you written any new songs?"

"Only on the piano, and I can't fit that in the car."

"Bring your guitar, then, and we'll go over your old ones. None of that self-indulgent shit, though. What was that song? The awful one."

"I can always count on you to let me know."

"Someone has to."

"See ya, Dutch."

"Bye, Gigi-girl. Have the chemo."

"You're incorrigible."

"I like you alive."

Mum confides to me, in racking tears, "If something happens to you, I don't know if I'll be able to love the baby. I just don't know, Gi. You're my baby. You'll always be my baby."

Kim Farrant, my wildly talented film director friend, laughs and cries at the same time when I tell her about the cancer.

"Gi," she says, "when you were waiting to come into this body, the angel at the gate stopped you with his clipboard and asked what experiences you wanted in this life. You just said, 'Tick every box.'"

Dad's eyes well. I've never seen him look helpless, ever.

"I'll be okay, Douggie," I say. "I've got this."

"Good," he says, but his eyes stay wet.

Twelve weeks pregnant and I'm back to the medical center for a nuchal test referral, to check if the baby has chromosomal abnormalities. This time I'm seeing another doctor, husband to my first GP. He reads my patient notes and shouts across the laminated desk covered in papers in his thick accent.

"I know about your case. Why you still pregnant?" he yells. "What have you been doing for last three months? Very bad. Very, very bad. We could not believe it. And you have not had proper treatment for breast."

I rock back on my heels.

"What?"

"Why you still pregnant? You have cancer, you cannot keep baby."

I start to explain that it's possible to have chemotherapy these days while pregnant and he cuts me off.

"Is very bad advice. Terrible. Who give you this advice? You should not be pregnant. We make appointment immediately for termination. If you have this baby, you will die."

Wolf Mother arrives.

"Stop talking to me like that," I say, heart beating a tattoo, voice blue ice, a little raggedy, a touch breathless, but diamond-clear.

"Your decision is bad one," he says. "Is it yours? You decide this alone? You and your husband? You have bad advice."

"We decided together with my breast surgeon."

"Oh," he says. "Doctor advise you."

"Yes," I say. "A doctor advised me, but the decision's mine. Mate, you can't sit there and tell me I'll die if I don't do what you think. I just want a bloody referral. Then you never have to see me again."

I'm still clutching the referral when I meet Lee for our first ultrasound of the baby, whom we've nicknamed Bean. Heavy blankets cover the windows in my heart. The waiting room is ghastly. Fluorescents carve sickly gray hollows into waiting patients' cheeks.

"Miserable bunch, aren't they?" whispers Lee, nudging me.

"Shhhh."

"That one there looks like *The Cat in the Hat*."

I choke.

"He does. Look. Even has the whiskers."

"Stopppp."

"That one's Scrooge. And look, Putin's hiding behind the pot plant. Asian Thor in the corner. What. I'm allowed, I'm part Chinese, so it's not racist. You're snortling, Gigi. That's really not appropriate."

"Chick? Gina Chick? I'm Kelly."

We rise from the ranks of the damned and follow the technician into a small room that smells faintly of chemicals. I lie down. She smears clear jelly over a funny-looking instrument, presses it into me, and a few seconds later a strange sound floods the room.

Thum ah thum ah thum ah thum ah thum ah thum ah.

Kelly smiles and turns the screen around and I hold my breath. I'm scared to look, scared to see a tiny collapsed shape motionless in black and white, it will break me, but I look anyway because that sound, what is that sound, it's so regular and fast it goes thum ah thum ah thum ah thum ah thum, and I know what it is now and I look and there is our baby, our Bean is jumping and wiggling and squirming and I see legs and arms, Bean is waving hi mama hi papa it's me, I'm okay, and that sound is a heart, a clever little heart beating fast and strong and sure, and I burst into tears, trying not to squeeze my eyes shut in case I miss something and Lee's crying too, we're transfixed, our fingers wrapped around each other so tightly they'll leave red marks later but for now we notice nothing but that little wriggling shape dancing on the screen. This is our baby, our baby is real, is *real* and growing and a miracle of life like all life is a miracle. Bean is alive. Alive, alive, alive.

We're two normal parents in raptures over some scribbly white lines and pixels. That's a tummy, that's the eyes, and that's the heartbeat. Thum ah thum ah thum ah thum.

"That's our baby," I say.

Lee nods, eyes streaming. "Our baby."

In his eyes I see what's alive in my heart. We will fight every millimeter of the way to bring our baby into the world. Together.

"Look, there's Bean," Lee says, poring over the week-by-week pregnancy book we've inherited from someone.

"Hi, Bean," I say to the little figure in the photo. "Hmm . . . Bean looks like a fish."

"A clever fish."

"Very clever fish." I pat my belly. "Keep being clever."

"What's growing this week?"

"Ah, this week we have a host of new developments. Fingers and toes are forming, but they're webbed."

"So frog rather than fish."

I turn the page. "Yes. Actually, more alien than anything else. Here, look."

"Eek. I see what you mean."

"But it's our alien. Looks a bit like you, love."

"Let me see. Hang on . . . move your finger . . . oh, that's why. It says here that its brain is growing faster than anything else. Just like me."

"Wait . . . and it's growing an anus. Just like you. Ow!"

My belly feels strange. Full and heavy, even though the pregnancy isn't really showing yet.

"Want a cuppa, Lee? There's herbal, herbal, or . . . ooh . . . herbal."

"Nettle, thanks. You should have some too."

"Blah. Tastes like compost water mixed with cat pee. I'm making a chai. And please stop telling me what I should have. It's driving me bonkers."

"You should be eating brassica."

"I have morning sickness. Brussels sprouts make me want to hurl."

"Gina, you have cancer. Brassicas mop up the estrogens."

"I'll have some broccoli later."

I brew chai and some fresh nettle tea and stroke Lee's arm. "You don't know what morning sickness is like, love. It's seasickness with attitude, all day. If I'm awake, I just feel like I'm gonna puke, but I can't. I'll make sure I eat some brassica today."

He starts to say something, then sighs and drinks his tea.

"I hate calling Bean 'it,'" he says. "Should we find out whether it's a boy or a girl? I'll connect more with the baby if I know who it is. It's all right for you; everything's happening inside you. I have to watch and wait for the next six months before it's properly real."

"Ah, love. It must be hard for you, with everything going on, having no control."

"Yeah. It's working me. All I've got is brassica, and you won't even eat that."

I laugh. "I'd rather know too. Hang on, does it tell us in this silly book when we can do that? Twenty weeks. Seems like a long time."

"I'm sure there'll be plenty to occupy us."

"Don't remind me."

I've never been more awake. Every pore is open. At night I see myself, a huge white bear, wandering across an icy horizon, a small cub at my heels, batting at snowflakes. We've been roaming like this since time began. Glaciers chew mountains to rubble. Eternal days and nights circle like beetles. There is no home but here.

Danni drops in every single week with flowers. She stays for a cuppa, then drives back to the Northern Beaches.

"You don't need to do this, Dan," I say. "I'm doing well."

"Flowers are happy," she says. "I love you."

Sometimes I cry a bit when she leaves.

Lee sings to my belly and our little bump, makes me food, massages my feet. I chug green drinks, take supplements, meditate, laugh, cry, and pee on little strips to assess the acidity of my body.

All the tools in my basket come into play: breathwork, massage, primal sessions, family constellations, craniosacral with fellow therapists. The tens of thousands of hours I've spent learning to unlock a body's secrets now make sense; they were homework for this. I see myself unpicking the shroud cancer has me wrapped in. If I shine light into the shadows, maybe it will have nowhere to hide.

Parallel universes are real; they gallop along next to each other. Around me, normal people go through their normal lives. My old life has died. Nothing will ever be the same again.

Soon, I'll have to look chemotherapy in the face and really choose. I know it. I just hope to be as clear as possible, for myself and for the baby. The wrong decision could be fatal for either or both of us.

Ancient fears hammer me daily. The voices of my ancestors, women standing on the shoulders of women, reach up to whisper that the child will be born deformed, stunted, dead. I'm too old, chromosomes will split badly, cancer will eat us both, the child will fail.

Mum's first baby was stillborn at seven months. The nurses held a pillow over her belly so she wouldn't see the baby. A little girl. I still quail every time I think of that, her first! To be abandoned by her own mother, and then my older sister died in her womb. And then there's my tragic, beautiful grandmother, who never got over giving Mum up for adoption; she had three more children, who, by all accounts, she neglected in favor of her writing. Two of them killed themselves, and so did she.

All the women in my DNA who have lost children haunt me with their stories. They wail through my dreams and wring their hands and moan.

I cling to a faint straw of hope.

I'm the latest in a long, unbroken line of thousands of women who got it right. They birthed babes who birthed babes who birthed babes to get to me.

So many voices make up a human. We think we're a single thing, when really, we're so many things: a swarm of bees, shifting clouds, currents of dust; the illusion of substance.

When the doors of life and death fly open, we look for the safety of that which we know, for any anchor points, and are horrified to find that the closer we examine ourselves, the less we *know* about anything. Cancer is a great unmaking. So are pregnancy and birth. But really, this unmaking is happening all the time, if we choose to look. It's so terrifying that most of us never do, until we're pressed hard against the glass.

*

I've sacked two GPs, an oncologist, and a surgeon, all of whom treated me as a faceless statistic. In their places I now have my team, all of whom respect me as a human with intelligence and autonomy. My oncologist is the teaching professor at my local hospital. I have a wonderful alternative GP who sent my blood overseas for a test of circulating tumor cells. He says I need to be prepared to have chemo if the levels rise too much.

And then there are my magicians.

John is in Canada. If he lived in primitive times, he would be the village medicine man. Our Skype sessions are arcane, moving into the unquantifiable worlds of meditation and spiritual journeying. Together we visualize the relationship between my body and what we call Cancer Creature. We also explore my revulsion to chemotherapy, looking at ways to reduce my resistance should the day come when I need to take it.

Malcolm Ringwalt, from Tracker School, helps me find my center when I lose it.

"Gina, let go of your preconceptions and judgments," he says when I call him in a panic about the possibility of having chemo while pregnant. "There's merit in every medicine. All your doctors are your advisers, but you're the only one who knows your right timing. It's impossible to predict what may be right next week, or next month; there are too many variables that haven't yet come to pass. But if you're clear, you can know what's right, right now. There may come a time when you instinctively know chemo is perfect for you. Listen for that moment, and be willing to change from no to yes."

I practice with the surgeon and the oncologist.

"Chemo's not a no," I say. "But it's not yet."

Taking control of the timing for my medical procedures is a revelation.

Intuition is my primary sense. I've followed it all over the world. The only time it's let me down is when I haven't listened to it. This situation is no different. I see my path isn't to abandon the structure of logic, or the pull of the heart, but to hold these elements loosely so there's room for the intuitive leap, the flash of insight that comes from thousands of years of wisdom in my DNA. From Wolf Mother.

I walk around with an adage I read on the back of a toilet door: trust in god, but tie your camel.

Dutch is less esoteric. My blood tests show rising levels of circulating tumor cells. "Don't be a fucking idiot, Gina. Get the fucking chemo."

Strange things are happening to my senses. I keep turning around to hear what's ringing. Maybe it's this sky of beaten copper. Something on the other side keeps hitting it with tiny mallets. I know this is true because a cresting arrowhead of ducks beats a hundred wings in time to the shining rhythm, and I couldn't make that up. Could I? I stand like this a long time, head thrown back to let my throat catch the sound of their feathers. Such a vulnerable pose, but for all my fear, here I feel safe. Where the sea scratches at the sky, I know I'm home. I stroke my belly.

"Look," I say to the mysterious creature swimming inside, pointing to the place on the horizon where everything vanishes. "That's where you've come from." No answer from the spark in my belly.

The duck arrow strikes a growing sun, and for a moment, I wonder if they've all burned up, fallen into the waiting arms of the sea.

Everything leaves a track, even desire.

At twenty weeks we have another scan. Yet another waiting room. More cold goop all over my belly.

"Do you want to know the sex?" the technician asks. "Let's have a look here. Yes, you have a little girl."

"We're having a daughter!" Lee says later, and we cry into our sushi. We seem to spend my entire pregnancy crying.

"She's huge!" I say, seeing those long legs and arms again, the hand waving at us, her face turned as if she could see us. I cuddle my belly and say, "Clever girl. You clever, clever girl." She's huge, and healthy. A normal, healthy baby girl, dreaming her baby dreams, growing her strong bones and brain and nerves and her little heart a blinking light going pip pip pip pip pip, as steady as hope.

It's crunch time. The results of my latest blood test are horrible. My circulating tumor cell levels are off the chart. This cancer feeds on estrogen and progesterone, and my body is awash with both because of the pregnancy. I'm producing a high-nutrient soup and the cancer is sucking it all down.

"You need to do something," says my wonderful GP, who's been supporting me as I dance the line between conventional and downright out-there medicine.

I know he's right. My world crashes around me.

A bell rings in my bones. *Time.*

Wolf Mother pads the floors. *Time.*

Mowgli drums Bagheera's ribs. *Time.*

Modesty Blaise nods from the corner of the room.

Time for chemo.

Malcolm was right. The knowing is unmistakable.

I'm not ready. But I have to be, or I could leave my child an orphan and it will have all been for nothing.

Lee lopes in, smelling of wild summer and wood shavings. He prowls through the kitchen, opens the fridge, sniffs at it, closes it again, then glances to where I sit on the couch, staring out the back door into nothing, tears tracking my face.

"You okay?"

"I thought I was doing everything right. Now this. I'm so sad."

He settles beside me and I lean against his shoulder.

"I feel little," I say.

"That's okay, you can be little, love. I've got big covered for now."

"Thanks."

We sit like that for a bit, in silence. His body moves with slow, steady breaths. Outside, the magpies carol and a sea breeze tosses the pepper tree, which sighs.

"I've failed. Failed her, failed myself, failed you." I'm scared to speak it. "What if chemo hurts our baby?" My eyes leak, my face scrunches.

He moves his arm around me, pulls me onto his chest.

"Come here," he says. "Gigi, I am so proud of you. I don't know anyone who could have done this the way you have."

"Really?"

"Really."

"Am I doing the right thing?"

"Yes, love. It's going to be okay."

"Is it, though?"

"You're going to be a great mama."

"I don't feel like it."

"You *are* a great mama. I trust you. I don't trust much, but I trust you. You're doing everything right. If you need chemo, that'll be right as well."

"I hope so," I say. My voice sounds small.

"Hang on," he says, disentangling, and walks out of the room. "Don't go anywhere."

Familiar music, Louis and Ella, fills the back of the house as he returns, extending his hand to me with a flourish.

"Shall we?"

I take his hand and stand, and he twirls me. We slow dance cheek to cheek like it's 3 a.m. in a jazz club, and the night will never end.

"I love you, Lee Trew," I say.

"That's lucky," he murmurs into my hair. "Because I happen to be pretty crazy about you, Gina Chickerel."

I wake from a dream where I'm riding a dragon made of paper. Pages flutter. I lean my body, bank, and twist. Harsh, fluting cries pierce the skies from all around me. I'm at the head of a phalanx, thousands of paper dragons battling into the shriek of a hurricane. When one succumbs and drops in a tatter of paper, another takes its place.

When I wake, I say to Lee, "I know what to do."

The oncologist laughs when I ask for forty years' worth of double-blind clinical studies of pregnant women having chemotherapy, until he realizes I'm serious. He returns with a huge wad of pages and a dubious expression. He doesn't know I can read medical jargon. Lee sleeps in the spare room as I turn page after page, scribbling with highlighters. The chaotic turmoil of tables and statistics is tamed under my gaze. I regard my findings with a sense of rising hope.

It's possible to have a healthy baby after having chemotherapy. A glycoprotein in the placenta offers some protection to the fetus. Babies of chemo mums are usually very small, but they catch up across all the charts in the first two years. Chemotherapy has no higher rate of birth defects than a non-chemo pregnancy, as long as the chemo is given in the second or third trimester. Chemo is given with drugs to stop the inevitable nausea.

"Okay," I say to the oncologist. "Let's do it, but I don't want the antiemetics."

"The chemotherapy regime will make you very sick," he says.

"I won't get sick."

"And how are you going to do that? One of your witches' brews?" He's been teasing me about being a witch for weeks now.

"You'll be begging me to bring in my cauldron so you can give my recipes to everyone. I'm not going to get sick."

"Gina, everyone gets sick on this chemo. Everyone."

"We'll see."

There are three antinausea drugs in the treatment, and he's insistent.

"If you don't take these, it will be cruel. I won't treat you unless you do."

"I'm not having a steroid while I'm pregnant. Give me the other two."

For all my bravado, inside I'm a jittery mess. What if I'm wrong? What if all this madness hurts the baby?

Dutch calls.

"Gigi-girl. It's been awful. I've been dreaming about you every night, and every night you die. Please have chemo."

"Hi, Dutch, how are you?"

"I'm serious. Have the chemo. Please, please, please. They've been nightmares. All night every night. Don't die for an idea, Gi. It would be such a waste. Where else would I find an Amazon with cheekbones like yours?"

"It's okay, love, I got there anyway. My last blood test was a shocker. I've met with the oncologist and the obstetrician and know what drugs it'll be. I start in a couple of weeks."

"Thank god. I've been so worried. You aren't just saying that to make me go away, are you?"

"When have I ever?"

"So you'll have chemo?"

"Yes, Dutch. I'll have chemo."

It's time.

There's nowhere left to run. I dream of approaching trains, earthquakes, floods. Wake long before the birds, suspended in the obsidian slice of night where spirits dance.

All my clarity and confidence have evaporated. I'm sick inside, knowing that in a couple of hours I'll flood my system with chemicals so potent and powerful they kill dividing cells. What's a growing baby but a whole bunch of dividing cells? How can this be the right decision? How can this possibly turn out well?

There's not enough time, I need days, weeks before I can do this, I'm not ready, I have to be ready, the time is now.

Now.

I suck in a huge breath, big as I can, and hold it until lights dance like crazy fairies behind my eyes. I breathe out all the dread and preconceptions. If I'm going to do this, then let's do this.

I cradle my belly and murmur to our little one all the way to the hospital, telling her it will all be okay, although nothing is. Lee's a monsoon, barely contained. His eyes don't look like him.

The machine gobbles us up.

We flick through trash magazines among a cluster of bald people wearing scarves, hats, and wigs. All of us drink awful tea from polystyrene cups. The loveliness of the staff can't lift the heaviness of all these people looking death in the teeth and wondering how sharp the bite will be.

I'm calm. Lee's a thorn embedded far inside himself, which looks calm from the outside. We skate on the meniscus of a dark pool and eat white bread sandwiches from a tray, trying to ignore the too-loud daytime TV, inane American talk shows.

The oncologist calls us in. I sign forms, here, and here, and here, take the antiemetics, here's some water, see you soon. Next.

Lee and I curl on the bed like dried leaves. A big wind would blow us far away and out of here. *Please let my baby be okay*. Wolf Mother growls uneasily at the nurses as they whisk past.

The head nurse swishes in, diaphanous in her purple gown, cap, gloves, and mask, carrying a tray. Only her eyes show. This stuff is so toxic she has to wear a hazmat suit. The tray has three enormous syringes filled with what looks like bright red cordial. Each one is the thickness of my wrist. This red stuff is only the first of the three chemo agents. I dread to think what's still to come.

She inserts a cannula. Saline frost creeps up my arm. Maybe it will reach my heart, freeze me, turn my eyes to milk. My breath won't settle in my lungs. It keeps trying to fly away.

She attaches the first syringe.

I can't drag my eyes away from the impossible scarlet of the liquid. The color of wrongness.

This can't be good.

Gradually, I drop into meditation. Meditating through panic is like pissing into a fifty-knot wind and expecting to stay dry. But somehow, I do it. The red fluid going into my veins is medicine. Lee folds around me, almost catatonic. Every now and then the nurse changes a syringe, or attaches the next drug to drip into my arm.

Lee stirs, and I ask how he's doing.

"I want to punch the nurse, pull out the drips, throw you over my shoulder, and run out the door," he says, with such hopelessness and horror I resolve not to bring him next time.

"Ah," I say. "Doing pretty well, then."

"Well, I haven't done any of that yet, so I guess, yes."

The nurse rustles back with a cheerful little booklet of what to expect in terms of side effects. It's dire. I read it all and wish I hadn't.

On the way out, we hold hands so tightly it hurts. There's nothing to say. People bustle along the footpath, talking about inconsequential things. Normal is a planet I can't even see from here. I feel like chewing gum, stretched and twisted. Smacky and stoned and heavy, like moving through molasses.

We don't talk on the drive home. I go straight to bed.

In the morning, I feel heavy, slow, a bit tired, but no worse than many a weekend in my twenties after a big night.

"How are you?" says Lee, bringing me a cuppa on stealthy feet, as if he's afraid heavy footfalls will break me.

I feel into myself, gingerly, then with more confidence.

"I think I'm . . . all right. I am. Lee, I'm okay."

His face eases, but he still looks worried.

"And her?"

I stroke my belly. Inside, a spark shimmers and twists. Wolf Mother sleeps with her nose in her tail, snoring slightly.

"She feels good," I say. "She really does." I can't help the smile; it's wan, but clean.

Lee's face crumbles as he falls onto the bed and shudders, huge racking sobs that sound like the ending of time. I gather him into my arms and love him until the monsoon passes.

A male fairy wren throws his iridescent throat back, bubbling music. I lean against the smooth, mottled skin of an angophora, among snaking roots and ant nests and an explosion of pale feathers where a fox or owl fed last night. I pull my hair out in clumps, leaving bald bits and manky patches, then add these long ropes of hair to the feather graveyard, craning to see the result in a tiny makeup mirror. My scalp shines bright white where the hair isn't. Tufts stick out, others hang limp. It all highlights the purple bags under my eyes.

Lee recoils when he sees me, and I don't blame him. My beautiful mane is gone. I look *sick* for the first time, old and exhausted. I don't recognize my face in the mirror.

Stevie shaves off the patchy bits. Instantly, I feel honest. No more mangy dog. I walk around defiantly bald or wear bright silk scarves.

I find it hard to catch Lee's eye these days. He seems to be looking in any direction but mine. I can't escape the feeling that my baldness is the last straw, driving him further away than I can reach. I don't know how to bring him back.

Dutch gave me *American Gods* awhile back, and now I get to it, devouring the book in three nights. Neil Gaiman tattoos stories along the inside of my skull with small picks. Odin hangs from his tree, and now I'm suspended beside him, branches squeezing my chest and piercing my cancerous breast. The air runs thick with mystery. Doors peel open. Behind those, more doors, and more again. I tear the corners of pages, dawn-bright, like I haven't done since I was a kid. Book paper tastes different these days.

My sessions with John feel like chapters from that world, with the quality of ayahuasca dreams. Among labyrinths and catacombs, the thing we've named Cancer Creature stalks me on foul feet, watched by bored, assembled gods, a shifting nightmare of appetite in an uncaring pantheon.

Cancer is every place I've ever said no to love. It's the voice in the night listing hurts I've caused until I babble with shame. It's the loneliness of believing I'm broken.

I face the thing, tiny and defiant under its fetid jaws. Its eyes are flame and its form involutes. I feel it creeping under my skin, through my bones. I scream getitOUTgetitOUTit'sINmegetitOUT. Claw my flesh to ribbons, squeeze every drop of blood until I'm marble white, to be free of it. It creeps ice through my cells anyway, death to my kind, perfectly evolved to seduce my DNA into a dance of profusion. *More*, it thunders, advancing. *I will fill all your spaces until you have become me. Until your skin splits and I bubble out. Give yourself to me.*

No.

Wolf Mother holds her ground in the hall of the gods. At her side blazes a metal angel, Chemotherapie, all clockwork and filigree, animated only to seep through my blood and kill me with its saving.

I understand why people talk of fighting cancer, but Dutch is right: these are my cells run to riot. How can I fight myself? If I fight, I have to win, and this thing knows the battles of eons, while I am a mouse, facing a wyvern. I need the cunning of Anansi the trickster. I need to dance with the beast, distract it, and, while it looks elsewhere, slide between its claws and away. I need a riddle and three wishes. I need a golden ring of power. I need shaman magic and the red drums of my ancestors.

I beseech the watching gods, the furred, finned, scaled ones. Help me find the narrow path. Surely all things want evolution. Does Chemotherapie need to destroy everything it touches? Is there another way? An unspeakable thing nods, comes forward, drawing a splinter from the living machine of Chemotherapie. *Here,* it breathes without voice, *take this fragment. If you can find its better nature, use it.* I take the fragment and name it Little Brother.

In the long nights leading to the next round of chemo, I strike fire from cold stones and sit with Little Brother, stitching a robe of starlight to wrap my precious one in, so at the least she will be saved. While she sleeps, Little Brother and I share stories of the world; mine warm and fleshy, its of the abyssal beauty in the veils between life and death. I sing songs to wake the fallen, to kickstart a heartbeat in its metal chest, squeeze tears from chrome eyes. Take me, I say, but only what you need. You don't need a club; bring a feather. I won't fight you. Come all the way in, do your work, and leave like you were never here. Can you give me this?

Little Brother is soft now, its cogs have dissolved to silk. Ravens squall outside my window. Odin cackles from his tree.

I don't know if it will be enough, but it will have to do.

The oncologist calls me in for my interview before the second round of chemo, for which I've left Lee behind. I'll be fine, love, I say, and mean it. I've got this. Save your energy.

He ticks off questions. The walls are powder blue. I figure someone thinks it's a calming color.

"How are you? Any side effects? Nausea?"

"None."

His eyebrows raise. "No nausea at all?"

"Nope."

He scratches in his notebook.

"Ulceration? Mouth ulcers? Stomach?"

"None."

He writes some more.

"Your immune system only dipped by a third. We were expecting a much greater fall, to be frank."

"I wasn't."

He pauses, tapping his pen. "Muscle aches and pains?"

"Headache on the first night."

"That's it?"

"Yup."

"How are you feeling?"

"I feel fine. Pretty good, actually. Um . . . bald."

"There's the Look Good Feel Better program and a wig swap here at the hospital if you—"

"Nah, not interested. I'm fine with bald."

I don't tell him my husband won't look at me and I want to cry whenever I see my crisp-white noggin.

He agrees to halve the dose of one of the antiemetics.

This time, Little Brother rides at my side with Wolf Mother, not that anyone can see them. The chemo is both easier and harder. Easier to accept, easier knowing the shock-red fluid is coming rather than being terrified by the look of it.

Harder because I'm still rattled from losing my hair and losing Lee.

Harder to find my center. But still.

Humans can get used to anything; horrific can become banal, even boring.

Autumn days with cool edges. Sharp wind nips at tanned ankles. Warm sunshine hunts cool violet shadows. Lorikeets screech overhead like jeweled arrows, chasing summer away. Westerlies blow the ocean flat as a picnic blanket. Looping contrails stitch the blue into abstract shapes. Laconic laughter, the tourists going home; locals get to live here all year round.

I wander the beach, under toothy cliffs, away from the growing distance between Lee and me. As I walk, I turn over every stone I can find in the caverns of my psyche, where my shadows hide.

There's a sneaky pull in feeling special.

I have the story of all stories, not just cancer but also pregnant, dancing between life and death for my little one.

"You're amazing," I'm told daily by the people I encounter, but Wolf Mother growls her soft warning. Here be dragons. Cancer is a get-out-of-jail-free card. There are benefits. People make excuses for me, offer love, attention, money, time, kindness. If I don't find ways to get those needs met on my own, I won't want to let this go. I already feel that intoxicating seduction, of being the sumptuous heroine in a tragic tale. Being *amazing*. The size of my story and my warrior's journey make my life mythic. I need to remember I'm ordinary.

Sandstone ripples glow in the sunset. I breathe in salt and exhale slimy things, which vanish into purple cracks in the rock.

I fly to Melbourne to a weekend women's circle with a group of women committed to gathering three times a year. We dance and sing and share with breathtaking honesty. Most are mothers. I relax in ways I didn't know I needed, rejoicing at the wisdom of authentic sisterhood.

At the end of the final day, just as we're finishing up, the facilitator asks if anyone has anything to bring up before we close the circle.

"I do," I say, heart thumping. I draw a big breath. My voice shakes. I feel vulnerable, like a limpet turned over, surf tossing me around.

"I'm kinda terrible at asking for help, but . . . my baldness. It's the thing I've found the hardest to deal with. I think my poor head needs some love."

I bawl with grief and loss and terror and vulnerability as my scalp is stroked by so many hands it's impossible to tell who's who. I allow the love in, even though it hurts, surrounded by warm, soft bodies and gentle murmurs, a susurrus of trailing fingers bringing exquisite tenderness to my skin. My hairless head is the portal to my doubt and fear, to the little voice whispering, "What if you've got it all wrong? What if you've condemned yourself and your baby? What if you're just going to die, and it's messy and painful and awful?" I let myself feel it all, guttural, buckling under all that searing love. My head tingles and expands, and I see colored lights behind my eyes.

"Thank you," I whisper to these women I've just met. "Thank you."

Lee and I build a shelter from gathered objects on the property where he's teaching people how to survive in the wild. He tears huge armfuls of long grass by the roots, leaving patchwork commas of torn dirt in their wake, to the delight of a pair of yellow robins that dart around his feet, downing beetles dislodged from their dark and earthy homes.

Later, around the fire, while the rest of the village cooks and carves and weaves and works, I bundle the grass into wrist-thick clumps, which I tie off at one end with twisted grass string. Something about tying our relationship back together, one strand at a time.

Lee leans into me after the singing has faded away and everyone has drifted off to bed. Warm, so warm where our bodies touch. I rest my head on his shoulder.

"I'm sorry, Gigi," he says eventually, as the fire burns to embers. "I want to be there for you, but I can barely manage myself at the moment. I hate that I'm not able to give you what you need. You deserve better, love."

I turn away so he won't see the tears, but he pulls me to his chest anyway. "Shit," I say, wiping my nose. "I'm a snot monster."

"You're doing so well," he says. "I don't know how you're doing it."

"I miss you when you go away like that, Lee."

His voice is shaky. "I'm just so scared," he says, face twisting. "I don't want to lose you. I don't want to lose you. I don't know what I'd do if I lost you."

"I'm scared too," I say. "But you're not going to lose me."

Just like that he's back. Our little bush house with its grass roof and walls of tied branches takes shape, a womb of homespun hope. We work under the spotted gums, tying on thatching, falling into an easy rhythm, dreaming aloud the days when our daughter will play in this shelter. Time is lazy. Insects scream defiance. Heat thick as water. We amble down bush tracks to a clear, icy creek, so cold it steals our breath. Lee's eyes close as he drifts over the river stones. My belly soars proud as a mountain above the waterline, my ears underwater, the cicadas' assault muted. My bald scalp tingles under velvet fingerlings of water that twist into my stories and simply wash them away.

I can't walk fast any more; I have to stop every few steps to breathe through stabbing pains in my pelvis from the old appendix scars and adhesions.

My vast, twenty-eight-week belly pulses as the baby's feet push at its surface like some mysterious leviathan breaching from the sea.

"All healthy, she looks great. Good movement, and how about those long legs? A hundred and tenth percentile," chuckles the ultrasound technician. "She's a beauty."

Chemotherapy babies are usually tiny, around the twenty-fifth percentile. She's enormous. Chemo hasn't slowed her down at all.

Lee and I stare at each other, at the screen, our perfect daughter. Everything's going to be all right.

The oncologist says, before my final round of chemo, "You look well."

"I feel great," I say.

He records all my answers; despite ditching the antiemetics completely last time, I've had no nausea, no side effects, I'm effervescent with vitality. He puts down his pen. "All right. Tell me. What are you taking? What are you doing?"

"I thought you'd never ask."

"I'm asking."

"I told you you'd want me to bring in my cauldron," I tease.

"Yes, yes. Now what are you doing, Gina Chick?"

I'm doing things beyond your ken, my friend. Things the men in white coats would take me away for. I'm scratching at the footprints in the sky where the oldest stories leave secret trails. Bards from other whens stitch healing songs into my cells so deeply the cancer can't find a foothold anymore. I talk to chemotherapy like it's a lover and ask of it kindness. Lay down lights for it to follow so it doesn't sniff into the secret nest of my sleeping daughter, all wrapped in feathers and fur. I live in the spaces between breaths and find there a universe where the arrow of human will is a talisman. Magic is real, and it lives under my tongue, where tiny triangles of paper diffuse into a tapestry of the unwritten.

"Chlorella," I say. "It stops the nausea."

I lie on the bed and watch the last needles go in. My veins are agony. They're blue and bruised and ache constantly. Even the lightest drag of fabric on my skin hurts.

I drift into meditation, saying yes to Little Brother; come in, do what you need to do, then leave quietly, if you will.

This is it. After today I can focus on being pregnant and on the next doorway: birth. I stroke the tiny sole of her foot pressing against my skin. I can almost see her toes.

My perfect girl.

At home I feel like screaming, crying, and laughing all at once.

"We did it!" I sing to Lee, whooping.

"We did it," he shouts back, as we dance around the kitchen. Stevie arrives home from work to catch us jumping like lunatics. He joins in and the house rings to our shared joy. Rex and Lulu bolt into the backyard. I reckon the whole street can hear us. I don't care.

In bed, Lee can't fit his arms around my belly. He lies with his head against my bump, singing to our daughter. She kicks him through my skin until he makes funny faces.

Everything about me slows down. I understand geological time, the life cycles of stars, the birth and death of mountains. Our walks are glacial, the world whizzes by.

Lee says, "Why don't we call her Blaise?"

"We can't. Can we? What if she reads the books and thinks she has to be like Modesty Blaise?"

"By the time she can read, she'll know who she is. Anyway, as far as role models go, Modesty Blaise worked for you, didn't she?"

As an end-of-chemo celebration, Stevie books the Jean-Michel Cousteau Resort in Fiji. I'm so enormous I need to bring a letter from the hospital to say I'm still two months off and won't pop open on the plane like a jack-in-the-box.

At the resort, food to make the gods weep arrives while locals drink kava and sing harmonies around the pool. Stevie and his partner, Andy, sip wine and murmur over flavors. I finally don't have morning sickness or chemo heaviness, and it all tastes like ambrosia.

Lee scuba dives for the first time. I snorkel the tops of the reefs, frolic, and somersault, talking to the baby, telling her everything I see. Rainbow fish, curious, nip at my fingers. Temples of color coil down to pure blue.

I shuck the world of air, grow fins and gills, follow the bubbles of my husband and his dive buddy as they traverse the sea floor between two reefs, fifteen meters down. I angle until I'm just a few meters over them. Lee looks up, turns to face me. We swim like this, his bubbles enveloping me, masks close. His eyes are smiling. He blows a kiss and turns back to face the sand, while I kick and play.

Here, I'm home. I'm graceful without gravity flattening me; my belly doesn't get in the way. I'm a ponderous fat dugong. There is no time, only a lazy slide and glide through molecules of water, the heavenly joy of loop-the-loops and sideways rolls. I soar and whirl.

Everything. Vanishes.

Cancer, chemo, my relationship, the past, future—everything but the feel of my body dancing with slow, swooping kicks. I chase my bubbles up, then down. I fly, fins instead of wings, and breathe out the last months of worry, stress, fear. I give it all to She of the blue, and she swallows it, and me, entire.

At one point I look up at the rippling shelf, the sea's skin where water becomes atmosphere, and it's far, far above. I relax every muscle, spread my arms, and with one kick rise and slowly circle through whirling tunnels of fish, questing for the light. Shoals dart out of the way to make a path, reforming to scribble silver coils as I rise. I fall upward and inward, into the sun and the bubbles dancing all around and the light piercing my heart while my body spins, languid as a top, arms spread, crucifixion-style, face arched into the rising light, there's all the time in the world. My diaphragm convulses, just a little, from a long way away, but I tell it we're fine, it's all about staying relaxed, until I'm up and out with big heaving breaths and time starts up, the film's rolling, the world is known, while beneath me the timelessness is right there, right *there*, waiting for my next breath.

Blaise pummels my belly with tiny heels. She dives like this every day.

Lee monkey-climbs coconut trees with a couple of locals, who take us fishing in their little runabout and teach us Fijian songs, accompanied by the slap of wave against hull. A warm sea breeze steals the harmonies as we putter through crystal water. We make love on the beach, cook and eat our fish, and drowse in the shade.

I take photos. We're happy and brown, me huge-bellied against a sunset, bare-breasted, battered straw hat, looking back at the camera with the biggest grin you can imagine. Lee sleeping, tangled into white sheets beneath a huge window looking out over the tropical sea. Stevie and Andy with wide smiles, holding hands on a beach so pure the silence hangs in the light like ripe fruit.

It's a perfect Sydney winter day, with a sky to cut your heart on, lazy gulls hunting for tourists with chips. The ocean throws sapphires into the air with every wave's demise. All of Bondi is out in the sun, strutting, strolling, skating, surfing, yummy mummies on a pram jam, hipster arses hanging out of artfully ratty five-hundred-dollar jeans, old timers slowly loping across the bay from point to point, arms flashing semaphore, inured to the cold water, the same metronomic rhythm, wind, rain, or tempest, every day, winter or summer.

I'm heavy as elephants, lumber ten slow steps before stopping to let stabbing spiderwebs of pain subside through my lower belly and pelvis. Lee dodges through the crowds on his longboard, wheels click-clicking on the concrete. I lean on the esplanade rails, gazing out, inhaling the day, in love with the whole goddamn lot of it.

My white babydoll dress is positively obscene with the size of my belly. Scarf trailing down my back. At least my eyebrows didn't fall out.

"Get on," says Lee. "I'll push you."

I'm no great shakes on a skateboard at the best of times, but with my center of gravity shot to pieces right now, I'm wobbly as hell. I spread my legs, get my weight back.

"Let's go."

He pushes, which doesn't work. Then he moves in front of the board and holds my hand to pull, which does.

"Faster," I say, loving the feeling of freedom, of movement unfettered.

He trots.

"Faster."

He jogs.

"Faster."

He runs now, pulling me in his wake, my dress flying up and around my waist. I don't care, laughing so hard I might give birth on the spot. We hurtle through the crowd, a two-person train. If I come off, it will be ugly, and this makes it more exhilarating, the sheer stupidity of it all.

God, this is fun, proper-business fun.

"Look out!" I giggle, trying to steer around a slow walker. Somehow Lee gets me into some clear space and really turns on the speed. Rocket boosters, Thunderbirds are GO! My scarf gives up the ghost and flies off my head.

"WOOOHOOOOOO!" I yell and a busker jumps up, grinning so hard I think his face will crack as a gigantic, pregnant, bald, white juggernaut hurtles toward him, screaming to burst with joy, all belly and sails.

"You don't see that every day," he shouts, saluting as we shoot past. I wave and we're gone, clack-clack-clacking on the concrete. The day is sublime; everything is.

I don't know if passersby can see the spectral shape of Wolf Mother loping behind me, banners streaming, tail tangled in wind. Maybe they can.

It's all going to be okay.

Dutch calls.

"Gi-girl," he says. "Have you heard?" His voice sounds funny.

"No. What?"

"Oh. I thought you might have heard on the grapevine."

"I've been a bit busy, love."

"I just hadn't heard from you for a while and realized you must not know."

"Know what? What's up, Dutch? It's not like you to beat round the bush."

This doesn't feel good.

"We-ell . . . you know when I threw up all that blood and they didn't know why?"

"Uh-huh."

"I have liver cancer."

"Oh-kaaaay. You've had cancer six times and talked to it until it went away. This time the prognosis is . . ."

"There's nothing they can do."

I hear the words and a blank, silent space where meaning should be. It wraps me in thick wool. Then sound surges back into the world. Nothing they can do. As in, dying. This time for real. He's had so many near-death experiences I thought the Reaper had given him up as a bad job. Dutch, my wise, wonderful, funny friend, with more talent in his toenails than smart people have in their brains. Dying.

"Oh crap. Double bugger damn and shitfuck. How long?"

"Three to six months."

"*Months?*"

"Months."

"Shit, Dutch."

"Yeah."

"I'm so sorry."

We hold silence for a bit, then I ask, "So what now?"

"Now I get prepared. Can you help me?"

"Of course. Whatever you need. What do you need?"

"I need to say goodbye."

I visit Dutch in his little city apartment with the floor-to-ceiling books, straddling the chair to lower my belly down, panting. We sit, as always, at the glass table we've sat at for all those nights over the years, chatting and laughing and dammit, how can he be dying?

I'm so sad. My Dutch. I want to squeeze so much in.

"I'm planning a heck of a wake," he says. "Penelope's going to sing."

"Can I as well?" I ask.

"Yeah, that would be great."

His face twists. "Liver cancer . . ." he says. "At the end it's not good. You, you lose your mind."

"Oh, love." His mind is razor-sharp. It's his dance floor. His intelligence is a perfume. To lose this at the last, to die raving, is some cosmic joke.

"Hey, Dutch."

"Yeah?"

"You know you saved my life all those years ago, don't you? That if I'm in any way wise, it's because you took the shattered seed of me and watered and fed it until it grew strong and smart and brave again."

"I know, Gigi-girl. But you always were strong and smart and brave. Just incredibly stupid in your choice of men."

"Seems I may have finally got it right this time."

"Looks like it."

We cling to each other, surrounded by his towers of books and the echoes of every night around this table, the quiet, studied tap of his sculptor's tools, carefully shaping the living block of marble he found almost fifteen years ago, not a single conversation wasted. Somehow, he saw through the stone to a woman, chained, and freed her. He's my Willie Garvin, and he's leaving me. This is our goodbye, no matter what happens next. My Dutch. He squeezes, harder than he's ever held me, then pushes me away so I won't see the tears in his eyes.

I've never seen him cry.

I wrote a song years ago, one of the times he had cancer, and never played it for him because he'd strafe me for its sentiment. I sing it in the car on the way home, bawling like I'm a kid, lost and afraid, which, in a way, I am.

Friday morning, quiet street
Sun dripping through the blinds, autumn heat
And there we are laughing, talked all night again with you my friend
You're the lighthouse, I'm the wave
I give you a reason to shine

You show me how to be brave
But where will I be if you won't shine for me?
Please don't leave

Who will I run to if you leave me
Who will tease me into seeing, into being
And who will I run to when I'm run through, if you leave me
Who will teach me, who will reach me?
If you leave me
If you leave me
Please don't leave

Death. Everywhere, I see death. Death whispers in drifts of dried leaves stirred by the wind. Mutters in the small corpses of birds crawling with ants. Clatters hollow bones in the shiver of bare branches against a cold window. Headlines of murder from the dailies.

We're in winter's bone, and the earth turns inward, turns her gaze away from me, withdraws her sheltering heart. I shiver in the chill; I can't get warm. Dutch is dying. And here I am, preparing for birth. I'm impossibly stretched between the two doors, life and death, separated only by a hair's breadth, a held breath, a heartbeat, eternity. I'm an instrument played by forces beyond my ken. Water rushes through my red spaces. Sorrow sings me and joy blinds me. I feel the monstrous, momentous force of Birth preparing to turn me inside out, kill me forever, whoever I am will die and be dust as soon as I move through that portal. Birth. Death. The same door. The same damned door.

Hush, whispers Wolf Mother. This is the way.

"Honey," I say after lying with a dull pain for an hour or so.

Lee's deeply asleep.

"Honey," I say, pushing his back.

"Mmmph."

"Wake up. I think this is it."

He swivels, eyeballs popping. "Your waters broke?"

"No. Pain in my pelvis."

"Contractions?"

"Just pain. I think it'll be awhile."

I don't feel sublime or meaningful. I feel gross and uncomfortable, like I need to have a big crap. I practice my Calmbirth breathing. It doesn't really do anything. I probably should have done the workshop instead of just reading the book.

I lie awake, dozing a bit until it gets light. Through the morning, nasty, sharp pains trigger a crushing slab of fear.

I know this pain. Memories of morphine and madness.

What if I have a bowel obstruction? As the morning progresses, I become more afraid. All the adhesions and scars in my abdomen run with acid. Sharp pains in my thighs. The more convinced I am that I have a bowel obstruction, the worse it gets. The web of scar tissue crisscrossing my organs from my appendix infection doesn't have any give in it. I practically hear the ping as strands separate and snap.

Fear wraps me up like those bloodless ropes, with no give, no stretch. As the adhesions stretch, old stories filter up, of dying in the hospital, the sick hand of morphine pushing my head under until I suffocate.

Heidi the midwife takes one look at me and laughs. "You're in pre-labor, darl," she says. "It's your first baby. This'll probably start and stop for a couple of days. You might have a baby by tomorrow night, or next week. Go read a book, watch a movie. It'll be ages yet."

As my fear evaporates, so does my resistance. Within five minutes of Heidi leaving, active labor falls on me like a wall. Blam. Just like that.

My eyes grow heavy, my consciousness slews sideways. I'm in the grip of heavy-duty endorphins. Contractions come fast.

"I think I'm in labor," I say to no one in particular. Maybe to myself. Maybe to hear my voice: strange, muffled, thick.

And then I can't think about anything anymore.

My body's an avalanche. I surf it, barely. The pain is so huge, so catastrophic, that the only way through it is to scream into a pillow. I become an open channel of scream. All that exists is my belly and scream.

Our plans for a quiet, calm birth shatter in the force of these screams. They are my anchor. I follow each one into the next breath, the next surge, the next scream. The pain is so big the only way I can manage it is to go completely within myself. I can't speak to Lee or even think about him; having another person near me will knock me into the atmosphere. I'll crumble. Disintegrate into component atoms. My body is an earthquake; I'm rattling to bits.

I can't do this ever again. I can't do this now. This is too big, hurts too much. I despair as the feelings get bigger, faster. I can't. I can't. No break between screams, just enough time for me to catch my next breath and then the volcano that is birth does what volcanoes do.

I can't do this.

From some deep place, still vaguely attached to the rational world, a flag goes up. *When you think you can't do it any more, it's nearly over. You're in transition.*

"I think you need to call Heidi," I pant to Lee. "I'm in transition. We have to go now."

I lurch upright, make it as far as the bed, and the next contraction flings me down, bum in the air, the scream now a howl deep and huge, tethered by long bass notes of coal and obsidian. I dimly hear Lee on the phone.

"You'd better talk to Gina," he says, and hands me the phone.

"Hi," I breathe. "I think we should go in now."

"I just left you thirty minutes ago, darl, you were in pre-labor; you've got hours yet. You don't wanna go in too early. You're a first-time mum; it can take days—"

"Hang on," I say and scream, pure and diamond sharp. It trails on and long.

"That sounds a bit more promising," she says. "I know it feels pretty intense but it'll probably be ages yet—"

"Hang on," I say again, and throw the phone down as my body convulses around the gigantic living boulder, and I feel the shape of her, the hugeness of her. The convulsion goes on and on and so does the scream. Rattling bone, subsonic to supersonic.

"Well, you have progressed," she says. "But even—"

"Hang on," I gasp as the next wave hits, no break from the last one, it's a dumper, the scream is more animal, and at the end I feel her *move*, a seismic shift so huge there's an internal clunk as Blaise actually *shifts*, a juddering drop, and the scream turns into words. "THAT FELT LIKE PUSHINGGG!!!!!!!"

I pick up the phone to hear Heidi say in a very different voice, "If that felt like pushing, get in the car *now*."

Somehow, I stagger down the hall to the car, Lee loading the didgeridoo and drum and all the ridiculous things we thought we'd need to usher our daughter in. As I clamber into the front seat, I feel a pop and a warm flood and the pressure inside eases a bit.

"My waters just broke."

Peak hour, winter solstice dark, the wet patch on my dress steaming in the cold air. Rain mists the windscreen. Lee doesn't have his Aussie licence yet and our car is a rough-as-boots Land Rover Defender. I kneel on the front seat, facing into the back with my face between the seats.

I hang on: to Lee, to myself, to the incremental tectonic movement of our daughter kicking the rusty gates of my pelvis apart. I hear hinges groaning, forty-one years of scars and injuries and abdominal constrictions being given no choice.

At the hospital, we beeline for the elevator. I drop to all fours and bellow; I can't stand or walk, my face is in the floor, huge, wet patches on my gray dress where my waters have gushed.

This scream is the best yet, magnificent, operatic, box-office gold, and the elevator acoustics ripple and magnify it up the shaft. It arrives before we do. As the doors open, Lee practically does the splits to hold them apart while trying to help me up. The scream echoes and ricochets through the whole third floor of the hospital. Within seconds, masked and gowned figures appear. I still ride the contraction, hands on the floor, head down, can't stand yet.

"Just a contraction," I say, flapping a hand. "I'm okay."

"Do you want a wheelchair?" someone asks.

A prideful moment. No, I'll walk.

Who the fuck am I kidding?

I'm hustled into a wheelchair and whiz down the corridor at speed.

"Hey, wrong way!" I yell. "I'm going to the birthing center."

They do a 360 in a hurry as the next contraction hits. Hospital acoustics are pretty spectacular. I'm in full voice.

It's Meet the Midwives night at the birthing center. A row of pregnant couples listens as midwives talk about what pain-relief options are available, and what to bring, and how many pads to pack.

The sound of a minotaur tangled in a barbed wire fence resolves into a strange shape flying past in a wheelchair, one big trailing scream fading off as she's wheeled into a room, lumbers onto the bed only to find there's no bath, it's in the other room. Back into the wheelchair, another big, trailing scream as she's whizzed back past the midwives and all the open-mouthed, boggle-eyed couples into the right room and onto the right bed, thank god, next to the bath.

As I howl into the next contraction, I hear someone behind me say, "I hope someone's ready to catch because this baby is coming right now."

And then Heidi's voice, a bit breathless, "Goodness, you really did get a move on, didn't you? Do you want to get in the bath?"

In the bath, another contraction tears me into atoms. Heidi says, "Slow down, Gina."

Slow.

Myself.

Down.

My eyes are closed; they have been ever since active labor began. I've been barely conscious of Lee through the whole process. All my awareness is inward; I'm present inside myself at a cellular level. I know the shape of my insides. I know the shape of her. I feel the movements of her head, her shoulders, her pushing feet. I am the size of a mountain, inside. I am a meteor. Stars line my eyelids. I am the center of the circle, and around me, concentric rings of women chant their timeless joyous song of Birth, of Life. Wolf Mother prowls the perimeter. I am holding and held, dancing and danced. All the magic is real, and I am She.

"The head's right there, you can feel it," says Heidi. With my hand I feel the part of Blaise's head that's showing as my body stretches around her. A tiny rational part of me knows I can probably take another ten minutes to relax into this, breathe myself open, but birth is an earthquake, an elemental force that wants out, wants now, and I want her here. Knowing I'll tear, I push anyway, and the tear doesn't hurt. Pressure eases. I have all the time in the world.

"Her head's out, she's just sitting there, it's all good," says Heidi. "Do you want a mirror?"

A mirror?

I'm so inside myself, the thought of opening my eyes is like skydiving into another world. Participating so deeply that to even answer would pull me out. I struggle to think what a mirror is, or why I'd need one.

"No." Go away. Leave me alone. I'm so here. This is the rightness. This is happening through me, I don't need to see anything; I see with every cell in my body. I am made of eyes and they're all open. This is the most real thing that has ever happened in my life.

The next contraction tears me some more as her shoulders come through, and then there's a slither of slippery limbs. She feels like an octopus.

Here she is, sitting in Lee's hand, a chubby little sea creature, her open eyes slanted, watching. Calm. So much fat on her she looks like a seal. I want her on me, now now now, but the cord is short and as I try to pull her toward me it stretches tight from her navel. Her face is intense, like she's concentrating. She doesn't breathe for a little bit. I tug her up toward me but for some reason she doesn't move.

"You're pulling the cord, drop her down," Lee says a couple of times, but I can't focus, I'm too intent on bringing her to me. I tug at her, wondering why she won't come.

Heidi pinches her a bit, saying, "Come on, little one, breathe." She starts to go blue. Heidi runs off and a male doctor runs in and tries to take her.

Lee barks at him, "She's still attached, it's fine." The doctor steps back. Then Lee says to me, firmly, "Drop her down, Gi, the cord's pulling."

I finally register and do as he says, and she starts breathing immediately, her color changes from bluish to pink, she gives a fitful cry, and my heart cleaves. I will kill to protect this little spark, this perfect mystery, my daughter. Our daughter. Wonder made real.

Her eyes find mine. She is cut from the velvet face of darkness. Her eyes are filled with mystery, like the deepest forest pool on a night so quiet even the stars hush. I fall into them and dissolve.

"Hi, Blaise," whispers Lee, pressed against my body, stroking her tiny hand with a gentle, giant finger. "Welcome to the world."

She has his eyes. I could gaze into them forever. She doesn't blink when I kiss her.

"Hi," I breathe. "You're here."

Lee bounces around, all jacked up on adrenaline.

"You need a cuddle," I say, heading for a shower as he settles with her onto the bed, dim lights, nobody here but us, no voices but our own. Blessed hot water, my body quivering with aftershocks. When I emerge, they're nestled together, his face tender and hers tiny and wide, both of them sleeping, so quiet, so entwined, I can't tell where he ends and she begins.

The hospice is just another floor of the hospital Dutch has spent so much time in over the years. I stagger under two huge vases of flowers, Blaise a sleeping lump snuggled into the sling at my chest.

He looks terrible. Skinny and sallow, yellow tinges in his eyes. His smile is pure him, though, and lights up his face. I see the sixteen-year-old, the twenty-year-old, the thirty-year-old, and the seventy-year-old he will never be. All the versions of Dutch and all the people he's touched with his snarky wisdom.

Hold it together, Gi. This isn't about you.

His bed is by a window. I put one of the vases on it, but he says no, it's best not to have flowers, and I should take them when I leave. Dying people need stillness, not color. They don't need the reminder they'll be outlived by a flower arrangement.

Blaise gazes at him, eyes eternal. She's just come from wherever he's going, and she left the door open when she came through. Death, life, the same damned door. I barely hold the tears in.

"Ohh, she's perfect," he says.

"I wanted you two to meet."

"For every death, a birth," he says. "I'm so glad she's here. How's your cancer? You have to hang around now, for her."

"Blood test results came in yesterday. I'm in remission."

"That's fucking wonderful."

"I can't quite believe it."

"You worked so hard to get her here I'm not surprised you pulled it off. You've always had a touch of Wonder Woman to you."

"Fuck, love, why do you have to leave?"

"You don't need me anymore. And anyway, what do I know about raising a kid? You'll be all right, Gigi-girl."

"I wish you could see her grow up. I really wanted you to be her Uncle Dutch."

"I'll keep an eye on you both, don't you worry," he says. "Don't sing anything maudlin at my wake or I'll fucking haunt you."

"I love you, Dutch."

"Just go be brilliant."

Three days later, I call the hospice. The phone at the nurse's station rings. Rings. Rings. Suddenly, I know the desk is unmanned because the nurse is with him.

He's leaving.

I can't hear through a roaring ocean that's washed the walls of my heart away and only realize I'm already sobbing when a nurse finally picks up.

"You must have felt him. He passed, just now," she says. "His family was with him. It was peaceful."

Blaise will never know him. Dutch is gone. My wonderful friend no longer walks the world. Blaise nuzzles at my chest from inside the sling, unperturbed by the sounds coming from me. My perfect, precious miracle.

part seven Beautiful Girl

the year of 43

I tuck chilly bare feet under myself; I can't be bothered hunting for my Ugg boots right now. My body tracks the length of days, each morning the light's landing later, sending me slower, more inward. Seasons print themselves into anniversaries. According to my marrow, it's officially winter.

Blaise is about to turn two. This time two years ago I was huge and ponderous, yet to meet this mysterious creature who ignites my heart. I barely remember that Gina, left her crumpled on the birthing floor to disintegrate, as all shed skins do eventually. That Gina died. In her place rose a mother.

Morning chai. White flames of steam hunt the sun. It's not quite cold enough to light the fire; not far off, though, we'll be getting frosts soon enough. A male lyrebird sings his heart out somewhere behind the house, running through his repertoire of forest mimicry, a liquid mashup of every bird in the area. There's a new note in his morning serenade, a melodic puzzle. I nearly spill my chai when I realize it's the bubbling glee of my daughter's laugh. It's so pervasive it's become part of the song of the bush.

There it is again, from her this time, a piping, throaty chuckle flung unfettered across the grass. Wallabies barely look up from their grazing.

Lee's reading Blaise a story about a singing cat named Caruso, out on the wide timber deck that overlooks this little valley. The deck faces north, so it catches all the best sunshine. It's scattered with couches of every description, most scavenged from beside the road; a bit of a scrub and they're right as rain. Lee stretches across the long one with Blaise tucked into the curve of his body, staring intensely at the book.

When Caruso isn't singing, apparently the cat's Scottish. Caruso's Glaswegian yowling is fit to wake the neighbors, or would be, if we had any. There's a farmhouse a few hundred meters down the road, with sleek horses who accept Blaise's offerings of carrots with soft, whuffly lips. She even gets to ride one, clinging to the pommel with her head thrown back in glee. She's tiny on the huge creature, but not afraid. She thinks everything in the forest is her friend and talks to them all in the secret language of wild creatures.

We be of one blood, ye and I.

When she was born, we were both bald from the chemo. About three months later, a speckle of titian fire glistered on her skull, awakened by a trickle of sun. She's well named indeed.

It's a mop today, more dreadlocks I'll pour huge gobs of conditioner into and comb out later, though I don't know why I bother. They'll be a mess of sticks and leaves again, soon enough. There's a wondrous stillness to her; when I ask her to stay for these ministrations, she drops into a slow place inside herself, even when she's itching to get away. Her eyes are dark as an owl's. Sometimes when I stare into them, they seem to reflect no light at all, like she's grown from the breath of something vast.

We live in deep bush. Kookaburras sing us awake, and we sleep to the hectic cacophony of fighting wombats. Sugar gliders yip like fox kittens in the trees. The Milky Way spreads cold fire along the field. Our huge self-seeding veggie garden gives us organic food, which we devour around a fire outside, washed down with sweet rainwater from the tanks. Silence prowls around the house, seeps into our eyes and ears, licks the bush with color.

Blaise doesn't know any different. She hasn't had to compress into city walls; she knows the names of all the birds and their calls and greets them every morning like they're singing just to her, and maybe they are.

"Hello, black cocky! Hello, yellow robin! Hello, baby robin, did your mama give you nice worms and beetles this morning?"

She points out wombat tracks and wallaby scat with little fingers, eats golden, sticky wattle gum and sweet geebung fruits from the tree, stands barefoot in the dirt, face smeared, making king parrot sounds until the kingies land in her hair.

My wolf cub is wild as the winds, which know her name. Sometimes the nor'-easter twists and mutters through the casuarinas down by the creek, whispering, "Blaaaaaaaiiiiiiisssssssseeeeee," and I hang on to her extra tightly. I fought so hard to get her here. Nothing can take her away from me.

"Mama, mama, Daddy's found WITCHETTY GRUBS and we're cooking them on the fire NOW you have to come NOW they taste like EGGIES!"

I amble up past the tussock grass to the commotion. Blaise is so excited she jumps up and down.

"Hot," says Lee, blowing on a grub and shaking off the ash.

"I'm giving it to Mama," she says. Blaise is barefoot and dreadlocked, filthy in her beloved pink tutu, which I keep hiding and she keeps finding. She chomps down steaming witchetties like they're jellybeans. Not that she's ever had a jellybean.

Everywhere she wanders, the bush creeps in on tender paws to meet her. She rescues a blue-tongued lizard that's under the weather.

"Mama, look. Daddy's getting all the ticks off. The lizard's got lots of owwies."

She whimpers as Lee pulls fifty ticks from around its eyes, then kisses its scaly snout before releasing it back into its hole. She sings to bees and makes friends with the white cabbage moths decimating the kale, crying when I crush their little grubs between my fingers and flick them into the mulch.

"Mama, noooo, you're not allowed to kill them."

"I'm giving the birds some dinner, love, see? Everything in the world has to eat, and when something dies, it becomes food for something else to live. Like us. When we die, we'll give our bodies back to Earth Mama, and all the tiny bits of us will be regrown into the trees and the rain and the possums and guinea pigs and butterflies."

"Oh. Okay. Can I eat one?"

"These are yucky for us—we need to leave them for the robin."

"She's a mama robin, look, she's not so yellow as the daddy."

"That's right, love. Maybe she'll use it to feed her babies."

"Her eggs are blue. Daddy found a nest and we counted the eggs, there was one two seventy 'leven." Fingers splayed.

Every day I split open and more of the bigness of motherhood falls in. In the beginning it was her cute mixed-up words. "Baise ride bikicle, bikicle fall OHva." Her first word after "mama" and "dada" was "mau," back when we still lived in Bondi with Stevie. She learned it through many conversations with Rex and Lulu. Now any animal is called Mau, including her favorite toy cheetah. Her next word, "read-it-book," one word, is a noun and a command wrapped in one. She devours stories like they're oxygen, must have one every night.

Lee reads books with all the voices. I make up stories, the baby wombat so fat and round he can't walk because he trips over his paws, and bounces like a ball, so everyone calls him Ball. Of course he has endless adventures, even bounding over Old Man

Kangaroo, who shakes a furry fist at him. When she finally sleeps, as my voice trails to silence, I don't dare move. Her little body fits perfectly against mine, flame curls tickling my face. I'm smitten.

Easter holidays roll around. We have a full complement of kids for our Rewild Your Child program. Lee's on the hill with seven kids and the young couple who live with us and exchange work for rent. They help Lee mentor the kids when there's a program.

"Mama," says Blaise. "Where's Daddy? I want to play with the BIG kids and eat ALL the yabbies."

"We're waiting here, love. Daddy will be back in a minute."

"Or an hour," says Amanda, wiggling her toes in the sun. Her two boys idolize Lee like he's Zeus, following him so closely he almost trips over them as he teaches this crop of youngsters to weave grass into string, track wallabies and roos, make fire and shelter, and find snacks in the landscape.

Amanda's daughter Jami is too young to go up with the big kids. She clings to her mother's neck like a monkey while we gaze at the hill over endless cups of tea and the chuckling rivers of mother-gossip. Three trail bike riders careen up our dirt driveway. I wave them away, muttering, "Noisy bloody kids" under my breath. As they turn and blat down the road, Blaise waves frantically and screams, "BYE-BYE, NOISY BLOODY KIDS."

The sun drops behind the hill. Lee's still not back. The program is supposed to finish at 3 p.m., but it's more likely five by the time he remembers these kids have families to return to.

We hear them before we see them, singing down the hill.

Who are, who are,
Who are the wild ones, where do they come from?
Maybe your great-great-grandmother was one.

Wild ones are wise and strong they say
There's a wild one in everyone here today.

Finally, the wild rumpus crashes on excited muddy feet back through the house, bearing bounty and triumph on great fragrant gusts of smoke and clothes in need of a week of bleach, and even then, some of them will never come good.

Everyone's got swag. Fire kits, an old, weathered nest, something's mossy vertebrae, reports of scratches in the tree too deep for a goanna that therefore must be a panther or a yowie, crumbling clay pots, plaited string, a bird leg, tufts of feathers, pails of cooked yabbies.

Blaise bolts to her papa, who sweeps her into the air. "Yabby for ME, Daddy? Eat it now?"

He peels her one, then winces as she wipes yabby juice in her hair. I pretend not to notice. Lee and I have differing ideas about hygiene.

Lee loads the kids into his car to drive them back to their parents. While he's gone, Amanda's sons recite every one of Lee's stories word-perfectly and show their mother how to light a fire.

"Not on the deck," she says. "I don't think Lee and Gina want their house burned down."

Blaise captures Jami's hand and pulls her into the garden to find the guinea pig babies, while the boys make fires in the front yard, arguing as they do.

"I swear, they're on their best behavior for Lee, and I get everything that's left over," sighs Amanda. "Look at them. Little shits."

One of them is stamping his brother's fire out. Outraged cries echo, then slaps and howls. We watch them scuffle and tumble down the hill.

"Maybe they'll land in the dam. Can they swim?"

"Hopefully not," she says, dipping a biscuit in her tea.

After Amanda leaves and Lee's back to spend time with our daughter, I busy myself making a huge salad from the garden, then settle for a moment of peace and a cup of tea.

Lee's relaxed and happy now we're living in the bush and he's running the kids' program. He's found the place the jigsaw shape of his gift fits into, where he makes sense. Turns out he's a kid whisperer. Parents marvel at the change in their children and travel long hours to bring them back for the next holiday program.

I love this man. There aren't too many surprises anymore and certainly no rose-colored glasses. But I love him, from my earth and bones. It's maybe a bit quieter than the intoxicating, turbulent love of the first years. Less clingy and more tolerant. More truth and less marketing.

I love his smell, his terribly inappropriate sense of humor, his practical fashion sense, his inability to wash up, his wild creativity, his intricate theories of everything. I love watching him climb a tree like water flowing uphill. I love listening to him make our daughter almost pee herself laughing. I love it when he smiles just at me. He drives me completely crazy. He gets me laughing so my ribs hurt. He runs toward the cracks in himself where the darkness hides, leans into his sharp places, and holds me when I lean into mine. He takes responsibility for what's his and calls me on my crap. He's the best man in the world. We've been hammered white-hot in the anvil and come out stronger, though it was touch and go for a while.

I never thought I'd have a family, let alone live in such a haven of wilderness and peace and love.

I press on my breasts. Nothing sharp meets my fingers. Everything really is okay.

A commotion down in the paddock. Last light haunts grass tips and kisses the highest eucalyptus leaves, which blush pink. I cradle my cuppa and move from the comfy armchair, my current favorite, lean on the rail, and look into the veggie garden. The free-range guinea pigs squeak when they see me, asking for carrots.

There go my husband and daughter, chasing each other down the hill. Blaise's hair glows amber fire in the latelight. From here, she is a freewheeling picture of joy. Lee's a bear, or a wombat, or a giant, something big and growly. She squeals with the delight of being scared and comforted at the same time. My daughter looks up at me and her smile lights the house.

"Mama! Daddy's a DINOSAUR! Come DOWN. Come down here NOW."

Then she squeaks again and is off, trailing giggles and sunshine and her doting Daddy. I can't resist the magnetic pull of her. Stopping to grab a carrot for the pigglies, I descend the paint-peeled stairs to meet my family through a pale veil of dusk. I chew the carrot into pieces and toss the bits on the grass. Boo, the bravest guinea pig and the matriarch, is the first to come sniffing into the clearing.

"Pigglies," I call. "Dinner."

They all poke whiskery noses out from wherever they've been foraging. I count; they're all there. Their numbers regularly decline due to feral foxes and cats and possibly pythons, then the survivors have babies and bring them up to scratch again. I feel a happy glow watching them crunch their carrots. They won't be handled anymore, are wild around the edges. Like us.

Blaise barrels into me. "Mamaaa." I hoist her high and kiss her all over her face.

"Cheeky monkey," I say, flipping her over and tickling her tummy. Lee joins in and she squirms and laughs and says "Family," which is our cue for a group hug. Lee holds her, she wraps one arm around my neck and one around his, and we sing "Blaise and Mama and Dada, Blaise and Mama and Dada," over and over, skipping in a circle with her oh-so beautiful face wide and open and unfettered as she looks from one of us to the other.

Our daughter is a creature so immense and strange and wonderful I can't comprehend the edges of her. She keeps us real.

We laugh, chase, and play around the house, splash water fights in the bath, run with abandon at the beach. The bonds between the three of us are so strong and palpable you could trip over them.

After dinner, Lee carries her out into the darkness. "Ready? We'll wrap the night around ourselves like a cloak," he says. "And then you'll never get cold or scared. Now look, who's up there?"

"Grandmother Moon," she says, eyes huge, dipping her head into her father's chest.

"Goodnight, Grandmother Moon," he says, and she waves upward.

Snuggling in bed, I sing one of the lullabies I wrote for her.

Blaze on, blaze true
Blaze brighter than the brightest star, 'cause that's just what you are,
Blaze on, blaze true
And when the night seems so dark
Remember who you are
You are the star
That lights the dark,
So blaze on.

Her breathing slows. My daughter is a fragrant seed coiled into the pod of my knees, belly, and chin. Two conjoined parentheses, she and I. She's a restless sleeper, like me. I do laps, she does tumble-turns, we crash into each other in the night, waves settling into periods of slow, deep silence, ripples subsiding as we nuzzle and nestle. *Are you here? I'm here.* All is well.

How can I love this much? How can my heart tear apart and again to allow the fullness of life shared with this mysterious creature? I'm cut wide open to let the big sky fall in. Motherhood is a dying every day, dying to everything I think I know. This feeling is bigger than thought. It is the most mundane of mundane, most sacred of sacred. It is goodness.

the year of 44

Jilly the dog rests her long nose on the reclining chair with a big sigh. Her ears flop against her head. In the corner of the living room, Mum warbles as she drapes tinsel on the tree, arranging baubles just so.

"Be still, Jilly," scolds Danni's daughter, Amy.

"Yes, Jilly, be still," echoes Blaise. She stares adoringly at her older cousin, who wields the nail polish brush like a lightsaber.

"Hold her paw, Blaise."

"Okay."

Once Jilly's nails are rainbowed to the girls' satisfaction, Amy plonks reindeer ears on her.

"There. Now she's a Christmas Jilly."

"Is Jilly a reindeer? Will she fly in the air with Santa?"

"No, but if Santa needs a spare reindeer, she can help."

Lee's out the back, helping Dad with the barbecue. Kris has just arrived with Bear and his three boys. Danni's husband, Jonno, is asleep on the lounge, knackered from spending an hour chucking sticks at the resident koel, a giant migratory cuckoo that whoops in a continuous ascending crescendo above the top deck, just out of range. "Fuckin koel," he swears every year. "Always picks my fuckin window at 4 a.m." Danni's in the kitchen making Mum's birthday cake, with a mask over her face so she won't eat the mixture. I swoop in to scoop up a fingerful.

"GINA. Stop it."

"Shall we get the girls to decorate it?"

"Bloody hell, they'll be covered in icing."

"Yeah, maybe not. Blaise still hasn't had sugar. I want to hold that off as long as possible. Once that genie's out of the bottle . . ."

When we go to the supermarket, my feral barefoot daughter sits in the cart eating a capsicum the size of her head, dribbling red juice all over herself. If she finishes that, I give her a carrot. Passing mums twitter, asking how I get her to eat veggies like that. She doesn't know what sugar is, I reply, knowing as soon as she goes to school, it'll all be over.

"Lee seems much happier than he used to be about Christmas," Kris says, blown in on a tumultuous hurricane of teenage boys. I stick my head around the back door, following the sharp thwack of objects striking wood.

"That's because they're all chucking axes and other pointy-stabby things."

"God. As long as it's not chainsaws," says Mum.

We all share a dark look. Douggie's out there. It's a natural progression.

"Someone hide the chainsaw!" shouts Mum as we collapse into fits.

Bear ambles in, hands full of beers for the men.

"Ooh. Did someone say chainsaw?"

"Bear, out!" Kris points at the back door.

"Can I play with the chainsaw, Pinky?" says Blaise.

"Absolutely NOT," says Mum. "But I have some paint here just for you."

Jilly shakes off her reindeer antlers and trots after the human puppies and their grandmother.

"I'm going to paint your nose blue, Jilly," says Amy.

"No, green," says Blaise.

"Blue like water."

"With fishies. Can we bring Jilly to the treehouse?"

"She can't climb the ladder, silly, her paws won't work."

"Oh."

"But you can bring Mau and Scruffy Bear and all the Miffys."

"Just watch out for the blokes throwing axes, honey," I call after the girls as they run into the backyard. "And get Kai to help you climb the ladder."

"On it, Gi," says Kai, the youngest of Kristie's boys. They call Kris their Step-Chicken, and she organizes them with the same cheerful ferocity that she brings to coaching the dragon boat club she and Bear started, loving her entire family and in her spare time denouncing anyone who's an entitled wanker.

After dinner, which involves Dad tossing sausages onto Blaise and Amy's plates, with Mum shouting at him over the Christmas carols, we clear the table for a card game of Oh Hell! It devolves, of course, into shouting and recriminations, and accusations of cheating, none of it serious. Lee's right in the middle of it all, on a winning streak, palming cards up his sleeve, so I'm trying to take him down. Danni drinks a glass of champagne and goes, as we say in the family, rabbit. This time it means she makes dolphin noises for twenty minutes, then falls off the chair, half on purpose. Bear analyzes current events with anyone who'll listen. Kris bustles between washing up, prepping food for tomorrow, filling people's drinks, and delivering a running commentary on people's Oh Hell! scores. Dad drinks from a tiny glass, his enormous pinky raised. The contents change often. White wine, then red wine, then vodka, then Baileys, then whiskey, then cognac, then vermouth. The wine comes from a cask, and not one of the bougie ones either. I can smell it from the other side of the table: metho mixed with cat piss. How he doesn't get hangovers is anyone's guess. He says it's because the glass is so small.

"Yeah, but you drink ten of 'em," snorts Kris, pouring him another. "You're not getting the posh gear—it's lost on you."

"Bloody waste of money. What do you want to drink that expensive crap for?" he says, knocking back some more Chateau Cardboard. "Ahhh, this is the good stuff."

"Yeah," says Bear. "Go the goon bag, Douggie." The Bear Cubs cheer.

"He's Dorian bloody Gray," says Mum. "One day I'll stumble across the painting and die of fright."

Tomorrow is Christmas, our day of days. It's the first one where Blaise is old enough to understand what's going on. She and Amy plan to wait up to see Santa.

Wherever Amy goes, Blaise is there, face alight, watching with awe and wonder. Amy is all the big sisters that ever were. She has the best games, the most wonderful ideas, she shares all her toys and dresses. Danni and I tiptoe downstairs to find the two of them in each other's arms, asleep next to the plate of cookies for the reindeer. Jilly's painted nails twitch in her sleep, her nose close to the biscuits. The smell must be driving her crazy. Danni scoops Amy up to bed, and I carry Blaise.

"I still think Christmas is silly in summer," says Lee as we drift off to sleep. "But if you're going to have it anywhere, your family is pretty great."

In the morning, the biscuits are all gone from the plate, and Santa's milk has been drunk. I suspect Jilly. Mum's birthday champagne means we're all light-headed by the time we get to the presents. The girls have new bikes, with training wheels for Blaise. They ride them around the back deck for hours, in waves of frothing tulle. On the trampoline, the tutus look like wings. There's so much light I may just dissolve.

I find the lump the day Douggie, who's seventy-four but rides a hundred klicks a week and is fitter than me, is struck from his bike by a car and airlifted in a rescue helicopter to Sydney in an induced coma.

I spend hours on the phone trying to discover where he's been taken, desperately calling the chopper service and trauma hospitals, getting nowhere. On hold for eternity, not knowing whether he's alive or dead, in the air or in surgery somewhere.

Somewhere in those sticky hours I notice Blaise, running around bare chested in her purple tutu, and the thought that's been pinging at the edge of my awareness for a couple of months finally sharpens and takes form. Her belly is too big for a three-year-old.

"Come here, little chicken," I say. She dances over, twirling her fingers in the air.

"Have you found where Pa is yet?" she asks, her dark eyes worried.

"Not yet, love. He's flying in a helicopter somewhere and phones don't work in helicopters; they're too high."

"Oh. Does Pa have an owwie?"

"Yes, love, he has an owwie, but the doctors are going to fix it. Come here and lie down. I want to feel your tummy."

She lies down, trusting me always, and I feel her soft belly, and my throat closes to a tiny whistle as my hands hit something solid, that reeks of wrongness, lurking beneath her ribs. It is huge and hard like a river stone. I know what it is, instantly and completely.

Oh fuck. No. Oh fuck no.

Those countless hours rolling a pea-sized lump in my breast with my fingers. The unmistakable hardness of cancer. Once you've felt it in your own body, you know it forever.

Oh fuck no. No nonononono. This can't be happening. Not my daughter. Not her. Not this. Anything but this. Oh fuck.

Time does something strange, stretches and freezes. The hold music is tinny and trite in my ear. I keep my expression bland as my voice speaks from somewhere far away.

"Thanks, chicken. You have a beautiful tummy. It's perfect."

She skips away. I feel myself dissociate as an operator says, "Chick, is it? From the south coast? We have a helicopter arriving at St. George Hospital in the next half an hour. The trauma surgeons there will look after him. He'll be in the ICU."

"He's alive, then?"

"As far as I know, yes."

"Thank you," says robot Gina, hanging up.

I ask Lee to feel Blaise's belly. My face is tight and, after she has floated off to play with Mau, he says, "What do you think it is? Cancer? It might not be. Could be a cyst or something."

"It's cancer," I say, terror emanating from me in waves.

I feel wholly alone. I know.

Mum's just had a knee replacement and is shaky on Endone and shock. After fifty years of marriage, Douggie's her carer, her lighthouse, her other, and now he's smashed into small pieces somewhere, possibly dying. I scoop Mum and Blaise into my arms and drive to Sydney, not knowing if Dad will be alive when we get there or when we'll even be able to come back. I've packed for a long time. As I drive away from my beautiful life, I already know it's gone forever.

After an hour, the car shudders, then thumps and knocks. It dies without fanfare beside the highway. I nearly break, but my mother and daughter both need me, so I sing songs with Blaise instead and laugh at the funny car, it's got an owwie like Pa, oh dear.

Lee drives up to meet us and rides back with the tow truck as we continue to the hospital in his car, where, it turns out, Dad's already in surgery, an operation that takes nine hours. The surgeons MacGyver as much of him as they can back together again, staples and stitches and pins of metal. Luckily, the rib breaks are within reach; if he lives, he'll be the bionic man, a crooked construction of titanium and blood.

Danni's already there with Amy, and Kris arrives soon after us. We cluster around Mum and tumble into the familiar shapes of the women in our family: life and laughter and tears and love and noise and fart jokes, because irreverence is what we do best. Amy and Blaise fall into each other's arms.

The doctor is grave. Douggie's rib cage is completely crushed. His lungs have been punctured multiple times and are full of fluid and blood.

He looks solemn. "Due to Doug's age, even if he does wake up, the pain will be so great it will probably kill him."

He's taken aback when we all laugh, even Mum, clutching her cane, her swollen knee still yellow with iodine.

"You don't know our dad," say the three sisters, almost in unison.

"He doesn't feel pain," says Danni.

"Yes, but at his age . . . he'll probably never wake up. You need to be prepared."

The doctor thinks we're delusional, but the next morning, sure enough, Douggie's not only awake but, unable to talk and frustrated by the tube down his throat, has taught the nurses sign language and is flirting with the pretty ones.

He looks terrible; drugged, bruised eyes and tubes everywhere, his face puffy as a bullfrog, but I can't keep up when he signs through the alphabet and tells me with flickering fingers that the doctor over there is a bit of a wanker, and those are his acolytes, who follow him everywhere, and that nurse is his favorite.

He spells "acolytes" with his fingers the day he wakes from a nine-hour operation that should have killed him, when being smashed to smithereens by a speeding car didn't do the job.

I know then that Douggie is going to be all right and I'm no longer needed.

Blaise and Amy are playing in the fort they've made under the couches in the ICU waiting room. Their laughter fills the halls.

"Come on, love," I say, packing Blaise's toys into a bag. "We need to go to another hospital to have a look at your special lump."

"Why is my lump special?"

"Because it's yours, love, and not many kids get to have a lump. We're going to take some pictures of it."

"With an inside camera?"

"Exactly. An inside camera."

"Will it hurt?"

"No, love."

"Okay."

At the hospital, Blaise is recalcitrant in the face of patronizing adults trying to do things to her. After days of tests, each seemingly more traumatic than the last, the oncologist finally delivers the news I already know in my bones. It's cancer, but they don't know which kind and need to do a biopsy so they can plan treatment.

Cancer. My daughter has cancer. I wrap the implications in velvet. There's no time for me to fall apart; Blaise needs me to be her guide through this nightmare. My wild daughter, who never wears shoes, talks to the sun and the birds, and doesn't understand walls, will be here for weeks. She needs major operations, then probably radiotherapy and chemotherapy. We could be in and out of the hospital for years.

All I can do is focus on the day's challenges. Blaise must be sedated for imaging and fights every procedure so hard I'm exhausted.

Lee brings extra books for her from home and a fresh breath of wisdom when talking to doctors and explaining things to Blaise. It takes all our skill and patience to help her understand we need to do these things. She's scared, and I can't take the fear away. She's not even three and her body is being invaded: first by cancer, and now needles and biopsies and X-rays and ultrasounds and MRIs and blood tests. The horror of trying to explain what's going on breaks my heart, daily.

Lee and I never let her hear what we're discussing. One of us plays with her outside the room while the other talks to the doctors. We don't want her to think she's sick and defend that boundary fiercely if anyone's careless enough to talk about surgery without clearing the language with us first.

"The doctors are going to take out your special lump, love," I say.

"Why?"

"Because you don't need it anymore."

"How will they take it out?" she says, looking at her tummy.

"How do you think?"

She ponders for a moment, then her face lights up.

"With a spoon."

"Exactly, darling. With a spoon."

A big shiny TV takes up half a wall in Ronald McDonald House, or Ronnie Mac, as we call it, the charity accommodation for families with kids who have to spend months in hospital. Blaise has never watched TV, apart from David Attenborough documentaries on Lee's phone. My heart breaks a bit to see her plonked in front of the enormous screen, eyes huge, eating her lamb chops.

"Whatever gets us through," I whisper to myself, and download the entire catalogue of *Peppa Pig* onto my laptop.

Lee and Blaise need me to be clear, so clear I will be. The screaming, yammering voice of terror that my daughter has cancer and may die is picked up by the scruff of its neck and placed firmly in a box, for later. I simply do not have space for it now.

Finally, after the biopsy, the diagnosis comes in. Neuroblastoma, and the operation is tricky because the tumor is wrapped around her kidney. Neuroblastoma isn't the worst childhood cancer, but it isn't great either. The muffled voice from the box kicks and thumps in the night.

I squeeze into her bed as she recovers from her second major operation, having the tumor removed. The surgeon saved her kidney but punctured the tumor, which spilled its contents through her belly. The doctors reassure us that this isn't a problem, but my dreams tell me otherwise. Blaise tries to pull out the catheter and the drips in her arms. Holding her is like keeping a wild creature in a cage and asking it to understand where the sky went.

Once she's released, we check back into Ronnie Mac to wait for the results. Lee heads home to our wonderful life in the bush, to begin packing it into boxes. The owners are moving back in. On top of all this, we have to move. The idyll is over.

Blaise turns into someone I have never met before.

We're playing in our room at Ronnie Mac when she begins screaming. Her body thrashes, she shakes and screeches. For ninety minutes my child screams like her arms are being torn from her body. And I, cool, calm woman that I am, don't know what to do. First, I try to hold her, but she'll have none of it; she punches and pushes me away. So I sit close and murmur loving words, but they infuriate her more and she screams louder. By the time thirty minutes has gone by, I wonder if she is broken. She throws her body around, thrashing, thumping against the walls or hard floor if I don't intercept.

After ninety minutes I'm angry and upset and done. I tell her to stop, please stop. She screams. I beg her to stop. She screams. She throws herself off the bed again and her head bumps on the floor and it shocks her eyes open.

The trance breaks. She sees me.

"Mama, I need a cuddle."

I break into pieces, scoop her up, and hold her. She burrows into my chest, falling asleep almost instantly, while I kiss her neck and her hair and her face and whisper, I love you, I love you, I will always love you, you are my heart.

Later, while she sleeps a good sleep, calm and peaceful, I realize what I just witnessed. She was expressing the trauma of the operation, of hospital, the fear and rage, moving it out of her body with the innate intelligence of the antelope that bucks and twists after breaking free of the lion's deadly embrace, that movement we've marveled at in the David Attenborough documentaries she loves so much.

Her body knows exactly what to do. I know how to hold this, have done so for decades with adults in breathwork and bodywork sessions. It isn't something to be afraid of or shut down; it's her healing mechanism.

When she wakes, it's like the fit never happened. She's cheerful and hungry. I make dinner and ask how she feels now she's let the big inside-owwie out.

"Good, Mama. Can you make a heart, please?"

I squirt tomato sauce onto the plate.

"That's a goood one, Mama."

"Love, I just want you to know that it's totally fine for you to let your inside-owwies out. I'll sit with you while you do it."

"Oh. Okay. Can I watch *Peppa Pig*?" she says, and dunks her lamb chop in the heart-shaped blob of tomato sauce, and that's that.

Until the next day, when it happens again. Twice. And the next day. These storms become part of her rhythm. I never know when they'll arrive.

While we wait for medical results, we escape on excursions to Bondi so she can wade in the water and ride her red tricycle around the streets in her new Giggle and Hoot pajamas, visiting all her favorite shops and getting an almond milk babycino from Dan at Gertrude and Alice Bookstore. She pulls up her T-shirt to show him the huge scar across her belly. He pulls up his T-shirt and sticks his tummy out until she laughs and covers her eyes.

Cyclones tear through her without warning. I sit in an empty shop doorway as she convulses in my lap and screeches. Again, in the car, fighting against the seat belt, her face purple. In the bedroom at Ronnie Mac, again and again. All I can do is reef the sails and wait it out.

Finally, she picks a fight with me.

She wants to go downstairs to the communal area at Ronnie Mac, naked. She knows this will be a "no" from me.

I block the door while she tries to pull me away from it. She wrestles the handle, yanks and tugs and roars.

I know now. Her feelings are a tsunami. She needs me to be the cliff she can crash onto, a mountain mama with roots to the center of the earth, rearing high enough to touch the clouds. Big, bigger, biggest. I'm the safe place for the hugeness inside her to land. My job is to be larger than her feelings. She needs her inside and her outside to meet, and I am her reflection made huge.

I become implacable. I don't meet her eye, plant my feet, and every time she hits me, I soften my body, but don't waver. When she pushes at me with all her strength, I am immutable. I am a forest in a high wind, a tree clinging to a mountain, a cliff pounded by storms. She is a comet, and I am the planet onto which she falls, over and over.

I tell her I love her, always. She is safe. And though my heart is in ten thousand shards, I don't rescue her from this pit; it isn't for me to save her. This movement is hers, and she really, truly knows what to do if I just stay out of the way and let her move it. This is her dance.

She howls and my heart splinters further, but still I don't move.

Finally, after railing for an hour, she sits back, and her eyes fly open and she says in her baby voice, "Mama, I need a cuddle."

I laugh and whirl her around, my delight, my sunshine, my incredible wise daughter. She wraps her arms around me and we squeeze each other, partners in this terrible, wonderful dance.

"You're so clever, little chicken. You have such a clever body; it knows what to do! You taught your mama something today. I'm so proud of you. I love you to the moon."

She chuckles as well, a quiet, exhausted laugh.

She feels clean. Some huge, festering boil has popped and the worst of it is done. She's processed her horror. The storms go from twice or three times a day to once a day, to twice a week, from an hour each time to thirty minutes to ten.

My own locked box catches in its corners a fallen star, and with it some light. But the true journey is only just beginning.

★

The pathology results come back in. The margins of the tumor are clear, lymph nodes and bone marrow also. Come back in three months for a scan, the oncologist says.

On the drive home, I'm too scared to breathe in case I shatter this miracle of miracles. I was prepared for two years of chemo, to become another shuffling zombie parent in Ronnie Mac. Instead, I bring her to Mum and Dad's, where Douggie's recovering from his accident. My tender little family takes over the big back room until we find a townhouse on the beach in Huskisson with views to the horizon. We move in to the sound of waves, a view of the beach and the possibility it's all over. As far as I'm concerned, it is. Blaise sleeps on my body every night, and when she wakes and says, "Mama, I'm scared," I cuddle her and tell her she's safe now.

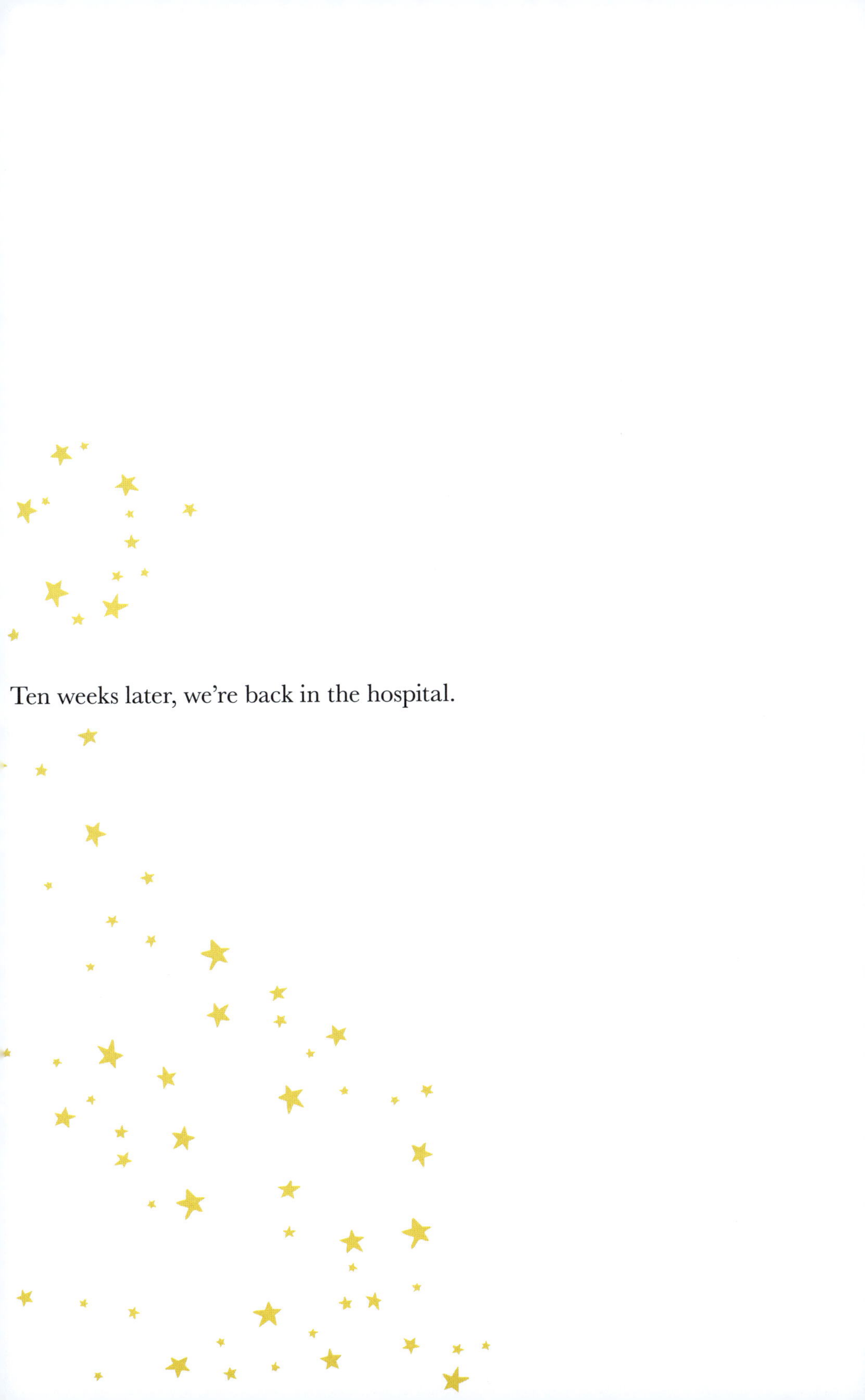

Ten weeks later, we're back in the hospital.

Nine days after that, she is gone.

part eight Song of the Wolf Mother

the year of 45

Baoooooow
This is the song of the Wolf Mother,
Howling at the fell moon
Not cold, yet to me it seems so
Cold as my little one's lips
As the marble forehead I kissed a thousand thousand times
As the limp body I nudge with my long nose,
Get up. Get up.
No life hides there.

I long to be a stone
Plunging end over end into the cool deeps of my grief
Lie still at the bottom
Darkling
Untouched by time or tide.

Against my urges
Life bears me up and out
I pop and bob in the frothy margin

The sunlit slice between ocean and air
Sea and sky
Huge as tangled mountains
Vast as galaxies
Over and over I fill
Breath after breath
Each larger than the last
Each one a rain of blessings
Each one the whisper
The shout
Of her name.

A drift of leaves against the blue. Negative space. The last faint chime of a fading bell. Skies spun from glass. A drift of leaves against the blue. Breath. The faint shout of squabbling children. Spun glass. Three pelicans, south to north. A necklet of clouds, crumbling. A drift of leaves against the blue. Sea-breeze feathers. Negative space. Bleached bone.

Gone.

Before we danced in this here-and-now, perhaps she and I floated together in the mystery. Hovering in the Between. In whatever form we take when we're not in these bodies, just amorphous balls of energy or whatever. Hanging out. As you do.

Perhaps she came bounding, or rolling, or phasing between planes of existence. Perhaps she said—not in words, of course—but trilled or hummed or sang or vibrated:

"Hey. I've got a great idea. How about we go do the human thing again, you and me. And this time, you'll be the mama, and

I'll be the bubba, and you'll teach me about love, and I'll teach you about grief. Isn't that the best idea?"

I've squelched or zoomed or sung, "Fuck yes, let's do it. That'll be fun."

And then we squeezed into strange, heavy bodies that walk and talk and eat and shit and know time and confusion and desire for chocolate and world peace, and we forgot all about our arrangement. Mostly. Well, I did, except for those moments just before I sleep when the walls fall away and I remember I'm more than my skin and then forget again in the morning. I wonder if maybe she remembered the whole time. Half of her was always in the silence.

Now here I am, in the brutish dumb punch of the Real.

I taught her about love, and for the rest of my life, she'll teach me about grief.

While we're here, in the downright horrible part of it all, there's one more part to the story. It's bone-hard but also beautiful, if you can bear it. If this is all too much, though, skip ahead. I understand. I'll catch up with you in a moment. I just have to place coins on her eyes so she can make it across.

We're in the ICU. She's not awake, my little love; she's in a prison of beeping, hissing machines. They breathe for her because there's no room in her lungs for oxygen. It turns out, in those ten weeks she was home, playing on the beach, sleeping in bed with us, over two hundred tumors grew in her small body.

The doctors are grim.

"There's only one faint hope. We give her a huge dose of chemo, try to melt the tumors in her lungs so we can wake her up and treat the cancer properly."

Yes, we say. Whatever you can do.

I watch them pour into that little body more chemotherapy in three days than I received in three months.

It lands on her like a tectonic event. She drops deep into herself, further than I can feel, curled into a tiny spark in the center of an ocean of darkness. She's not questing outward anymore, not searching for me. The drugs are a huge, heavy hand, holding her under.

In that moment, I know my daughter is going to die.

If you are a parent, you know this is the unbearable, the unspeakable, the unthinkable. Every cell in my body retreats from the knowing of it. My flesh tries to crawl off my bones. The resulting no is a howl from some other place, pure white defiance at the gods, rejecting any and all parts of this.

You will not take my baby. I will. Not. Let. You.

I cannot bear this. If this happens, I will die.

And then.

From somewhere beneath time, a voice arrives. That wild, wise voice. Raksha the Wolf Mother, higher self, Gaia, intuition, Dutch haunting me like he promised, whatever you want to call it, I hear it, clear as you whispering a poem of love into my ear right now, clear as the tart joy of a winter apple, clear as light through honey or petrichor or the stunning silver agony of a splinter under your fingernail.

"*Is she a gift?*" says the voice.

Lee sleeps next to me in a cracked coma of despair. We're in Ronnie Mac again, a smaller room this time. I look to see if he's spoken, but his breath whuffles from the other world and my heart breaks for him, for me, for her.

"*Is she a gift?*" the voice says again.

"Yes. Of course."

"Is she the greatest gift of your life?"

"Yes."

"Then everything that comes from her is part of that gift. Even this."

Every hair on my arms is on end.

"And if you say yes to the gift of her, you need to say yes to all of it, even this. Especially this."

These aren't just words, they are a phalanx of birds carrying a net behind them, and in it is contained something boundless. They fly through the holes in my nose and ears and eyes, deliver it into me, complete, older than knowing. The last jigsaw puzzle piece falls into place and I see what I thought was a picture of a forest is actually an ocean. I am the forest. I am the ocean. I am the waves and the breeze and the clouds and my daughter in her hissing cage and, further out, all the children and all the mothers and, further out, every choice that led me here and, further out, all the versions of me that made different choices, and all their lives, spreading out further and further and all I know is that this child is my heart made real, and I do not want to reject one iota of her, ever, in any of the versions of me that may be scattered along endless cresting beaches between the slow dance of stars that make up the cosmos.

All at once, I get it, a ka-chunk so loud I think it will wake Lee.

My daughter is going to die, and I need to say yes to it, simply because it's real, and true, and if I say no, I will miss her last gift to me.

There is nowhere left to fall. I am alive into every single part of myself, and everywhere I look, she is there too.

This is the palace of the real. This is capital-R Reality. Not the reality I want, or think is fair, or think I deserve. This is simply what is.

I am the only person awake in the whole world. The earth breathes with my ribs. Through the floor of this room, stippled with despair and hope and the never-ending prayers of the parents who have slept here before me, I tumble down, down, into clay that stops my eyes and nose, suffocating me.

"Please let me die with her," I beg, but the voice is calm.

"*Even this,*" it says, and my struggles cease, and I know what to do. All noise falls away. All that is left is silence.

If this is my journey with you, little chicken, then I will say yes to it. Pick up my bundle, hold the shards of my shattered heart in my hands, and give them over for you to take with you as you walk your last steps in this body.

Because this is how much I love you. There is nowhere in the whole universe my love cannot reach.

I say,

Yes.

*

And Everything. Falls.

Quiet.

I walk into the ICU wrapped in a cloak of stars and stillness, on a blanket of velvet moss, steady as forgiveness. Kiss my daughter's face, tell her the stories that made her laugh in our other life, already a husk on the breeze.

I release Lee from his relentless vigil.

"I've got this, love. Look after me, and I'll look after her?"

He brings sushi, massages my shoulders, deals with all the messages from people desperate to come visit, then peels me away to watch movies and make love. He tells me terrible, edgy jokes until I laugh, reads *The Wee Free Men* again, with all the accents, me in stitches over the antics of the small, blue, homicidally brilliant Pictsies. We cling to each other and cry together in the small bed, and through it all her tumors don't get smaller on the X-rays. They get bigger.

Yes, I say from the center of the quiet golden pool.

Yes, my daughter is dying.

I know how to speak medical well enough, and it's clear, the chemo hasn't worked.

Yes, it's time.

It's time to let her go.

There are so many tubes, so many places her body has been pierced. Without their snaking stories she is herself again, my little girl, my darling.

"There you are," I cry, pulling her limp body into my lap and wrapping myself around her. "There you are." She's home in my arms at last, but boneless, which feels so wrong. She isn't reaching out to wrap her arms around me, breathe in my ear, whisper, "I love you, Mama." The homecoming is one way; she's somewhere else already, further than I can touch.

I howl, an unearthly sound that bursts from me like skin splitting, like bones tearing.

It is time.

We told the ICU staff we will do this thing. It is not for strangers. We'll midwife her from this world with the same presence and love with which we brought her into it. No extra voices, no doctorly advice.

I administer the sedative, just the touch of a button, watch the fluid drip into her veins and take her one step closer to the dazzling dark. The nurses leave us to say our goodbyes. Blaise is still present; I feel her reaching up to me from whatever deep hell she struggles through, ghostly fingers against the glass, mine pressing from the other side.

I'm here, love. I will always be here.

"Nearly there, my darling," I whisper, kissing her face.

"You're giving your body back to Earth Mama," says Lee, kissing her fingers. "But first, remember to wrap the night around you like a cloak so you never have to be afraid. Grandmother Moon's waiting for you. We love you always and always."

Lee pulls the respirator from her nose. It beeps and the tube hisses, so he stuffs it under a pillow. The nurses probably weren't expecting us to do this bit without them. The beeping is distracting but we can't do anything about it, so we ignore it and focus on her, our beautiful cub. This is the most important moment in all our lives.

I curl around her and he holds me, and it's like when she was born, when I couldn't tell where any of us began or ended. Just one merged ball of love. Birth, death, it's all the same damned door.

I feel the small shudders as her body tries to breathe, but her lungs are collapsed; without the magic of machines, they do not work at all. Tiny little movements deep inside, like a bird caught behind her ribs, her diaphragm doing all the work. Valiant to the last.

I want to open a place in her to let the fluttering bird out, set it free to soar around the room trailing phoenix feathers, escape through the window into the night, cheating this whole story in true trickster fashion. I almost hear her laugh. See, Mama? I was only joking.

It takes a couple of minutes. Not long. The only thing that's been keeping her here at all is the fierceness of our love, willing her to stay.

We let her go.

Blaise dies, in my arms, with Lee wrapped around us both. We sing to her as she flies, our voices strong and true, singing her out of the world as we sang her into it: together. Light paints the walls with promises and the clock ticks as if nothing is happening at all. It's just a normal hospital room, and in it a child is dying and somewhere another is being born and another is eating breakfast and another is weeping and another laughing, playing, growing, falling. . . . There's nothing unusual in any of this, we're part of a great dance, and this is . . . what? Pure fluke, grand design, cosmic joke . . . that our dance floor is lined with mourning bells and ravens, while a breath away a family dances on a carpet of butterflies. We're all connected. Death to life to death.

Lee and I expand to fill the room as she flies away, trying to grow big enough to catch her wingtips and fly with her. We throw our heads back and sing as if to burst the moon; we wail from another world, already in two places at once. We have the room to ourselves; it could be anywhere, anywhen.

The room fills with her presence, her huge light.

The room is empty. She is gone.

She is everywhere.

Silence.

A silence so thick and alive that I almost swim through it to hide my head in Lee's chest. A stillness so rich every atom feels charged with the dynamic fingerprint of her. A darkness of indigo and honey and tears.

I feel peace, and love, diamond awareness in every movement. So much grief I'm turned inside out. Endless, boundless gratitude.

I cover her body with love. The enormity of it all is a constant arrival. Here. Here. Here. I wonder if this will keep bringing Lee and me together or if it will fracture us, grief taking us down separate roads where we can't find each other any more.

I hope not. I don't want to do this on my own.

She's the best thing that has ever happened to me. The best thing I have ever done.

How can I bear it? I feel euphoric in my expansion, so much presence and wonder in the space of death. My heart is so open the tiniest puff of wind reveals its edges.

Lee dresses her with exquisite tenderness in her favorite rainbow skirt and purple shawl, and suddenly she is Blaise again, time resumes its march. It seems impossible she won't wake up, our one precious cub. We have to let her go. Grief swells in us both again.

Lee carries her through the hospital to the morgue, the purple shawl covering her body. No plastic bag for her milk skin, just his warm arms, his father love. The nurses pull all the curtains closed in the ICU so other parents won't have to see their darkest fear made true.

I sing softly as we proceed. We make a strange procession; people look back at us, it's obvious something monumental is going on but there are no real cues. Our favorite nurse walks with us.

Sacred isn't a place outside us; we carry it in our awareness, in our movements, in our intention. We bring it to this walk: every step, every breath in honor.

The attendant comes to meet us at the entrance to the morgue, solemn as a monk. Waits for us to say our goodbyes and hand her to him.

We sing the song I wrote for her when I was pregnant. "Beautiful Girl." The nurse weeps next to us. Lee hands Blaise to me for one last embrace. Her body is cold now, her face marble against my cheek. I kiss her eyes, her forehead, as if I can kiss the life back in, but I can't, she has already flown away.

"I'll miss you every day, love," I whisper. "Thank you for choosing us. Thank you for walking with us for a while. Thank you for changing our lives forever. You're off to have an adventure, my darling, and one day I'll find you so you can tell me all about it. Wherever you go now, know you are loved. Until the end of time, I will love you."

It is time.

The attendant takes her inside. The doors close.

She is gone.

She is gone.

I say yes to that, as well.

Yes, and yes, and yes.

My second day back home. Her laughing ghost streams wild hair and silken fairy wings. Dark eyes flashing urgency: come play with me, now now now now now.

"Come ON, Mama, come outSIDE." Tugging at my hand with both of hers as if the world will suddenly end before she can get into the middle of it and she'll miss something hugely important like a sunrise, or a baby lorikeet wheezing from the gnarled banksia, or a unicorn that is really a shell, all white fluted edges, scrubbed clean by the sea.

She's in the dappled shadows of the trees, peering at bugs in the bark, giving them all names. Her silhouette wavers along the beach, letting sand trickle through her fingers to be caught by the wind.

"Look, Mama, the sand makes wings. Can we make a sand bird? Can we?"

"Of course we can, love."

She hovers in lost ordinary rituals, the everyday ceremonies of cups of tea gone cold, lamb chops and veggies and tomato sauce in the shape of a heart, lights out, hurry up and read-it-book, Mama.

Read-it-book read-it-book read-it-book.

I see her so clearly it's baffling that I can't hold her. Her handprints are all over the glass door; there's a small smeary dot where her nose pressed against it like a puppy's, pining for release into the unfolding goodness of sunny days. How can she not call out from upstairs? How can the bed be so bereft of her warmth?

Blaise's dancing ghost trails me down the main street of our little seaside town. Since coming home, I've been wrapped in the gentle, tender arms of this community. The whole town grieves. They all knew Blaise; she was a glowing fixture along this street, and I see she's mourned in red eyes and hushed conversations, in compassionate glances and mothers hugging their kids extra tight, kissing tops of heads, and forgiving tantrums where there would usually be a scolding.

Strangely, I seem to have the most solid roots of anyone I meet. I feel no sense of wrongness, injustice, or cruelty at her loss. People leak tears as I pass, yet in public I am straight-backed and supple, dry-eyed, cloaked in certainty that everything is in its place, this is simply what happens sometimes. Life is. So is death. People die.

I sink into the acceptance that I inhabit a world without her exuberant form skipping through it.

Yes, she is gone. The world still has beauty.

I'll survive this.

One man says to me, "You're in shock. It hasn't sunk in yet."

I flash with anger. My daughter just died in my arms and you're telling me how I feel?

Then I realize I'm not presenting with his picture of a grieving mother. I should be tearing my hair from my head, catatonic and paralyzed. My calm is suspect, is other.

My experience is of the silence in the center of a heaving weather cell. I'm huge and quiet and reverent until a wave sweeps in to dump me and then the tears come all at once, a sudden flash flood of raw, puling chaos. I do my weeping in private, where nobody's drawn to comfort me, because really, they try to comfort that lost place inside themselves, not me; their comfort is akin to a "hush, hush," and I do not want to halt these waves, their rhythm makes sense, each one is a gift from her and therefore sacred.

I'm protective of my grief, which can be derailed with a well-meaning hug. I need space to expand into the guttural honesty of howling, need to shout myself hoarse and beg and plead into an uncaring universe.

"Give her back!" I scream, lying on the carpet at home. "Give her back give her back give her back!"

I feel like the arctic peoples, with their myriad words for snow. I wear all the beautiful colors of sadness, each with its own flavor, its own perfect time. My snow cloak.

My mama self misses her with every fiber. I risked all of myself loving her, and that's now how big the pain is. But it is also the gift, so I say yes to every shred of feeling that comes with loving her. Grief moves through me and on the other side is simply grace.I walk down the street and smile at her ghost, so grateful it's a joyous one, looking back impatiently at me from the bike path where she's scooted ahead, curls on fire, legs pumping madly, her grin infectious.

"I win, Mama. You couldn't catch me because I was SO FAST I was faster than an EAGLE and a BEAR and I was FLYING, did you see? I win."

Yes, love. You do.

This is no white Western funeral marked by people in scratchy clothes. No stranger casts sprays of stilted words to land on a wooden box covered with flowers of the most cloying scent.

This day is a goddamned Viking funeral, a stupendous shout to the heavens that life must be celebrated and the life of a child must have color and music.

We begin with a gathering, a making, and a feast.

Our little place fronts onto the beach. A strip of reserve stitches the two together. The reserve is grassy, with tall old trees hugging the sky and a bike path winding through. Random sounds of tinkling bells and laughing children form a backdrop to our activities.

Lee's a monkey, climbs trees like he was born in one. He shimmies up the largest of them with a fat, heavy rope around his bare torso, carrying it up, up, making it look easy. This tree opens rough arms and welcomes him, offering hand- and footholds where before there were none.

Kids watch in awe. He's Spider-Man, for real, already a god in their eyes. He spends a long time fixing the rope; fail-safes and U-bolts and double attachments, and a ripple goes through the kids as they realize he's making a swing. But this is a swing like an eagle is a bird, like a whale is a mammal. It's the swing of all swings, the essence of swing, what all swings want to be when they go to heaven, a giant finger tracing an arc so large he's attached a climbing harness to its nether end so nobody can fall out.

It's a symbol, a defiant signpost.

It says: Today is going to be fun.

I carry a giant multicolored Afghan rug and some cushions out to the reserve; this rug can fit a multitude of well-padded bottoms. Tubs of colored cardboard and markers and scissors and ribbons and more tubs filled with strips of paperbark and even more tubs filled with a riot of pink and purple flowers.

The bottom level of the house has been co-opted by my mother and Lee's. It's festooned with tables and giant pieces of cardboard. Mum bustles around with a hundred enormous photos she has printed of Blaise. The photos must go on the cardboard and be decorated; here is glitter and stickers and more markers; we need volunteers, who's feeling creative?

Mum's a force of nature, weeping and laughing prodigiously as each photo brings my daughter to life. Surely Blaise will leap off the pages to run through the whole chaotic spectacle, clapping her hands in delight and shouting, "Pinky, there are so MANY PEOPLE!" The kettle never stops boiling; tea is ministered like medicine, and there's a limitless supply of tissues.

The circus has come to town. Not a single person wears black. Some of the kids clutch invitations to the biggest party of the year: wear pink and purple, fairy wings optional.

A friend skips along in a multicolored striped Lycra bodysuit with tiny wings, looking like a demented *Alice in Wonderland* bumblebee. Stevie twirls his purple tutu and fairy wings, muscular legs gorgeous beneath bubbles of fabric. He made it all, of course. Someone paints faces in the sun next to the house; sprays of cherry blossoms wind along cheekbones, kids and adults waiting in the queue, weaving sprigs of flowers into fantastic creations until it's their turn.

A sigh rustles through the party. Lee runs backward, pulling on the rope from the bottom of the swing as the current lucky kid dangles higher and higher. It's like a ride at Luna Park when he lets go. The true majesty of the swing unleashes its physics and, if you're in the harness, it's impossible not to squeal.

Men do important things, setting up extension cords and speakers in the beach shelter that is our base, figuring important logistical stuff in little groups, hips akimbo, pondering how to hang Mum's photos so everyone can see them and is there a ladder and whose turn is it to push that bloody swing?

On the Afghan rug, a Greek mama holds court. She lost her husband a couple of years ago, and she does widow like nobody's business. Her widow has a multitude of generations of entitled mourning behind it; she dares anyone to out-grieve her. At one of my women's circles, she encountered another, younger friend, also bereaved, and for the first time, the Greek mama had competition. They had a widow-off.

"My kid doesn't have a father," she declared passionately, eyes watering.

"At least you got to HAVE a kid," countered the younger woman, and so it went, the rest of us goggle-eyed and afraid to breathe in case we broke the spell and halted this magnificent spectacle of gloves-off, smackdown female mourning.

This morning, all three of us commandeer the rug. I hold my hand to my ear, theatrically listening to something in the distance, and say, "Hear that? That's the sound of me taking the gold medal in the grief Olympics. Give up your titles. I win." We collapse into giggles at the wrongness of the joke, and also the rightness of it, because god, it's good to laugh and death can be funny.

Chattering mothers push flowers into strips of paperbark, others glue photos and glitter to cardboard. Colored ribbons are wrapped around a giant twisty branch to create a Story Tree. People hang written offerings; poetic leaves twist from its beribboned fingers. All around, kids flit like garnets in the sun.

For a moment my heart thumps and breaks because Blaise would have loved this so much; it would have been every birthday rolled into one, which in a way it is.

Food happens. Pastries and rolls and casseroles and dips and fruit and tarts and delicate wings of meat and sauces and each is more mouth-watering than the last.

More and more people arrive, clustering in the shelter at the top of the beach where the photos now hang. Blaise is breathtaking with her titian curls and huge smile.

A new pink stripe shines through my hair in my daughter's honor. My pale silk dress ripples and flutters in the cold wind.

A child I barely know approaches me shyly, holding out pink flowers.

"I made this for you," she says. "You need a crown."

I cry for the first time. She has woven me a crown of dark pink roses, and it's true, I do need a crown. This one is perfect. Thorns protrude. They help it stick to my hair.

The transition from party to ceremony is organic. Laughter fades, and we grow solemn. The sun retreats. An icy wind raises gooseflesh from scantily clad arms and legs; fairy wings and tutus may be the order of the heart, but bodies beg for coats and beanies in this wind. People huddle together for warmth and all faces turn as Lee and I stand before the throng of two hundred people. I falter a little. This is the hard part. Words come, simple and clear, then we sing the song I wrote when she was slumbering in my belly. The last verse is new, and I hope I can make it through without crumbling.

Beautiful girl, we dreamed you
Now you are dreaming yourself a life
And it all makes sense, for the first time
How can I have taken so long to know
That home is here?
Beautiful girl
Beautiful girl
When you came my heart grew wings and flew
And wrote your name in clouds and stars across a brand-new sky
When you came I died
A thousand times each minute
To be born again every time you smile
Beautiful girl, you've flown now
Leaving no footprints on the sand
And it all makes sense, for the first time
How can I have taken so long to know
That home is here?
Beautiful girl
Beautiful girl.

My sisters and mother are magnificent, speaking without scripts. I marvel at the women in my family, seeing them clearly, this tumbling ocean of female power that roars in from both sides: from the deep mists, through my mother's mother, Charmian, and my father's six-foot matriarch, both long gone but present in their fiery granddaughters and departed great-granddaughter. Here is the sole surviving carrier of all the genes, my niece, Amy, who was Blaise's best friend and has essentially lost her only sister.

Lee's father and sister read touching tributes. And that is it, really. But it isn't.

I take the microphone back.

"I know this is hard for everyone. We're nearly done here, but bear with me a minute longer."

I gather my words.

"When a child dies, I think we're presented with a gift. It's so devastating, so huge, it kicks down the doors and walls in our hearts and reveals our own unmet sorrows. We finally have an excuse to let them out. Blaise was the greatest gift of our lives. Her passing can be your gift too, if you like."

Every face is still; they're turned toward me like flowers to the light.

"After this ceremony, we'll release flower rafts into the ocean. We're inviting you to release a raft for your own story of grief, whatever that is. We're big enough, together, to hold this, for each other."

I turn to Lee, who squeezes my hand. Nods among the throng. I exhale; it's enough.

"Thank you," I say, my own tears falling, and I wonder at how much liquid is carried in the ocean of the human heart.

Lee takes the microphone.

"To conclude this ceremony, we're going to sing a song. It's a difficult song to remember, so if you're struggling, just pick up the words as you go along, okay?"

Lee and I raise our hands in the air, palms out, and wiggle our fingers. As we begin to sing, the shelter rumbles with laughter and two hundred voices raise the roof in a crescendo as four hundred hands tickle the sky.

Twinkle, twinkle, little star
How I wonder what you are

The sea of singing faces shines with sorrow and love and my heart expands. People hold each other's arms and waists, people who don't know each other but will never again be strangers lean heads against shoulders, hold hands, while the biting wind flaps hanging strips of cardboard and the photos of Blaise dance.

Up above the world so high
Like a diamond in the sky

The wind drops at the last. So many voices in unison soaring up, up, carrying to my little one this simple message of gratitude.

Twinkle, twinkle, little star
How I wonder what you are.

The cheer is a roar that spreads down the beach. We follow its momentum, carrying baskets of flower-bedecked rafts as a bizarre procession of pink and purple dances and sings along the white sand to where the mouth of the creek enters the sea.

As we round the point, we collide with the full force of wind, blowing up from Antarctica, straight into our faces, whipping hair and wings alike into a frenzy. It's not pretending any more. A cold and ravenous beast hunts us. I blanch.

I place a raft in the water where the creek rips into the sea, and my offering blows back onto the rocks. The weather is a club, pounding our plans to ruin.

This is not going to work.

Two hundred people slip around and up the creek bank, hesitating. We need to be on the other side, but the wide lagoon is waist deep and the wind is ice. Everyone hovers. Hesitates. What now? If we lose momentum, the magic will be lost.

And then, my father makes it all okay.

He simply wades into the water, and just like that it's decided.

We shall cross, all two hundred of us, to the other side, where we can do this thing right.

I weep tears of awe and joy as children are hoisted onto shoulders, grandmothers helped across shoals, and lines of people pick their way to the shallowest crossings like migrating animals.

I'm one of the first across and point my camera back. The sun appears, briefly. The lagoon seems strewn with backlit flocks of wading water birds, walking on water. Someone at the back has a huge bubble maker, and clouds of rainbow bubbles whip along the water like transparent balloons. Well-dressed matrons sink to their waists; the wind is freezing, and still they come, everyone helping everyone else, hands clasping hands, men handing women handing children across, pointing out deep holes, guiding fingers indicating easy passage. A handful stay dry on the other side, and this is also perfect; we form an archway of love down both sides of the river. I snap photo after jubilant photo, my grief forgotten, this is honest-to-god magic happening right here and now.

A dear friend and one-time lover grabs my hand. "Gina. You have to watch this."

The rafts fly.

Clouds bruise the horizon, low and dark as wrath. Wind whistles and roars like an animal. The tide screams out as rafts spear into standing waves. Hundreds of rafts, each bearing bright flowers, drops of blood glowing against the gray day. Big rafts, little ones, capsized ones, rafts with sails and messages and offerings; one is even on fire until a wave swamps it.

I hand my camera to someone and wade into the water. Deeper, deeper, until I am up to my waist, my silk dress tugging at my legs. The rafts are beautiful. People spent hours making their own creations. They whistle past me like her life, here and then gone, to tumble and crash in the waves. Some make it through to deep water, others are washed back on the beach like broken butterflies, and this is also perfect.

My daughter is dead.

My daughter is dead.

My throat opens and from some other place I sing a Hawaiian healing chant given to me by Kahuna elder Aunty Dawn long ago on a trip to O'ahu, my voice deep and raw and cracked, a pure channel from my toes to the heavens. My love pours out. I sing into the waves and the wind and feel everyone holding me from the shore.

And then I falter.

I have no raft, no flowers to offer.

But I do.

The crown of roses, pricking my scalp. A gift for my baby.

I lay it in the water. It floats downstream, a circle of scattered blood; she is drifting away from me.

She is dead. My daughter is dead.

My hands cover my face, and I buckle.

In the maelstrom of wind and wave, waist-deep in arctic water, surrounded by ranks of my extended family, I finally break, and it is the shattering of a huge ship, the melting of a planet, a mountain sundered. I howl and thunder, it is like no noise I have ever made before. If grief has a sound, this is it, and it is the rending of a universe tearing in two.

I feel a presence and turn. Dad stands next to me, up to his thighs in the water, ready to wrap me in his arms, rescue me from this pain, but he cannot, nobody can. I reach out my hand to squeeze his. He moves to hold me, but I stop him with my fingers; I'm okay, and he gets it, stays where he is although every instinct in him is to rescue his baby. He leaves me to my breaking.

I wail until my wailing is done. The rafts peter out and then there are no more Viking missives. Just like that, it's over. The day is icy and we're freezing; time to get inside, get warm, have a cuppa.

We make a huge circle on the white sand flats. Holding hands, we start low and, with one voice, raise a shout that culminates in our arms high, screaming, laughing, cheering.

Clouds that held their breaths this whole time bless us with a pelt of cold tears to add to our warm ones. Everyone scatters for the cars.

There is one more part to this long day.

Our local community hall has great acoustics and a sprung wooden floor, perfect for dancing. Now warm, showered, and fed, a revived throng of revelers appears. People bring drums and shakers and candles and rattles because damn it, if there is a party, there must be dancing. An African woman leads us; she accepts no mis-rhythm, singing and thumping her drum like she's pounding the bosom of the earth itself, until everyone is in time. Her teeth flash white, her body shakes; this is her people's ancient magic and she brings it like the priestess of the real that she is.

We dance, whoop and roar, stomp and twirl, form circles that merge into conga lines that morph into crazy expressions of individuality. This is not a dance of moves, it's a dance of being moved. We are danced and in our dancing are reborn.

I see Blaise in the middle, dancing with us all, twirling around and around in her favorite tutu, feet barely touching the ground, face turned up to the skylight, a universe dancing through her. Lee does his funny wobbly-leg dance, I'm a snaking wave, and she twirls between us, through and around; she is the space between dancers, the softness between beats, the silence beneath the music, the matrix through which every one of us is woven.

She is everywhere.

We dance in shuddering bliss for hours until there is no sweat left in us. One by one, revelers peel off, replete.

I lock the hall after everyone has gone and gaze up. A gap in the clouds frames the face of the pale moon gazing back. Grandmother Moon.

"Hi, love," I whisper. "Did you like your party?"

And then I weep again, soft tears like feathers falling down my exhausted cheeks, because I know it was the best party ever. We did it right.

We did it so right.

I marvel my skin doesn't split with how huge my insides are.

When I was a mother, all my pathways led back to Blaise. I made of myself a shape, a huge castle of mother-ness, complete with minarets and towers and halls, tiny nooks under the stairs for hide-and-seek, trellises to climb, swings of woven vines and flowers. Together, we romped and played through every inch of it.

Now a vast wave has washed away that sandcastle, swept it into a ceaseless ocean, and all that is left is a smooth beach as far as I can see, wide and white, unmarred by wind or wave, no footprints, no paths, just possibilities. The sea reflects sunlight into showers of brilliant discs. No cloud tears the blue. Silence howls in my blood. I can walk in any direction, but nothing calls me yet. So I pause, like a heron, head cocked, and listen, and wait.That space, that structureless plane of possibility, feels necessary. I know life will call me into action at some point, but for now it feels important to be very, very still and listen to that silence. Not to fill it. In the silence I hear the tiniest whisper inside myself. I'm caught in an eddy where time no longer exists, entranced by the invisible.

Leaves show me the shape of the wind: here a squall, there a calm, now a gust ruffles the surface of the ocean, shapes like giant fingerprints upon the skin of the sea. I see the wind as a huge questing creature, pressing against the world with colossal paws, licking at creation with a raspy tongue, urging and asking, can you be moved? Limbs the size of hills, fur streaming with leaves.

I hum with the rhythm of trees, the generous stillness of their dance, gathering sunshine in willing nets, catching light from long-dead stars, breathing out life, each tree a planet homing birds and insects and critters in hollows and ridges. Gravity calls me into the cool honesty of roots, drinking the dark.

The ocean consumes me, down, down. Here I float, suspended, and above is a shimmering circle of light, where ripples and waves tell tales of wind and current, but down here there is no movement, only stillness, and in that stillness I feel everything, every child, every mother, every loss, every joy, layers and strands in a giant web flung out on the breath of trees, catching all life in its tendrils, all the journeys of love and pain and the infinite struggles of existence.

Time is pliable. Nothing is important but to be in the exquisite silence of her gone-ness and honor whatever arises from there.

I sing the siren songs of a mother bereft, the sweet, sweet lullabies of a woman finding her way, and the deep drumming drone of ancient silence that rings me like a giant bell, changing me forever.

The Quiet wraps its arms around me and whispers, *I love you.*

I'm secretly afraid.

An edge grows sharper in Lee, daily. Part of him polishes the blade like a samurai sword with which he can cut away his sorrow, and I fear he's going to cut me away with it.

Lee and I traverse very different landscapes these days. Most of the time we're partners. We lean on each other, but not too much, make love with a passion we haven't shown through the years of parenthood, wander together for lunch and coffee, watch films and laugh. We talk about Blaise often, and occasionally one of us cries and the other holds.

Most of the time this feels true: we're still friends and lovers, and the huge and terrible truth of our daughter's death won't grow spines that slice the space between us.

However.

There is less to hold us together when darkness strikes. We have our places in the too-quiet house. I sit upstairs to gaze at clouds, stars, trees, sunlight dancing on the bay. He sits in his office with the blinds drawn, watching *Breaking Bad*; he needs the darkness of it. I don't want to hear about the show, so we can't share the experience.

This is true of grief; everyone's experience is so different. Grief is absolutely selfish. We can't comprehend anyone else feeling as deeply as we do, nor can we understand anyone else's version of its dance.

For me, something unlooked-for has happened. My awareness has developed new senses, perceives notes on the spectrum of feeling previously hidden to me. I am simultaneously conscious of the tiniest shells on the beach of my heart and the flotsam sweeping back and forth with every wave and the standing lines of water moving inexorably in from the horizon, indifferent clouds in communion with the sun so far above. I feel so many things; grief has so many colors. Woven through them is the powerful thump of missing her. It is a dull roar, a fist in the night, a delicate shower of ice, a furnace of pain. A longing so deep it never leaves. But no matter how big grief is, I am bigger. I don't understand the why of her passing, but I can hold it. Say yes to it.

Lee's journey is not so kind to him.

Here, quietly now, I wonder whether Lee and I will make it.

I miss the easy friendship of our relationship.

He traces circles into his flesh with a small black thorn. The chemo I took to save my life may have caused the cancer that killed her. And although the oncologists say there is no pathological evidence for this, and I know he doesn't really believe it, it's in the corners of his eyes sometimes when he looks at me.

If he can't let it go, we're done. The thought fills me with panic. I've already lost her; I can deal with that, just. But him as well? Not that. That would be too much. Nothing else can die, not ever. I can stretch as far as grieving her, but any more and I'll untether from the earth and float free into space, and perhaps if that happens, I will not mind at all.

The dog paces the back of a big caged enclosure, like a wolf in a zoo, never taking her yellow eyes off us. She traces infinity in the air with the effortless floating glide of wild predators and ballet dancers. I feel like an intruder, just watching her. She doesn't belong in a cage; she belongs under an untamed sky, ghosting across grasslands, lifting her pointy muzzle to howl all unearthly with the rest of her kind, then hunting till the hunting is done.

Sophie, the handler, is chatty. A few people have come to see the dog, but because she's so skittish and terrified, no one will take her.

She's breathtaking. Her tail is bushy and white tipped, the rest of her skinny and fox-like, ribs taut and trembly as she breathes. Russet pelt with a darker saddle, white paws and a blaze on her chest, a white strip down her muzzle. She's the most beautiful dog I've ever seen. Eleven months old, found in the bush as a ten-week-old wild pup, having missed the bonding period with humans, after which she'd be tame. Hopefully someone will take her who can work with her shyness, her fear.

Sophie looks at us.

Oh, and by the way, the breed assessor just came in, and she's not a dog after all. She's a dingo, Australia's version of a wolf. Do we still want her?

Mowgli howls in my belly, drumming leathered heels on Bagheera's ribs. Baloo's mournful snout tastes the air. If it would take a slaughtered bull to buy her, I would wield the knife myself.

Lee and I barely check with each other, both alight with her beauty and wildness. She is a lost young creature needing a home, and we are a home that lost a young creature. We're instantly in love.

Yes. Yes, we want her.

Her ears lie flat to her head as she pants, the whites of her eyes showing, cowering at every sound as we lead her to the car. She crawls into the footwell and doesn't move until we finally get her home. Now she hides in the laundry, her long nose visible behind the washing machine. She will not come out, not even for chicken.

"How about we name her Star?" says Lee, looking at the flash of white on the back of her neck, and Star she is.

She is wild, proper wild, like a wolf cub. Touch is earned and barely tolerated; one hurried move and she bolts or bites.

Star is a lean Houdini, all ribs and angles, chewing through leads and slipping collars, and has to be lured back with raw chicken and crossed fingers. She slinks home eventually, wrapped in darkness with her tail down, her body language scared; it seems for her the night is indeed dark and full of terrors and our house is only marginally less appalling than the stormy chasm of sky, under which she flattens herself completely with her legs splayed, staring up as if it will suck her away.

She needs loads of exercise or she eats the house, so she gets two big runs each day. The first is at cold dawn, after we wake to the sounds of her gnawing the wooden stairs into matchsticks or tearing the curtains to shreds in ripping tugs. I come down one morning to find her wild-eyed in a field of snow. The beanbag offended her in some way; she took it on and won. Resoundingly.

Still, she will not come to us and has to be cornered to get a lead on for walks. Lee feels rejected, and I despair. What have we done? This feels like a huge mistake. We desperately want to love her, and she won't let us.

Then one day she pounces on one of Blaise's colored balls like it's prey, and her tail curls up over her back, bouncing with every move. I roll the ball and she chases it, batting it with her paws, nudging it with her nose. She looks to me to keep tossing the ball to her when I stop.

I don't realize I've been holding my breath for weeks until I let it out. Play means she's relaxed. She trusts us.

Lee loves her instantly and completely and talks about her as if she's a deity. He rises early every morning to run with her, researches dingoes for hours on the internet, mining the annals of dog whispering. He tries out techniques, buys toys and better leads to replace the ones she chews to bits.

I feel ashamed that, although she's wonderful, I resent how much energy is required to have her. How much work she is. How damaged she is. Then she looks at me with liquid eyes in that narrow fox-face, and I see she is a scared baby whose world just turned upside down, and I hate myself for not being able to give her my whole heart.

After these blessed months of space and silence, the house bursts with the chaos and life that comes from a young thing needing love. I'm not sure I have it to give, though I suspect she'll win me over soon enough. She's a symbol of life moving on, calling me out to play.

I'm not quite ready, little pup. I'm sorry you don't understand I can't love you properly yet. Maybe we can be two broken things muddling through until enough of the pieces glue back together to make one good one.

I give Blaise from my heart to the void, from my belly to the world, from my eye to the sun.

Hush, Mama, she whispers. *It will all make sense soon.*

I hear Lee before I see him, clattering *takakakaka* along the concrete, and here he is, crouched low on his longboard, whizzing along the bike path, pulled by Star in her dogsled harness. They split the air to atoms, buzz me at supersonic speed, then vanish around the corner, scattering curses from outraged locals, wobbling on their bikes to avoid them. Lee's cheeky face pokes around a tree, pulling faces to make me laugh while the locals ride past and I pretend to hunt for galahs in the casuarina. Once the coast is clear, the raiders gallop back, unrepentant. I swear Star's in on it from the way she looks up at Lee.

"Whoops. I think they hate me," he says.

"Only when you take a blind corner on the wrong side of the path with a bloody dingo coat-hangering them with her lead."

"Yeah, that was a bit dodgy."

"You think?"

I still have grazes from taking a tumble off my bike when Star went one way around a signpost and I went the other and the lead snapped tight to spill us both onto the concrete.

Everything about her is fraught.

She chews halfway into her lead while our attention is elsewhere.

"Oi. Stop that."

She doesn't.

Lee flips the board under his arm and grabs her collar. Our feet squeak in blinding sand as we nestle into the shade, lying back on a carpet of casuarina leaves. The bay peals azure to cobalt, sea breeze not yet kicked in. Star flops beside us, far enough away that we can't touch her, startling at every noise. She leaps upward at a low lorikeet, spinning in mid-air like a cat, her jaws snapping shut on tail feathers. The bird screeches as it flies away, leaving her to spit out emerald feathers like they're cotton wool. She sneezes.

Lee sighs like a lovesick teenager. "Fuck, she's quick. When the zombie apocalypse comes, I reckon we get three of her."

"There go our plans for chickens and goats. She'll eat 'em all."

"She's magnificent, isn't she?"

"I didn't say that like it was a good thing."

I unpack the picnic: salad and hard-boiled eggs, with an extra one for Star. Lee mixes everything together in his bowl with last night's pasta and pours peanut butter over the lot while I pretend-retch. Star traps her peeled egg between her paws to nibble with the primness of a Victorian aunt.

Blaise's ghost gambols around chasing butterflies.

Lee and I have been talking about starting up the Rewild Your Child program again. Lee's keen. I'm not sure how I'll be around happy families. *Go on*, says Blaise, leaving no footprints on the sand. *Take me with you.*

Lee persists. "How about we just go camping for a few days with Camilla and Amanda? I can't bear to tell those kids it's over, Gi. We can keep it super casual, no program, throw up some tents, hang out with them, maybe take the kids out for some low-key activities."

We haven't spent any time with kids since ours flew away. Blaise fades into shadows, reappears again. Other kids feels like betrayal.

"Won't it hurt too much?"

"I think I'll be all right. It'll be good for me. I need to do something, and town life is killing me."

I feel into the place Blaise left, that Star's trying to fill, that Lee and I dance around.

"It's so soon. What if we lose our shit?"

"Everyone'll understand. We can introduce the kids to Star. They'll love her."

"If she bolts into the wilderness, we'll never get her back. The wild dingoes will have her."

"She'll come back. We're her family now."

Star helps me pack the new canvas bell tent by nipping my ankles whenever I pass her and biting through one of the handles. The tent is supposed to be her hidey-hole. We can zip her inside when she starts chewing through all her leads, although I doubt it will hold her long. She'll eat her way out.

The property we're heading to lies in a gentle haven of soft ferns and huge eucalypts, on a river so clean we drink from it. It'll be Star's first time properly out in the bush. I reckon she'll do a runner; it'll be the last we see of her, once she gets the wild in her eyes.

Despite my doubts, as soon as we immerse in the wilderness, I relax. I love being out with the families, setting up the bell tent, filling water containers from the river, eating under the stars. My heart lifts to see Lee with the kids, chasing each other with plastic swords, Lee doing his crazy high-stepping run with his ridiculous *Wallace and Gromit* face as the kids all charge him, shrieking with laughter.

Star stays as far away as her leash will allow. The kids are all fascinated and want to stroke her, but she snarls if they come close, so they keep their distance. After six weeks with her, my forearms are already striped with scars from her teeth, each one a reminder to slow down and ask permission.

The weather's perfect. Backlit afternoons, mundane conversation around the fire watching Amanda systematically burn every meal for her kids. The mothers hover around me, ready to catch me if I crumple. Survivor guilt shines from worried faces.

Before dawn, I wander to sit in the bush among waves of birdsong, missing my little one. Mostly, though, it's just nice to be outside with friends, the sky our ceiling, the green our walls.

"My womb's all yours, Gi," Amanda says, as she chars toast to a smoldering ruin for the third time on the fire. I had a miscarriage last month, and the women tut their sympathy.

"Amanda, not in the flames. Use the coals, love," I say. Again.

"Good thing I'm better at birthing than cooking," she laughs, patting out the fire and handing the charred remains of perfectly good bread to her daughter, who rolls her eyes.

"I'm surprised my kids have survived this long. Ohh. Sorry, Gi. You know what I mean. But I'm serious. Just give the word."

I hug her tight.

The kids make fire with flint and steel and build a shelter from logs and leaves. Their faces hang rapt as Lee tells *Monkey Magic* stories with all the funny voices. He's more alive than he has been in months. I see how he needs this, and the kids need it too. This is his fatherhood now. At the end of the camp, he cries openly. The kids come up to hug him, solemn as priests, one by one.

At the regular women's circle in Melbourne I've been attending since I was pregnant, I lose myself in our communal dance, ending up outside under a huge gum tree. Grief takes me. I thrash in a trance in the dirt, howling like a banshee. Afterward, all the mothers hover with eyes full of tears, which almost hurts more than the grief.

Kim Farrant, my brilliant film director friend, is thoughtful over lunch. She's directing her first feature, *Strangerland*, which stars Nicole Kidman, Hugo Weaving, and Joseph Fiennes—a huge coup. She leans forward to wipe dirt from my face with her napkin and says, "How would you feel about meeting Nic? She's a bereaved mother in my film; her kids get lost in the desert. That rawness, you're so honest. Would you share it with her?"

One of the worst things is helplessness. Here is a way I can help.

Two months later we're filming in the Aussie desert, in the middle of nowhere. There's a fence around the set to stop gawkers and paparazzi. Nicole can't even go to the newsstand to get some mints without being mobbed. She's always so gracious. I reckon I'd lose my shit.

Filming moves into her character's bereavement. Even between takes, palpable loss radiates from her in crackling waves that bring shivers to my skin. Some archetypal tuning fork vibrates us into communion. Her eyes well when they meet mine. On a day off, in a quiet room we talk about grief. Stories of motherhood. Children always fly away, one way or another. They crawl, then they walk, then they run, then they take wing. Every day we have to let them go a little more.

"I can show you, if you like," I say.

"Really? Do you mind?" She's so quiet inside, sitting with her is like being in a forest.

"Not at all. It's a relief, because it means I'm telling the truth, all the way through."

I lie on the bed and let the wave fall on me. It's like coming home. Afterward, Nic hugs me. "Dear Gina," she says, over and over, trembling.

In the cooling desert, circled by cameras under a falling sky, she claws at her body and screams at the last fading spit of sun.

"Bring her back!" she howls, calling for my Blaise, for her own children, for all of us. "Bring her back!" She doesn't even exist any more. She's a mirror made of broken mothers, but her spell is alight. Maybe it will work when she does it. It's strange watching my grief come out of someone else, but also impossibly beautiful.

Six months after Blaise flew away, I burn to rage.

Towers of anger reflect not in the high clouds I so regularly gaze into, or the lulling water-songs of my beach, but in the padding paws of Star.

When I was Mother, everything revolved around that state. Non-mother was a reality I could dance with, a beautiful, terrible emptiness.

Since welcoming this four-pawed creature into our lives and our pack, I'm now almost-mother, kind-of mother, nearly-mother, and it's too hard to bear.

Rage circles the fire of my heart, a deeper shadow in the inky night, trailing tendrils of ice and fury. I howl into the baleful dark, creeping with shadows. Twin red discs stare back at me. It's a relief to dive into them.

I pick up the sword and pant with long teeth, daring any predator to come and find me. Bring me your cruelties, that I may mete out justice. Bring me that which is ready to die, that I may smite and smite some more. I am storm-bred, raise waves the size of mountains to drown ships and their passengers, and cast birds from the sky. I am a stone banshee stamping her feet and clapping her hands until entire villages fall from cliffs into the sea.

Bring me anything, everything, to fuel my unquenchable fury about the one thing you can't bring me, no matter how I beg and plead and bargain, so instead I must rage until there is no "I," there is only rage.

You cannot bring back my daughter.

I punch pillows until they surrender, scream until whispers float from my throat, but still the truth is bigger.

I can't bring her back.

Rage cannot last forever, all waves must tumble and foam, and in the aftermath spreads a silence so still and profound that I lie on my back and feel the blessing of light weeping from a million, trillion stars, filling me with the force of creation. And as I lie, beneath me spreads the full magnificence of my snow cloak, in all its resplendence. I see threads of red running through it now, ochers and ambers and the devastating beauty of blood.

I am weaving such a thing of beauty, bringing life into every corner of my being, simply by saying yes to it all.

Eight months now. Time keeps rolling over, carrying her further away, or maybe just carrying me further from her. I barely remember those first weeks of emptiness, staring at the sky. Life has well and truly picked me up.

Blaise's legacy now extends to this.

Our little camps have ignited into something far bigger than Lee and I could have dreamed. What began as a simple gathering of three families under a small canopy of forest has turned into a huge event, touching hundreds of lives. We quickly outgrew the glade in the blue gums. Our venue is now a big field on a private property surrounded by wilderness. It meanders along a kilometer of river that streams straight out of the mountains, so pristine we swim and drink at the same time. Kids surge up a little track every day to the secret bush camp they built themselves with their mentors. For four hours each morning they learn to be at home in the wild while their parents hang out around the fires, dropping into slowtime.

Lee and I slide into new roles as we midwife this village into being.

I reek like some happy forest creature: a wallaby, or a bandicoot, perhaps. Hair of smoke and earth. Burn scars crisscross my hands from wrangling heavy camp ovens in the blistering heat of the fires. Splinters and cracks stud my bare feet. Good dirt blackens my nails.

Everything aches, but it's a delicious hurt, the best kind: from sleeping scant hours on lumpy ground, chopping huge rounds of hardwood into manageable pieces, lugging endless crates of food tins, digging slippery trenches and compost holes. Bush stories scratch my skin, rattle my bones. Wombats scronch and chomp on grass around the tents at night. Vast, brooding cliffs with ten thousand faces encircle the camp, tall enough to hold back the stars trailing fire across the sky as they fall to earth. Our local Aboriginal elder blows sweet eucalyptus smoke into every face and welcomes us all, one by one, to this country.

I'm not sure how it happened, but I'm the matriarch of a village, and somehow, I know how to do this thing in my DNA. It's not just me awakening to this ancient wisdom. Lee's always said he makes sense in service to a tribe, and now I see it. He's magnificent, leaping around the fires as a troubadour, weaving stories so fantastical that even the adults' faces are breathlessly rapt in the firelight. He's come into himself, bringing elegance of thought and an innate understanding of social technologies to curate a program that brings hunter-gatherer skills to modern humans.

The camps follow a timeless rhythm; humans gather, move apart, regather. We're all fisher folk, sailing out across the landscape, then coming together to share our catch. Nights ring with stories as we congregate around the fires in our longhouse without walls, where every voice is as important as every other.

Songs bubble up from the land and through my cells to emerge in three-part harmonies I pluck from the air in golden strands that wind through the trees and cliffs and chuckle from the river. I teach them to the village gathered nightly around the fires. Songs of wind, water, earth, and connection. Songs of celebration and renewal. My heart leaps when the different melodies click together and the song becomes something alive, weaving our little family together in one triumphant voice. Dutch nods from the shadows, his twisted smile approving of the music pouring from my heart into 150 others, and from there into the welcoming bosom of this land we love so much. Behind him, the ghost of Blaise twirls in her tutu out under the moonlight.

I take a break from the spoon I'm carving with my gorgeous new hatchet and lean my head against Lee's shoulder, surveying our school without walls from the top of the hill, as afternoon sunlight lines the tents and joyous faces run through the camp.

"Blaise would have loved this. All these kids here to play with her."

He kisses my hair.

"And her in the thick of it, teaching them what all the animal poos are."

"She's here anyway, though, isn't she?"

Fifty kids with muddy faces and sticks in their hair romp and play. Shrieking piggyback racers tumble down the hill, beneath the line of kids taking turns on the mega-swing. Star rests beside us on the high side of the field.

"I heard the teenagers planning a game of spotlight," I say. "We'll have to let everyone know about headlamp etiquette again. Those things are bloody lightsabers."

"I'll sort that tonight if you like, before the story. You doing a song after dinner?"

"Yup, a new one, a three-parter. It found me on the drive in. It's a cracker, called 'Love This Dirt.'"

A bunch of kids share apple slices to cook on long sticks over the fire, others group around a freshwater crayfish someone caught in the river. Mentors break out musical instruments for an impromptu jam that turns into a flash mob.

Wherever I go, voices sing out "Camp Mama!" and hands wave as I pass. Kids line up in the morning, around the fire, for Camp Mama hugs. Some of the adults line up as well. I've stopped being a mother to one child and have instead become mother to a whole village.

the year of 46

The first fragile light calls me into wakefulness, tangled in bedclothes and the memory of this dawn a year ago.

It seems surreal, that it's been a year since Blaise flew away.

In the early days, each second lasted an hour, each hour a week, each week, months. And yet already the jasmine is flowering again and the scent of it takes me back into her room, the stink of hospital chemicals not quite overpowered by those little white flowers doing their valiant best.

Time has become truly fluid for me. Streams of it interlace around and through me. Depending on which of those rivers I inhabit, time lifts, lulls, fetters, or flattens.

In one stream it gallops, whitecaps cresting like eager horses, urging faster, faster, and I see her shimmering form in their foamy faces, her body straddling broad equine backs. Hair flying, elated, she flies along the mouth of the current astride her brilliant white steeds of air and mist, turning back to call, "Mama, quick, come look, there's so much beautiful, hurry UP, Mama."

In another stream I flow with glacial slowness, tracking every scratch of grief, my movements gluey and honey-stuck. I have time to notice each exquisite nerve ending as my heart fires a different terrible shade of pain; my skin burns and crisps with the flames of missing her, my belly thuds hollow and heavy in her absence, my bones rattle and echo in the space she left.

In another, I skip across the stepping stones of daily life without her: sleep, wake, eat, cry, dance, cry, eat, dance, sleep, repeat.

I inhabit these entwined strands simultaneously, time shifting and distorting until I have no inkling which when is the one other people live in. Grief is really love; this is the truth I keep coming home to. This is how big my love for her is, this country of grief, this place where I live. It has no boundaries and its horizon is a true one, one I can never catch. No matter how hard I run, it lopes endlessly further, the days rolling on their backs and the clouds floating carelessly above, dreaming of rain.

So here I am, a year on. Losing her has not destroyed me. In the quiet light that echoes that other liminal October dawn, I feel the space at my belly that is forever hers. Her back listening to my softest songs, hair tickling my nose. We could lie like this for hours, snicksnug and safe. But not safe, because safe is an illusion. Nothing is ever safe, not really; safe is just a series of stories we tell ourselves so we can sleep at night.

Our only true safety lies in our own resilience and honesty, in being able to look our darkness in the eye and say, yes, you are part of me, a segment of my deepest mystery, even if I don't understand you yet. Safe is being willing to reach through our fear to clasp the hands of our demons and welcome them in. Not hiding from any part of ourselves.

I remember Blaise saying, "You can't die, Mama. Because then you'll go somewhere and I can't come too."

She's gone somewhere I can't reach, but I catch a tendril of suspicion that I'm already there, that I always have been, I just don't know how to stretch my senses enough to feel it.

Time marches on. I can't reason or bargain with it. It takes her gone-ness and makes it years. There's no pact I can make, other than freezing in my grief, stopping my life force from moving on, choosing to die in this single moment over and over rather than let Time carry her further away from me.

I see a future where I choose this path, keep a house as a shrine to her three-year-old self, tending and dusting, trimming its lawns, and lighting its candles, a house where neither of us ages. I could hide here forever, cutting myself open again and again on memories and regrets and the shame of the undone and unsaid, the actions I can never rescind.

I see why people crystallize around pain. It holds their loved one close. By being carried by grief rather than carrying it, I am swept away from her, which feels a little like betrayal. My memories of our life together have faded; to keep them fresh I'd have to go over and over them, tracing them anew each time, but when we do that, we don't trace perfectly. We change things a little, until the memory we cherish is a poorly scribed leaf of history.

It would be so easy, in a way, to walk this path. End my days in a room of love and loss, caught in an Escher loop of what-ifs. But to choose this is to say my life is done, that without her I am over.

I'm not done.

Life is so precious I can't squander mine. This child has touched and transformed me in ways I cannot fathom. Can she reach through me into the world, the two of us now blended into one? Surely that is what we're designed to do, transform our pain into art and give it to the world like a shout in the dark.

The space at my belly, where she isn't, is cold. I thought I'd spend today folded into myself as a small, quiet bundle, nose to tail, soft and reflective, but I'm restless and need to move. I open my laptop, check the news, social media.

Then.

Time freezes. In that stasis I stare at the familiar layout of my Facebook newsfeed. There's something strange about all the posts, from people all over the world.

They all wear my daughter's face.

Am I mad? Hallucinating?

I don't know what I'm looking at, at first, but after a few seconds I understand.

I scroll faster, feeling my heart burst into a thousand shards, and every fragment is alight, resplendent with love. Radiant with her.

Everyone I know, it seems, has chosen a photo of Blaise to use as their profile picture for the anniversary of her passing. Hundreds of people honoring my daughter this way. Some of them with words, or memories, some of them just a photo. Like a flock of starlings exploding into a high sky, her essence has showered across the internet and each photo is a note in a shining song celebrating my lost daughter, now in hundreds of hearts.

Here she is in one of her amazing outfits, too-large sunglasses pushed back on her titian curls, mismatched socks pulled to her knees, one tutu tucked over the other so all the colors show. Here again, standing in the bath covered in charcoal after a day cooking witchetty grubs in the backyard, impish face black, holding a bar of soap, which is also filthy.

Here she is on Lee's shoulders, waving her chubby arms in the air, both of them flying across the grass against a Prussian-blue sky. Now giggling on the sand, making sandcastles she can jump on.

Here she is on the trampoline with her cousin Amy, their faces alight, skirts like flamenco dancers. Cuddling a guinea pig that has just peed all over her, and she can't stop laughing, it's the funniest thing ever. Riding her new bike, her legs pulled up and feet waving in the air, training wheels rocking. On Mum and Dad's piano, calling music from the air, biting her lower lip as she concentrates.

Here she is with cutout pieces of paper that are her "fish"; fishing from a big tin can and serving her catch to us on a plate.

Here she is in my arms, our faces so close you could draw a line between our eyes and balance on it forever.

Here she is. Here she is. Here she is.

I scroll through post after post, each one a mirror of my daughter's life and our love for her, many from people I've never met. Person after person singing my daughter's name. She is not lost. She is not gone. She lives and she dances and a reflection of her shines back at me in the choice of photos that made people smile, or cry, or chortle. In the revelation that anyone cares enough to make this gesture.

I see the path of her presence as a network of stars igniting a glittering web that stretches around the world. I've swan-dived backward off a high cliff and been caught by a thousand gentle arms, soft as whispers, strong as hope, as my renewed faith in humans, in our capacity to love and share, to truly hold and support each other through anything.

Blessed be.

the year of 47

Deserts suck at the watery insides of things. Nothing's alive by accident out here. A single cough and the desert could shrug me off and nobody would find the bones, except maybe the ravens.

Red dust floats in the space kicked by my dancing feet, in a circle of hulking stones, hunched over their own violet shadows like they're hatching plans for my demise. Maybe they are. I'd better keep an eye on them.

I've been dancing for days through sun-smashed heat at a 5Rhythms workshop in the ancient heart of this country, just outside Alice Springs. It's a long way from my party days on Oxford Street, podiums and lights and the fizz of chemicals lifting me skyward. Now the only chemicals are ones I generate myself and my makeup is an accidental smear of red earth.

"Come into the desert," Rivka had said. "We dance about six hours a day. You'll love it."

I've fallen into 5Rhythms dance meditation as though it's a lover. After all my decades of sniffing under every rock in myself, sitting at the feet of gurus and charlatans, keeping the crumbs that felt real and useful, throwing away the dross and delusion, this is the practice that calls me home more fully than any other.

Dance threads a perfect pathway through my sorrow. 5Rhythms is a practice not of moves but of being moved. There is no choreography, nothing to get right or wrong, just the simple honesty of a body in motion, moving what's true.

My aching feet scribe poetry into the dust. The desert doesn't care about my stories. It just wants to drink my water. Hills mutter and shift, dislodging pebbles from trackless heights to clatter into waterless gorges. If I'm not careful, the invisible old ones might throw a rock at my head or call a snake to my swag. I stamp my feet to let them know I'm here, shout echoless that I'll be gone in three more days, singing thanks for my safe passage.

I wish I was here with a mob of this country's original dancers, sixty-five thousand years of culture coiling into my toes through ice ages and epochs, learning songlines at the feet of wise grandmothers, taught from birth to read the book of Country, every track and wrinkle a story as compelling as any I've chewed from a page. My colonial feet dance on stolen ground. Local elders gave their blessing and blew smoke over us before we began. I'm humbled by their generosity, ashamed of my reaving ancestors. I'll say all this with my hips and my heart.

The generator coughs, then revs. Rivka's giving us music for this session, and I stifle a whoop; she knows what she's doing. There's enough of the podium queen left in me that I still love a cracking good trance track. Bass echoes from yellow rocks, lands in my sternum. Each track leads to the next. I give shape to my feelings, make repetitive movements as emotions arise, and something unlocks inside the soft, fleshy basement of my body. What was stuck moves; what was held releases.

I follow that movement as my body shakes and webs of old stories release their grip, falling away one after another. Sweat leaves trembling tracks for insects to follow. I soar into gilded mercy as the notes trail away to stillness and the desert takes over with its eternal deepsong. Music drips from spiky leaves. Silence so bright it's thunder. Even the air tastes alive.

I finally fall exhausted onto the sheltering earth to sleep, breathing in dirt, spread-eagled under the cold velvet kiss of darkness. An eerie sound pulls me lucid from deep desert dreams. Part ululation, part harmony, part savagery, all wild.

Dingoes push at the stars.

I understand how people go missing in wild places. I've laid myself along this land over days now, spread thinner and wider, as far as I can hear in any direction.

A dingo pack runs over the rolling stone hills of my body, paws on my back, snouts in rocky ribs, sniffing into the ticklish valleys behind my knees. I lope with them, nip and am nipped, run until my pads are bloody. Tall, ghostly shapes woven from deeptime drift past the pack, hunting the small and squeaking creatures that only poke whiskers from safe holes when the monstrous heat has faded and the light is kind.

I run and run and run.

I wake properly, and of course the dingoes are miles away in old desert, their song cutting through the icy night air to lodge uncomfortably in my pelt and belly. I lie back to let the barbs work their sweet torment.

Revelations rise.

Mowgli squats in the sand at my head, throwing sticks into my hair. I hear Frankie's voice, from so long ago.

"Sometimes a book understands you. I think this one will understand you very well."

I thought my first true book was *The Jungle Book*, but I'm wrong.

Death is the book I've been reading this whole time.

From the small speckled egg I cooked, trying to hatch a honey-eater chick in a Milo tin, to the blue-ringed octopus whose neon I darkened, trying to hang on to its brilliance. Dad's wide hand encircling galaxies as he gave me the mysteries of a universe of elegant laws and sweeping scope. My winged daughter leaving me bereft and earthbound.

All the books that live in my cells have the same story in their bones.

Death is the fulcrum of every lever. Each moment only survives as long as it takes to notice it, and then it dies into another. Nothing ever stays the same. Not ever.

The rocks chuckle, purple shadows twist.

Everything must die. Otherwise, nothing can be born.

A familiar feeling prickles my scalp as unearthly strands of dog-music weave and soar and vanish.

I am a wild thing in a tame skin, restless between worlds.

Lee throws weights around in the downstairs dojo. It's his den, and I leave him to it. We've fallen into our own uncomfortably comfortable flight paths these days, sorrow our invisible, freeloading roommate. Sometimes it's a well-behaved tenant; at others it finds our pressure points, poking them relentlessly until we spit and yowl at each other like cats in an alley. We rarely sleep in the same bed, what with me tossing and turning and his need for uninterrupted sleep. Some days we don't speak until after lunch, then drive to town to watch a movie, or make a fire on the beach while Star chases rabbits and a susurrus of waves soothes our prickles and we're home to each other again.

A horrible sadness chews my bones. I can't have another child, and Lee won't be, can't be happy until he's a father again. My last miscarriage, the fifth in a year, drove another wedge between us. He's desperate for another child, it's all he talks about, while my aging body is abundantly clear I'm done with birthing. Our twelve-year age gap was never an issue while we were both on the same sloping face of fertility. Now I'm tumbling down the other side of that mountain while he's still ascending, and the steep summit blocks our view of each other.

We wrestle possibilities, talk about inviting a younger woman into our dynamic so we can bring up a child in community. He doesn't want to adopt, talks of donating sperm to a lesbian couple we could co-parent with.

I do my best to consider these options. Deep down, I already know co-parenting is a line I can't cross.

"I can't do it, love. How can I watch you parent with another woman? It'd hurt too bloody much."

"But it'd be ours, Gi."

"It wouldn't. You'd be in love with the baby, and whoever birthed it, and I'd be stuck on the outside with my heart in my hands, doing all the washing. I'd be shattered, every single day. It'd be utter shit for me."

"We'd make it work."

"Fucksake, Lee. You're asking something that's impossible."

"How are we going to have another kid, then?"

"IVF."

"Grow our kid in a Petri dish."

We escalate, our screaming faces ten centimeters apart, slam doors and clatter dishes.

Just as quickly we circle back, sotto voce, find each other, talk it through as we've always done. I understand his need for parenthood; he understands the bleak reality of my inability to give him this gift. We batter ourselves against the immutable. It's nobody's fault; it's just reality. The relationship lurches on.

I take the afternoon walk with Star, as usual. She throws her lead around in frustration when I take too long to find my day pack. Chews holes in the carpet until I bark at her, stern, then drops flat to the ground in that strange, splayed shape only dingoes can manage, chin on the floor, eyes whirling, seemingly obedient.

She doesn't fool me for a second; as soon as I turn my back, the carpet will have more holes. Today's a hunting day, and she feels it already, although I won't decide for sure until we're wandering the limpid trails of the bush. Our freezer is empty of meat, and I ate no breakfast or lunch, so my belly is sharp with hunger. These are my rules. Killing an animal while my belly is fat and slow with calories, or we already have meat, feels disrespectful to any animal we might take.

For Star, every day is hunt day. Keeping her by my side when an animal bolts takes every ounce of training we've poured in.

I'm firm with her. My inner matriarch is louder than my need for her to be my friend. Also, dealing with the consequences of a badly behaved dingo is a daily grind. If we're not careful, she stalks the neighbors' cats and chickens, roams the neighborhood making untold mischief, nips a passing stranger's ankle, shakes small velvety dogs in her jaws until they behave like the wolves she knows they must be, somewhere under the pretentious haircuts. She's disgraced us with all these transgressions. I hold her will tightly in my fist lest she enact some lupine carnage that means we have to euthanize her. It's only a matter of time, really. She's a bloody headache. It took awhile to love her completely, but now I can't imagine life without her.

I drive forty minutes into the wilderness where deer are a pest, wreaking untold havoc on native trees by ringbarking them. Today's the reward for Star's obedience. If we see a small male, I'll let her have it and we'll eat for a month.

I strap on the radio collar, checking the batteries on the handset so I know I can find her when the wild stains her fur with lightning and her eyes are full of prey. She scratches at the door, whining, tongue unrolled, then nips my ankle.

"Grrrrr. Star. No."

Finally, we're in the car. She pokes as much of herself as she can out the window.

I park in state forest, among trees half blackened from old fire. As soon as I open the door, she's out.

"Oi. Come back here, ya bloody ratbag. Walk."

I call her to heel along the path while she watches my hands for the flickering signal that she's free. Her tail bobs a jaunty circle over her back as she sniffs untold delights: wallaby tracks, the cedar tang of stringybark, a mélange of volatile oils in the unique flavor of sclerophyll forest. She tastes the air, as do I. It's a good day; the bush beckons.

"Off you go."

She streaks away, a pale bullet, nose to the ground, while I sing to myself and jump over eroded crevasses and runnels, marveling at how big the tadpoles in the puddles are, tracking Star by explosions of frenzied alarms from wrens and honeyeaters.

She circles back, checking I'm coming, hurry up you slow human, then her ears prick as muffled thumps announce a fleeing deer. It's a juvenile male, small, maybe twenty-five kilos. Fair game.

"Go on, then." I throw my hand out, flinging her loose to the chase.

By the gods, she's made of air. I lose the chase in an eyeblink and angle to follow, glancing at the screen every now and then to make sure my direction is true. I don't run until I hear rough yelps. Dingoes don't bark, and Star holds true to this, except when she's cornered prey and calls me to finish the job. I am her pack; she can't make the kill alone; she needs my hands and my knife.

I run barefoot through the forest, swearing over sawgrass, through a swamp, under tangles of lawyer vine. Bloody dingo. The barking shifts intensity. *Hurry up.*

She's got the deer down. I approach carefully, call her off, and jump onto the panicked animal before it can scramble up, staying away from its kicking legs and throwing a leg over from behind to pin it with my full seventy-five kilos of body weight, jiujitsu style. It struggles and kicks, a fleshy fairground ride, as I encircle it with arms of iron, meeting its force with my own, relaxing when it relaxes, rewarding it for softness.

This is the part that breaks me every time, being the architect of terror. I cradle the animal, my chest along its body, feeling its hammering heart against my own, and take my time to love it completely. As it calms, I stroke the soft russet pelt with its creamy spots, caress its long ears, slide my fingers down its body.

"Look at your gorgeous coat, your beautiful eyelashes, these clever ears that hear so much. Thank you for your meat, your skin, your sinews." I speak in a low voice, the voice I used to talk to birds when I was a child. Tears burst and roll, this is never easy, my heart rips and tears, I feel this oncoming death as if it is my own hand that's dying. As I murmur, Star idling in a patch of lomandra, the deer's heartbeat slows from drumming terror to something less frenzied. Its breathing gentles, its struggles cease. Still I stroke and croon, holding it in my arms, tears falling on fur. I hate this, but it's the necessary part of taking a life. If I'm to eat the meat, I have to feel every part of the pain of this. I refuse to hide.

Finally, the deer's heart beats a slow drum and its body completely relaxes. Its neck droops to rest in my arms. Long eyelashes flutter on half-lidded eyes.

And then the magic thing I've been waiting for happens, as it does, every time.

The deer gives an enormous sigh and turns to gaze right at me, huge, peaceful brown eyes reflecting my silhouette against the light. Then it goes completely limp.

I'm yours, the sigh says. *Now.*

My knife is quick and deft. Sadly, I've learned to kill well by killing badly—it's the way of all hunters, the consequences of a blunt knife so terrible I only made that mistake once. Ghosts of bad kills haunt my nights and leave me nauseous and heartsick.

I know where to cut, now, and sing Aunty Dawn's kahuna healing chant as life leaves this jerking body in a river of hot blood that sinks into the earth and my clothes, my voice breaking and cracked through tears as I sing out my vigil and the bush breathes close. Then the eyes fade, the body stills, and my stroking resumes, thank you, thank you little one, thank you for the gift of your life, your meat will feed my cells, thank you for your hide and your bones, we're part of each other now and forever.

As the last tremors subside, the moment comes that always breaks me into wonder, knowing that in my decades-long journey as a hunter, I've touched some pure truth that can only be found through slowtime.

An invisible force streams out and away in all directions from the deer's body. It breaks like a huge wave through the bush, which silences under it. The ceaseless drone of insects turns off like a tap; birds hush, trees cease their endless whispers, and the lilting breeze drops to stillness. For a moment everything . . . pauses.

Wherever I look, color dances in fiery streams. Rivulets of nutrients glow in the veins of grass and lomandra, while swallows trace lazy love songs into the blue. I ring bright as a clear bell as nature bows her head to receive this shift in the dance of life, or that's how it seems to me, tears drying on my cheeks, my hands sticky with blood and my belly warm from the fading heat of this little creature giving its life for me. Life dances as death welcomes it home.

The wave dissolves. It is done. I embrace only cooling meat. Insects sear the sky again with noise, breezes toss hanging leaves, and birds whir and dart. Star rises from her resting place, smooth as a dancer, sniffing at the sightless eye of the deer. She knows the next gift of my knife.

I give her the guts, filled with the probiotics she needs from the fermented contents of the herbivore's belly, followed by luscious strips of dark liver. I take my tender time to skin the beast, salt and roll the hide, and wrap it in a bag. Cut meat from bone with careful precision, every scrap precious. I'll make jerky from most of it, and we'll eat the other cuts over the next weeks.

The backstrap and heart are special, reward for the hunters.

I make fire with rubbed sticks, and once the banksia logs burn down, I roll sweet chunks of backstrap and crimson heart in the ash until they sizzle. The smell is maddening. Star abandons the stringy ropes of intestines she's been gorging on. Her belly is round as a drum. I thank her for the hunt, feed her a juicy piece of cooked meat, which she takes with delicate politeness. A piece for me, then for her, until it's all gone and I belch, lick my fingers, poke the dying fire, and sing myself songs of forgiveness while Star cracks bones to suck the marrow and the dying light tells me it's time to head for home.

We trot together back down the path toward the car. She sleeps in the back seat, waking as we turn through the rows of houses compressing us into concentric shells of civilization. When we park at the house, she leaps out. Her tail's a banner. Mine also, although she's the only one who can see it.

Lee holds me close, sniffing the wild blood in my hair. In the adrenaline of the hunt I'd forgotten our fight. He smells like home.

"I wish I didn't need to be a dad so badly, Gigi. We can figure this out, love," he murmurs. "We have to. There has to be a way."

Two months later, car loaded to the rafters, after a tearful hug for Star, I drive away.

Separated. It sounds so easy, like using the curved shell of an egg to smoothly scoop out the sunny yolk, one deft move, no mess. There's nothing easy about this.

I half expect Lee to run out, flatten himself across the hood, crying, "Don't go."

He's not going to. We both know this is the end of the road.

We've navigated cancer, chemo, birth, family, the death of our child, and the growth of a community from first seeds through to a verdant forest. Eight years wound entirely into each other's lives and now we have to unravel those ribbons.

Star watches me from the top deck with Lola, her new pack sister, a scrawny black kelpie whippet pup with enormous ears that angle toward me like radars as I call out with a cracking voice, "Bye, scallywags. Don't eat the next-door chickens, okay? Or if you do, don't leave any evidence."

I've found an apartment in Sydney and can't have animals there. Only what I can fit in my car. I'm leaving everything behind, truly untethered.

Lee ghosts around the car, looking lost.

"Got everything?"

"Yeah, think so. If I've forgotten anything, well . . ."

"You know where I live."

"Yeah. Yeah, I do."

It's never been awkward between us, but we don't know how to do this. No matter how deeply we've torn at each other, implicit in our darkest arguments is the understanding we'll always circle back, talk things through until they're done, pick apart our projections and beliefs until some deeper truth shines raw as polished bone. Our love lies deeper than any tumult. Love is where we live; it's kept us together. We're both as stubborn as the other, yet when it's needed, we'll admit we're wrong as we dig for what's real, because love is not lying to each other, even when it hurts.

What's real this time is insurmountable. I can't argue with desire. Desire just is. He yearns to be a dad again. And underneath my grief, much as I wish I could hate him for it, I want fatherhood for him as well.

This is all part of the gift of Blaise's parting. If I'm to say yes, I have to say yes to all of it. Even this. Especially this.

He hugs me. I don't let myself soften. He's not my harbor anymore. We're dry eyed for this parting, which feels surreal. My car's packed to the gills with clothes, a massage table, and some books. Nobody to consider now but myself. I don't know what it is to put my needs first; it's been so long since I've been single.

"Righto, that's it, then. I'm off."

"Bye, Gigi."

"Bye, Li-li."

I'm not sure what to feel as I drive away from the house on the hill, one last look back on the wide opalescent ocean of my childhood, no sound from the hounds wagging their tails. They probably think I'm just off to the shops for some lunch.

I wish I could cry. My heart is a stone.

All those years ago, wrestling with the idea of marriage vows, I saw Lee and me as two sandstorms, sometimes overlapping, sometimes whirling away across the desert. I committed to the space we make between us. Even though I no longer see the whirling wonder of him on the horizon, the space between us is still alive. I drive away, feeling the pull of him through every part of me, like an elastic band stretched tight. I reach into myself, pull the cord out by the roots.

He's not mine anymore. Deep down, I know he never was. Nobody ever is.

Grief is the flipside of the coin of love. Both are proof we breathe.

For all my strivings, I am at the mercy of my own wisening heart. Humans don't fall in love with the person; we fall in love with the lesson they're here to teach us. When that lesson is done, it's done.

Surprising beauty moves into the space Lee leaves in me. Sunlight falls to the forest floor, calling new growing things to strive and stretch for the light. I take lovers. Men, women, and those who don't fit into easy categories. Wide, lean, scruffy, manicured, dark-skinned, pale as milk. I love them all, cherish every moment of discovery. Bodies are a wonder, to be rolled around in, shrugged on and off. Internet dating is a revelation. Festivals are a joy. How much life can one woman swallow? A lot, it seems.

I live in an apartment overlooking the silver-hammered ocean over Tamarama Beach, where my massage table is the only piece of furniture apart from a couch. I make music, write songs, and find communities of fire dancers, drummers, poets, and artists. In quiet moments I grieve Lee, but in truth the pain is a slow hum. He still walks the world. All that's changed is our shape, and in the aftermath of that breaking I see how necessary it actually was. We've freed each other.

Lives don't make sense, looking forward. It's only when we look backward that we see the true reasons for our choices. When Blaise was in the ICU, the voice that spoke of her gift was right. Her passing has sculpted me. The huge space I've carved out in myself by saying yes to every part of losing her reveals a hidden strength. I have enormous capacity to hold others. I'm bigger, brighter, clearer, kinder. Less pushy, more loving. I'm not afraid of anything I might find inside.

I live sniffing. In this new freedom, Wolf Mother is insistent. She points me across the seas, following the meandering trails of 5Rhythms workshops that count toward the teacher training. Stories about what's possible evaporate. I can bound in any direction, and do, with a fierce glee that rains sparks from my paws.

Lee and I still come together to run our wilderness camps and Quest programs. We finish our decade of training with Malcolm when he visits Australia. We'll be Quest Protector teacher trainers after this. In that week, a gorgeous woman flirts with him. I approve, and nudge his ribs when she wanders away, vivacious and vital and voluptuous.

"Are you going to let that arse walk out of your life?" I say. I know what he likes.

He laughs, but his attention sharpens as Hannah flashes a huge smile back to him, and later, he gets her number.

We're no longer lovers, but I get to keep my friend, mostly without the screaming arguments that peppered our relationship, although Lee still has the singular ability to press my buttons until I explode into an insane batshit-crazy hurricane banshee.

But now, whenever this happens, and after we've made up, I get to drive away.

the year of 48

The first night of Rewild camp is always a little chaotic. All afternoon, families brave the jolting, muddy logging track that regularly claims the suspension, tires, and sometimes axles of city cars. The empty field gradually blooms into a garden of tents and shelters.

After the nuts and bolts of logistics, Lee asks the whole village if we want to try an experiment. To see if we can look after each other, no matter what. Everyone raises their hands to agree, except for a couple of cheeky kids who giggle and dig each other's ribs with glee at their rebellion.

"If you didn't raise your hand, that's fine," says Lee. "You don't have to agree. But if you don't want to try, you'll need to leave. 'Cause otherwise, what are we even doing here?" The recalcitrant kids look horrified and push the sky with eager hands while their parents laugh.

"How does that feel?" says Lee. Smiles around the circle.

In the morning, kids and mentors stream up the hill for their morning's activities, leaving the longhouse peaceful for the adults gathering for our first parent circle.

It seems Lee didn't let that arse walk out of his life, after all. Hannah plonks a slab of clay down, cutting chunks off and tossing them across the circle to waiting hands. She sticks her thumb into a ball, then pinches to create a cup shape. She's huge bellied and slow, and beautiful with it. The mothers who've been coming to camp for years slide their eyes between us as they mold their clay, searching for tension between the old wife and the new. They won't find any. Hannah and I have an instant easy connection. She gives Lee and me space when grief breaks us into communion. I love her because she loves him. Plus, she's funny as fuck. Sometimes we gang up on Lee, which he pretends to hate, but he bloody adores it.

After the parent circle, I amble up to bush camp, alive with groups of kids playing, building shelters, making bows and arrows, blowing coals into flame, hunting fish in the river, skipping stones, telling jokes, and galloping through the bush in an epic multiage game of Capture the Flag.

After the kids have been handed back to their parents and the mentors debrief the day's happenings, we have a couple of hours to rest. Lee and I eyeball the camp, probing for places that need our attention.

Hannah waddles across the field to their bell tent. Star snakes three meters behind, chin low, sniffing the molecules of air she leaves behind.

"You okay with this, Gi?" he says.

"I'm happy for you, love," I say and lie on my back to stare at clouds.

"Really?" He joins me, grass prickling our backs.

"Yeah, really. Hannah's awesome. You'll be a great papa, and she's good for you."

"What if something goes wrong, Gi? The bigger she gets, the more scared I am. What if Blaise's cancer came from me? What if Hannah has trouble with the birth?"

I crane my head to watch her.

"It won't. Look at her. She's born to be a mama, and she loves the shit out of you. You hit the jackpot again, you lucky sod. So don't fuck it up, hey."

He barks laughter. "Don't suppose you want to be at the birth, do you?"

"You serious? Fuck, no. I'll probably disappear for the first year as well, in case the baby looks like Blaise. After that, we'll see."

We pick out morphing shapes tumbling far above in a jet stream. This one a dinosaur, that one a whale. It's a game we played with Blaise.

"I'm really sorry, Gigi," Lee says, tears in his eyes, holding my hand, squeezing. "You know I love you, right?"

Tears prick my eyes.

"I know, Lee. I know."

Mum's Christmas trees are smaller these days but still immaculate. Somehow, she got old. Douggie never will; we're all convinced of it, especially Douggie.

Stevie helps Mum with the Christmas tree. He's down for the day and accepts the swarms of hugs, beaming. He and Mum sing songs from *Joseph and the Amazing Technicolor Dreamcoat*, which Mum produced when she was a young teacher. We all sing along when we remember the words.

"Jilly-bean," coos Amy. "What color do you want your nails today?" Jilly wants her usual shiny black, but Amy will have none of it. We must all have reindeer headdresses to match Jilly's and wrap tinsel around the poles and banisters.

Mum arranges the huge bowl of Christmas bush, kisses her fingers to the various framed photos of Blaise, and scans the house with a critical artist's eye. "Douggie, that painting needs a light; it'll make the lilies glow. Could you rig something up for me, please?"

He disappears into the garage, and soon the sounds of banging and sawing rise through the floorboards.

We descend on the local café, Chick-style, Jilly's reindeer horns hanging around her chest. Mum's just been interviewed for a story about Charmian Clift and shows the barista the photos Douggie took; she's surrounded by lights and camera crews, photos of young Charmian all over the table.

"Just think," she says, "what Christmas must have been like for Charm every year. Remembering the baby she gave up. Never being able to tell anyone why she was sad. And now here she is, so alive in her granddaughters and great-granddaughter." She points to my sisters and me, and Amy.

"She'd be proud of them, for sure," says the barista, handing over the coffees.

"And a bit jealous, probably," says Mum.

Half of Jervis Bay says hello to Mum as they file through getting their Christmas Eve coffees. Would Charmian have been such a matriarch, if she'd lived? Or did her singular dedication to her craft preclude having a true community?

"Mum, we need to get back to make Pinky's secret birthday cake," says Amy at the top of her voice. Chuckles from the café.

When we pile back up the stairs, Mum lets out a horrified shriek.

"DOUG! What have you DONE? I said I wanted a nice little light on the painting, not a bloody horrendous suspension bridge."

We elbow each other out of the way to see what Douggie's come up with this time. It's a cracker.

A huge chain protrudes from the ceiling and snakes along, hanging in descending loops, fixed to the roof with frayed cable and gaff. The final light is held together with bright yellow electrician's tape.

"It works fine," he says proudly, flicking the switch. "And look, if you need to change the angle . . ." He pokes it with a broom handle and it turns lazily, spraying light onto different sections of the painting.

Kris can't speak, she's holding her sides, and Danni's legs are crossed in the way she does when she laughs so hard she pees herself a bit.

"FUBUF as always," says Bear, cracking a beer and toasting Dad.

"FUBUF?" asks Stevie.

"Fuckin Ugly But Functional," says Bear. "It's his trademark."

"Mum, are you crying?" says Danni. "Are you okay?"

"No," sobs Mum. "He does it on purpose."

Hannah and Lee drop in to visit. Danni looks worried, watching me check out Hannah's pregnant belly. She hugs me extra hard over the washing up.

I poke at all the tender places inside myself for feeling. Blaise's sister is about to be born, the child I can't have with the one-time love of my life. Surely I should feel bitter. Am I in denial?

I can't find anything but happiness for him, and, surprisingly, gratitude it's not me. I'm done with birthing and relish the freedom.

Blaise's ghost is close, mostly hovering around Amy, who's outgrown the toys they used to play with. The treehouse still gets a good workout, though.

"Little chicken, you're going to have a sister," I whisper to Blaise when nobody's looking. She's not really there, it's just a breeze from the front deck tinkling the Christmas decorations, shaking Dad's bog-ugly light into slow, defiant circles.

More and more, I'm called into the wild places. Sometimes when I'm out past the lights, I forget who I am; at other times I've never felt more myself. Quick trips into thick bush to sleep straight on the sand, next to the river, just a day or two but it feels like weeks. Carving spoons from bush cherry, munching on bitter greens, cooking eels straight on the coals until their skins crisp. Longer adventures, climbing cliffs to find a cave to sleep in; if I fall, there's nobody to rescue me, so don't fall, Gi.

This is an extended trip. After a month without walls, sleeping on the ground, my hair and clothes reek of fire smoke and freedom. My attention snags on a soundscape of bird calls, goannas rustling, shivers of wind turning the leaves silver, then green. I feel far beyond my body in all directions. This is what it must be like for hunter-gatherers and First Nations people, attuned to the seasons, to the many languages of the living planet, knowing they're part of something infinitely larger than themselves, dependent on an innate sensitivity to the symphony of information that nature gives all living things who live hunting.

My steps are slow and light, while my awareness sweeps wings along the trail into the bush on either side as I amble. I greet everything as friend: the grasses and stones, cool sand giving up the shifting tracks of forest creatures.

Three glossy black cockatoos creak and moan in the trees to my right. I call to the nearest one, fifteen meters up.

"Little sister, will you give me a feather?"

The bird looks at me for barely a second, then reaches her beak to her tail and preens one tail feather, which she pulls out and spits into the tree.

I'm dumb and ecstatic and disbelieving, but there it is, catching the light. The bird watches me.

I beat a trail down a little ravine and up the other side to the base of the tree and look up. The feather is stuck to the branch, way above me. The trunk is smooth and featureless; I could never climb it.

The bird raises up on the branch and flaps both wings at once. The wind from her wings picks up the feather, which spirals down like an autumn seed pod to land at my feet, glowing orange and yellow, striped like a tiger's pelt.

My experience keeps taking me further into the many possibilities inherent in any moment. My world keeps expanding, filled with earth magic; events I cannot explain with logic but in my deeper language, the language of seasons and fires and waves and weather and stars and infinite space, these happenings make perfect sense.

My idea of what it is to be human is changing. Animals I cannot see pad alongside my bare feet, next to the Wolf Mother and Bagheera and Mowgli. The wind whispers that I should stop here, change direction thus, and I understand in my bones. I'm made of a billion antennae that don't see but instead know, and when everything lines up in rightness, I ring like a giant bell and understand exactly what to do; now, and now, and now.

My footprints are sometimes paws, sometimes claws, sometimes human, sometimes simply not there.

Star's luck finally runs out at camp. We find the snakebite on her swollen paw, but it's too late to save her. She dies under a tree with the sun on her fur. Lee digs a hole near the longhouse. The whole camp turns out for the memorial. Kids lay offerings on her body. Sticks tied together in the shape of a dingo, bush flowers gathered into posies, string woven from bark, wood carved into knives and spears, other votives. One by one, village members share stories and poems about our beautiful dingo. Lee is bereft and collapses on the dirt, while the kids and mentors circle around to hug him. Someone starts filling in the grave as I sing for Star like I did for Blaise, farewelling my hunting companion, the wolf of my heart. Mowgli's tears fall from my eyes. It took me a while to love her, but now she's so far inside me she's part of my cells. I see Blaise and the dingo running through the field together, pouncing on blown leaves.

Look after each other, will you? I call to my winter ghosts.

Hannah's belly is huge as she kneels to gather Lee into her arms.

Birth. Death.

The same damned door.

With Hannah about to give birth, suddenly Blaise is loud in the corners of my heart.

"Your sister's nearly here," I say to her. "Please help me love her."

My hands move in patterns, from my heart to the floor, over and over, letting Blaise go. Every ending is a beginning and every beginning an ending, from womb to tomb to womb.

How deep is grief? It is a bottomless ocean, and this is the dance, to know that endlessness and not be overwhelmed by it, but rather to learn to swim like a dolphin, make it my home, undulate from the deeps to the shallows and know the fierce joy contained in my well-muscled tail; one swift flick and I break the skin of the sea, roll my sleek and laughing eye toward the sun.

Water and air, tears and blood, fire and rust, earth and mystery, all these things are mine—and beneath this, Blaise is part of me, as I am of her. I kick with her tail and she lands back into the ocean with my body.

I visit Lee and Hannah not long after their daughter is born. Taiga comes into the world folded completely in half, bum first, and as her spine relaxes over the first days, she shrieks her fury to break the walls of the house Lee and I lived in, now peppered with Hannah's clay pots and mugs, art I've never seen before, new stains on the carpet. Lola, now an only dog since Star died, wriggles into my lap in an ecstasy of recognition.

I'm terrified to hold the baby in case my heart shatters when I see how much she looks like my lost daughter. If she does. Maybe she won't.

Taiga turns her squished newborn face to me, and my belly skips.

She doesn't look like Blaise. She looks like Hannah. Oh, thank god.

I'll be able to love her.

"Gi," Hannah says, squeezing Lee's hand as I coo. "We want to ask you something."

"Uh-huh?"

I rock the squalling bundle and give her my finger to suck. Taiga's not impressed and spits it out, shouting at me for my stupidity. Hannah smiles and scoops her back. She's twelve years younger than Lee, which makes her twenty-four years younger than me and elastic. She's already bounced back from the birth, is relaxed with the baby like she's been waiting her whole life for this.

They keep swapping furtive glances.

"Jesus. Spit it out, you two."

"Gi. Will you be Taiga's godmother?"

Godmother means if something tragic happens to them, I look after this little scrap of mewling fury, grow her up, give her whatever she needs, prepare her for life. Godmother means they're inviting me to be part of their family.

"Is it too much?" says Lee, when I crumple. They wrap their arms around me as I sob, Taiga squished between us, screaming blue murder about this obviously ridiculous turn of events.

"No, you great berk. It's not. It's wonderful. She's wonderful. You all are."

part nine We Are the Stars

the year of 49

Esalen perches on the northern Californian coastline, a network of buildings sprawled across grass and wild gardens. All the paths lead to terraces of natural baths built into the cliffs. Sulphuric hot water pipes straight out of the ground into the baths, which splosh and splash with acres of pink-skinned, steaming flesh. Bones soft, eyes half-lidded, I pull myself to the edge and lie with my head on my arms, sunshine pummeling my shoulders. Cliffs fall away to the smack and slurp of ocean. Otters float on their backs, cracking shellfish with rocks. Orcas glide near the horizon. Strange birds call in foreign tongues, but the meaning is universal, shaped by the ceaseless gavotte of wind and wave. Salt air hangs heavy with breeze-borne tales from the edge of the world.

A big clock on the wall marches relentlessly on. I pull myself out, dragging feet cleaner than they've been in years, wrap a towel around myself, and walk up the path to my hut. Flowing pants, light singlet, ready to dance for six or seven hours, I make it to the yurt with ten minutes to spare. Jonathan's already there, stretching on the wooden floor.

He's the son of Gabrielle Roth, who founded the 5Rhythms dance meditation. Gabrielle gathered somatic wisdom from the archaic bones of trance dancing, in which humans have taken refuge since we first ritually stomped and whirled around fires, hundreds of thousands of years ago. By freely expressing her inner world with movement, she found she could track into the deep wilds of her psyche and instincts, releasing old beliefs, judgments, and hurts in a rain of sweat and whirling feet. She turned her suffering into art and in the process mapped pathways to the stillness and presence that lie at the heart of every spiritual discipline.

The mirror of the body, she found, cannot lie.

Gabrielle systematized this wisdom into an elegant and teachable practice that, in turn, seeded most modern conscious dance. She held and taught it with the devotion of a martial artist, then flew away, leaving teachers all over the world to continue her legacy.

And now I'm about to become one of them.

This workshop finishes my necessary 120 days of dancing all over the world to become a 5Rhythms teacher. Following 5Rhythms has given me a family and another pathway through sorrow.

Jonathan lays down a carpet of music, breadcrumbs into the forest, and I follow into the dark. My arms lengthen into black wings. Other dancers glimmer through them, but I barely notice. I'm in my body, aware of the beat and the weight of my heels, but my cells are made of smoke and time. My skin splits to volcano, blistering white at its heart. Tiny flame-ravens fly out, each bird a dancer, each breath a dance.

Sweat lodge softens me further, eerie songs and rattles in the dark melting away my idea of who I am. In the space that remains, I hear the call to write, to sing, to share. Footprints lead away from everything I know.

Into a gentle palm of silence, a pause in the hot, humming darkness of the lodge, I sing the lullaby I used to croon for Blaise, spiraling her into the quiet.

Sleep, my little one, sleep
Close your eyes, go down deep.
There is nothing to do, and nowhere to be
So sleep, so sleep.

Afterward, the Native American elder taps me.

"That lullaby. I have not heard it before."

"It was for my daughter. She's gone ahead."

"Ah. She clears a path for you," she says, and her eyes are so kind I'd cry, but there's no water left in me. I gave it all to the lodge.

My old life is a toss of bleached shells, crackling underfoot. Where before I used to walk, now I dance the flesh back onto my bones, and with it, creativity blooms. Songs flower. Music threads into me at all hours. Words fall from my fingers onto pages. Pages grow into books. I stick greedy fingers into the ether and skeins of stories wrap themselves down into my heart. I can't type fast enough to keep up with them. These stories are fully formed creatures, woven from earth and lightning. All I have to do is seduce them in, if they'll consent to come.

It's been years since I've read *Dune*, or *Modesty Blaise*, or any of the thousands of books I've devoured over the decades, but these tales are so much a part of me it's hard to remember they didn't happen to me. Paul Atreides rides sandworms through the desert of my life. Mowgli waits in jungle shadows for the moment I turn my back on the city and fade into the bush. Ayla hunts horizons for the dawning of an age of ice. Modesty Blaise stands at my shoulder, my valiant protector.

What is life but a series of stories?

Lee tells one, of a group of shaman gathering to break bread and sing songs, all the necessary business of planning for the prosperity of all the tribes. After the gods have been prayed to, births have been celebrated, dances performed for future hunts, and everyone's bellies are fat and full, someone suggests a competition to see who can scare each other the most.

The first shaman stamps her foot to summon a cyclonic wind, which shakes the camp and blows out all the fires. The second shaman dances, and birds sing in the tongue of beasts and beasts in the tongue of birds. The third shakes his hair and ten thousand flower petals turn to flame. And so it goes, into the night, around the fires. One by one the shaman bring their best efforts, while the congregation shakes its collective head, shudders and cheers and mutters, wondering how to choose who is the scariest.

Finally, when the last breath of night has almost blown itself out and the first fingers of dawn are yet to tickle the sky, the last shaman walks up. He's well known as a trickster. He's small and old and crooked, with one milky eye looking inward and one piercing blue eye looking out.

He doesn't dance, or shake a rattle, or chant.

Instead, he tells a story.

It's a story of a people who have forgotten the song of the earth. Gradually, they pierce her flesh and hunt her creatures, pouring poison into the air and stealing all the life from the oceans. They dig into the bones of her body to gather precious stones, leaving deep, ragged scars that bleed putrid mud, choking rivers until they turn yellow and stink of corpses. They swarm into ancient forests and fell the oldest grandfathers and grandmothers with axes, leaving their bodies to decay after taking scant handfuls of wood for their fires. They enslave their brethren, chain mothers, and murder children, sing fierce, harsh songs of ownership, count themselves chiefs of all the creatures who swim and fly and crawl and climb and run. Animals are kept in cages and pools no bigger than five men standing arm to arm and made to perform tricks for their enjoyment. They make magic fabrics that never rot, which fill the air and land and sea and even the blood of all living things until strange diseases bloom. Eventually there are no more grassy plains, no more forests, no more herds of creatures covering the sky and the earth in their glorious migrations. The oceans and rivers are baked bare of life. Still, they feast and sing and devour, giving nothing back. The earth hangs her head, her beautiful songs lost, and all the old people's wisdom burns on pyres while the new humans dance and roar until they fall in insensible heaps under a blackened sky.

The shaman's voice trails off. His blind eye gleams in the last embers of firelight. All the shaman wait, but there are no more words. The darkness roils with chittering shadows.

"This is the worst magic I have ever heard," shouts one. "Take it back."

"Yes!" the rest chorus, angry and wailing. "This is terrible. What have you done? Take it back. Take this story back."

"Oh," says the shaman. "I'm sorry. I thought you knew. It's a story. I can't take it back."

Clarissa Pinkola Estés knows this bone truth. Stories are alive. They live and breathe and take root inside us, follow our fractures and fault lines into dark and secret holes where our lost ones hide. They metabolize, metastasize, create their own ecosystems. We have to be very, very careful about which stories we allow to live in the cathedrals of our hearts. It's up to us to choose the ones that serve us best.

Who is the foolish girl who loved Shere Khan and lost her life? She is a ghost around a fire. Who is the child who shrugged out of her clothes to run into the storm? She is the seed of all that comes after. Who is the wildling who sang to the birds and listened to the deepsong of stones? She is the heart of the morning. Who is the mother who gave up her crown of roses? She is the vine twining to the sun, casting petals of such ambrosia that a single drop of nectar soothes her ravaged soul.

So many voices make up a human. They are all true, and none of them are.

Every step I take brings me closer to the time when my own story grows wings.

For the first time, I begin to see a future beyond grieving Blaise. I have been shaped by forces beyond my ken, forged into something useful.

An instrument.

Play me.

Fourteen of us pad into twisting dawn light to walk five kilometers into the wilderness, each wearing only shorts and a light singlet, with a blanket wrapped around our shoulders, tied at the waist. It's survival, Lee-style, familiar from when I first wandered into his tepee and catalyzed this strange life that now has me entire.

Lee grins at me through the gloom, and I know my face is also alight as we usher the group off the trail. Nobody breaks the silence; it's pure reverence, with a healthy dash of fear. We're falling off the edge of the known, and every single one of us will be forever changed when we return.

This Survival Quest, which we call Thrive, is a group adventure. Each of us carries a single basic survival item, but we chose them together as a village. Three small pails to boil water, four folding saws to cut our firewood, a few fishhooks and line to try to catch bass or eels. A ferro rod and a hand-carved fire kit. Three knives. A scant daily handful of rice and nuts each, mainly so everyone's blood sugar is stable enough that nobody falls in the fire.

Together we'll solve the challenges of shelter, water, fire, and food for the next six days. Hunt and gather our food. Nights are cold for people in bathing suits, down to five or six degrees. It means our communal shelter has to be very efficient and our woolen blankets are life-giving, at once both warm coat and sleeping bag.

Lee and I have first-aid kits and emergency supplies in our backpacks, plus a couple of walkie-talkies to connect us back to the main house, although to make contact one of us would have to leg it half a klick up a ridge to get reception.

We teach hunter-gatherer skills of village survival by inviting people to live them. This group will learn more in six days than they would in years of YouTube videos or rewilding workshops.

The fog lining the path muffles our footsteps. We drift through changing landscapes in silence. Birds chide and chatter, passing on the news of our passing. We ford a river, then loop back across a kilometer upstream, holding the tails of our blankets high. Black cockatoos beat heavy wings and drop ragged creaks on upturned faces. All is right in the quiet of morning.

This group is an even spread of ages and genders. We guide them gently, letting them discover the mistakes that are the biggest teachers. Once they feel properly hungry, the reality of our situation will galvanize true learning. The greater the need, the greater the result. At a pinch, Lee's usually guaranteed to bring back game, and I'll probably catch an eel, but who knows. Nature has her own ideas.

Our camp is a clearing next to the river, far into the wild places. Bodies fan out; for all the beating heat of the day, rain is forecast tonight, which means we only have these hours to build our shelter, and only from what we find in the bush.

After an exhausting day of building, the shelter is almost complete. It's covered with layers of debris and cabbage palm leaves to shed rain. Beds of bundled fern radiate around a central fire to keep us warm. Hungry, sweaty bodies flop where they fall. A couple head out with fishing lines to try to snag a dusk fish, although we won't start hunting food properly until the shelter is complete.

The sacred order of survival, as taught to us at Tracker School by Tom Brown, is shelter, water, fire, and food. A human will die fastest from exposure, so shelter is the first priority, which includes the clothes on our bodies, or in this case, being near-naked, our woolen blankets. Fresh water burbles in the river beside the camp, and half the group is off collecting firewood. Tonight we'll sleep warm and comfy with some nettle tea for dinner. Tomorrow we'll try to find food.

I love the pure freedom of Survival Quests. If I'm honest, I prefer to be solo or with one other. Roaming the landscape barefoot with only a knife and a day pack of predried jerky and basic gear, hunting and gathering with no sleeping mats or sleeping bags, making shelter and fire for warmth, finding water by following the birds, learning by doing, where my choices have consequences and I learn more from a night of true cold than I could in a decade of reading about it. Hypothermia is a great teacher.

I'm no master or expert in survival, not even close. To be an expert I'd be able to live completely wild, gather all my calories from the landscape, be self-reliant without any technology. Read the book of nature as it flows across my senses, absorb the intimate tales of wind and weather and season without thought, without translation. Track and trap and weave and tan and shape in the flowing dance of an untamed creature, listening to what's true. Understanding the pure poetry encoded in the high flight of a hawk, the silver flash of a fish, moonlit waves of cloud marching single file from south to north, promising rain in three days; make shelter, take cover.

Everything is fractal. Everything in nature teaches us everything, if we know how to listen.

Gaia sings in a song I still only half hear. I don't know all the words; I have grown in a petri dish of culture estranged from her deep roots, a culture of boxes and measurable outcomes and entitlement and food in packets and addiction to convenience and the reckless splurge of energy that comes when you don't have to hunt for everything you need.

I don't speak my Mother Tongue. This makes me sadder than I can ever express.

But still, somehow, my life is a marvelous creation.

Four months of the year, I sleep on the earth, next to a fire, running Rewild camps and wilderness rite of passage programs with Lee, or going off on my own barefooted bush adventures, following tracks only Wolf Mother can see. Smelling always of fire smoke and freedom. Panting into the deepest green trails, tongue lolling, ears pricked.

I spend four months a year traveling the world, facilitating 5Rhythms retreats, classes, and workshops, dancing in the French Alps, the Spanish coast, the Central American jungle. Taking women into week-long journeys exploring power archetypes, shooting bows and arrows, dancing six hours a day. Shaking loose the structures that keep humans small, weaving tapestries of music as a conscious dance DJ, all those years of podium dancing now come full circle, no drugs required; a life lived awake is the best drug there is.

Four months of the year I live in my seven-meter Toyota Coaster camper-bus, driving up and down the coast, blown hither-thither by sunrises and wind and work and the siren call of lovers. Strumming my guitar with fresh chai warming the cozy interior of the bus. Tapping away at my laptop. Christmas always at Jervis Bay in the glorious, tumbling chaos of my family.

"Woah. Gi, concentrate," says Lee, balancing precariously two meters above me, snapping me out of my reverie.

"Shit, sorry." I push hard on the base of the wobbling bush-woven ladder that it's my job to steady, as he places the final waterproof plug on top of the shelter.

He lands lightly next to me.

"What happened there?"

"Just spacing out. I'm back now."

There's a cheer as the youngest member of our little band walks into camp, bearing a small flapping fish. Between fourteen people, it's not even a bite, but the broth will be delicious with the nettle. Firelight casts young faces into old ones and old faces into naiads and dryads. Hands get busy weaving string and baskets from grass and carving utensils from green wattle. Someone begins a song; other voices pick it up. We could be anywhere, anywhen.

I remember waking with Lee in his tepee, to the spectral sounds of a village. A decade later, here it is. Here we are. He smiles at me across the fire, and I could not love him more.

The soup comes around in a pot that's too hot to drink from. I quickly carve a rough spoon to sip with, splinters and all.

the year of 50

The desert sings a white and lovely song, underneath all the chaos.

Alkaline dust in all directions, pulling me out and up to the deep-rooted mountains cradling the fervent heart of Babylonian insanity that is Burning Man festival. A Dalí painting in every eyeblink. Black Rock City, built from nothing every year, calls me to teach 5Rhythms at Rhythm Wave, the conscious dance camp. It also calls me into the desert to die.

Here, everything is true.

At the end of the week, tens of thousands of people gather to watch a towering effigy of a man burn. It's made of plastic and wood and spews rancid smoke high into the desert air. I perch with friends who are family on top of an RV, away from the chaos, but there's no such thing. It's all chaos.

My attention skitters off the lights. They shock my nervous system repeatedly with lurid pulses, each one a violent slash of color slicing the air to ribbons, and with it my heart. It's a terrible beauty; creativity gone rampant; giant children's squiggles tearing the night with turbulent whips. I can't look but can't look away.

Lightning dances through my veins and sinews in waves of creation and destruction. The Man in the center of the city burns inside me, and I burn with him in a sacred unholy conflagration. This spectacle is utter madness. Oily clouds drift to the far mountains. A frenzy of humans howls as the Man collapses.

Doors open inside me, where all the stories I've ever eaten live and breathe.

I see the world as I know it burn. Maybe Grandfather is right and in scant years it will be up to those who remember the old ways to flee into the wilderness and hunker down until all this madness is no more.

Ayla swings her sling, ululating, on horseback, shooting me a feral smile as she gallops by. She's followed by Mowgli on lumbering Baloo. Bagheera hisses at the smell of burning plastic.

Flames roll high and the sky blooms with venomous plumes. Waves of cheers roll across the playa to buffet me. Babylon burns. I'm so sad, that humans will snuff ourselves out and celebrate as we do it. We scorch the earth and poison the sky, creating even in this ceremony of healing the very thing we rail against. The earth rocks and groans and the mountains hide their faces, uncaring of our schedules. In their time it's not long until we're done.

Under the melee, the planet whispers to me much as she whispers to the spider to weave her web and the baby to suckle and the cell to divide. All other living things on this planet hear her without effort. All I hear is my own foolish voice.

Humans. We think we're alone and call into the night in our fear so our voices echo through the darkness and drown hers into the scratching of beetles in the sand, quiet as sorrow, soft as feathers, unmet, unmet.

I can't bear this for one more second.

I snuggle into a huge fur, smear makeup from my face, and kick off heavy boots until my bare feet kiss cold playa dust. Tracks fall away into icy desert, which I lick with the lolling tongue of the earth's wild creatures. If I am not only a human in the world of humans, what else am I?

I roll my bushy tail over my back, trusting my belly, my whiskers and fur, and the pad of my paws, sniffing deep into the meat of things.

The noise of Babylon fades as I run into the desert, without a flashlight; there is no need, the night is bruised with flame and neon. Modesty Blaise keeps pace, out where the moon shines white.

At the foot of the mountains, finally I am far enough. Here, under the jagged teeth of Gaia, I dance on the dinosaur skeletons of my chains. I dance through shapes of bondage. I dance on the eggshells of my stories in a wild, laughing swoop.

And then I see my daughter again, seven years and eternity after she flew away.

There is so much light. She hangs in space in front of me, not that she is a she anymore. Someone has pinched the fabric of the universe and folded it into impossible fractal shapes of dazzling focus. Radiance. Radiant. Blessed.

She hangs in front of me, inside me, turning and turning, light upon light, and I tell her I miss her. I tell her I love her more than all the stars.

"*But I am the stars,*" she says.

"I know, love."

"*Remember I am the stars,*" she says again.

I laugh and cry at the same time. "I remember."

The light in front of me is mesmerising. The logical part of my mind tries to make explanations but can't. She's just here. I feel her in my heart, in my cells, in the place where I held her close and sniffed the good scent at the nape of her neck with her back snuggled into my belly and her head resting on the soft inside of my arm. I feel her where we danced barefoot down the street past all the shops that played music, her face alight, her starfish hands clapping "More, Mama, more." I feel her where I cuddled her until her breathing deepened and she finally slept after the umpteenth bloody story, and I couldn't, wouldn't move until she started twitching, although my neck cricked and my back hurt. I feel her where I covered her body with my own on sweltering summer nights with the sheets thrown back, so the mosquitoes would bite me and not her, each tiny sting meant another one was full and would rest on the ceiling all night. I feel her in the place that felt frustrated when she froze, entranced by that bee with his fat yellow pajamas, legs heavy with pollen, I had somewhere to be and there isn't time, chicken, we have to go now. I feel her in all the places where I love her, which is all of me, my precious cub, I love her to the edge of forever.

"I have to let you go, love," I say, weeping.

"But I'm always with you."

She's insistent. She says it again before she leaves. "*Remember I am the stars.*"

"I know, love. I'll remember."

I don't feel the cold as I lie back on hard rock.

Remembering.

When we took her to London, six months before she died, she was astounded by the staggering hordes of humans.

We got off the Tube one morning at peak hour, where heaving throngs were almost running on their way to work. A river of furrow-faced, black-clad people streamed past in one direction; another tide like a school of fish came in the opposite one.

Blaise was traveling at her usual pace, so people had to swerve to go around us, which they did with an unconscious, morphic intelligence, like starlings in flight, not even slowing.

And then.

The haunting notes of a saxophone wound into the tunnel; some busker everyone had heard before but nobody paid attention to, a familiar backdrop to the morning rush-hour clack of heels and scuffle of feet.

I saw the music strike Blaise like lightning, and she stopped still, entranced, and oh-so-slowly started to gracefully dance.

One arm floated up and started to coil, then the other, her fingers twinkling like glacial stars. She turned a slow twirl, head cocked, eyes rapt, music falling on her upturned face like manna from heaven. Each movement was exquisitely slow. It was like watching a flower bloom.

This is when magic happened.

She dropped to a halt, and now the streaming waves of people had to actually look at her to avoid her.

When they looked, they *saw* her.

It was like watching a lightquake.

She was oblivious to them all, deep in her own trance, and I watched the incredible beauty of her presence startle them awake, break them out of their own trances into the perfection of a child dancing to music they hadn't even heard.

Stressed faces broke into delighted smiles, at her, at us, making eye contact with each other. Incomers, noticing the disruption, focused and the smiles spread. I heard giggles whoosh past. Delight exploded around us, and the shock waves spread out and away.

A woman in an immaculate suit and perfect makeup laughed and twirled as she went past. A man doffed an invisible hat as he raced by. A little girl clapped her hands and tried to stop, but her mother tugged her away. The child looked back over her shoulder until they disappeared from sight.

Blaise was like an unearthly being, dropped from some other planet, who had brought the atmosphere with her, alien scents and exotic energy and some new crackling form of life. Nothing existed for her but the music. She was utterly in the moment, being danced.

Joy ignited in the reflection of her simple presence. Joy leapt from heart to heart, flames in the dark, and that joy was swept out and away, like a shout in the wind, where I could no longer hear but I could feel it, feel the energy of it traveling, radiating, as people carried it into their day. I knew there would be conversations around water coolers about the flame-haired girl in the rainbow skirt, dancing in the Tube tunnel.

I knew people would bring their smiles to work and those ripples would move out, colliding with other people, further and further.

One single moment can change the world.

We all do this all the time; we are immensely powerful, more powerful than we know. In every single interaction we completely change reality; it's a living co-creation, again and again, over and over. We can co-create by radiating stagnation and darkness, or we can take responsibility for our stories and live in the real. This is teaching by being. I saw that by being truly present for just a few seconds we create ripples, subtle and profound, that move out in ways we can never track, but those ripples make other ripples and those ripples make waves and those waves make bigger waves until that one moment can level mountains, part oceans, unite humanity, or make a single flower bloom.

Since Blaise died, her power has radiated into the world, through me, through Lee, and through everyone her light touched. Every word I write, every move I make, every time I speak, it is partly her message, her dance, her music, because everything I am is her, and she is me; we are one.

I am who I am because of her. Everyone I touch is who they are, in some way, because of her. We are all who we are because of each other.

I saw a clip a while back on YouTube, of a crowd gathered for a Green Day concert in London. Maybe you've seen it too.

The viewpoint is from the back of the stage, looking out at the crowd. The drum kit is in the foreground. Roadies do roadie things. A cymbal moves in the breeze. There are sixty-five thousand people, all pressed together, shoulder to shoulder, waiting. Breathing, sweating, chatting, and laughing, joined by anticipation and proximity and the febrile promise of being part of something bigger than the sum of its parts. Massive banks of speakers play music to weave a common thread, keep people entertained—classic crowd control, because a bored crowd is a dangerous crowd.

And then.

A familiar piano riff floats over the park and something extraordinary happens as people realize which song is playing. "Bohemian Rhapsody."

Suddenly, spontaneously, like a flock of starlings exploding into the sky, like thousands of dolphins weaving in and out of each other's wakes at breathtaking speed but never colliding, like the startling revelation of a meteor shower in a cold night sky at 3 a.m., sixty-five thousand people raise their voices together and sing every single word of this epic modern opera. Every. Single. Word.

Together.

It's chilling. Staggering. The tiny hairs on my arms and the back of my neck prickle and rear like I am some primal creature in the presence of something that can eat me and I will let it. I want to bow in homage and shudder with wonder and awe. Tears stream down my cheeks within seconds. I sob uncontrollably as I feel that bone-deep yearning for oneness being met. Here it is, here is the human animal in complete harmony.

Sixty-five thousand throats open, sixty-five thousand hearts meld, and it is so fucking magnificent it sweeps me away, and I feel it, that incredible sensation of oneness. I feel and know what it is to be connected to every living thing, where there is no me or you, no "I"; just the awareness that happens to be arranged through and around the general vicinity of my body, and it's the same awareness in the tree I lean on, rough-skinned and old; and in the zooming dragonfly, lit up like an emerald dart, that just touched down in my hair before vanishing into the sky like it was never there; in the hanging mystery of mist suspended like ancient perfume on the delicate wrist of the morning, in atoms vibrating like fun-park rides with all the lights on.

What if creation is made up of gazillions of tiny little bits of awareness: neurons and synapses in the mind of something greater than we can comprehend? When you look with enough magnification, none of us exist; we are made of atoms, which are essentially made of space. What if space is awake and it's what we really are, under our pretty skins? Space. What if we are the nothing that is the everything?

Explaining this is hard. I have to not think, un-think, even, because thinking is logical, and this is a soul koan. It's about all the lessons on the way to something incomprehensible. It's the journey of an egg that will hatch into a billion stars.

Despite our brittle smiles and chitter-chatter, I think most of us feel in some way lost. Alone. Misunderstood. Like we don't belong, in the world or in our bodies or in our lives. We believe this dream that we are substantial, have mass, and are therefore separate; there is a me and a you, and because I can touch the me and the you and they feel different, therefore you are other. We dream that mass is all we are: we believe the evidence of our physical senses, which are really just one frequency of information in a radio with infinite bandwidth. We listen to that one station and think we are apart because all the songs are of heartbreak.

And yet we ring with some deep knowing that we are the same. This feeling of separateness hurts because it isn't true, and lies are painful, just ask any child whose parents say "I'm fine" when inside they howl into the night, and the kid feels the truth beneath, can see the wolf shadow on the wall, and knows she is being lied to.

We identify with this body, knowing it's going to die, and this terrifies us because we think it's all we are and when it dies, we'll end, and life is so fucking precious we fight for it with fang and talon, fight to give our lives meaning, to leave our scratch in the sand, some mark to say that we were ever here at all. All of this suffering and brilliance because we think we're separate from each other and from the universe. We think. And think. And think.

Then there are those precious moments when we happen to be awake for that molten sunrise, or are captivated by the underlying pattern of light as it dances on water on a spring day, or a seal visits us while we paddle on a glassy ocean and it just hangs there with its fishy halitosis for breathless minutes and its dark liquid eye gazes into our soul like it's trying to tell us something. Or the sound of a kid's laugh splits us in two, or the music from that artist somehow makes time and our heart stop, or that wave we've been waiting on for months appears right in front of us and we catch it, hallelujah, soaring into a pellucid tunnel of stillness for what feels like weeks, knowing our balance is pure, we're centerd all the way through, and invisible hands guide us along its shimmering face and back out into sunlight and salt, lifted on a crest of eye-watering ecstasy.

These are the moments when everything lines up and for a minute, or an hour, or a day, we feel instead of think: feel connection, feel oneness, feel unity, not as a concept but as something innately true in ourselves, something more real than real. The place where we are loved and wanted and enough. The place where we don't have to try anymore. Where we know we are part of something infinitely bigger than us and we don't need to figure anything out because it's all doing a bloody good job of being perfect exactly as it is, and maybe we are too.

"*Remember I am the stars.*"

I have an idea of myself as a thing or a person or a set of ideas or a series of emotions that feel like me.

If I turn this around so that what I truly am is space, everything feels very different. I'm not my body, my heart, my mind, my spirit.

I am the spaces between.

If this is true, then she is the stars and so are we, all tumbling and dancing together in a cosmic snow globe, shaken over and over by the winds of life and death in a movement designed to make us continually lose our balance so we can relax our death grip and see beyond the certainty of our thoughts and catch a glimpse of other realities, even if just for a moment.

Can I let go into the river of this? I hang on to the parts that still think I am real, dissolving only so much, because I'm not ready to fully die to myself just yet. But I feel the knowing of oneness as a truth, and my heart aches with melancholy and expands into peace.

I die just a little more each day. Every ending a beginning. Every death a birth.

She is the egg that hatched into a billion stars and so am I and so are you, and this is our dance, to keep turning up, over and over, saying yes to however much of it as we can, and hopefully know it is enough, and cut ourselves some slack.

We are enough. I am enough.

I remember, love. I remember.

We are the stars.

acknowledgments

If there is a wolf, there must be a pack. Here is mine.

We Are the Stars was first published in Australia, and, to my absolute wonder and delight, the ember ignited. I've had a roller-coaster ride authoring an Aussie bestseller, and everything that came with it; a humbling, overwhelming, beautiful experience. Stretching further afield became a no-brainer, and you're holding the result in your hand. This is the US edition of *We Are the Stars*, and with it comes a huge new wave of thank yous.

The publishing gods smiled on me (again) with this edition. I landed into the seemingly endless wisdom, care, and oh-so-loving skill of the team at Andrews McMeel. We're talking old-school brilliance. They publish from a profound belief in the transformational power of story, and I'm so grateful that that vision includes this book. They work beyond the brief, making a stand for stories that stretch the reader into new shapes of tolerance; archetypal tales to crack open the doors and windows in the human heart so a deeper wisdom can grow. They do it for the love of books, and that love shines through on every level. Richard Morecroft and Alison Mackay, bless you for introducing me to Andrews McMeel's CEO and president, Kirsty Melville, and my extraordinary editor, Melissa Zahorsky. From our first meeting, I knew this book had a new home.

Kirsty and Mel, you two are da best. I'm so grateful to have found you. Thank you for loving this book as much as I do, and pouring so much care into bringing it to deeper life, even when the maelstrom of my chaos was made even more challenging by time zones and distance. Mel, in particular, I'm sure you're hiding a halo somewhere.

Huge gratitude to the rest of the team: Diane Marsh, Brianna Westervelt, Julie Skalla, Kate Zimmermann, and Kathy Hilliard. Thanks also to Devon Ritter, for coming in to help tame my incomprehensible Aussie slang into something digestible to American palates. And a gigantic, grateful thank you to Arsh Raziuddin for the incredible cover, which I adore.

Another person who has helped this edition find its way is Michele Schweitzer. Mich, your unswerving love and belief is nothing short of divine.

And of course, to Hugh Jackman, who the rest of you apparently know as some kind of movie star but to me will always be just Hughby, and a colossal dag at that; thank you for all the ways we keep finding each other, across decades and distance, and life and death. Your love and support means everything, as does the next desert horizon with another endless conversation, pushing the boundaries of reality, under rivers of stars.

Andrews McMeel wouldn't have had a book to publish, if not for the Aussie midwives.

My literary agent. Jeanne Ryckmans of Key People Creative Management, how in god's green earth was I lucky enough to land in your arms? Oh, that's right: Bradley Trevor Greive, the Fairy Godbear himself, padded in like a huge hairy angel and swatted us both on the bum. *Oi, you two,* he said in his growly bear voice. *You belong together. Get it done.* And we did. BTG, you are a treasure beyond price, and Jeanne, you are this book's first midwife and my literary ride or die. I couldn't have done any of this without you.

To Jane Palfreyman, my incredible first publisher, my deepest gratitude. Thank you for allowing my newborn to breathe without knocking the stuffing out of it. Thank you for your faith, finesse, and mastery. I always knew yours was the heart into which I needed to deliver this book, and I am beyond grateful for the opportunity to do so. Thank the heavens for you.

This book was first published by Simon & Schuster in Australia. A heartfelt thank-you to everyone at S&S for your unflinching belief and backing, and for scooping me up with absolute commitment. It takes a village, and yours is warm and kind and the soup is always bubbling, with tea and hugs at the ready. You're an amazing home for my book and me, and I feel so blessed to call you family. A special shout-out to Anna O'Grady: You aren't just a publicist; you are an honest to goodness old-school champion. King Arthur got nothin on you.

Ash, you wrangled my chaos (and a surprise book auction) from the beginning, when neither had a bloody clue what we were doing. For a couple of rookies, I reckon we aced it. None of this would have happened without you.

Catriona Mitchell of The Mythic Feminine, my dear friend and fellow dancer, you were the final editor I needed. Holing up in the Historic Blue Moon Hotel in New York for a week, interrogating the book, was in itself bookworthy. Your laser eye and keen sense of story shook its pages until everything that didn't serve fell away. You sliced with such kindness and love it didn't even sting. You are a rare creature and a bloody genius editor. Thank you for pushing me (for years) to write until I finally did, and then pushing me even harder to bring my best.

Kirsha Kaechele and David Walsh, your patronage in the form of a single gesture of kindness meant I spent three divine weeks writing the bulk of this book in your gorgeous beach house. Jane Turner, you let me outstay my welcome in the green velvet chairs at Gertrude and Alice Cafe Bookstore, writing and editing in a trance while drinking buckets of chai and eating endless squashed cheese croissants. Your love never wavers. What author could ask for more?

Sue and Douggie, thanks for blowing on every ember in my creative heart and then feeding the flames with anything that came to hand. Sticks, leaves, love, random bits of unwanted furniture, old stories, new ways of thinking. You believed in me so strongly I never doubted myself, and you taught me to dare beyond dreams. Not to mention you gave me endless grist for the mill with your free-range parenting choices.

Danni and Kris, I have only this. Fanny farts and snufflupagusy camel-scrotum wankle rotary engines. Great big flabby puftaloon tits. You're the best sisters a chick could have. And Amy, you have no idea what you mean to me. I love you forever.

Stevie/Angel, you are my rock. The teapot chakra will be our home forever. Kimba, Mishae, John, Steph and Karina, Cam, Bam and Camilla, thank you for holding me when I was losing my shit. Karina, in particular, you were there through the thick of it, with red wigs and the odd camel toe, and the sweetest harmonies at 2 a.m.

Jilly, Jazz, and Elvis . . . woof.

Thank you Hannah, Taiga, and Koko, for being the family I couldn't have but who love me like I'm blood.

Lee Trew, what a ride we've been on. We've never shied away from the deepest relating humans can embark on, and I'm the better for it. No matter where you go in the world, know that you are always in my heart. This book is a love song to our journey in all its iterations. Thank you for being the best father Blaise could have.

The extended Chick/James/Willis family absolutely belongs in this book, but I didn't have enough words to spare. Instead, you have my love.

My Bluegum family: you know who you are. Camp Mama love to you, in three-part harmony around a crackling fire.

Thanks to Shar and Shiv and the UTS crew and of course my '90s queer family, with whom I still dance. For those of us in female bodies, where we used to display smokin-hot derrieres, now our post-menopausal cleavages have pride of place. We go to bed a bit earlier these days but can still tear up a dance floor, and I'm looking forward to our next reunion.

My sisters from other misters, you know who you are. I offer you a boob salute, in a lush haze of chocolate, sunshine, and coconut oil.

My brothers from other mothers, thank you for being the reason I don't choose the bear.

An acknowledgment of gratitude to my many teachers, especially: Tom Brown, Malcolm Ringwalt, Gabrielle Roth, Jonathon Horan, Chris O'Brien, and Gyanamala. Your wisdom is woven into every page. To the Aboriginal custodians of this stolen country, those I have met and those I have not: my deepest respect, acknowledgment, and gratitude. Thank you for your sharing, your generosity, and for teaching me how to walk the right way. I'm still learning, step by step. Thank you, Frankie, for the book that understood me; Dan, for teaching me to be wise; Charmian, for the lightning; Blaise, for every gift; and Star, for the wild hunt.

And finally, to the lovers of story, the authors and poets and wordsmiths, the publishers, booksellers, and readers, and in particular to you, dear reader. Without you it's all for naught. May this tale link hands with the stories in your heart and in some small way help to light your path. And if all else fails, may you go outside, look up, and remember that the atoms that bind you first grew in the heart of a star.

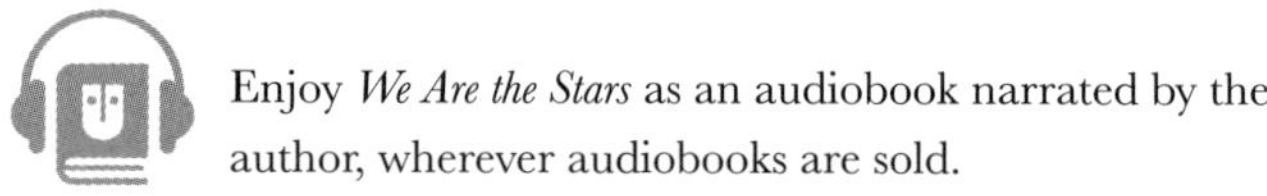

The authorised representative in the EEA is Simon and Schuster Netherlands BV, Herculesplein 96 3584 AA Utrecht, Netherlands. (info@simonandschuster.nl)

Amber Lotus
an imprint of Andrews McMeel Publishing
a division of Andrews McMeel Universal
1130 Walnut Street, Kansas City, Missouri 64106

www.amberlotus.com

First published in Australia in 2024 by Summit Books Australia,
an imprint of Simon & Schuster (Australia) Pty Limited
Suite 19A, Level 1, Building C, 450 Miller Street, Cammeray, NSW 2062

Summit Books and colophon are trademarks of Simon & Schuster, LLC

Cover illustration by Arsh Raziuddin

26 27 28 29 30 SDB 10 9 8 7 6 5 4 3 2 1

ISBN: 978-1-5248-9990-5

Library of Congress Control Number: 2025948845

Chain saws, children, and risky behavior. Life with Douggie. What could possibly go wrong?

This. Falling out of a car backward at 100kph with Douggie at the wheel.

The eras of sisterhood. Bowl cuts, big mouths, and bridesmaids. Gina left, Kris middle, Danni right.

Ballet sisters in bonnets and twee. I still don't understand how this happened. Danni left, Kris middle, Gina right.

Dress-ups with whatever comes to hand; in this case, Mum's silk scarves. Gina left, Danni middle, Kris right.

I can't even. Eye shadow all the way to our eyebrows and what are those hideous leotards? Gina left, Kris middle, Danni right.

The Great Duckling experiment. Everyone thought we were boys, because we didn't wear bikini tops and had short home-cut hair. Danni left, Gina middle, Kris right.

The now grown-up ducks followed us to the beach like dogs. Chick sisters with cousins Sharyn, Kellie, and Margo.

Budge the cockatiel and Ooka the kookaburra supervise Gina playing the flute.

Gina goes crab hunting with cousin Jarrad. Good tucker for blue-ringed octopuses.

Knickers the cocker spaniel and Mrs. Cat share baby duties. Mrs. Cat is off having a toilet break so Knickers is in charge. Gina left, Danni right.

It's perfectly normal to feed your baby birds this way, isn't it? Why does everyone think I'm a weirdo?

Sisterly mud fight on the Murray River. Because, mud. Danni left, Kris middle, Gina right.

How many cousins does it take to sink a canoe? From left to right Sharyn, Gina, Kristin, Margo, Kellie, Danni.

Sisters reading. In the jungle room: Kris bottom bunk, Danni top bunk. Ocean room: Gina in the clouds.

Frankie said, "Sometimes books understand us better than people. I think this book will understand you very well." *The Jungle Book* changed my life.

Raksha the Wolf Mother holding Shere Khan at bay.

Sisters read in the family van. I'm on *Lord of the Rings* for the tenth time.

Possum magic. Gina in Mum's dressing gown pouch, Danni's in for cuddles as well.

First day of primary school, I'm so excited to be such a big girl. On display: Douggie's homemade safari jacket, '70s mustache, and a whole lotta hair.

Sue in her happy place with her water babies. Gina left, Danni middle, Kris right.

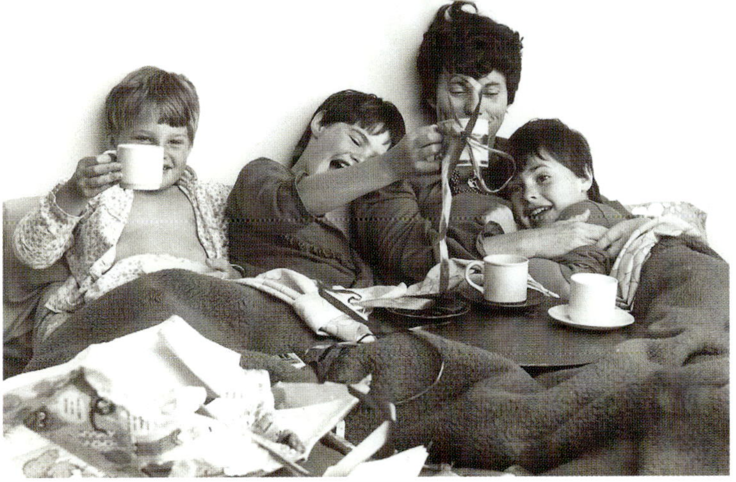

Mothers' Day ritual; breakfast in bed with cups of tea and Daddy's Biscuits. Kris right, Gina and Sue middle, Danni right.

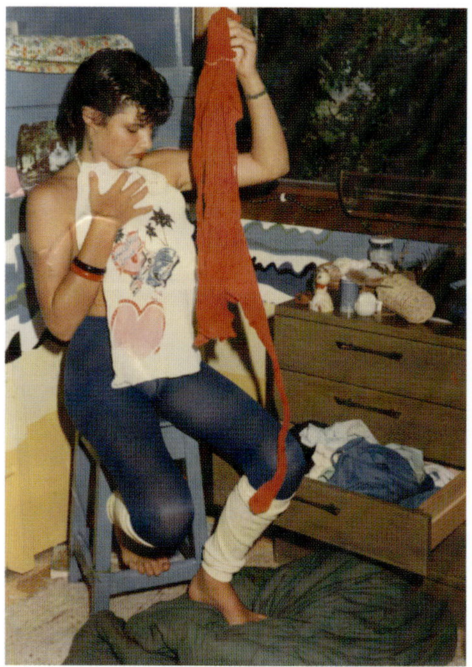

Eighties dress-ups in the ocean room. Hair gel, leg warmers, and too many choices.

A 14th birthday party with real live friends. Angela helps blow out the candles.

We walked around the neighborhood wearing this. On purpose. The '80s has a lot to answer for.

Marrying Dean. Wedding day, aged just 23.

The wedding reception. Hugh (Jackman) and Gina, Dean and Maggie.

Wedding night. A small crew headed to the Deception, an underground secret warehouse party where we danced all night. *Photo Mazz Image @mazzimages.*

Stevie/Angel and Gina running wild at the Opera House, early '90s.

Gina and Stevie on our way to the Gay and Lesbian Mardi Gras, 1999.

Gina aka Cherry Bomb on my way to Harbour Party for Mardi Gras, late '90s.

The morning after. Chai to recover.

Gina at D.C.M. nightclub. Anyone who was around in the '90s remembers Carl and the snake. 1994. *Photo Mazz Image @mazzimages.*

Gina and Dean on our way to Mardi Gras party, 1993.

Inquisition party (my favorite event).
Photo Mazz Image @mazzimages.

Gina in the Royal Hall of Industries with 15,000 family members at Mardi Gras party, 1998.
Photo Mazz Image @mazzimages.

Getting ready for a night out, body honed from dancing 25 hours a week.

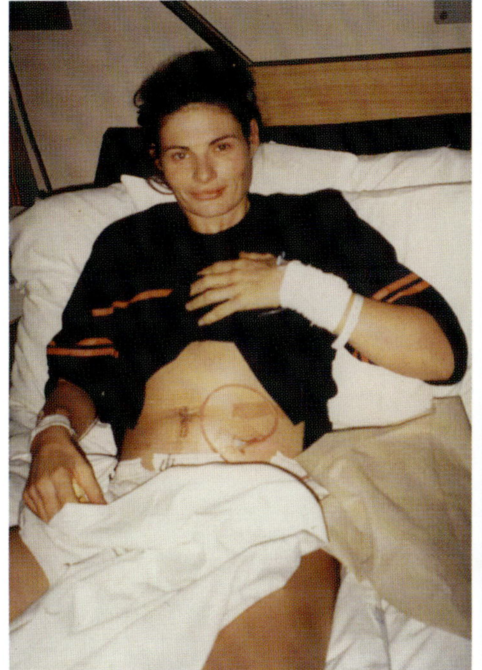

A ruptured, gangrenous appendix and pelvic abscess saw me spending over three weeks on a morphine drip, losing 30kg in body weight and nearly dying. My body decided to live. Just.

On pristine, remote Haggerstone Island I lived in a tree house for a year, healing my body.

This photo was taken during my first visit to Haggerstone Island, straight out of hospital, courtesy of Stevie. We made outfits from what we could find on the island, and wore them to dinner. Left to right Gina, Victoria, Pascal, Captain Cama, Stevie, and Jimbo.

During my thirties Haggerstone Island became my refuge. Free diving was homecoming. I dived like a dolphin and remembered how to be alive.

Obsessed with hunting (and eating) delicious painted crayfish.

Sometimes I stayed in The Beach Hut, a fairy-tale dwelling made almost entirely from driftwood.

My girlfriend, Kiri, was a roller-coaster Peter Pan adventure. Mud fight, standard.

Happy days in the Jeep.

Kiri and Gina on Haggerstone Island.

Storm Girl.

Above: Sue and Douggie. These two are my haven.

Left: Douggie and Gina.

The Chick women. *Clockwise from top* Sue, Gina, Danni, Kristin. Unbreakable bonds.

Top left: My wild, brilliant grandmother, Charmian Clift.

Top right: My mother, Suzanne Chick, Charmian's daughter, adopted out at birth.

Me aged 16, and aged 30. The genes say it all.

Charmian writing on Kalymnos, 1955. *Photo from Cedric Flower.*

Tom Brown Jr.'s Tracker School, Gina meets Lee Trew. 2008.

Our scout team The Hoboninjas in full camouflage, ready for the night's shenanigans before sleeping in holes in the ground.

The Tracker water hole where Lee and I hid between classes. The narrow log in the background was where students would stickfight with long bamboo staffs, blindfolded, while everyone cheered.

He followed me home, so I kept him. Lee and Gina's wedding on the rocks at South Head, January 2009.

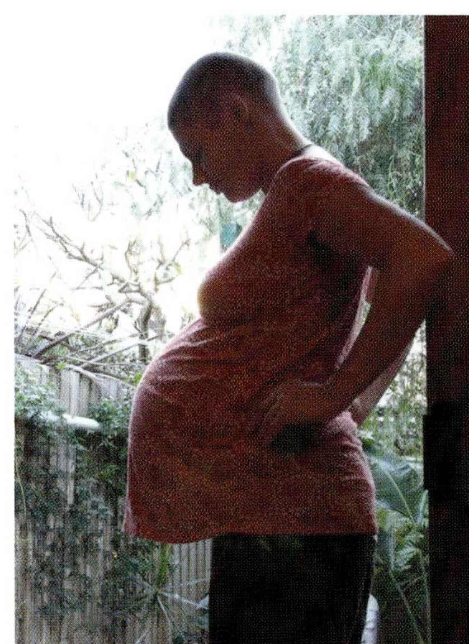

Hugely pregnant and bald from chemotherapy in the doorway at Stevie's Bondi cottage, early 2010.

Building a bush shelter in between chemotherapy sessions. Lee and I tied every piece of thatching to create a cozy nest for our bubba.

Pregnant, bald, and blissful; an amazing pic from Lea Hawkins.

Blaise arrived healthy and huge June 23, 2010.

Lee is smitten.

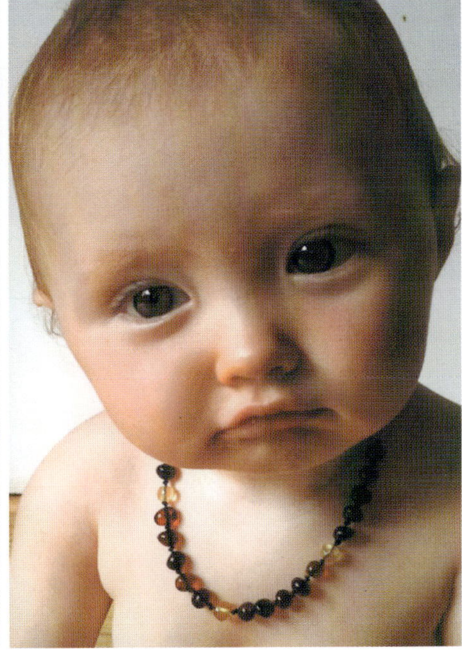

Manga baby Blaise.

Blaise was pure joy. My hair grew back super curly from chemo.

Sugarplum fairy.

Lee and Blaise waiting for the train in London. Blaise was amazed by everything.

Gina and Blaise in the ocean at Jervis Bay. She was such a water baby.

Outfit 100% Blaise. I kept all her clothes in a huge basket, and let her choose her outfit every day. Sometimes she took hours getting the ensemble just so, with layered tutus and accessories. She let me take her photo, but never smiled for these pics. Her style was inimical.

Grubby happy bush family playing together after one of Lee's burnoffs.

Cousin Amy and Blaise play with Amy's guinea pigs. Amy was her best friend in the whole world.

Sue aka "Pinky" gets a cuddle.

Douggie aka "Pa" delights Blaise.

The Chick women, a month before Blaise flew away. *Clockwise from center* Sue, Danni, Amy, Kris, Blaise, and Gina.

Kris and Blaise.

Danni and Amy in the water.

Blaise and Amy are inseparable.

Three generations of Chick women. Gina, Sue, and Blaise candle gaze.

Doug, Sue, and Christmas Jilly.

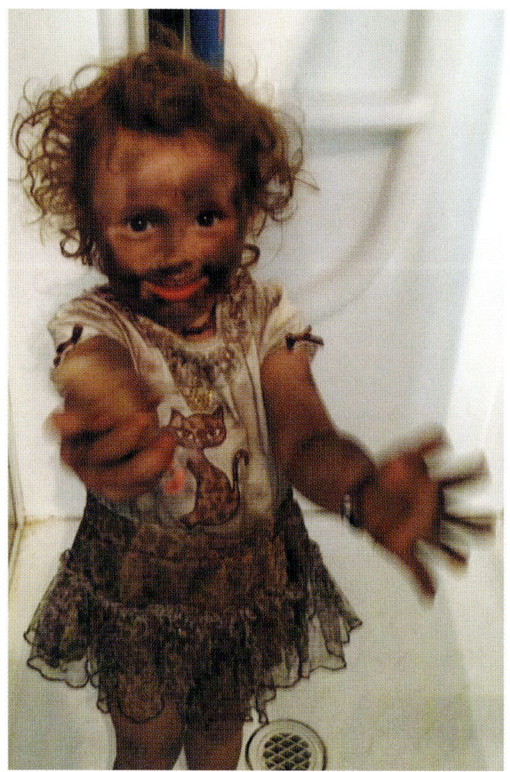

I don't think that soap is going to do much, kiddo. Blaise after a day eating witchetty grubs.

Living up to her name. Blaise is alight.

Lee and Blaise with their rescued blue-tongued lizard, sans ticks.

At Blaise's farewell ceremony, Lee and Gina sing "Beautiful Girl."

A forest of photos of Blaise's life. So much love here.

The mob reaches the creek and stops. What shall we do?

Everyone wades across because it's what needs to happen.

I release my crown of roses, farewelling my one wild cub.

Lee and Gina make a life without Blaise.

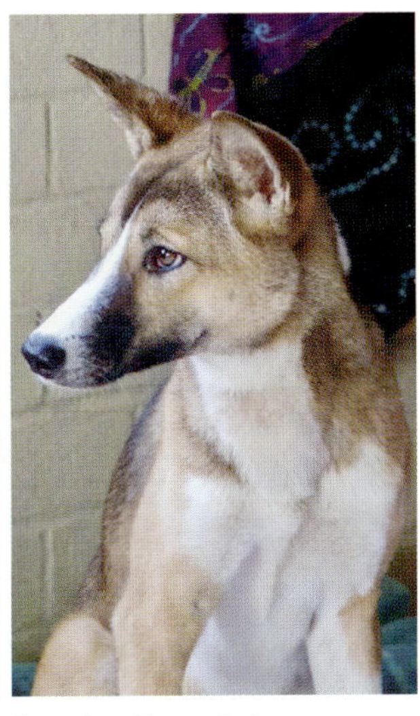

Star the dingo shakes everything up.

Bluegum Bushcraft Rewild Your Child camps become wildly popular. Here, Lee tells stories under the longhouse.

In the wilderness, during a Thrive group Survival Quest, Gina weaves an eel trap. Muddy, dirty, happy, and connected to nature.

It's impossible to be apart from wild nature, because we are made of earth and stardust. Life is beautiful.